Buddhist Iconography
in The Butsuzōzui of Hidenobu

BUDDHIST ICONOGRAPHY

in the Butsuzōzui of Hidenobu

Translated and edited by

Anita Khanna

Chairperson, Department of Japanese
Jawaharlal Nehru University
New Delhi

Foreword by

Michaela Appel

State Museum of Ethnology, Munich (Germany)

Prologue by

Lokesh Chandra

Director
International Academy of Indian Culture
New Delhi

D.K. Printworld (P) Ltd.
New Delhi

Cataloging in Publication Data — DK
Cortesy: D.K. Agencies (P) Ltd. <docinfo@dkagencies.com>]

Butsuzōzui, 17th cent.
[Hidenobu. English]
Buddhist iconography in the Butsuzōzui of Hidenobu / translated and edited by Anita Khanna.
p. cm.
Translated from Japanese.
Includes bibliographical references.
ISBN 13: 9788124605424
ISBN 10: 8124605424

1. Buddhist art and symbolism — Japan. 2. Painting, Buddhist — Japan. 3. Gods, Buddhist, in art. I. Khanna, Anita, 1953- II. Title.

DDC 704.948 943 095 2 22

First published in India, 2010

ISBN 13: 978-81-246-0542-4 (HB) ISBN 10: 81-246-0542-4

Published and printed by:
D.K. Printworld (P) Ltd.
Regd. office : *'Srikunj'*, F-52, Bali Nagar
Ramesh Nagar Metro Station
New Delhi – 110 015
Phones : (011) 2545 3975; 2546 6019; *Fax* : (011) 2546 5926
E-mail: inology@dkprintworld.com
Web: www.dkprintworld.com

Foreword

THE *Butsuzōzui* or "Collected Illustrations of Buddhist Images" was first published in 1690 (Genroku III), but an enlarged edition of five fascicles was printed in 1783 (Tenmei III) by Tosa Hidenobu. This edition became very popular and was reprinted several times, in 1796 (Kansei VIII), in 1832 (Tenpo III) and with some additions in 1886 (Meiji XIX).

The version on which the present English translation is based is a complete set of five fascicles printed in 1783 (Tenmei III). It was collected by the German scientific explorer of Japan, Philipp Franz von Siebold between 1859 and 1862 and is now held by the State Museum of Ethnology Munich, Germany. Siebold first published the German translation of the *Butsuzô-zui* in his monumental work in seven sections "Nippon. Archiv zur Beschreibung von Japan und dessen Neben- und Schutzländern" (Leiden, 1832-52), and thus this translation was the first scholarly work published on Japanese Buddhism in the West.

Philipp Franz von Siebold (1796–1866) was born in Würzburg, Germany as the second son of Christoph von Siebold, professor of Gynaecology at the University of Würzburg. From 1815 to 1820 he studied medicine, chemistry and botany at Würzburg and was awarded his medical doctor's degree in 1820. After he had practised as a medical doctor, he entered the colonial service of the Netherlands as medical officer of the East Indian Army in 1822 which was nothing special at that time, as many young German doctors worked for the Dutch East India Company from its foundation onwards. On his arrival in Batavia (present-day Jakarta) in the Dutch East Indies (present-day Indonesia) Siebold was sent by the Dutch to a mission to Japan to conduct a detailed and holistic study of Japan, its culture, history and natural environment and also to improve the trade relations with that country. Between 1639 and 1854, during the period of Edo, Japan was closed to outsiders and only Dutch and Chinese merchants were allowed to reside in Nagasaki. Siebold arrived in Japan in August 1823 and stayed there for six years, mainly at the Dutch settlement on the little island of Dejima (Deshima). He was allowed to open a doctor's practice in the suburb of Narutaki and to teach Japanese doctors who were especially interested in surgical methods at that time. Soon after his arrival, von Siebold started with his research. He was supported by his European colleagues and his Japanese students and first concentrated on Japanese fauna and flora. His patients paid him in kind with a variety of objects and artefacts which later became the basis of his large ethnographical, botanical and zoological collection. These everyday household tools, woodblock prints and hand-made objects used by the Japanese people of that time have gained historical significance. In 1826 Siebold participated in the so-called "court journey" to Edo, had discussions with famous scholars, studied in the Shogun's court library and among many other objects he acquired several detailed maps of Japan from the court astronomer, which was strictly forbidden by the Japanese govern-ment. As a consequence, two years later, when this fact was discovered by the Japanese authorities, Siebold was imprisoned and finally had to leave Japan in January 1830.

His collections were all given back to him. They included 200 samples of mammals, 900 birds, 750 fish, 170 reptiles, over 5000 insects, 2000 plants and 12,000 dried plants. His ethnographic collection contained about 5000 objects which he had arranged in four groups each divided in ten sections. Siebold went back to the Netherlands and settled in Leiden. Between 1830 and 1859 he started to work on his collections and published the results of his research. As adviser to the colonial ministry of the Netherlands he worked for the peaceful opening of Japan which was finally forcefully achieved by the Americans in 1854. In 1831 it was decided that his ethnographic collection should become a Dutch acquisition and in 1832 it was exhibited for the first time. In 1859 the "Rijks Japanisch Museum Von Siebold" was opened to the public. As early as 1835 Siebold heard about the plans for the foundation of a general Ethnographic Museum in Munich and wrote to King Ludwig I of Bavaria with a proposal for the foundation of such a museum. He wanted it to be a scholarly institution for comparative studies of foreign cultures for the people and wanted to supplement it with objects from his Leiden collection, but the plan was not realized at that time. From his second journey to Japan, between 1859 and 1862, Siebold brought back a second ethnographic collection which he largely collected in Edo. It was exhibited in Amsterdam in 1863 but the Netherlands state did not buy it. It was transported to Würzburg and finally to Munich and was exhibited there from May 1866 onwards. In October 1866 Siebold died, but his second Japanese collection was finally acquired by the Bavarian state in 1874 and integrated as a separate section, the "Sieboldsche Japanische Museum", into the Royal Ethnographic Collection that had been founded in 1868.

In 1830 Philipp Franz von Siebold met Johann Joseph Hoffmann (1805-78), a German scholar who was also born in Würzburg and had studied theology and philology there, but from 1825 onwards he worked as a singer in theatres. Due to his accidental encounter with Siebold, his interest was diverted to East Asia and Asian philology. From Siebold he learnt the rudiments of Japanese, and in order to take advantage of the instructions of Guo Zhangcheng, a Chinese teacher Siebold had brought home with him, he made himself acquainted with Malay, the only language except Chinese the Chinaman could understand. Within a few years Hoffmann was able to contribute articles and translations to Siebold's work "Nippon" which gained him recognition in the scholarly world. In 1852 his annotated German translation of the *Butsuzô-zui* appeared as the fifth section of "Nippon" with the title "Buddha-Pantheon von Nippon." In 1855 he was appointed Professor of Japanese and Chinese Studies in Leiden and later became member of the Netherlands and the Prussian Academy of Sciences. He was the only European scholar of the Japanese language of his time. His major works are his unfinished Japanese dictionary, begun in 1839 and later continued by L. Serrurier, and his Japanese Grammar published in Dutch in 1867, in English in 1868 and in German in 1877. Hoffmann died in Leiden in January 1878.

It should be noted that according to Bernard Frank (1991) the edition which Hoffmann used for the translation of the *Butsuzô-zui* seems to have been the Kansei edition of 1796. Bernard Frank also found out that Hoffmann's Buddha-Pantheon of Nippon obviously served as a guide for Emile Guimet, the founder of the Musée Guimet in Paris when he went to Japan, China and India in 1876/77. In a nine-week stay in Japan between August and November 1876 he had the opportunity to buy, among other things, three hundred religious paintings and six hundred divine statues. A copy of Siebold's Nippon and a copy of the *Butsuzô-zui* with the annotations of Emile Guimet's Japanese collaborators are still to be found in the library of the Musée Guimet.

In his introduction to the *Butsuzô-zui or* "Pantheon of Nippon" Seibold mentions the old Shinto religion which he calls "Kami service," the Buddhist religion and the cult of Sjuutoo (Shu-taó) which is grounded on the moral philosophy of Khung-fu-dsü. He also gives sketches of the Shinto religion and the Buddhist religion according to the European understanding of his time. In a footnote he gives the contents of the complete work *Butsuzô-zui* as it is printed in his "Nippon":

- Buddhist teacher in China (Fu dai si)
- The founder of Buddhism represented in four phases of his life (birth, enlightenment, first teaching, death) (Sjaka)
- Mida in nine forms (Ku bon-no Mida)
- The seven healing Buddhas (Sitsi Buts jak si)
- The sixteen great Bodhisattvas (Zju rok dai Bosats)
- The twenty-five Bodhisattvas (Ni zju go Bosats)
- The seven Kwan won (Sitsi Kwan won)
- The six helping deities (Bodhisattvas of Compassion?) (Rok Dsizoo)
- The five mighty Bodhisattvas (Go dai lik Bosats)
- The immovable helping deity (Fu too)
- The five great venerable Kings (Go dai son mjoo woo)

- The protective deities (Buddhas?) of the thirty days (San sjunitsi hi buts)
- The Gongen in the seven halls of the mountain kings (San woo sitsi sja Gongen)
- The light spirits of the four halls of Mount Kooja (Kooja san si sja Mjoozin)
- The sixteen sons of Benzaiten (Ben zai ten sju rok doosi)
- The eight great Doosi (Hatsi dai doosi)
- The ten revenging goddesses (Raksasi?) (Zju ra sets njo)
- The universe (Soo ten)
- The seven shining stars (Ursa major) (Sitsi juu sjoo)
- The nine shining stars (planets) (Ku juu sjoo)
- The twenty-eight houses of the moon (*nakṣatra*) (Ni zju hats sjuk)
- The twelve palaces or signs of Zodiac (Zju ni kju)
- The images of the thirty-six animals (San zju rok kin geo zjoo)
- The twelve gods (Zju ni ten)
- The four gods of heaven (Si ten woo)
- The six gods of riches (Rok Dai kok)
- The ten kings of the underworld (hell?) (Zju woo)
- The twelve heavenly Jaksi (jak si zju ni zin sjoo)
- The sixteen gods of the highest wisdom (*prajñā*) (Dai hannjo zju rok zen zin)
- The twenty-eight disciples of Kwan won (Kwan won ni zju hats bu sju)
- The protective deities of the life cycle (Itsi dai mamori hon zon)
- The thirteen Buddhas (Zju san buts)
- The five great Kouuzoo (Go dai ko kuu zoo)
- The twelve light gods (Buddhas) (Zju ni kwoo buts)
- The Kwan won images of the thirty-three places of pilgrimage (San zju san sjoo no utsi kwan won)
- The gods (Buddhist saints) of the six days of purification (Rok sai nitsi hon zon)
- The seven gods of luck/riches (Sitsi fuku zin)
- The goddess of sea farers (Funa tama kuu)
- The sixteen Arhan (Rakan) Patriarchs (Zju rok Rakan)
- The ten disciples of Sjaka (Zju dai dezi)

In this list of the content of the fifth section of the *Butsuzô-zui*, i.e. the enumeration of the monks, priests and masters of the various Buddhist sects, is missing, as well as the enumeration of the musical instruments and implements. Instead different appendices, e.g. of the Chinese and Japanese works cited in the Japanese Buddha pantheon, and an index of the proper names and theological expressions occurring in the Buddha pantheon are added.

Michaela Appel
State Museum of Ethnology
Munich, Germany

References

Frank, Bernard 1991: *Le panthéon bouddhique au Japon: Collections d'Emile Guimet.* Réunion des musées nationaux, Paris.

Kammer, Reinhard 1972: "Hoffmann, Johann Joseph, Japanologe." In: *Neue Deutsche Biographie,* Bd. 9, Berlin 1972: 426-27.

Kreiner, Josef (Hrg.) 1996: *200 Jahre Siebold: die Japansammlungen Philipp Franz und Heinrich von Siebold,* Deutsches institut für Japan-Studien, Tokyo.

Kreiner, Josef 1996: "Die drei "japanischen Siebold" und ihr Wirken." In:*200 Jahre* Siebold, Kreiner, Josef (Hrg.), Tokyo 1996: 15-17.

Noever, Peter (Hrg.) 1997: *japan yesterday: Spuren und Objekte der Siebold-Reisen.* München, New York.

Richtsfeld, Bruno J. 1996a: "Philipp Franz von Siebolds Japansammlung im staatlichen Museum für Völkerkunde München." In: *Miscellanea der Philipp Franz von Siebold Stiftung* 12: 34-54.

Richtsfeld, Bruno J. 1996b: "Philipp Frenz von Siebolds Japansammlung im Staatlichen Museum für Völkerkunde München." In: *200 Jahre* Siebold, Kreiner, Josef (Hrg.), Tokyo 1996: 202-04.

Richtsfeld, Bruno J. 1997: "Die Sammlung Siebold im Staatlichen Museum für Völkerkunde, München." In: *japan yesterday*, Noever, Peter (Hrg.), München et al. 1997: 209-10.

Wieninger, Johannes 1997: "Das ideale Museum: Die museumsgeschichtliche Bedeutung der Sammlungen Philipp Franz und Heinrich von Siebold." In: *japan yesterday*, München et al. 1997: 21-28.

1832 Nippon : Archiv zur Beschreibung von Japan und dessen Neben- und Schutzländern jezo mit den südlichen Kurilen, Krafto, Koorai und den Liukiu-Inseln, nach japanischen und europäischen Schriften und eigenen Beobachtungen bearbeitet von Philipp Franz von Siebold ausgegeben unter dem Schutze seiner Majestät des Königs der Niederlande Leiden 1832

1897 Nippon : Archiv zur Beschreibung von Japan und dessen Neben- und Schutzländern jezo mit den südlichen Kurilen, Sachalin, Korea und den Liukiu-Inseln von Ph. Fr. von Siebold

herausgegeben von seinen Söhnen
Erster und zweiter Band, 2. Auflage
Würzburg und Leipzig 1897

1930 Philipp Franz von Siebold

Nippon. Archiv zur Beschreibung von Japan
Vollständiger Neudruck der Urausgabe
Zur Erinnerung an Philipp Franz von Siebolds erstes Wirken in Japan 1823-1830
In zwei Text- und zwei Tafelbänden, dazu ein neuer Eragänzungs-und Indexband von Dr. F.M. Trautz

Prologue

A CALM exterior combined with the most intense introspection is enshrined in the Buddhist images of Japan. Elegantly resolved into form, they are a delightful harmony of man and the divine, hallowed in temples on remote mountain tops of angelic essences. A temple dedicated to the greatest cultural mastermind of Japan Kōbō Daishi in the monastery at Mount Murō is called the "Remote Pavilion of the Honourable Shadow" (Okuno-in Mieido) where his statue casts its ethereal aura on pilgrims. Statues are the manifestation (*mūrti*) of the Unmanifest (*Amūrta*). The images are mystic dedication to the supreme and eternal principles inherent in the different *Buddha*s, *bodhisattva*s and *deva*s. One meditates on them in a natural ambience where rock invites to ecstasy, water to tenderness, and tree to thoughtfulness. The images guide man towards *prajñā* that transcends all dualisms. In the words of Enō (636-717):

> The body is the *bodhi* tree
> The mind is like the bright mirror's stand.
> Clean your mirror continually
> Lest the dust make it dim.

The famous German doctor Phillip Franz von Siebold stayed in Japan from 1823 to 1828, a bygone age when there were several temples to Gaṇapati (Shōten) in the Tokyo area. The Gaṇapati temple in the Asakusa area of Tokyo was built in the ninth century and was still functioning when I visited it in 1970. Young couples thronged its precincts to gain success in courtship. He is also called Kangiten or Nandikeśvara, "the God of Pleasure." The area is named Shōtenchō, "Gaṇapati Township." Siebold was impressed by the rich Buddhist ambience of Japan in his times, and he became the first modern scholar to bring home to Germany five fascicles of the *Butsuzōzui*, "Collection of the Illustrations of Buddhist Images." It was an enlarged edition xylographed in 1783. Ever since its publication by Siebold in his *magnum opus* "Nippon" (Leiden 1832-52) it has remained a primary source for the Buddhist iconography of Japan in particular, as well as for the study of Buddhist art in general. It has been used extensively by Louis Frédéric in his *Flammarion Iconographic Guides: Buddhism*, published in 1995. The richness of iconography in the *Butsuzōzui* will sustain it as a work of constant reference. A photocopy of the five fascicles was most graciously made accessible by Dr Michaela Appel, from the State Museum of Ethnology, Munich where she is the presiding Sarasvatī over the treasures of Asian art. Prof. Anita Khanna, one of India's most eminent Japanologists, has translated the entire work and provided fresh insights into Buddhist iconography for Indian scholars who hardly have access to Japanese source materials. As the first original iconic pantheon of Japan done for international academia, it will generate a fresh interest in the several other iconographic manuals of Japan, dating from the ninth century down to our times. They shed light on several iconic forms described in Sanskrit texts like the *Mañjuśrīmūlakalpa*, but whose illustrations, either in the round or in the flat, are not to be seen anywhere. The Ten Great Disciples of the Buddha, the Sixteen Arhats, or the Thirty-three Avalokiteśvaras can be seen in this compact volume. No historian of art can ignore this treasure-trove of iconography, as is evident from the brilliant iconographic guide of Frédéric. The margins of his book are illumined with line sketches from the present pantheon. Prof. Anita Khanna has brought to light a *sine qua non* work, which had remained unknown to India's art historians. She deserves the gratitude of scholars for verily becoming a Sarasvatī to unravel the Benzaiten (= Sarasvatī) of Japan where she has several popular forms. In this pantheon she is depicted playing a *vīṇā* with both hands:

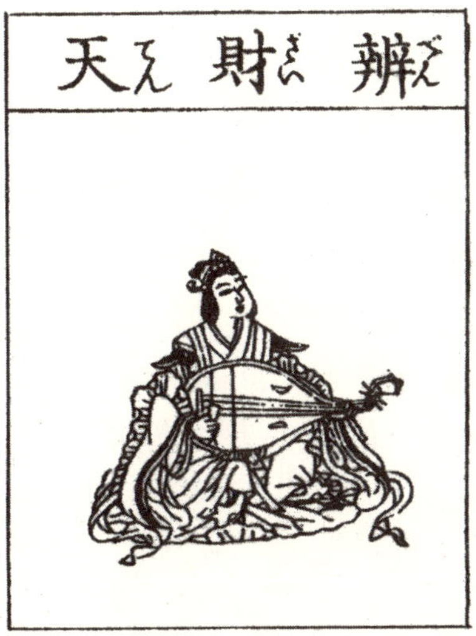

As a comprehensive manual of Buddhist iconography it depicts the four major events in the life of Lord Buddha, his Ten Great Disciples and his Sixteen Arhats (Rakan) who live in *dharmakāya* and keep the light of *dhamma* kindled in the hearts of humans. The two most important *Tathāgata*s or Transcendental Buddhas shown are Amitābha, a metamorphosis of the solar deities, and Bhaiṣajyaguru, the Buddha of Healing along with their entourage. *Bodhisattva*s who practise the six *pāramitā*s and do not go into *nirvāṇa* to serve suffering sentient beings are worshipped either as independent deities or as acolytes of a Buddha. Several series of *bodhisattva*s are delineated in this pantheon, e.g. the *bodhisattva*s in the Lotus Sūtra. Avalokiteśvara began as an attendant *bodhisattva* of Amitābha, but later on he came to be revered on his own as the Bodhisattva of Compassion in the 25th chapter of the Lotus Sūtra. This chapter has been circulating as a separate *sūtra* in Japan. Thirty-three emanations of Avalokiteśvara are depicted. This pantheon shows several categories of *bodhisattvas*. A number of Kṣitigarbhas are delineated. Vidyārājas, Acala along with his eight acolytes, ten *rākṣasīs* of the Golden Light Sūtra, and the Esoteric Buddhas of the Thirty Days are highlights of this collection of iconographic richness of Japanese Buddhism. Sarasvatī and Sixteen Kumāras attending on her show the wide vogue of this goddess from the Golden Light Sūtra. Temporal deities of the seven days of the week, nine planets, twenty-eight constellations and twelve signs of the Zodiac are drawn as they were important for astrological purposes. Deities specific to Japanese shrines, the founder teachers of various Japanese sects of Buddhism, and ritual accessories render this pantheon an all-embracing collection of Buddhist iconography. These images are deities necessary for the ceremonies which prescribe that only one who has divinized himself may be able to adore the Transcendent Divine: *nādevo devam arcayet*. They are the supreme essence that transcends the world of form into the luminous matrix of the *dharmakāya*.

Lokesh Chandra

Contents

Introduction

Butsuzō-zui is a collection of iconographic sketches of various *Buddha*s that falls under the genre of Zuzō Collections of the iconicdrawings in black and white. It was inspired by the Chinese style of paintings called Paihuo or Hakubyō in monochrome that flourished in order to emphasize the purity and power of brush. This style has been primarily associated with the drawings and sketches of the Buddhist icons in Japan with a few exceptions like Makurano soshi Emaki, the scroll painting in monochrome of the famous literary work Pillow Book (CE 1000).

The landmark work of this genre was compiled in 1175 under the title of *Besson Zakki*, i.e. The *Miscellaneous Records of Classified Deities*, in fifty volumes. It was the work of a Gazō, i.e. a painter-priest by the name of Shinkaku (1117-80), and the sketches were arranged on the basis of the treatise of the Shingon sect of Buddhism. With the development of wood block prints, the Zuzō collections were reproduced in large volumes to cover the entire gamut of Buddhist icons rather than a particular sect and finally these culminated in the work *Taishō Shinshū Daizōkyō* (1924) in 100 volumes.

The present collection of *Butsuzō-zui* is a prototype of this genre of collections which was first compiled in early Edo period in 1690 in 3 sections. The present collection is the enlarged edition in five sections of the original work compiled in 1783 by a minor official Tosa Hidenobu. The collection unfolds like an encyclopedia of Japanese Buddhism especially from the standpoint of populous Buddhism and the unique amalgamation of the Buddhist and Shinto gods. The later addition of section 4 includes the groupings of the protector deities of Buddhism and the section 5 gives the names of the various patriarchs of the Japanese sects and it also covers the list of implements used by the monks. Such a comprehensive and well-classified collection of the *Buddha*s, *Bodhisattva*s, *Deva*s, *Mahābala*s, incarnations (Gongen), various patriarchs, etc. was compiled, as remarked by the compiler in his foreword because "the very appearance of these icons is extremely befitting to inspire veneration and faith among people."

It has also inspired the interests of western and European circles, as pointed out by Lucia Dolce in her paper on Japanese Buddhism. As mentioned by her also it would have inspired Emile Guimet's decision to establish Musee Guimet, one of the foremost museums devoted to Buddhism in Europe.

*Butsuzō zui re*presents the complex weft and woof of Buddhism as it has been adapted in Japan. Buddhism reached Japan through Korea and China and evolved over the centuries to gain its distinct forms.

In this collection of Buddhist icons in five parts, in section one the list of sources especially the Sūtras is covered. The section two begins with the Chinese icons of Fudaishi and his sons who are popularly known as the laughing *buddha*s. It is followed by a brief reference to the historical Buddha, with the sketches of his birth, search, *saṁbodhi* and *parinirvāṇa*. Subsequently the groupings in Japan starting with the nine categories of Amida are given which has been widely adapted in Japanese culture and aesthetics as the yardstick of its quality. Then the classification of the Seven Buddhas of healing (Shichi Yakubutsu) is given followed by an exhaustive list of the *bodhisattvas*, *avalokiteśvara*s, *kṣitigarbha*s, incarnations, esoteric deities, etc.

In Japan the number of *bodhisattva*s has outnumbered that of *buddha*s as the protectors of Buddhism, and the founders of various sects are incorporated in the Buddhist pantheons as *bodhisattva*s. The five *mahābala*s are fierce-looking generals and have been closely associated with the role of Buddhism as the protectors of nation (Chingo). A symbol of compassion in Japan is Jizo, a popular folk deity originally Kṣitigarbha, and represents the six realms of Naraka, hungry spirits, beasts, *rākṣasa*, human beings and (Svarga) heaven.

Thus having arranged the grouping of the most popular Buddhist deities in Japan, the next section three introduces the amalgamation of Buddhist and the native Shinto deities, a unique feature of Japanese Buddhism. It is represented by the Sanjunichi Hibutsu, the secret *buddha*s of each day, of a month which is said to have come from China whereas the corresponding Sanjubanjin are the Shinto gods. Here in this translation the *buddha*s and gods for each day are listed serially in two parallel rows of above and below. So two separate series of numbers are assigned to each row, with the secret *buddha*s on top and the Shinto deities below.

This amalgamation of the two is carried further in the classification titled as Shinbutsu Gongen, the fusion of Buddhism with Shinto gods. It includes a long list of the Shinto gods regarded to be of Buddhist origin like the gods of the seven shrines of Sanno, Mt. Koya, the incarnations of Kumano, the Red kumara of Kasuga followed by the cosmic paraphernalia of stars, constellations, Zodiac and the lesser gods like Ḍākini, Hārīti, *yakṣa*s, *deva*s, *rudra*s and concludes with the ten kings of Naraka.

Subsequently in sections four and five, appended later with the aim of expanding the scope of the collection, the protector gods associated with the Japanese beliefs and culture as well as are added. The deified historical personalities associated with the various sects of Buddhism in Japan. So section four begins with 12 protectors of Yakushi (Bhaiṣajyaguru), the 16 protectors of *Lotus Sūtra*, the seven Japanese gods of luck, 28 *gaṇa*s, 16 *rakan* (*arhat*s) and concludes with the illustration of Prince Shotoku (Shotoku Taishi: 574-622), the foremost and fervent promoter of Buddhism in Japan. Here in the collection he is illustrated as the young boy of six and adult of 49, to denote that he devoted his whole life to promote Buddhism there. The seven gods of luck truly represent the amalgamation of Buddhism with the native gods without any conflict.

Next, section five, deals with the shapers of Buddhism in Japan starting with icons of the Indian, Chinese and Japanese patriarchs of the various sects. In the latter part of this section the list of various implements used in the rituals and the robes and other accessories worn by the monks are included. This section five begins with the ancient-most Japanese sect of Hossō based on the Consciousness only doctrine (Yuishikiron) with the illustrations of its Indian and Chinese masters. This is followed by Sanron-shū, the three treatises doctrine based on the teachings of Nāgārjuna, his disciple Āryadeva and transmitted by Kumārajīva. Based on the Mādhyamika and Satsastrya (Hyakuron), it holds that only by overcoming the fallacy caused by the outward appearances the truth is perceived in the state of *ku* or *śūnya* which is the only static factor (nitya) as others are always in a state of flux. It was propagated by Dōji. Next the Indian and Chinese patriarchs of Kuśa shū, the Kuśa sect based on the Indian work of the same name *Abhidharma Kośa* are listed. It was transmitted by Monk Dōshō who also transmitted Hosso teachings in Japan and it upholds the existence of *dharma* as essential and substantial. Subsequently the Jōjitsu-shū, also based on the concept of *ku* or *śūnya*, especially the one conceived by Harivarman is given. Then the Ritsu sect, based on the teachings of Mahāyāna Vinayas, the precepts for ordination that was propagated in Japan by a Chinese monk Kanshin in 754. Next the clerics of Kegonshū founded on *Avataṁsaka Sūtra* based on Shinnyo (*tathatā*), the essence are listed. It was introduced by Chinese monk Dōsen in 735. It holds that all things are interlinked being connected by the omnipresent Buddha nature.

These six sects together formed the Nanbu-rokushū, the six Buddhist sects of Nara (710-84). Subsequently in the Heian period, the religious sects of Tendai shū and Shingon shū flourished. The various patriarchs of Tendai are illustrated followed by the one of Shingon shū based on the true-word (*mantra*) the sect was established by monk Kukai on Mt. Koya.

In Kamakura period (1192-1333) marked by constant warfare and chaos, the religious sect associated with warriors, i.e. Zen shū is listed first followed by the popular sects like the Pure Land sect. Zen is based on the Indian *dhyāna* tradition and introduced in China by *Bodhi Dharma*. It was the monk Eisai who studied and practised it in China and propagated it in Japan in 1192. The other sects of Kamakura period like Jodoshu, the Pure land sect with a list of its Philosophers in India like Nāgārjuna, Vasubandhu, Bodhiruci, Chinese patriarchs like Tánluán and the great teachers in Japan like Kūkai, Honnen, Shinran, etc. are included. In the second half of this section five a long list of implements and accessories associated with the veneration of Buddhism in Japan particularly the objects placed in a temple, robes used by the priests, etc.

Buddhism in Japan

In Japan Buddhism was introduced as the new wave of religious thoughts and philosophies that gave birth to a new set of rituals and concepts, novel forms of art, architecture, implements, etc. that deeply enriched the weft and woof of Japanese culture. Initially the information about Buddhism was brought to Japan by the Korean migrants settled there, long before it was officially introduced. According to the *Chronicles of Japan* (Nihon Shoki (720)) officially Buddhism came to Japan in the year CE 552 with some official gifts from the Korean Kingdom of Kudara (Pekche) that included a tall image of Shaka Butsu (Śākyamuni) in copper and gold, several *piṭaka*s (flag and umbrellas) and some *sūtra*s. In the same work under the entries made in the year 545, it is noted that the king of Kudara got an image of Jorokubutsu (Standing Buddha, 16 ft tall) made along with a commemoration that praised the virtues of constructing the images of Buddha. Then in CE 552 King Seimei (Seio) despatched some officials with these presents to Japan. The citation praised the merits of Buddhism, "this doctrine excels all other doctrines. It is like a Cintāmaṇi jewel that fulfils all the wishes to one's hearts content." The idea of sending such a gift could be explained as "to transmit it to the Imperial country and to diffuse it abroad throughout the home provinces, so as to fulfil the recorded words of Buddha, "My law shall spread to the East."

Buddhism in Japan appealed to the ruling class and aristocracy and its development was initially facilitated by the arrival of Korean monks, nuns, and skilled artisans in Japan.

Nihon Shoki also notes how the emperor was elated with joy on hearing the *dharma* and consulted his ministers. One of them named Sogano-Oomi Inameno Sukune responded, "In all the Western countries, Buddha is worshipped then why our country only should refrain from doing so?" On the other hand some ministers opposed it stating, "Our emperors have worshipped the myriad gods in each seasons. Now by worshipping the gods from another land we shall be inviting the wrath of our native gods."

Due to such opposition the emperor handed over the statue to the minister Sogano-Oomi Inameno Sukune who installed it in his house in Oharida and converted the house into a temple. Soon after an epidemic ravaged the country and many people died. The minister Mononobe and other opponents attributed it to the wrath of the native gods and so the emperor ordered to discontinue its veneration. As a result the idol was thrown in a canal in Naniwa (Osaka) and the temple was completely destroyed.

In due course of time the antagonism calmed down and Buddhism spread in Japan with little resistance.

The emperor Yomei had faith in Buddhist law although he revered Shinto. It was during the reign of the empress Suiko (593-628) that Buddhism flourished in Japan with the efforts of Prince Shotoku (Shotoku Taishi) and the arrival of learned monks from Korea starting with the monk Eji from Kokkuri and Eso from Kudara. Empress Suiko asked him to preach the Shomangyo and then Hokkekyo and later Yuima gyo, the three texts on which he scribed commentaries as well. During her time the number of temples was 46, with 816 monks and 569 nuns.

From CE 607, the dispatch of official Japanese Embassies to China (Kenzui-shi) facilitated an active import of Buddhist culture. In due course of time the initial antagonism between Buddhism and the Shinto was completely reversed to the point of the amalgamation of the two resulting in the doctrines of Shinbutsu-shugo or Ryobu-Shinto. In Nara period the six sects, discussed above, were introduced from China collectively called Nanto-rokushū.

The exchange of official missions with China brought home the knowledge of other Buddhist doctrines like esoteric Buddhism, Pure-land Buddhism, Zen Buddhism sects, etc. which blossomed there.

The most magnificent event of ancient age and a milestone in the development of Buddhism in Japan was the construction of Daibutsu, the mammoth statue of Buddha in bronze, 18 m in height in a seated posture in the temple of Todaiji in Nara by emperor Shomu in 789. The "eye-opening" ceremony was attended by not only the monks from China, Korea, India, but also Vietnam and Cambodia.

The Tang priest Dax-Xuan came along with a number of monks from China as well as the Indian monk, Bodhisena, who presided over the ceremony.

Until the Heian period Buddhism continued to be the religion of upper classes and aristocracy and regarded as the protector of the nation. So such an amalgamation contributed to the growth and consolidation of the native Shinto as well. The concepts like Honji-suijaku holds that the Buddhas and gods were *avatāra* of Vairocana (the Tathāgata), i.e. traces on earth of the original substance of divinity.

During this period there were two main monastic centres, i.e. Hieizan (Mt. Hiei) of Tendai sect and Koya san (Mt. Koya) of Shingon sect. The former sect was inspired by Tien-tie sect in China that was based on the concept that all beings have the potential for Buddhahood as given in the teachings of *Lotus Sūtra.* Monk Saicho known by his title of Dengyō-Daishi introduced it in Japan. He went as a part of the diplomatic mission to study Buddhism to China in 804 and after his return founded Tendai sect with its monastic centre on Mt. Hiei.

The second one was based on esoteric Buddhism which had a strong influence on Kukai through Ākāśagarbha Maṇḍala and later upon his visit to China in 804. He first learned Sanskrit and studied it under the teacher Hui-Kuo, who taught Womb-Store

Realm, Diamond Realm and the rituals. When he returned home he spread it to Japan and brought back hundreds of volumes of Chinese translations on esoteric Buddhism, various iconical works and implements, especially Kukais. Shingon sect with emphasis on aestheticism and closer appeal to aristocracy and also with its emphasis on the *mantras, bīja-akṣara, maṇḍalas, dharaṇī, samādhi,* etc. also contributed to the development of art, iconography, calligraphy, and literary traditions in Japan.

In the subsequent Kamakura period there were far-reaching changes in the political situation, economic conditions, ruling power, etc. The social conditions of chaos, warfare, natural calamities affirmed the faith of people in the Buddhist concept of Mappo, the end of law (*dharma*). As the existing sects failed to reach out to the people, a number of new sects like Jodo-shū (Pure land sect), Jodo shin-shū, Jishū appeared which emphasized the simple practice of "Nenbutsu" among common people. On the other hand in order to garner support it merged with Shinto that resulted in Ryobu Shinto in case of the former and Sanno Shinko in case of the latter. Zen-shū also developed due to its popularity among the warrior class and support of the ruling military generals. The Zen monks contributed largely to the native art and paintings.

Among the artists there were talented monks who made paintings on Buddhist subjects in order to gain religious and spiritual merits. Some such painters of the esoteric Buddhism gained prominence due to its emphasis on iconographical drawings. Besides such amateur painters, there were the professional painters called Ebushi. They were specialized in Buddhist paintings and also undertook the jobs of decorating the religious works. There was another category of professional artists called Oshi who accepted secular commission. A number of Obushi came from Takuma-ha family. They were otherwise laymen although the distinguished Ebushi were given religious status and also awarded court ranks in recognition of their skill.

Takumaha was one such school of Ebushi, priest painters who specialized in Buddhist themes in Kamakura period. The founder was Takumaha, the priest painter who specialized in Buddhist subjects and was active in Kamakura period. The founder Takuma Tameto was the founder who was awarded the title of "Hoin." His son painted Jūniten-screen depicting the Hindu gods adopted in esoteric Buddhism at Zenkoji temple and Ryokai Maṇḍala at Toji temple in Kyoto. Another prominent name is Tori Busshi mentioned in Nihonshoki who was entrusted with Prince Shotoku. With the development of esoteric Buddhism, the amalgamation of new Shinto deities gave an added dimension.

This was closely related to the developments in the faith of Amida, Miroku (Maitreya Bodhisattva), and Yakushi (Bhaiṣajyaguru, the Buddha of Healing) in Japan.

With the collapse of Ritsuryo system the authority of aristocracy was on decline and the constant warfare among the various powerful families vying to rule, the situation of chaos prevailed. It was worsened by the successive natural calamities and led people to believe in the prophecies of Buddha about Mappo, the period of the degeneration of Buddhist law and so relied more and more on the saving power of Buddha. Like this the base of Buddhism limited to aristocracy now spread out to include the masses with emphasis on Nembutsu, i.e. to invoke the name of Amida with complete devotion in order to be reborn in the pure land of bliss. It was Honen, also known by the names Genku and posthumous title, Enko-Daishi, who taught people to recite Nembutsu in order to give solace to them. There was a sharp rise in the believers of Jodo sect from all parts of the country which also invited the wrath of the clerics from the other sects. His disciple Shinran founded Jodo Shinshu that emphasized mere invocation of the name of Buddha to attain salvation. It was Nichiren who extolled the *Lotus Sūtra* as the ultimate teachings of Buddha and founded Hokke shū that emphasized the chanting of the name of *Lotus Sūtra*, Namumyoho renge kyo.

At the same time Zen-shū gathered attention among the Samurai class due to its primary emphasis on meditation and discipline rather than metaphysical contemplations. It was introduced by monk Eisai who studied it in China where it was introduced by the Indian monk Bodhi Dharma in 520. He founded Rinzai School of Zen, and Dogen founded Sōtō School of Zen that emphasized Zazen.

The Zen monk Eisai introduced tea to Japan that was cultivated into a ceremony. Even during the Edo period when the authorities adopted Confucianism the Buddhist temples continued to be the centres of popular education called Terakoya (temple schools) and were run by Zen monks.

These developments resulted in the adaptation of Buddhism as a part of its culture with the construction of temples and objects associated with the rituals and prayers and so the list of implements is a long one.

Hymn to Vairocana Buddha

稽首毘盧遮那佛
一切如來金剛身
廓周法界無邊量
隨方應現滿虛空
能以一身為多身
復現多身一身相
有身有相權來化
非身非相是無為

Preface of the Japanese Editor

神佛靈像圖彙序

古德云。逢佛殺佛。逢祖殺祖。其一機一用。一棒一喝。以摧疑團。破執取名相者。或如丹霞和尚。燒卻木佛像。了雖然凡夫庸俗。豈能徹向上玄旨耶。故

Illustrations of images of
Devas, Buddhas, and Miraculous beings

There is a saying of wise men that, kill the Buddha if you meet him, kill the patriarch when you meet him. With a single strike, complete concentration, and one aim crush all illusions and attachments. So a priest named Tanseki burnt the wooden images of Buddha and destroyed them. However it was an act of one who was ignorant and unaccomplished. Is it a fine purport to withdraw the objects of veneration?

大覺世尊以大悲心。方便利導。使
彼凡庸赴漸修也。一日有客。圖畫
諸佛菩薩乃至諸天諸神之靈像。
來請倂予爲序壽于梓矣。予斂袵
危坐從頭拜覽之。端嚴和雅之慈
相。忿怒勇猛之威容。自然令人歸

As the most reverent one with the heart of great compassion expediently lead and guide the men to advantage. Buddha gradually led this man to faith. One day the man had a visitor. He drew the images of Buddhas, *bodhisattvas*, gods and other celestial beings. He asked me to write a foreword and get it printed. In order to pen it as I sat down and observed the drawings minutely I saw that there was expressions of solemn elegance, compassion, majestic expressions of valor, anger, fury and rage that would naturally draw any person to Buddhism and be in awe.

敬心潑而警畏意厚。夫描寫之巧。
不可言焉。然有名同而相異者。名
異而相近者。至于樂器兵物之品
彙多。一繙看之。則雖童蒙能知其
名相能辨其異同。實緇侶之所宜
貴重也。嗟呼向善之徒。拜其靈像。

There are no words to praise the skill of the artist in depiction. There are cases of similar names with different expressions and there are others with similar features but different names. Further I observed minutely the whole range of objects held by them from musical instruments to weapons. In other words, having gone through it anyone even a novice can learn the names and tell the similarities and differences. A monk will hold it in high esteem and revere it without fail. Look, all the seekers of virtues observe the divine images.

唱其尊號眞修實行而得神佛不
二之理則利益廣大者耶於是不
顧管窺蠡測終爲之書
時
元祿三歲舍庚午夷則穀旦

chant the names of gods and Buddhas and practice to meditate on it, in order to understand the logic of non-duality of Shinto gods and Buddhas. Those who grasp the fact that both are the same shall be benefited enormously. With no regard to my narrow vision, I have penned the preface for this book.

Time: 3rd year of Genroku Era (1690) seventh month of (Lunar calender), An auspicious day

Preface of Hidenobu

肇公曰法身無象而殊形並應然則
上自諸佛下至天龍八部無非無相
法身矣此書選集蓋在其意乎先托
木行世久矣以故尊形磨礲印相難
分咲怒叵辨見者苦之書肆請余改
寫余思其有補信人休暇舐筆且增

The monk Sosho in the commentary on the Vimalakiriti nirdeśa remarked: "Although the Dharmakāya is formless, it manifests in ineffable forms." In other words it is not true to say that right from the various Buddhas, down to the eight kinds of guardians of the lower realms starting with Nagarājas, are formless. The objective of this collection perhaps is to support this fact. The wood blocks used for the print of this work were worn out since they had been in circulation for a long time. Thus the figures were are not well defined and the impressions were blurred, so much so that it was difficult to make out whether one was happy or angry. This would confuse the readers. So the publisher

寫金剛王大勝金剛等一百一十八
尊再上梓恐人不識其由爲之記
天明癸卯秋八月
畫工　土佐將曹紀秀信謹識

asked me to remake it. When I started working on it I added another 118 illustrations including the Vajrarājas, Mahāvajra etc., and made this enlarged edition.

Fearing that the readers of this edition, being ignorant of this fact, may fail to understand the real reason behind it, I have appended my comments.

Tenmei Era (1781-1789), 8th month (Lunar Calender), Autumn — Artist: Kin Hidenobu
Shoso (official of lower rank), Tosa School

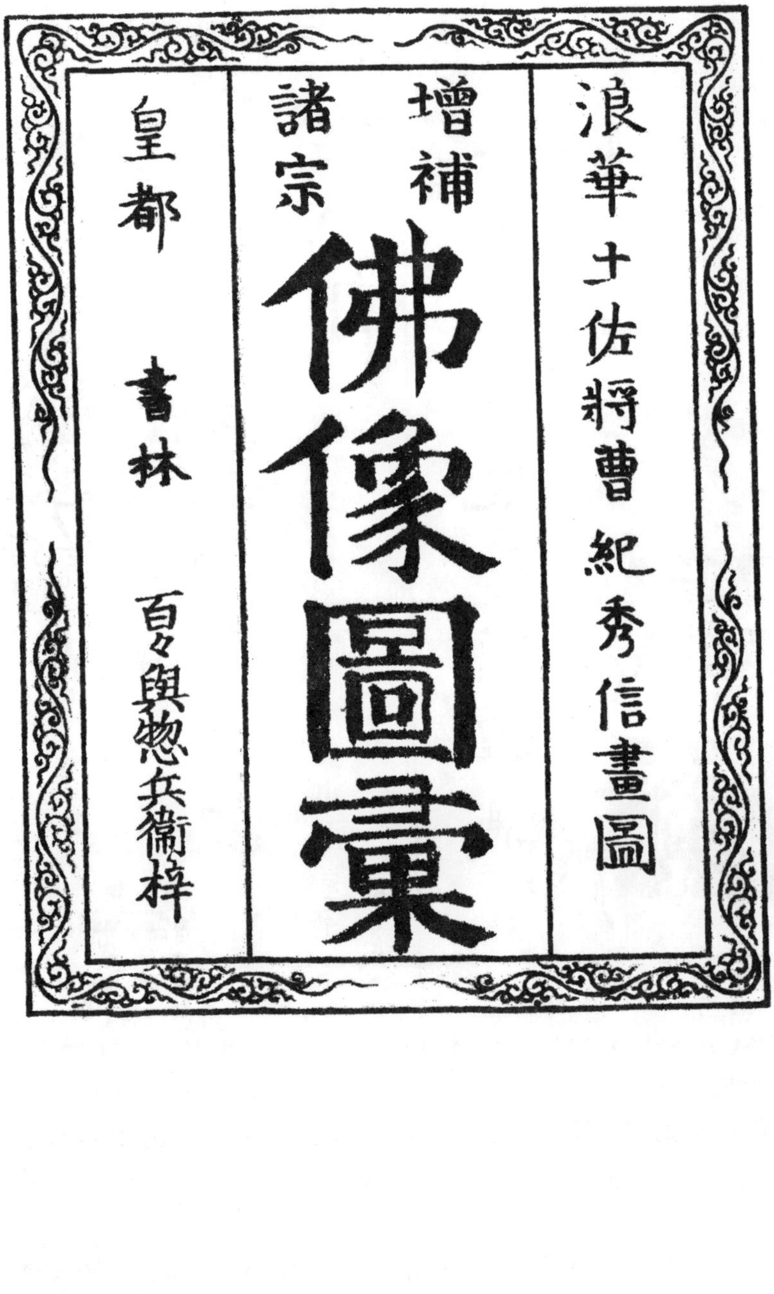
浪華士佐将曹紀秀信畫圖

增補
諸宗
佛像圖彙

皇都 書林 百々與惣兵衛梓

Naniwa = Osaka

Tosa Shōsō ; Junior officer of the Tosa School

Artist Kino Hidenobu

Kōto = Kyōto

Publisher Shorin

Printer, Momokō Sohyōe

增補諸宗佛像圖彙 壹

Fascicle – I

佛像圖彙所引用書目録

	A	B	C	D
1	阿含經	梵網經	虚空藏經	仁王經抄
2	方等經	楞嚴經	造天地經	大日經抄
3	涅槃經	維摩經	地藏十輪經	觀音經抄
4	法華經	十王經	七佛功德經	曼陀羅抄
5	大集經	千手經	造像功德經	諸經要集
6	般若經	淨名經	法華懺法	往生要集
7	華嚴經	愛染經	同科注	名義集
8	大日經	莊嚴經	同定珍抄	西谷名目
9	孔雀經	舍利經	同文句	光明疏
10	彌陀經	大黑經	圓覺注疏	六物圖
11	藥師經	錫杖經	彌陀經疏	稽古畧

List of the References

	A	B	C	D
1.	Agon Kyō Āgma Sūtra	Bonmō Kyō Brahmajāla Sūtra	Kokūzō Kyō Ākāśagarbha Sūtra	Niō Kyōshō Vajra-Sūtra in summary
2.	Hōdō Kyō Vaipulya Sūtra	Ryōgon Gyō Sūraṁgama Samādhi Nirdeśa	Zōtenji Kyō The Sūtra of creation	Dainichi Kyōshō Essence of Mahāvairocana Sūtra
3.	Nehan Kyō Parinirvāṇa Sūtra	Yuima Gyō Vimalakīrti- Nirdeśa Sūtra	Jizōjūrin Kyō Kṣitigarbha Sūtra	Kanon Kyōshō Essence of Avalokiteśvara Sūtra
4.	Hokke Kyō Lotus Sūtra	Jyūō Kyō Dasarāja Sūtra	Shichibutsu-Kudoku Kyō Sapta Buddha Guṇa Sūtra	Mandara Shō Essence of Maṇḍalas
5.	Daishū Kyō Mahāsamnipāta Sūtra	Senju Kyō Sahasrabhujā Sūtra	Zō Kudo ku Kyō Sūtra of the Guṇas of images	Shokyō Yōshū Essence of various Sūtra
6.	Hannya Kyō Prajñapāramitā Sūtra	Jōmei-Kyō Avataṁsaka Sūtra in Chinese	Hokke Senbō Lotus Sūtra Confessions	Ōjō Yōshū Essentials of Pure Land
7.	Kegon Kyō Avatamsaka Sūtra	Aizen Kyō Raṅgarāja Sūtra	Commentary on Raṅgarāja Sūtra	Myōgi Shū Dictionary of Buddhist terms in Chinese characters explained in Japanese
8.	Dainichi Kyō Mahāvairocana Sūtra	Sōgon Kyō Vyūha Sūtra	Commentary on Vyūha Sūtra	Nishitani-Meimoku Names of Niśhitani
9.	Kujaku Kyō Mahāmayurī Sūtra	Shari Kyō Śarīra Sūtra	Wordings of Śarīra Sūtra	Kōmyō Gisho Commentary on Mahāvairocana
10.	Amida Kyō Amitābha Sūtra	Daimoku Kyō Mahakāla Sūtra	Zukaku Chūgi Notes on Illustrations	Rokumotsu Zu Illustrations of six objects of a monk
11.	Yakushi Kyō Bhaiṣajyaguru Sūtra	Shakujō Kyō Khakkhara Sūtra	Amida Kyōgi Commentary on Amitābha Sūtra	Keīko ryaku Acomplishments in some Art

	12	11	10	9	8	7	6	5	4	3	2	1
A	傳燈録	碧巖録	宗鏡録	出家論	唯識論	起信論	俱舎論	十住心論	毘婆沙論	大智度論	佛祖三經	觀音經
B	法界安立	祖庭事苑	五燈會元	袾宏往生傳	三國傳記	元亨釋書	佛祖統紀	法苑珠林	高僧傳	了義燈	虚堂録	辨財天經
C	年代記	拾芥抄	壒嚢抄	神代巻	種類集	諸尊種子	増無縁双紙	諸天傳	感通傳	太子傳	八宗綱要	理趣經抄
D							藍藍	天易	論語	廣雅	三才圖會	三藏義

	A	B	C	D
1.	Kanon Kyō Avalokiteśvara Sūtra	Benzaiten Kyō Sūtra of Lakṣmī	Rishu Kyō Adhyartha Śatikā Prajñāpārmitā Sūtra	Sanzō Gi Trīpiṭaka's Commentary
2.	Busso Sankyō The Buddha, Patriarch & three teachings	Kyodō Roku Records of Chinese monk Hsü T'ang	Hasshū Kōyō Essentials of Eight Religions (Japan)	Jūnisai zue Sansai Zue pictures at the age of 1243
3.	Daichido Ron Mahāprajñāpāramito- padeśa Śāstra	Ryōgi Nita-arthā	Taishiden Biography of Prince Shotoku	Kōga A Chinese work
4.	Bishamon Ron Vaiśravaṇa Śāstra	Kōsō Den Biographies of High Priests	Kan Tsūden Memoirs	Rongo Confucian Analects
5.	Jūjū shin Ron Ten stages of mind	Hōon Jurin A Chinese work on Buddhism	Shoten Den Accounts of various Devas	Teneki Book of Divination
6.	Kusha Ron Abhidharmakośa	Busso Tōgi Records of Buddhist Patriarchs	Zōmuen Zōshi Fiction	Hoki The baskets (Piṭakas)
7.	Kishin Ron Śrāddhotpāda Śāstra	Genkō Shakusho History of Buddhism in Japan (1322 CE)	Shoson Shūji, Bīja representations of various Buddhas	
8.	Yuishiki Ron Vijñapti mātratā	Sangoku Denki A collection of Buddhist talks (1407 CE)	Shurui Shō ū A *Bīja* typology	
9.	Shukke Ron Pravrajyā Śāstra	Ōjō den Accounts of Salvation	Jindai Kan Age of god in Kojiki (712 CE)	
10.	Shūyō Roku Religious Mirror of Zen Buddhism (961 CE)	Gotō Egen Origin of five Lights of Zen	Ainoshō Encyclopaedia on Buddhism (1530 CE)	
11.	Hekigan Roku A Japanese work on Zen Buddhism (1100 CE)	Sotei Jien A collection on Zen Buddhism (1108 CE)	Shū Kai Shō Encyclopaedia on Buddhism (1532 CE)	
12.	Dentō Roku Accounts of transmission of lights; A work of Zen Buddhism	Hōkai Anritsu On Establishment of Dharmadhātu World	Nendai Ki Annals	

増補佛像圖彙目録

巻之二

	A	B	C	D
1	傳大士 普建 普成	誕生釋迦	出山釋迦	正覺釋迦
2	涅槃釋迦	九品彌陀	妙觀察智	曼陀羅
3	五劫思惟	山越	多寶○寶生	金剛界大日
4	胎藏界大日	七佛藥師	日月燈明佛	二萬燈明佛
5	三萬燈明佛	不空成就	一字金輪	佛眼佛母
6	般若菩薩	不休息菩薩	文殊菩薩	普賢菩薩
7	兒文殊	兒普賢	七字文殊	無盡意菩薩
8	虛空藏菩薩	福一滿虛空藏	金剛界十六	大菩薩
9	二十五菩薩	妙音	滿月	七觀音
10	三十三體觀音	十二體地藏	六地藏	滅惡趣

Index

Fascicle - II

	A	B	C	D
1.	Fudaishi Mahāsattva Fu kyu with two sons	Tanjōno Shaka Śākyamuni at birth	Shussan Shaka Śākyamuni leaving the Mountains	Shōgaku Shaka Saṁbuddha
2.	Nehan Shaka Nirvâṇa Form of Buddha	Kuhono Mida Nine Grades of Amitābha	Myōkan Zacchi Pratyavekṣanā Jñāna	Mandara Maṇḍala
3.	Gokō Shui The Five Kalpas of Amitābha	Yamagoshi Ascetic Yamabushi	Tahō Hōshō Ratnasaṁbhava	Kongōkai Dainichi Mahāvairocana of Vajradhātu World
4.	Taizōkai Dainichi Garbhadhātu of Mahāvairocana	Shichibutsu Yakushi The seven Eminations of Bhaiṣajya Guru	Nichigatsu Tōmyōbutsu Candra Sūrya Pradīpa Buddha	Nimantōmyō butsu Twenty thousand Pradīpa Buddha
5.	Sanmantōmyō Butsu Buddha of Thirty thousand Lights	Fukū Jōju Amoghavajra	Ichijikinrin Ekākṣara Uṣṇīṣacakra	Butsugen Butsumo Buddha Locana
6.	Hannya Bosatsu Prajñā Bodhisattva	Fukyūsoku Bosatsu Bodhisattva of Infinite Life	Monjū Bosatsu Mañjuśrī Bodhisattva	Fugen Bosatsu Samantabhadra Bodhisattva
7.	Chigo Monju Young Mañjuśrī	Chigo Fugen Young Samantabhadra	Shichiji Monju Saptākṣara Mañjuśrī	Mujini Bosatsu Dharmadhātu Bodhisattva
8.	Kokūzō Bosatsu Ākāśagarbha Bodhisattva	Fuku Ichiman Kokūzō Ākāśagarbha of ten thousand *puṇya* (West)	Kongō kai Jūroku Dai bosatsu Vajradhātu Ṣoḍaśa Mahasattva	
9.	Nijūgo Bosatsu The Twenty-five Bodhisattvas	Myōon Gadgadeśvara	Mangetsu Full Moon	Shichi Kannon Seven Avalokiteśvara
10.	Sanjū santai Kannon/The Thirty-three forms of Avalokiteśvara	Jūnitai Jizō Dvādaśāṅga Kṣitigarbhas	Roku Jizō Six Kṣitigarbhas	Metsaku Shu Nirodha Durgati

12	11	10	9	8	7	6	5	4	3	2	1	
善財	童子部	藏王	愛宕	白山	三十日秘佛	卷之三	火焔	倶利迦羅	沉宅不動	金剛王	法華四菩薩	A
金剛童子	宇寶	飛瀧	伊豆	富士	三十番神		金剛童子	孔雀	愛染	大勝金剛	妙見	B
善尼師	八幡	渡唐天神	箱根	飯繩	山王七社		大元	烏蒭沙摩	兩頭	五大力菩薩	華光	C
庚申 同童子 四百剎鬼	春日赤童子	高野四所	湯殿	鈴鹿	熊野權現			六時	五大尊明王	明王部	大隨求	D

	A	B	C	D
1.	Hokkeshi Bosatsu Four Bodhisattvas of Saddharmapuṇḍarīka	Myō ken Pole Star (Ursa Major)	Kekō Padmaprabha	Daizūgu The Great Zuigu
2.	Kongō ō Vajra Rāja	Daishō Kongō Mahavajra	Godairiki Bosatsu Five Mahābala	Myōō Bu Vidyārāja
3.	Chintaku Fudō A Protector Acala	Aizen Rāgarāja	Ryōda Both Bags	Godaison Myōō Five Vidyārājas
4.	Kuri Kara/Black Dragon, a symbol of Acala	Kujaku Mayūri	Uzusama Ucchuṣma	Roku Jí Six Times of Day
5.	Kaen Jwala	Kongō Dōji Vajra Kumāra	Daigen Aṭavika	
6.	Fascicle - III			
7.	Sañjūnichi Hibutsu Esoteric Buddha's of Thirty Days	Sañjūbañjin Thirty Devas of Protection	Sanōshichisha Seven Shrines of Sannō	Kumano Gongen Incarnations of Kumano
8.	Hakuan Mount Hakusan	Fuji Mount Fuji	Izuna Izuna Incarnation	Suzuka Suzuka
9.	Atago Atago	Izu Izu	Hakone Hakone	Yu Tono Yu Tono
10.	Zoō Incharge of Sūtra's in Zen Monarstry	Hiryu Hiryu	Totō Tenjin Protector Diety of Travellers to China	Kōya Shisho Four Landmarks at Mt. Kōyasan
11.	Dōji no Bu Section of Kumāra	Uhō Ratnavarṣa	Hachiman God Hachiman	Kasuga Akadōji Red Kumāra of Kasuga
12.	Zenzai Sādhanā Śreṣṭhī dāraka	Kongō Dōji Vajra Kumāra	Zennishi Abbess	Kōshin Dōji, Shimen Setsuni Nīl-Vajra with both Kumāras & Four Dogmas

巻之四

	11	10	9	8	7	6	5	4	3	2	1
A	五道冥官	訶利底母	金光明辨天	刀八毘沙門	如來荒神	韋駄天	四天王	二十八宿	北斗	十羅刹女	十六童子
B	倶生神	寶藏天女	妙音天	吒枳尼天	吉祥天	堅牢地神	摩利支天	十二宮	明星	天部	不動八大童子
C	葬頭河婆	波利采天女	六大黒	八臂辨天	菩提樹天	夜叉	歡喜天	三十六禽	七曜	日輪	五道天
D	十王	優塡王	三面大黒	二臂辨天	非想天	三寶荒神	大形星	十二天	九曜	月輪	鬼子母神

	A	B	C	D
1.	Jūroku Dōji Sixteen Kumāras	Fudōhachi Dai Dōji Acala in form of eight Mahākūmāra	Godō Ten Five Realms of Heaven	Kishimojin Hariti
2.	Jūrasetsu Nyo Ten Raksis	Ten Bu Devas	Nichirin Halo of Sun	Getsu Rin Halo of Moon
3.	Hoku To Plow Star	Myō Jō Aruṇa	Shichiyō Saptagraha	Kuyō Navagraha
4.	Nijūhatsu Shuku 28 Nakṣatra	Jūni Kyū 12 Zodiacs	Sanjūroku Kin 36 Beasts	Jūni Ten Twelve Devas
5.	Shitenō Four Guardian Kings	Marishi Ten Marīci	Kanki Ten Nandikeśvara or Gaṇeśa	Daigyō Shō Big Star
6.	Idaten Skanda	Kenrōjishin Pṛthvī	Yasha Yakṣas	Sanbō Kōjin Kōjin of Three Treasures
7.	Nyorai Kōjin Tathāgata Kōjin, a Buddhist-Shinto God of Fireplace in the house	Kichijo Ten Śrī Mahādevī	Bodaijū Ten Deva of Bodhi tree	Hisōten Deva of Formless World
8.	Tōhatsu Bīshamon Vaiśravara with Eight Swords	Dakini Ten Dākiṇī	Hatsuhi Benten Eight Armed Sarasvatī	Nihi Benten Two Armed Sarasvatī
9.	Konkōmyō Benten Sarasvatī of Golden Light	Myōon Ten Gadgadaśvara	Roku daikoku Six Mahākālas	Sanmen Daikoku Three headed Mahākāla
10.	Haritei Bo Harītī	Hōzō Tennyo Ratna Devi	Harisaī Tennyo A Devi	Uten ō King Udayana
11.	Godō The Official in the retinue of Ten Kings of Naraka	Kushō jin The being, born with indivdual, called ĀlayaVijñāna	Sōzugawa no Baba Old Woman of the River of three Crossings (Hell)	Jū ō Ten Rajas

	1	2	3	4	5	6	7	8	9	10	11
A	藥師十二神	十三佛	延命尊	多羅	善光寺如來	十二光佛	七福神	摩竭	迦陵頻伽	葛由	十大弟子
B	十六善神	龍樹	胎虚空藏	普賢延命	因幡藥師	三十三所內	舩玉宮	飢竭	偓佺	西王母	維摩居士
C	廿八部衆	地藏	五大空藏	烏瑟膩沙最勝尊	嵯峨釋迦	觀音變像	猩猩	前鬼後鬼	赤松子	扁鵲	役行者
D	一代守本尊	藥王	求聞持		天王寺庚申	六齋日本尊	天狗	天人	馮長	十六羅漢	聖徳太子

巻之五

Fascicle - IV

	A	B	C	D
1.	Yakushi Jūnijin 12 Marshals of Bhaisajya Guru	Jūroku Zenjin Sixteen Yakṣas	Nijūhachi Bushū 28 Guardians	Ichidaishū Honzon Main deities Enshrined in Temples
2.	Jissan Butsu Thirteen Buddhas	Ryūju Nāgārjuna	Jizō Kṣitigarbha	Yakuō Bhaiṣaja Guru
3.	Enmei son Buddha of Longevity	Taikokū Zō Ākāśa Garbhadhātu	Go Daiku-zō Five Evolvers of Ākāśa Garbhadhātu	Gumon ji Gumonji, Worshiped in esoteric ritual
4.	Tara Tara	Fugen Enmei Prolonged Life Samantabhadra	Uzunisha Saishō Son Uṣṇīśa of the Revered One	
5.	Zenkōji Nyorai Tathāgata of Zenkōji	Inaba Yakushi Yakushi of Inaba	Saga Shaka Śākyamuni of Saga	Tenōji Kōshin Kōshin of Tennōji
6.	Juni kōbutsu Amitābha's 12 titles of Light	Sanjūsan Shonouchi Kannon Henzō Deities of 33 temples of Avalokiteśvara		Rokusainichi Honzon Main Deities of Upoṣadha
7.	Shichifuku Jin The seven gods of fortune	Funadama kū Guardian deity of ships	Shōjō Hanuman	Tengu Long nosed Creature
8.	Makatsu Rahu and	Kekatsu Ketu	Zenki Goki A pair of goblins	Tennin Celestial beings
9.	Karyūbinga Kalaviṅka	Okusen Ascetic Okusen	Shaku Shoshi Ascetic Sekimatsu	Fuchō Ascetic Fuchō
10.	Katsuyu Ascetic Katsuyu	Seiōbo Queen Mother of the West	Henjaku Chinese Healer	Jūroku Rakan Sixteen Arhats
11.	Jūdai Deshi Ten Great Disciples	Yuima Koji Vimalakīrti	Enno Gyōja Ācārya Enno Ozuno	Shotoku Taishi Prince Shōtoku

	12	11	10	9	8	7	6	5	4	3	2	1
A	○禪宗	善无畏	龍猛	智證	妙樂	○天台宗	俊芿	○律宗	道空	道融	慈恩	○法相宗
B	達磨	一行	龍智	惠心	傳教	南岳	○華嚴宗	菊多	○成實宗	惠灌	○三論宗	護法
C	慧可	惠果	金剛智	檀那	慈覺	智者	華嚴	鑒真	跋摩	○倶舎宗	青辨	戒賢
D	僧璨	弘法	不空	○眞言宗	元三	章安	惠藏	叡尊	善無畏	世親	羅什	智鳳

Fascicle - V

	A	B	C	D
1.	* Hossō shū The Hosso Sect	Go Hō Dharmapāla	Kaiken Śīla Bhadra (529-645)	Chi Hō The Chihō
2.	Jion Kuei Chi	* Sanron Shū Sanron Sect	Sōben Bhāviveka (490-570)	RaJū Kumārajīva
3.	Dōyū Chinese Monk Doyu	Ekan The Founder of Sanron in 625 AD	* Kusha shu The Kusha Sect	Sesshin Vasubandhu
4.	Dōkū A Chinese Monk of Kusha Sect	* Jōjitsu Shu The Jojitsu sect	Batsu Ma Hari Varman	Zenmui Subhakar Siṁha
5.	* Ritsu Shu The Ritsu Sect	Kikuta Monk Dharam gupta	Ganjin The Chinese Monk Gañjin (688-763)	Ei-zon Japanese Monk Eizon (1201-1290)
6.	Shunjō A Monk of Ritsu sect (1166-1227)	* Kegon Shu The Kegon Sect	Kegon Hua-Yen	Ezō Mastu Ezō
7.	* Tendai Shu The Tendai Sect	Nan Gaku Chinese Monk Nān-yue Huāi-rāng (677-744)	Chisha The Founder of Tendai School in China Chih-i Chēn (538-597)	Shō An Chinese Monk Guān-ding (561-632) of Tendai Sect
8.	Myo Raku Chines Monk of Tendai Sect named Tannen (zham-rān) (711-782)	Den-Gyō Dengyō Daishi, the title given to Monk Saichō	Ji Kaku Monk En Nin (794-864)	Gan Zan Posthumous name of Monk Ryo Gen of Tendai Sect
9.	Chishō Chinese scholar of Buddhist works	E shin Monk Genshin (942-1017) of Tendai Sect	Danna Monk Kakuun	* Shingon Shū The Shingon Sect
10.	Ryū Myō The Chinese name of Nāgārjuna	Ryū chi Nāgabodhi	Kongō Chi Vajra Bodhi	Fukū Amoghavajra (705-774)
11.	Zenmui Śubhakarasiṁha (637-735)	Ichi gyō Yi-Xing (683-727), a Chinese monk	Kei ka Chinese Monk Hui-Guo (746-805)	Kō Bō The Posthumous name given to Kūkai
12.	* Zen Shu The Zen sect	Daruma Bodhi Dharma	Eka Chinese Monk Hui-ke (487-593)	Sō San A Chinese Zen Master

12	11	10	9	8	7	6	5	4	3	2	1	
延鎮	空也	大燈	普門	道元	性空	泰澄	婆羅門	親鸞	曇鸞	馬鳴	道信	A
唱念	辨阿	文覺	壹演	百丈	聖寶	良辨	明恵	○日蓮	道綽	龍樹	弘忍	B
一遍	良忍	中將法尼	榮西	夢相	臨濟	興正	行基	○玄昉	善導	天親	恵能	C
俊乘	證空	永觀	慧玄	聖一	隱元	覺鑁	解脱	智泉	法然	流支	○淨土宗	D

	A	B	C	D
1.	Dojin A Chinese Monk of Zen Buddhism	Kōnin Hung-jen (643-716) A Patriarch of Chinese Zen	Enō Priest of Chinese Zen (638-713)	* Jōdō Shu The Jōdō (Pure Land) sect
2.	Mu Myō Aśvaghoṣa	Ryū jū Nāgārjuna	Ten jin An Indian Monk, Vasubandhu	Ru shi Bodhi Ruci
3.	Don Ran T'an-Luan (476-542)	Dō Shaku Tao-ch'o (562-645)	Zen Dō Chinese Monk Shan Tao (613-681)	Hō Nen Priest Hōnen (1133-1212)
4.	Shin Ran Priest Shinran	* Nichi Ren The Nichiren Sect	* Grembō A Priest of Hossō Sect	Chisen High Priest Chisen
5.	Bara Mon Brāhmana	Myō E A Priest of Kegon Sect	Gyo Gi Priest Gyogi (668-749)	Ge Datsu Monk Jokei (1155-1213) of Hossō Sect
6.	Tai Chō Ascetic Taicho	Rō Ben A Monk of Kegon Sect of Japan	Kōshō Priest Eizon of Ritsu Sect	Kaku Ban Monk Kakuban (1095–1143) of Shingon Sect
7.	Shōkū Jonin Priest Shōku	Shō Bō (832-909) A Priest of Shingon Sect of Japan	Rinzai Chinese Monk Rinzai Gigen	In Gen Monk Yin Yuan (1592-1673)
8.	Dōgen Founder of Sōtō Sect in Japan	Hyaku jō Monk Hyaku jō Ekai of Chinese zen	Mu Sō Priest Musō of (1275-1351) Rinzai Sect	Shō Ichi Monk Bennen (1202-1280)
9.	Fu mon Samantamukha	Ichi En A Monk of Rin zai Sect known as Mujū	Eisai Priest Eisai (1141-1215) of Rinzai Sect	E Gen Zen Masler E-Gen
10.	Dai Tō An abreivation of title given to Priest Myōchō of Rinzai Sect	Mon Gaku Priest Mongaku	Chūjō Hōni The Chūjō Hime associated with Taima Maṇḍala	Eī Kan Priest Eīkan
11.	Kūya Founder of Kūya School of Tendai Sect	Ben A Another name of Monk Bencho (1162-1238)	Ryōnin Priest Ryōnin (1071-1132)	Shō Kū Priest Shōkū (1177-1247)
12.	Enchin A Priest of Tendai Sect	Shō-Nen Nichiren	Ippen Monk Ippen (1239-1289)	Shunjō Monk Chogan (1121-1206)

	12	11	10	9	8	7	6	5	*4	3	2	1
A	梧桐角	鉢子生飯板	鳴槌	木魚	磬	風鐸	幢幡	佛座	舍利塔	道具部	覺信	國阿
B	鷄婁	華籠	槌碪	銅鑼鼓	雲版	鐸	佛殿旛	瓔珞	**佛龕		眞佛	西山眠像
C	角子	鼓	齋堂前飯擲	佛前鐘鼓	銅鉢	鈴	鐘	花曼	***舟御光		寒山	日像
D	銅角	寶幖	錫杖	虚鼓	鈸	鈴杵	鐘版	天蓋	***輪御光		拾得	日興

	A	B	C	D
1.	Koku A Monk Koku-A of Jishu	Seizan Nemurizō Reclining Posture at Seizan	Nichi Zō Monk Nichizō (1267-1342) of Nichiren Sect	Nichi-Kō Nikkō, a Priest of Nichiren Sect
2.	Kaku Shini Bīkuni Kakushin of Jōdo Sect	Shin Butsu Priest Shinbutsu	Kanzan Hanshan Kumāra	Jittoku Shin-tẽ Kumāra
3.	Dōgu Bu; Implements and Accessories			
4.	Shari tō A Stūpa	Butsugan Buddhist Altar	Funa gokō Boat shape Halo	Wa gokō Round Halo
5.	Butsuza Buddha's Seat	Yoraku Decorative Accessories	Keman Garlands	Tengai Canopy
6.	Dōhan Hanging banner in Buddhist Temple	Butsuden Hata Banner of the Inner Hall	Shō Hanging Bell	Shō han Bell used in monastry for signals
7.	Fū Taku Wind Bells	Taku Chimes	Rei Bell	Reikyo Bell Pestles
8.	Kei Large drum	Unhan Cloud shape bronze plate used as a Gong in Zen monastry	Dōhatū Copper Bowl	Hatsu Cymbals
9.	Moku Gyo A Wooden Drum in the Shape of a Fish	Dōrako Gong	Butsuzen no Shōko Drum & Bell in front of Buddha	Kyoko Drum
10.	Mei Tsui Mallet	Tsui Chin Mallet and wooden block used in Zen monastery	Saidō mae no-Hanteki Bell for Dinning Hall	Shakujo Staff
11.	Hachi no ko San han Ita Wooden tray for monks	Ke-ko Flower Basket	Ko Drum	Hōbyō Kalaśa
12.	Gotō Kaku Wooden trumpet	Keirō Conventional-Drum	Kakushi Trumpet	Dō kaku Bronze Trumpet

	12	11	10	9	8	7	6	5	4	3	2	1
A	花皿 (ハナザラ)	香爐 (カウロ)	扇 (セン)	如意 (ニヨイ)	座具 (ザグ)	絡子	廿五條袈裟 (ニジウゴデウケサ)	袍 (ハウ)	月琴 (ゲツキン)	琴 (キン)	尺八 (シヤクハチ)	律 (リツ)
B	佛供 (ブツグ)	香盒 (カウバコ)	引磬 (インキン)	護摩壇 (ゴマダン)	帽 (バウ)	淨土宗掛絡 (ジヤウドシウクワラ)	九條袈裟 (クデウケサ)	裳 (モ)	琵琶 (ビワ)	鼗 (トウ)	簫 (セウ)	笙 (シヤウ)
C	釣鉦 (ツリガネ)	花瓶 (クワビン)	線香臺 (センカウダイ)	經 (キヤウ)	嗩吶 (サ)	輪袈裟 (ワゲサ)	袈裟 (ケサ)	堂衣素絹 (ダウエソケン)	直綴 (ヂキトツ)	箜篌 (クウコ)	羯鼓 (カツコ)	笛 (フエ)
D	敲鉦 (タタキガネ)	鰐口 (ワニクチ)	鶴龜 (ツルカメ)	數珠 (ジユズ)	拂塵 (ホツシン)	鈴懸 (スズカケ)	七條袈裟横被 (シチデウケサワウヒ)	法服 (ホフブク)	衣 (コロモ)	阮咸 (ゲンカン)	腰鼓 (エウコ)	箏

	A	B	C	D
1.	Ritsu Rhythm notes	Shō A reed Instrument	Fue Flute	Shichi Rikoi Shinto Flute
2.	Shaku hanchi Japanese Bamboo Flute	Sō Flute with Several Pipes	Kakko Chinese Shoulder Drum	Yō ko Waist Drum
3.	Kin Koto Stringed Instrument	Tō Japanese drum	Kū ko Japanese Harp	Genkan A stringed Instrument
4.	Gekkin Round Moon shape Koto	Biwa Japanese Lute	Jikitotsu A casual robe of Monk	Koromo Robe
5.	Hō Coat	Mo Skirt	Dōe Soken Coarse silk Robe	Hō Buku Preacher's Robe
6.	Nijūgo Chō Kesa Twenty five pleated Monk's Stole	Kujō Gesa Nine layered Monk's Robe	Kesa Monk's Robe	Shichijō Kesa ōhi Seven lined stole
7.	Kaku shi Trumpet	Jōdōshū Kara Pure Land Sect Monk's Robe	Wagesa Round Robe	Suzu kake Loose Robe
8.	Zagu Cushion	Bō Cap	Sanō Pipe Instrument	Bucchin Clean Speck
9.	Nyoi Anuruddha	Goma dan Platform for Yagña	Kyō Sūtra	Zuju Rosary
10.	Sen Japanesse Fan	In Kin Percussion Instrument &	Senkō Dai Insence stand	Tsuru Kame Crane & Tortoise
11.	Kōro Censer	Ko Bako Incense Container	Kabin Flower Vase	Wani Guchi Temple Gong
12.	Hana Zara Plate for Flower	Butsu gu Altar for Offerings	Tsuri gane Hanging Bell	Tataki Gama Ceremonial Gong in a temple

	6	5	4	3	2	1
A	轅輿	燈籠	傘	講座	位牌	* 燈燭
B	寶輿	皮鞋	拄杖	倚子	出生臺	** 菓子盆
C	五輪石塔	率都婆	琉璃燈	水漉	經机	*** 供饗
D	石燈	山門外立石	提燈	淨瓶	香案	**** 三方

増補佛像圖彙目録終

	A	B	C	D
1.	Toshoku Candle	Okashi Bon small wood stand for	Kukyō sanbō dinner service sweets	San bō Tables
2.	Ihai Buddhist Memorial Tablets	Shusshō Dai A stand to hold new born	Kyō tsukue Table for Sūtra	Kōan Desk for Incense
3.	Kōza Lecture chair	Isu Chair/couch	Mizu Koshi Strainer	Jō bin Pure water jar
4.	Kasa Umbrella	Shujō Monk's wand	Ruri To Lapis lazuli Lights	Tei tō Hand Lamp
5.	Tō rō Lantern	Hia Footwear	Sotoba Stūpa	Sanmon no tateishi Milestone of a temple
6.	Nagae Koshi Palnquin	Hō yo Jewelled palanquin	Gorin Seki tō Five stage-stone pagoda	Seki tō Stone Lantern

End of Index of enlarged edition

增補諸宗佛像圖彙

貳

Fascicle II

§ 1. Fudaishi with two sons (1)

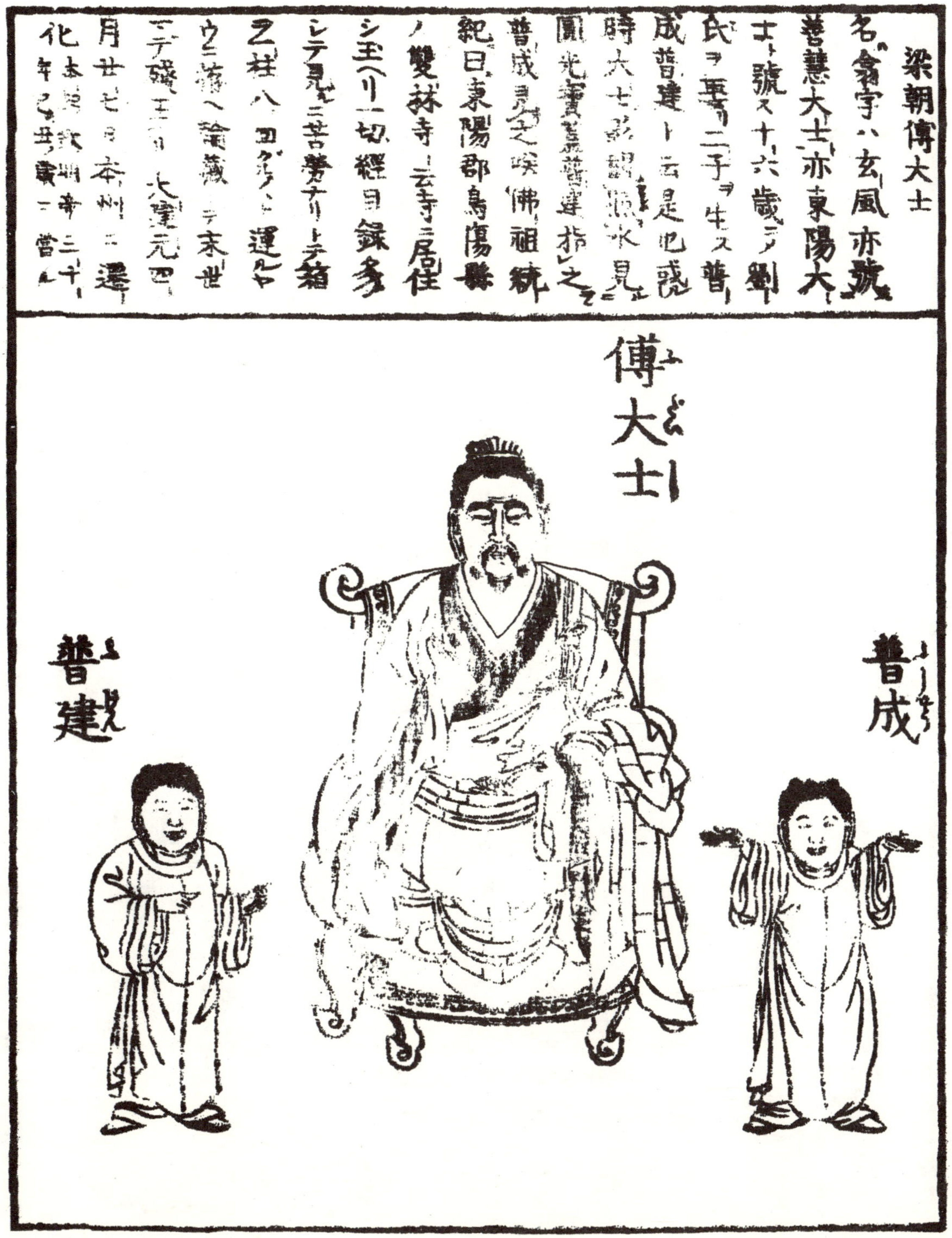

Fuken: First son of Fudaishi

1. Fudaishi: Mahāsattva Fukyu of China (CE 497-569).

Fujō: Second son of Fudaishi

§ 2. The four stages of the Śākyamuni (2-5)

4. Shōgaku no Shaka
Śākyamuni in Sambodhi

2. Tanjō no Shaka
Śākyamuni at Birth

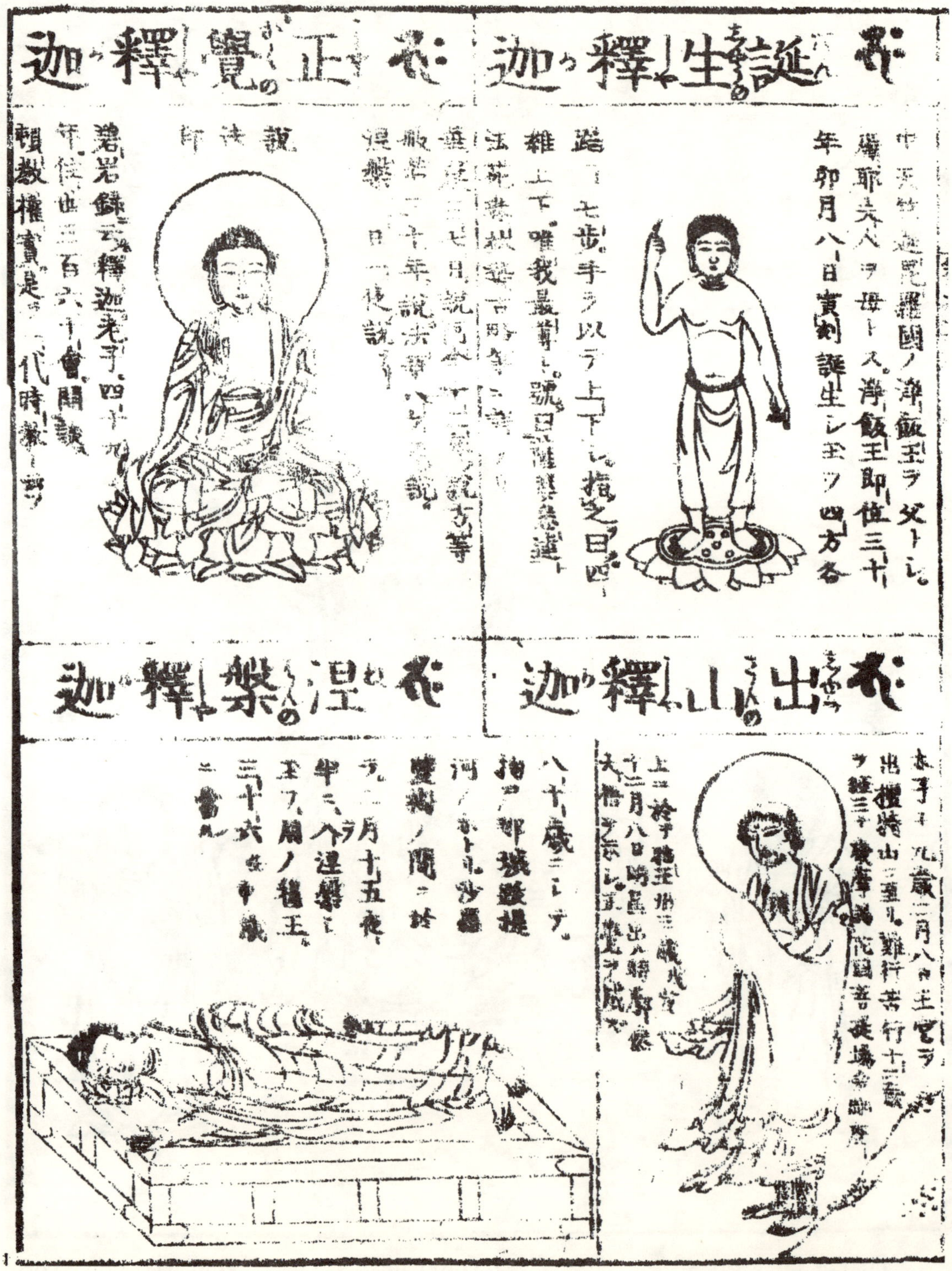

5. Nehan no Shaka
Śākyamuni in Nirvāṇa

3. Shussan no Shaka
Śākyamuni leaving the mountains

§ 3. Kuhon no Amida
Nine Grades of Amitābha (6-21)

8. Jōbon Geshō
Amitābha of lower superior grade
in Pure Land

6. Jōbon Jōshō
Amitābha of upper superior grade
in Pure Land

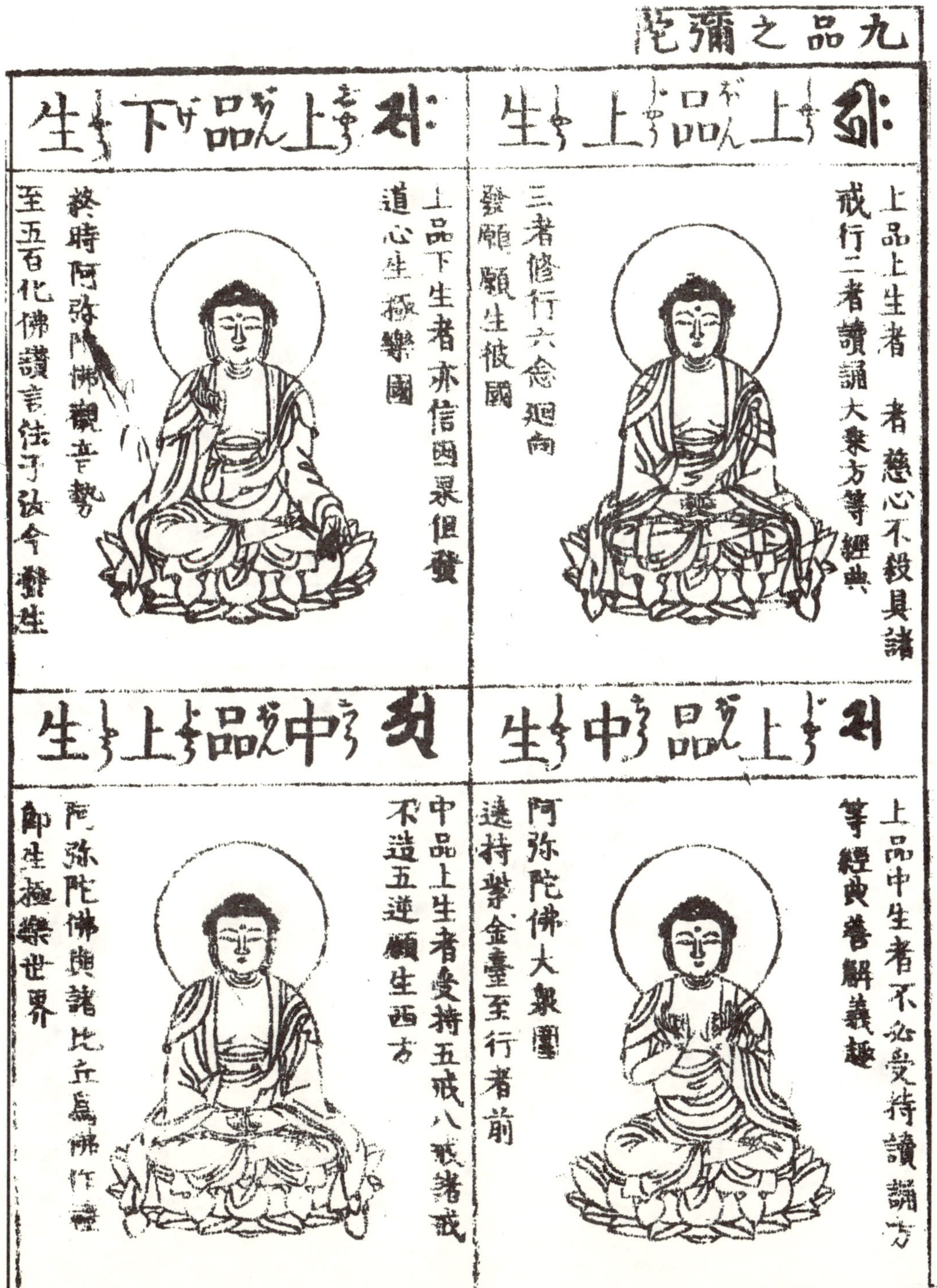

9. Chūbon Jōshō
Amitābha of upper middle grade
in Pure Land

7. Jōbon Chūshō
Amitābha of middle superior grade
in Pure Land.

12. Gebon Jōshō
Amitābha of superior lower grade in Pure Land.

10. Chūbon Chūshō
Amitābha of mid of middle grade in Pure Land.

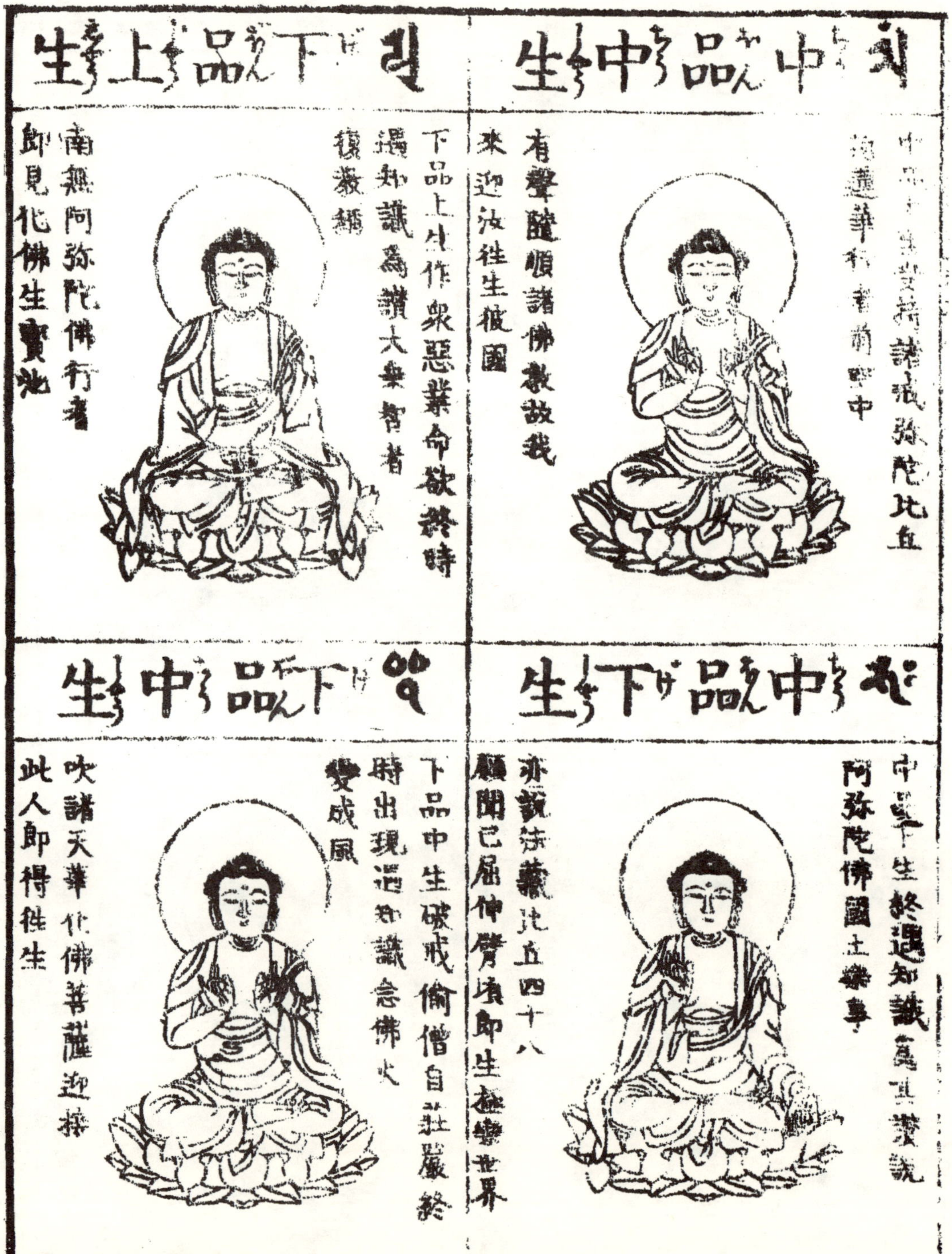

13. Gebon Chūshō
Amitābha of middle-lower grade in Pure Land.

11. Chūbon Geshō
Amitābha of lower-middle grade in Pure Land.

16. Mandara no Mida
Amitābha of the Maṇḍala

14. Gebon Geshō
Amitābha of lowest lower-grade of Pure Land.

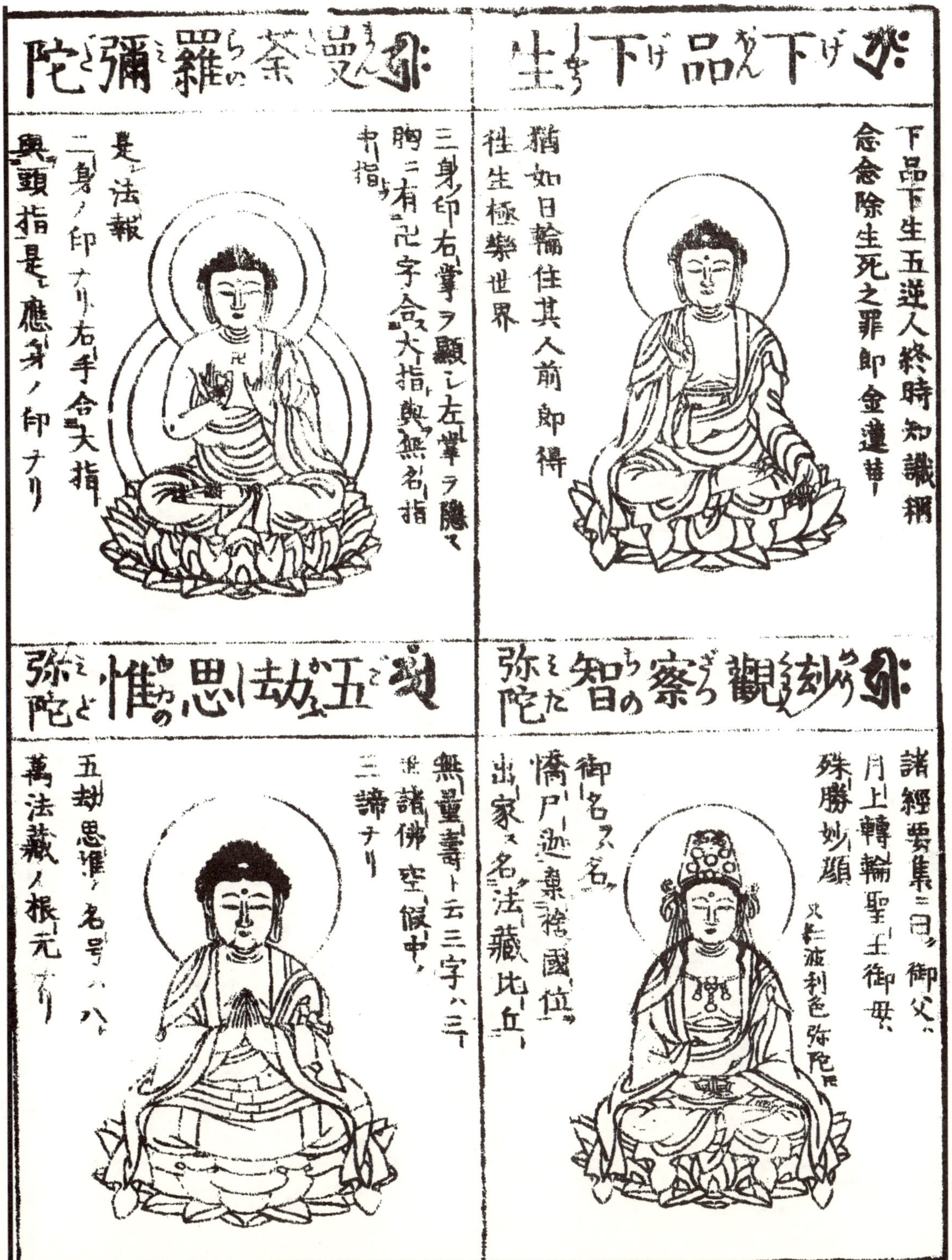

17. Gokōshui no Mida
Amitābha's vows of Five Kalpas

15. Myōkanzacchi no Mida
Amitābha of Pratyavekṣanā Jñāna

20. Kongōkai no Dainichi
Mahāvairocana of Vajradhātu

18. Yamagoshi no Nyorai
Tathāgata of Mountains

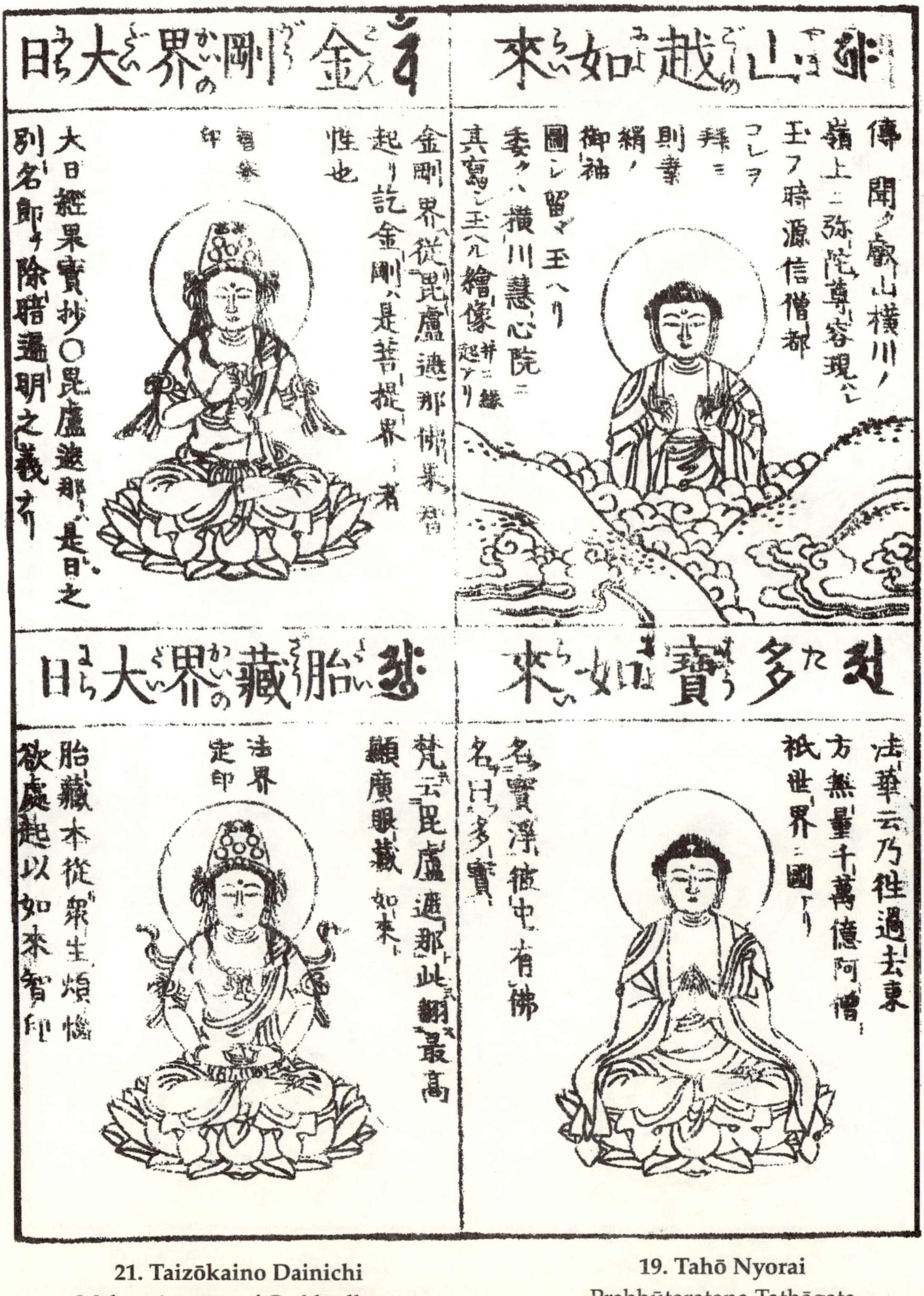

21. Taizōkaino Dainichi
Mahāvairocana of Garbhadhātu

19. Tahō Nyorai
Prabhūtaratana Tathāgata

§ 4. Shichibutsu Yakushi
The Seven Buddhas of Healing and Other Buddhas (22-28), (29-33)

24. Konjikihōkōmyōgyō Jōjuō, 3
Svaraṇaprabhāratna Siddhirāja

22. Zenmyōshokisshōō Nyorai, 1
Sarvasattva priyadarśana Tathāgata

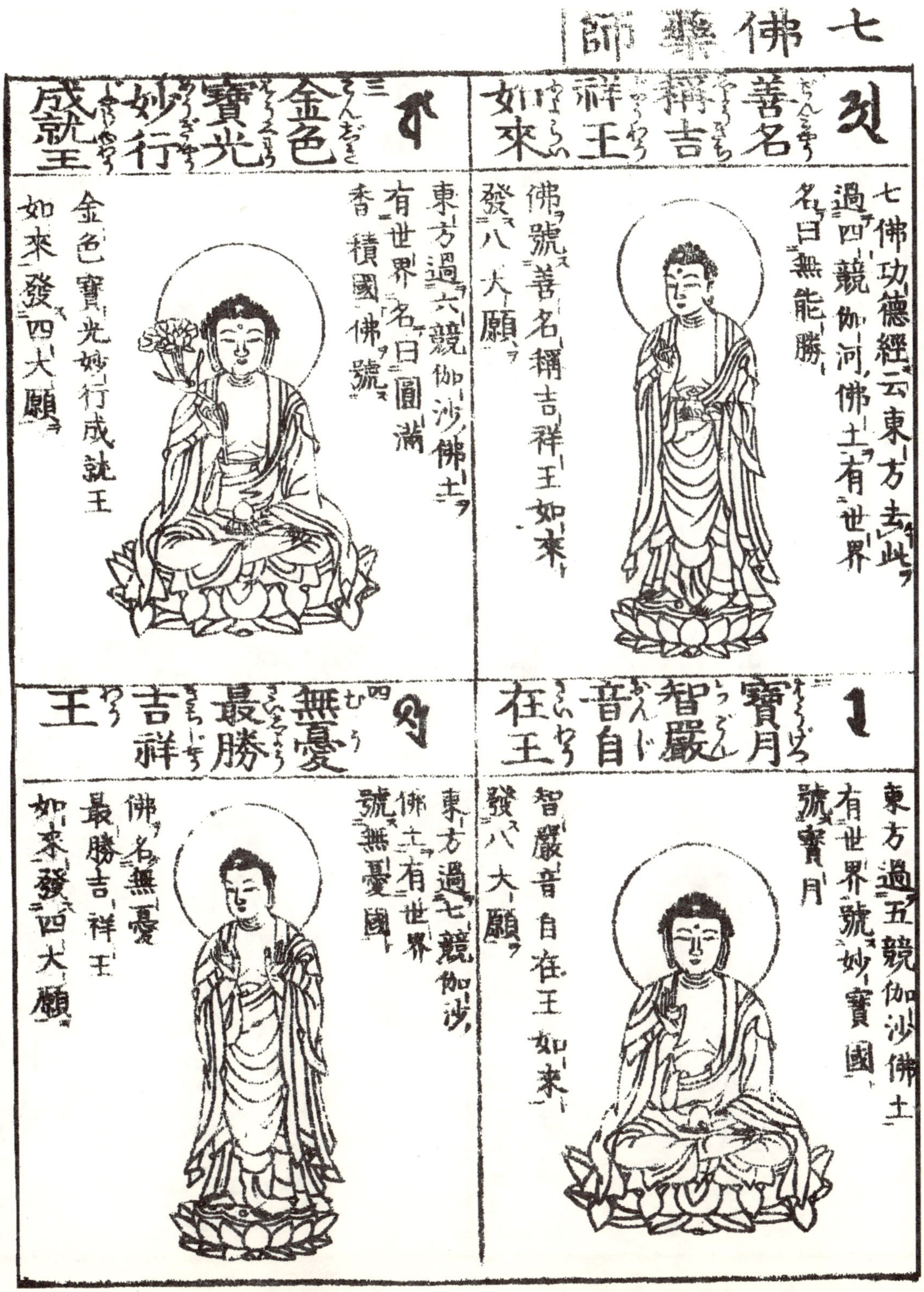

25. Muusaishō kisshōō, 4
Aśoka-Vijayarāja

23. Hogetsuchigenon Jizaiō, 2
Candraratna-janana Īśvaradeva

28. Yakushi Rurikō Nyorai, 7
Vaiḍūryaprabhā Tathāgata,

26. Hōkairaion Nyorai, 5
Tathāgata of thunderous roar

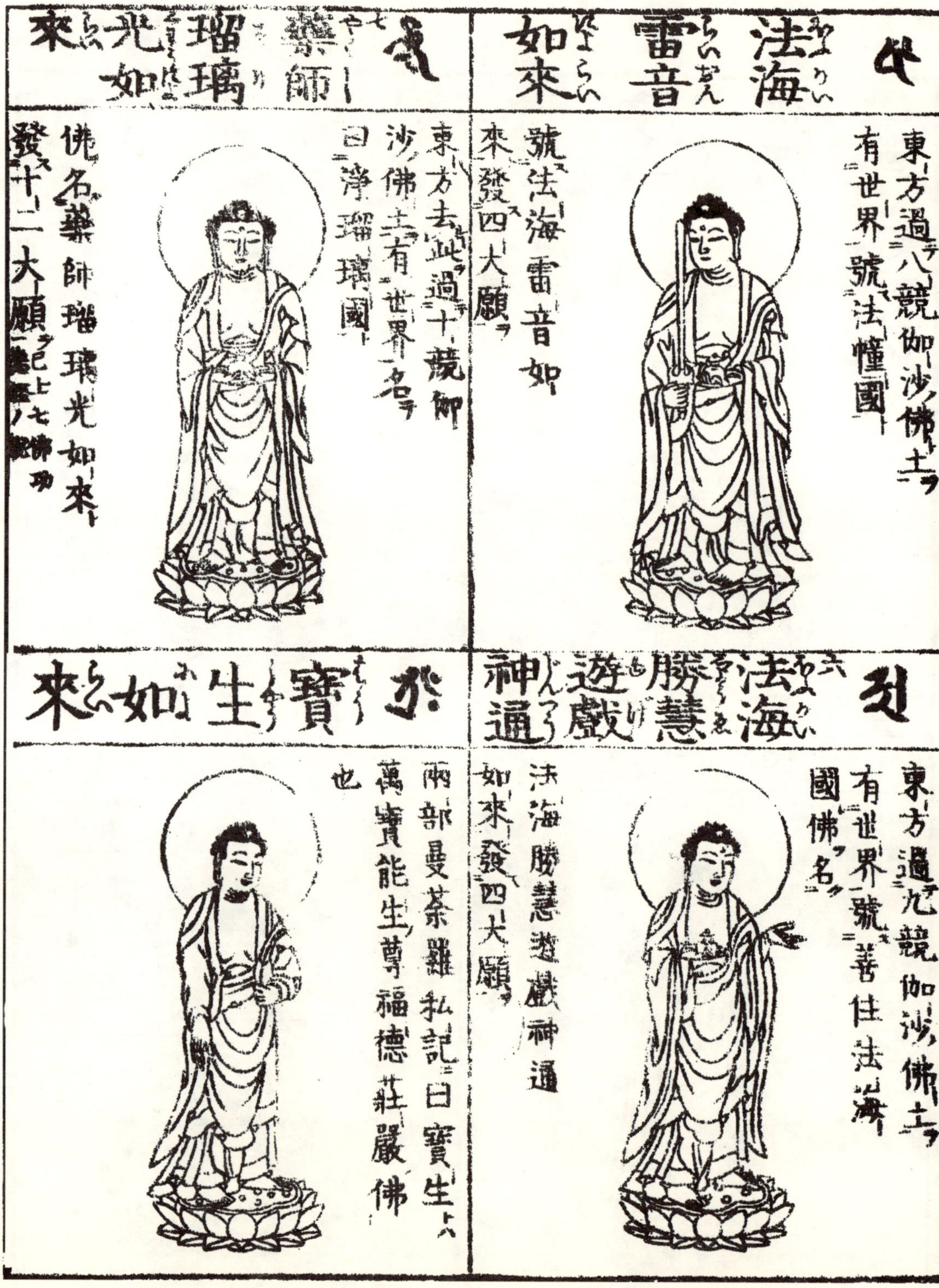

29. Chōshō Nyorai
Ratnasambhava Tathāgata

27. Hōkaishōeyuge Jintsu, 6
Dharmadhātu Vikrīḍita

32. Sanmantōmyō Butsu
Thirty thousand-Prabha Buddha

30. Nichigetsu tōmyō Butsu
Candra Sūryaprabhā Buddha

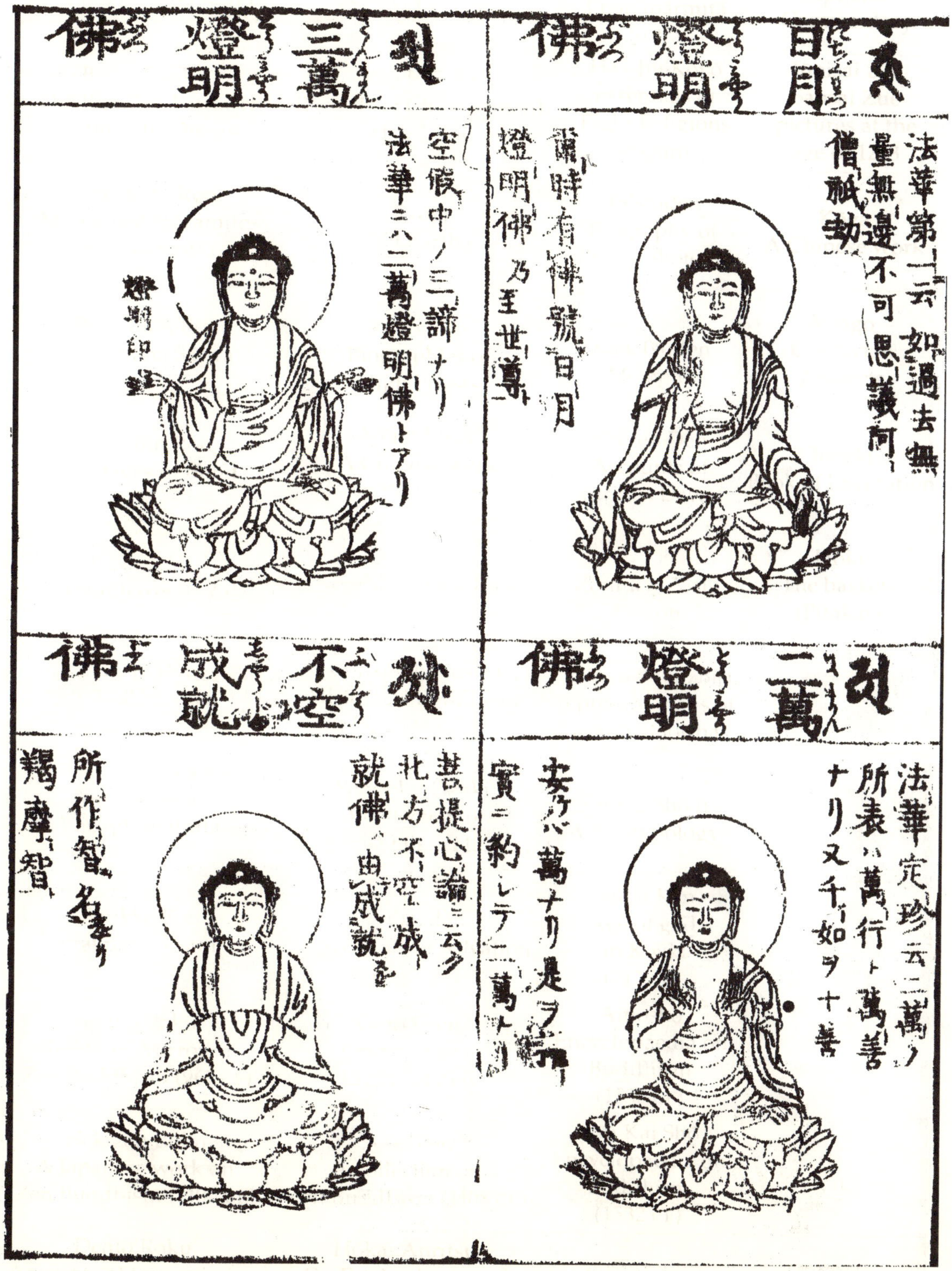

33. FukūJōju Butsu
Amoghasiddhi Buddha

31. Niman tōmyō Butsu
Twenty thousand Prabha Buddha

§ 5. The Eight Bodhisattvas and Others (34-45)

36. Hanya Bosatsu
Prajñāpāramitā Bodhisattva

34. Ichijikinrin
Ekākṣara Uṣṇīṣacakravartī

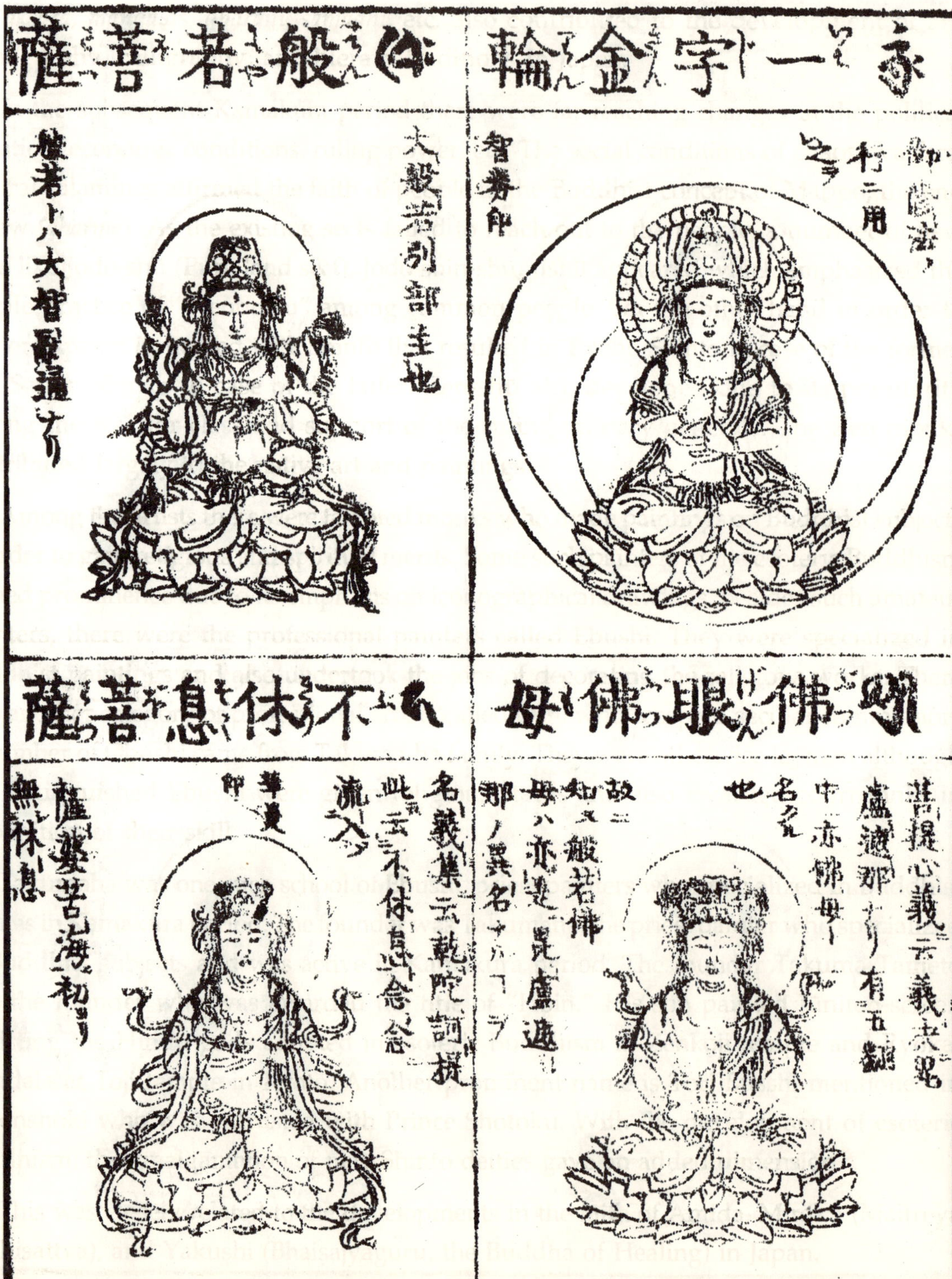

37. Fukyūsoku Bosatsu
Bodhisattva of Infinite Life

35. Butsugen Butsumo
Goddess Buddhalocanā

40. Fugen Bosatsu
Samantabhadra Bodhisattva

38. Monjūshiri Bosatsu
Mañjuśrī Bodhisattva

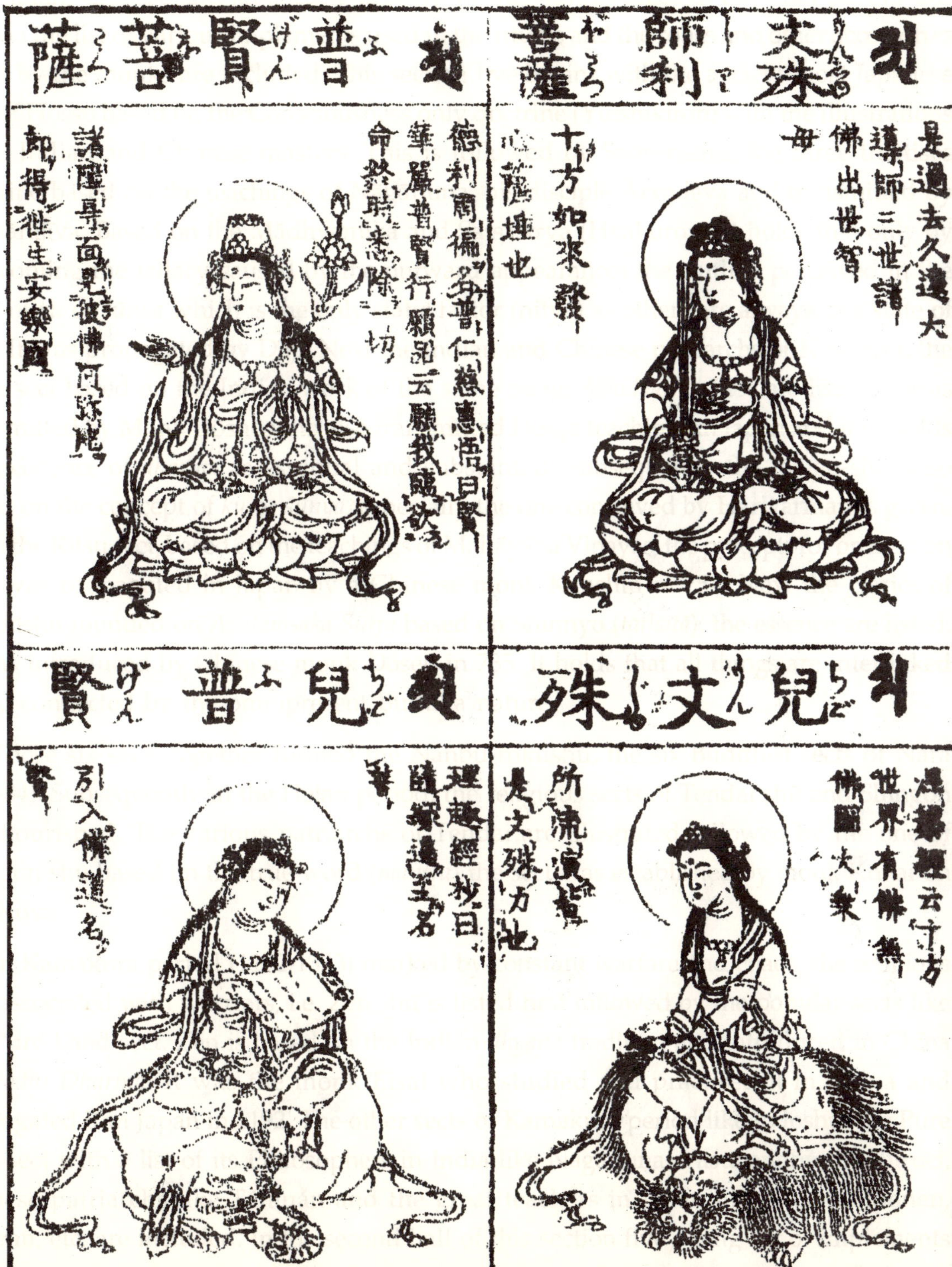

41. Chigo Fugen
Young Samantabhadra

39. Chigo Monjū
Young Mañjuśrī

44. Kokūzō Bosatsu
Ākāśagarbha Bodhisattva

42. Shichiji Monju
Saptākṣara Mañjuśrī

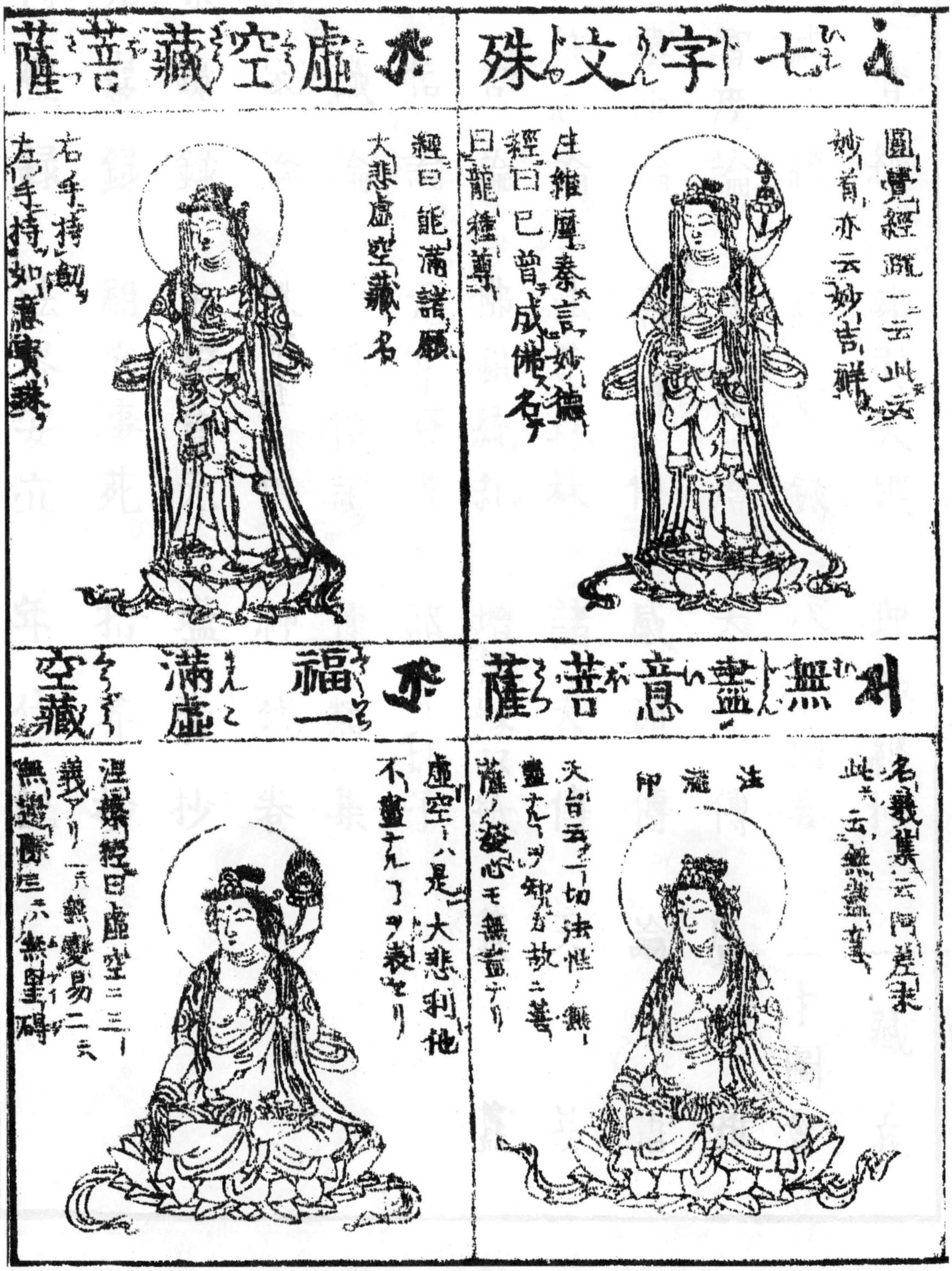

45. Fukuichiman Kokūzō
Ākāśagarbha of ten thousand Weal (*puṇya*)

43. Mujini Bosatsū
Cintāmaṇi Bodhisattva

§ 6. Kongō kai Jū-roku Daibosatsu Vajradhātu Ṣoḍaśa Mahāsattva (46-61)

48. Kongōai
Vajrarāga

46. Kongōsatta
Vajrasattva

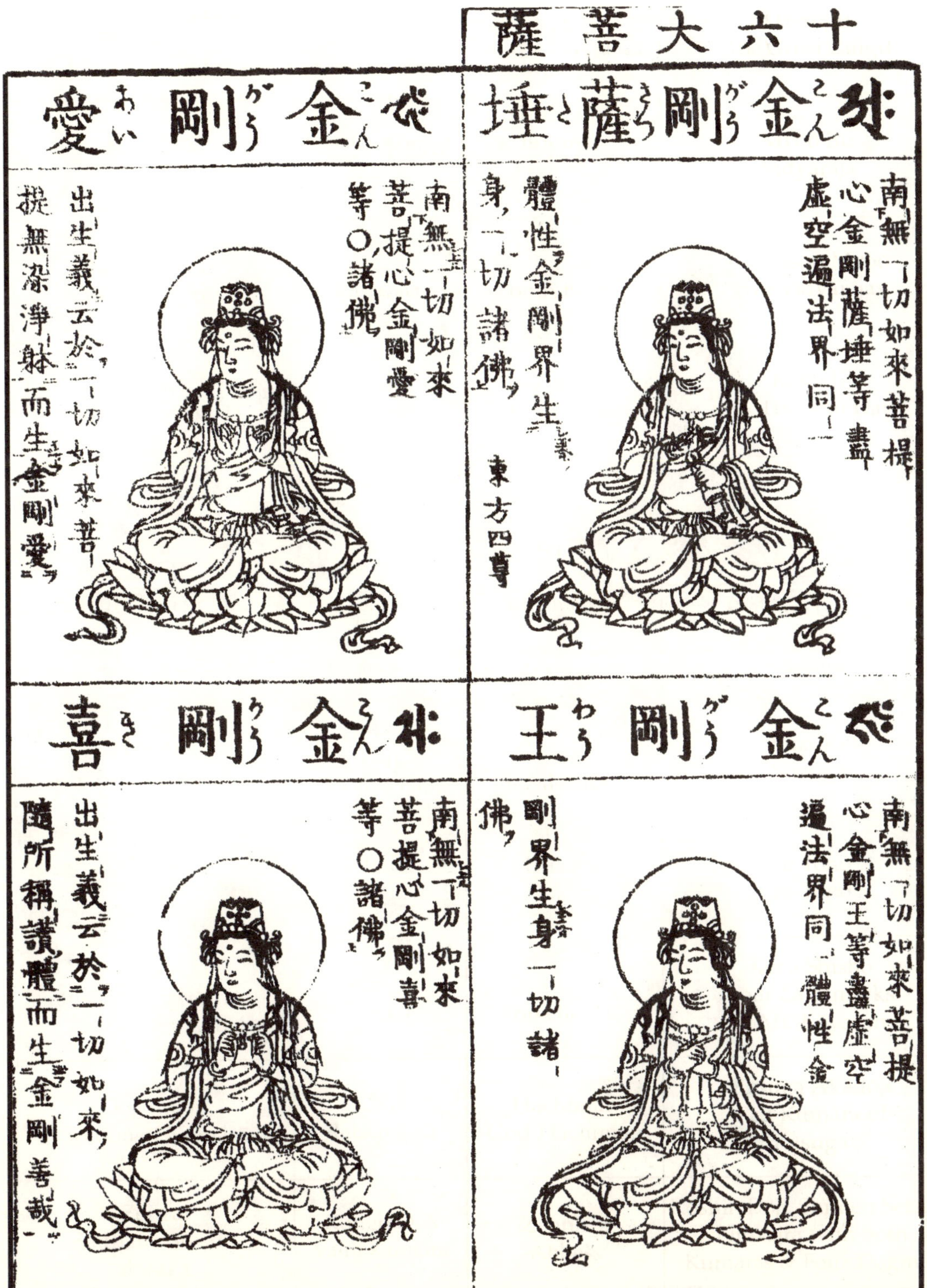

49. Kongōki
Vajraprasanna

47. Kongōō
Vajrarāja

52. Kongōdō
Vajrakumāra

50. Kongōhō
Vajraratna

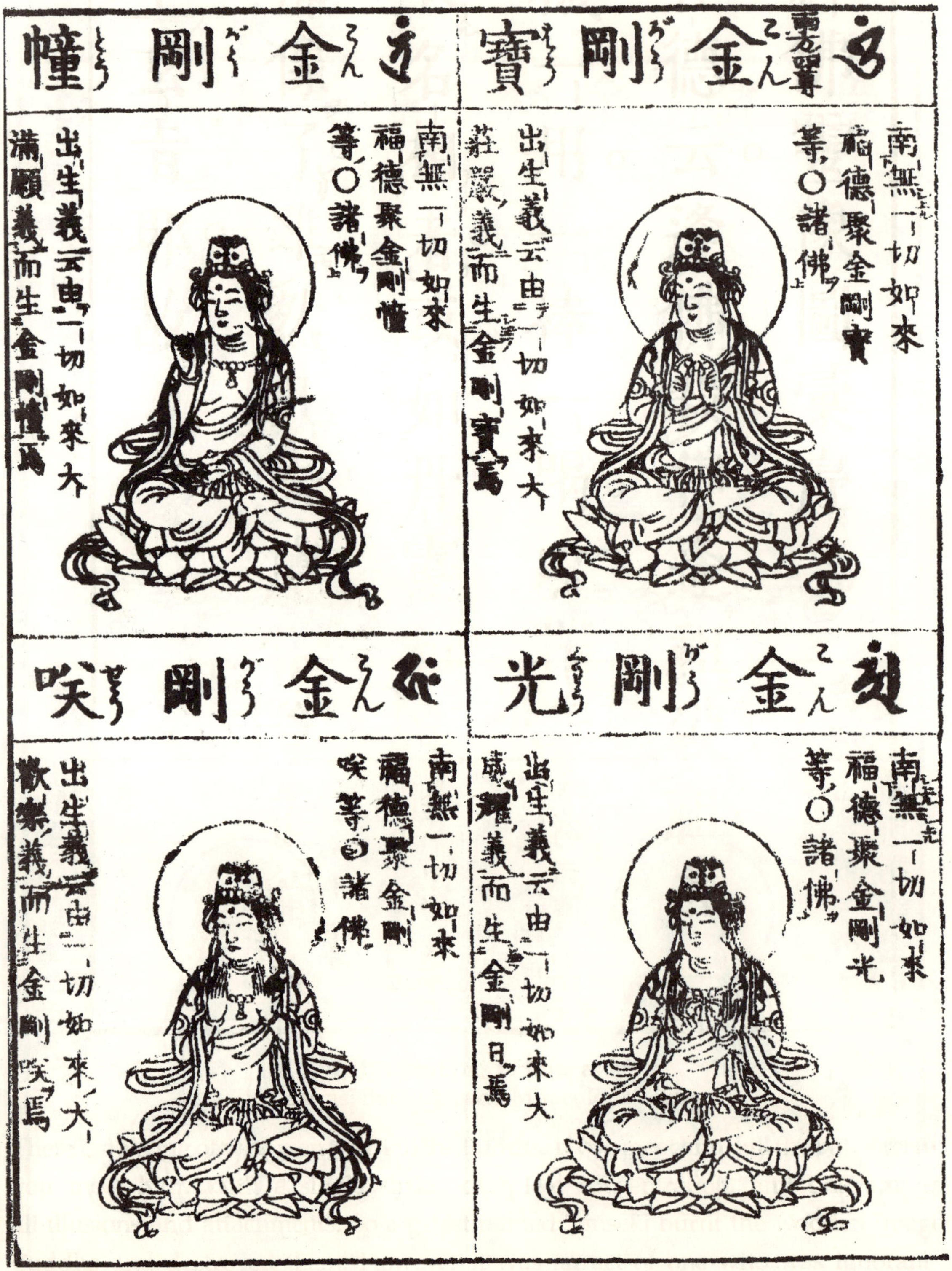

53. Kongōshō
Vajragandha

51. Kongōkō
Vajraprabhā

56. Kongōin
Vajrahetu

54. Kongōhō
Vajradharma

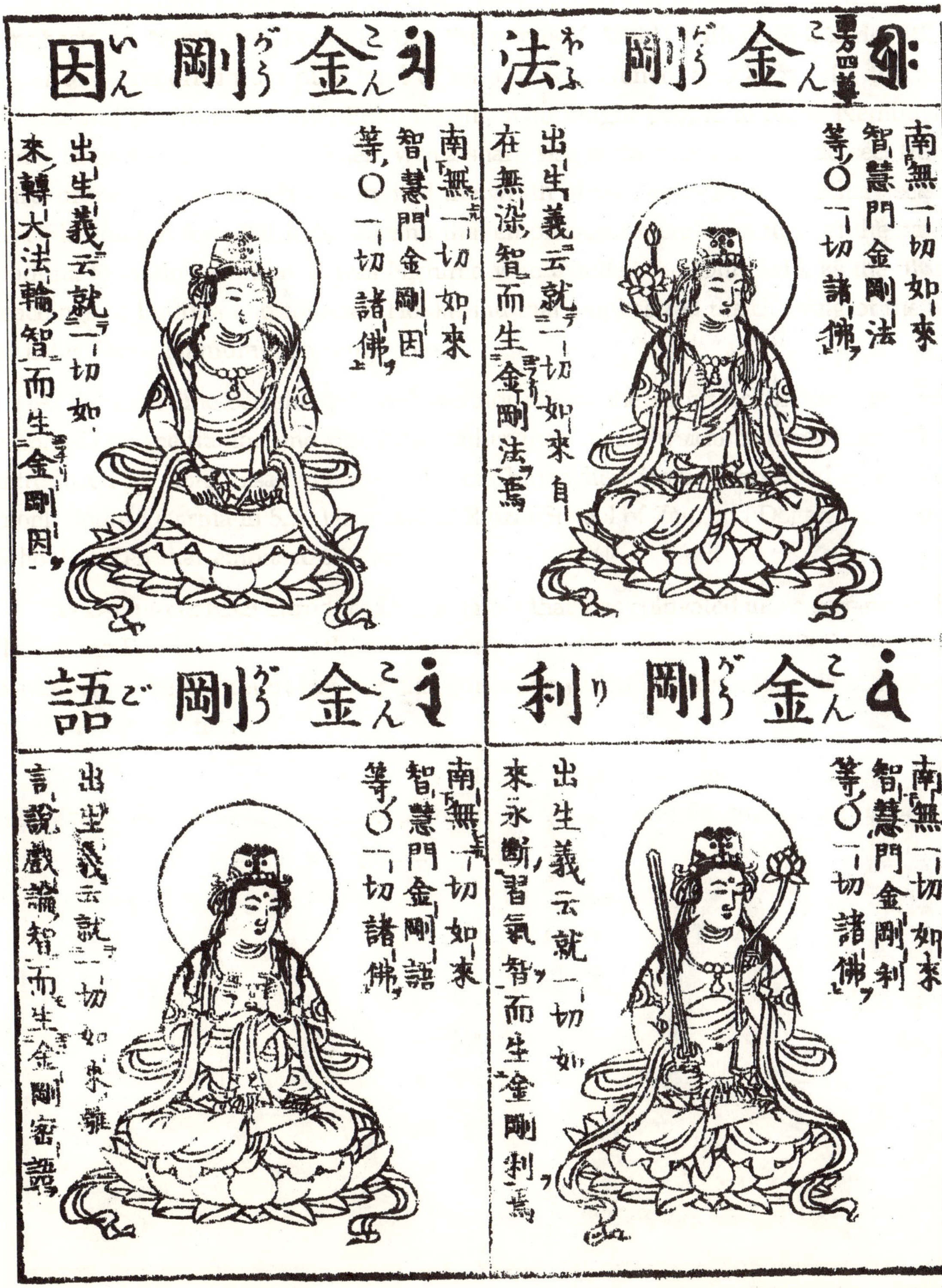

57. Kongōgo
Vajrabhāṣa

55. Kongōri
Vajralābha

60. Kongōge
Vajradanta

58. Kongōgō
Vajra-karman

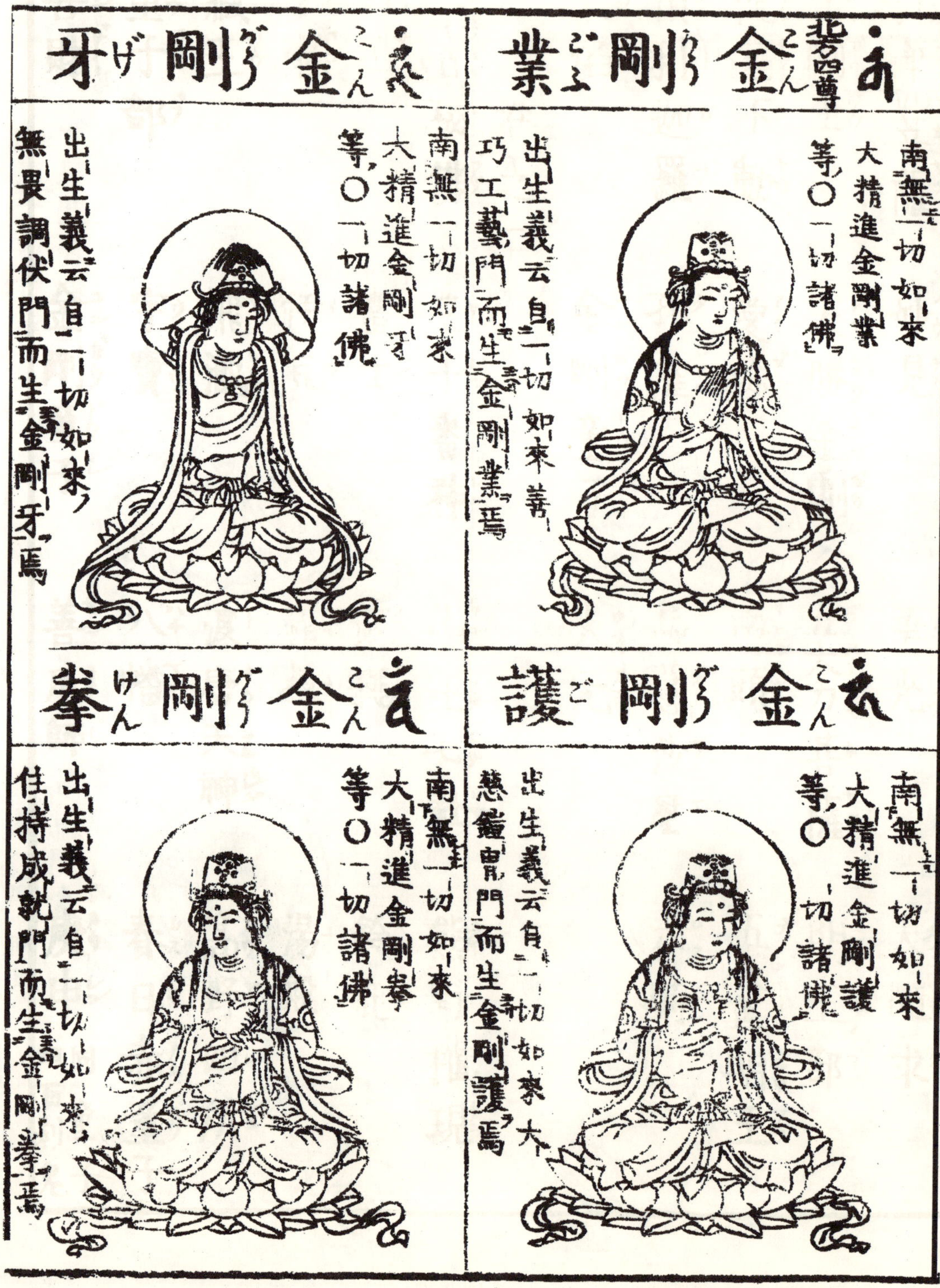

61. Kongōken
Vajramuṣṭi

59. Kongōgo
Vajrapala

§ 7. Nijūgo Bosatsu
The Twenty-Five Bodhisattvas and Others (62-89)

64. Daiseishi Bosatsu
Mahāsthāmaprāpta Bodhisattva

62. Kanzeon Bosatsu
Avalokiteśvara Bodhisattva

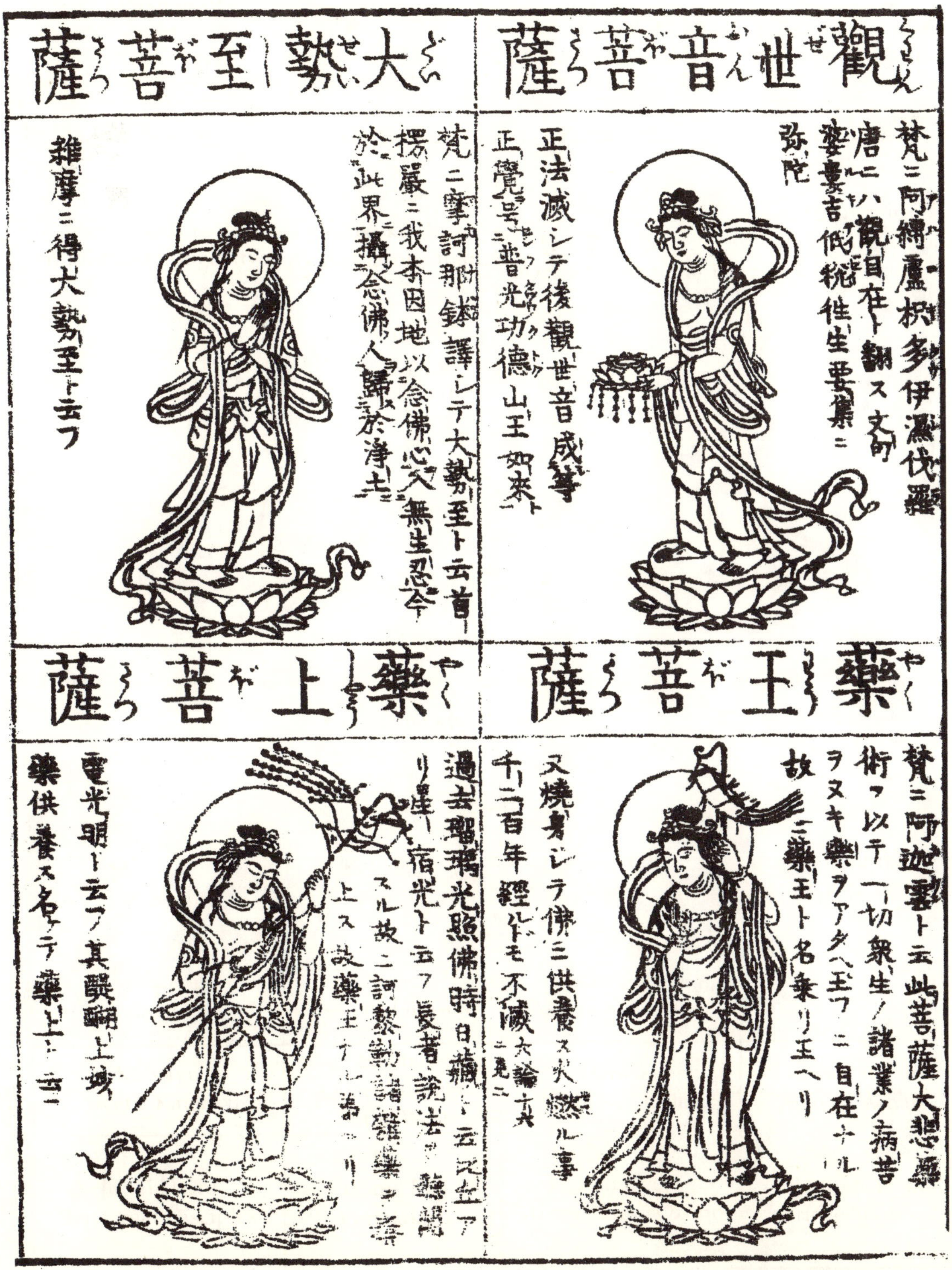

65. Yakujō Bosatsu
Bhaiṣajyodgata Bodhisattva

63. Yakuō Bosatsu
Bhaiṣajyarāja Bodhisattva

68. Hōjīzaiō Bosatsu
Dharmarāja Bodhisattva

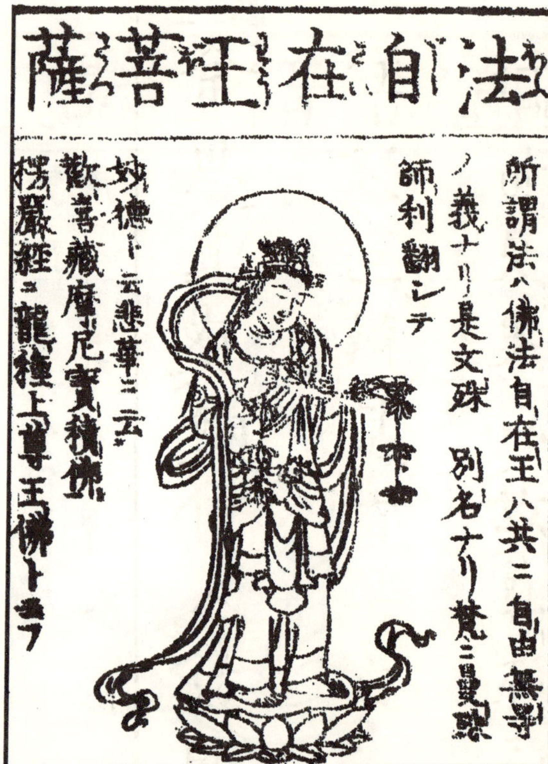

66. Fugen Bosatsu
Samantabhadra Bodhisattva

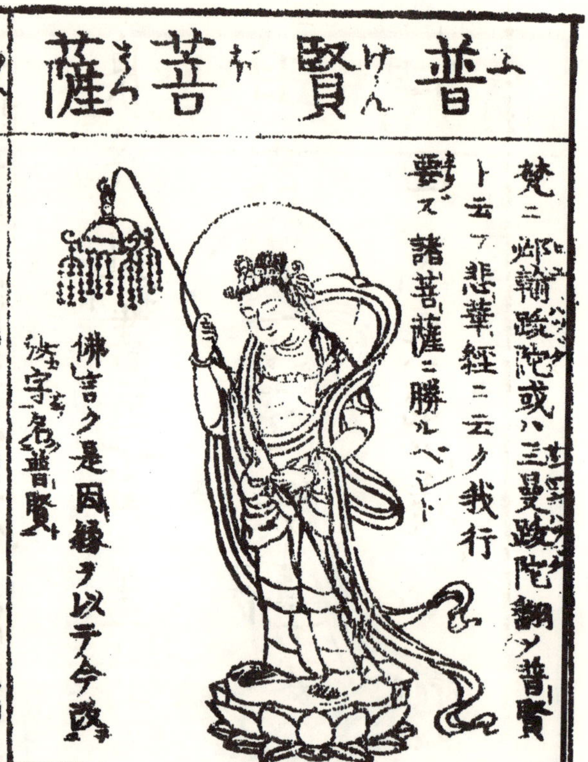

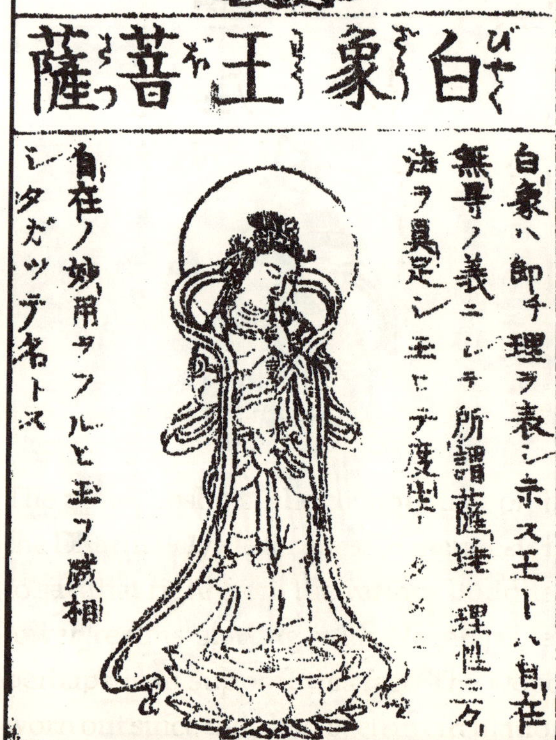

69. Byakuzōō Bosatsu
White Elephant King Bodhisattva

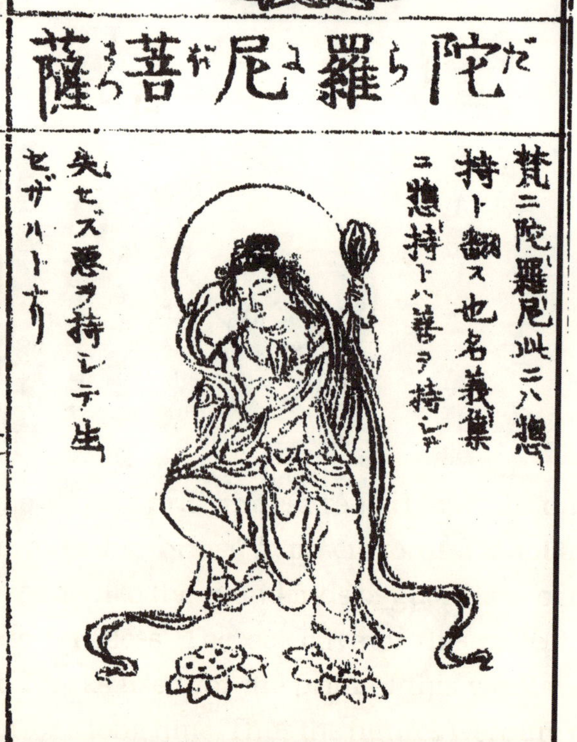

67. Darani Bosatsu
Dhāraṇī Bodhisattva

72. Hōzō Bosatsu
Ratnagarbha Bodhisattva

70. Kokūzō Bosatsu
Ākāśagarbha Bodhisattva

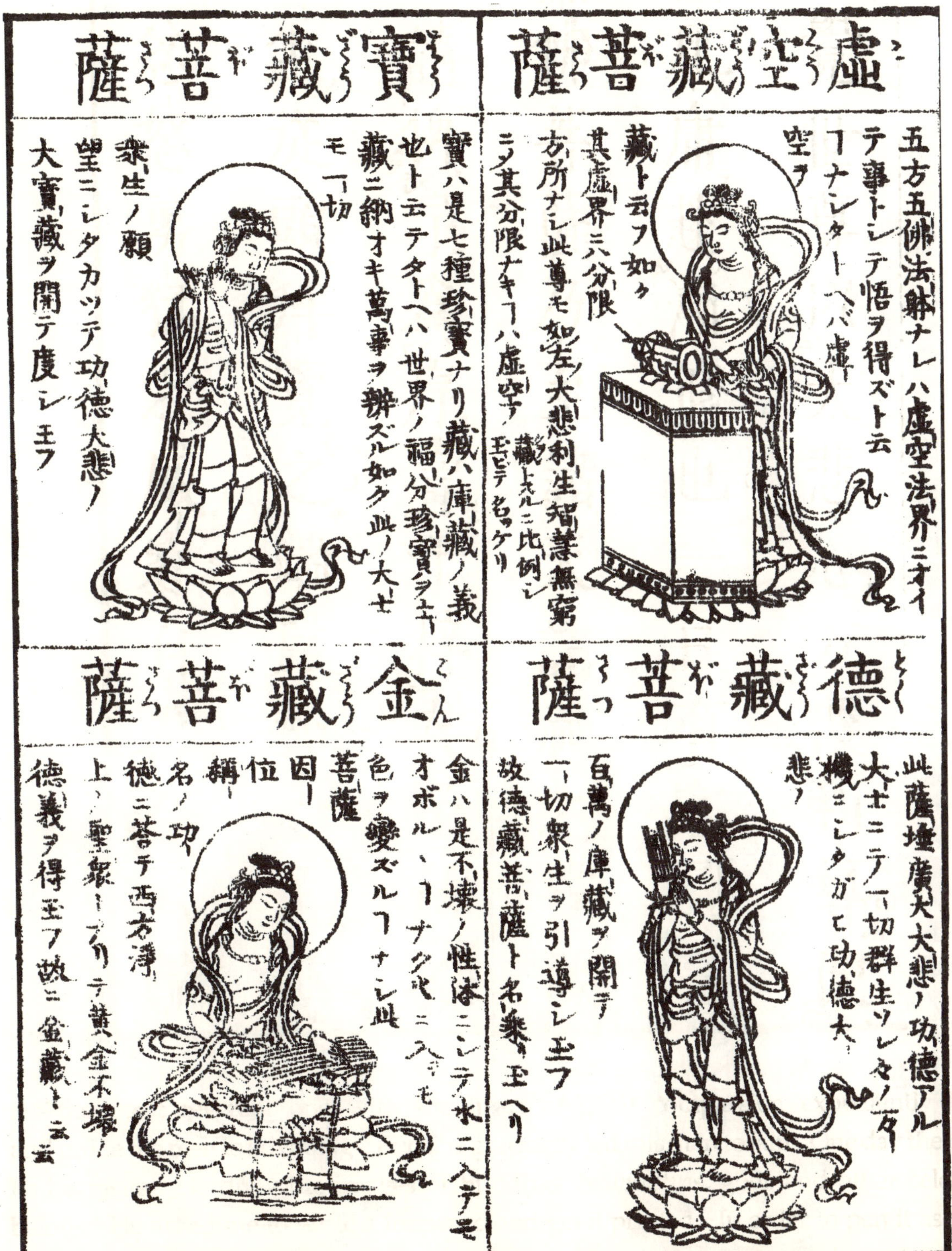

73. Konzō Bosatsu
Svarṇagarbha Bodhisattva

71. Tokuzō Bosatsu
Guṇagarbha Bodhisattva

76. Kongōzō Bosatsu
Vajragarbha Bodhisattva

74. Kōmyōō Bosatsu
Prabharāja Bodhisattva

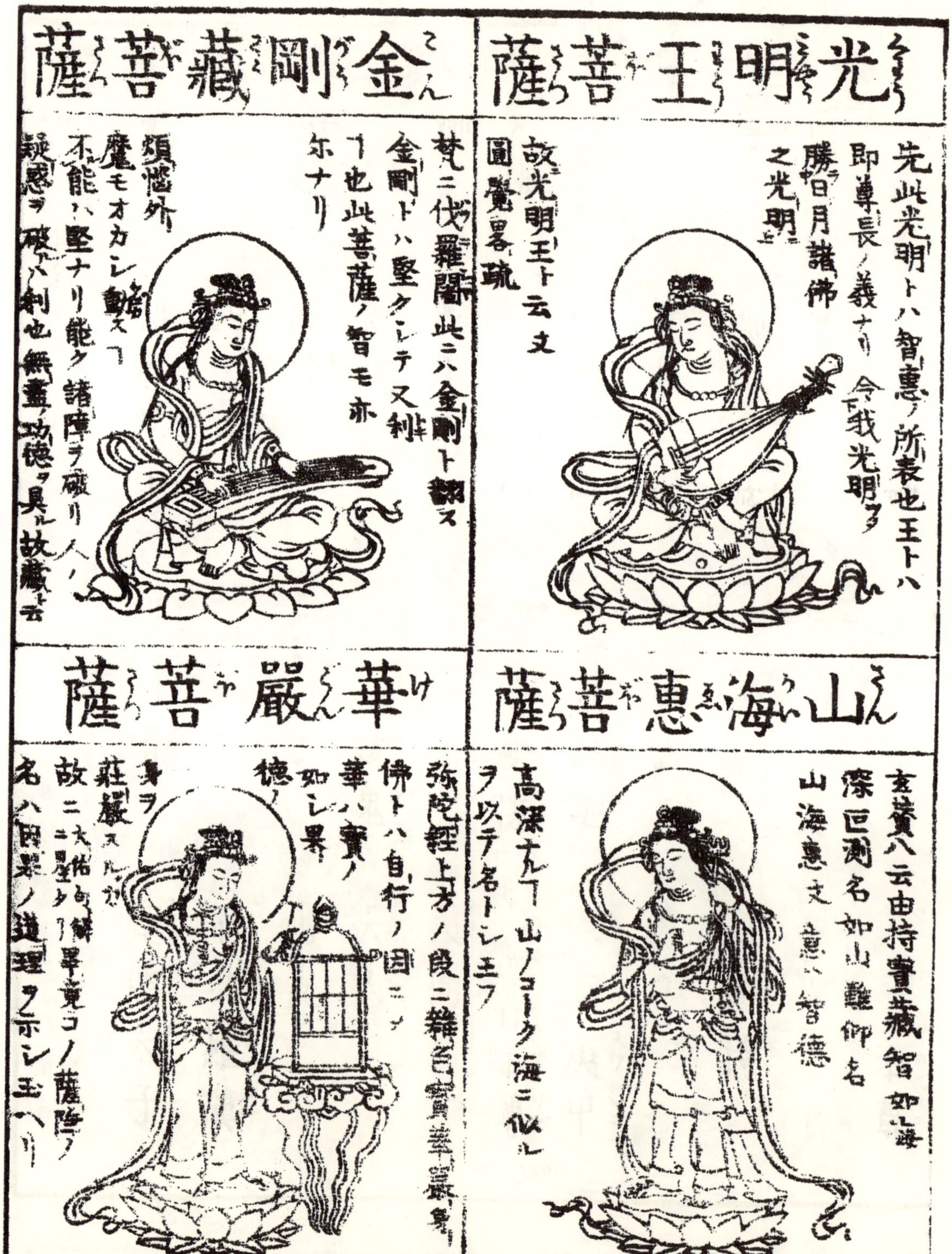

77. Kegon Bosatsu
Avataṁsaka Bodhisattva

75. Sankaie Bosatsu
Sāgara-Varadhara-Buddhi Bodhisattva

80. Gekkōō Bosatsu
Candraprabhārāja Bodhisattva

78. Nisshōō Bosatsu
Sūryaprabhārāja Bodhisattva

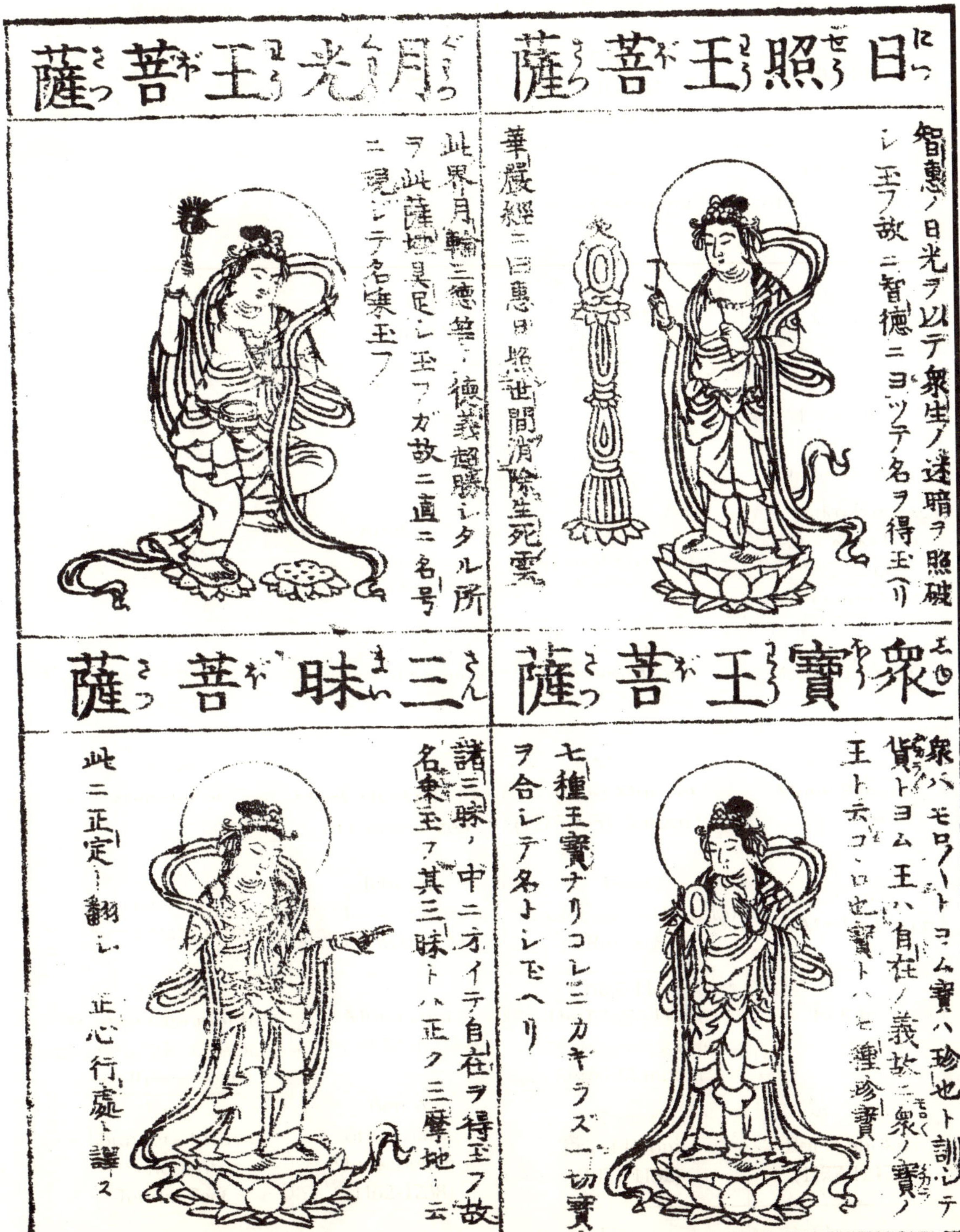

81. Sanmai Bosatsu
Samādhi Bodhisattva

79. Shūhōō Bosatsu
Sarvaratnarāja Bodhisattva

84. Jōjizaiō Bosatsu
Dhyāneśvararāja Bodhisattva

82. Shishiku Bosatsu
Siṁhanāda Bodhisattva

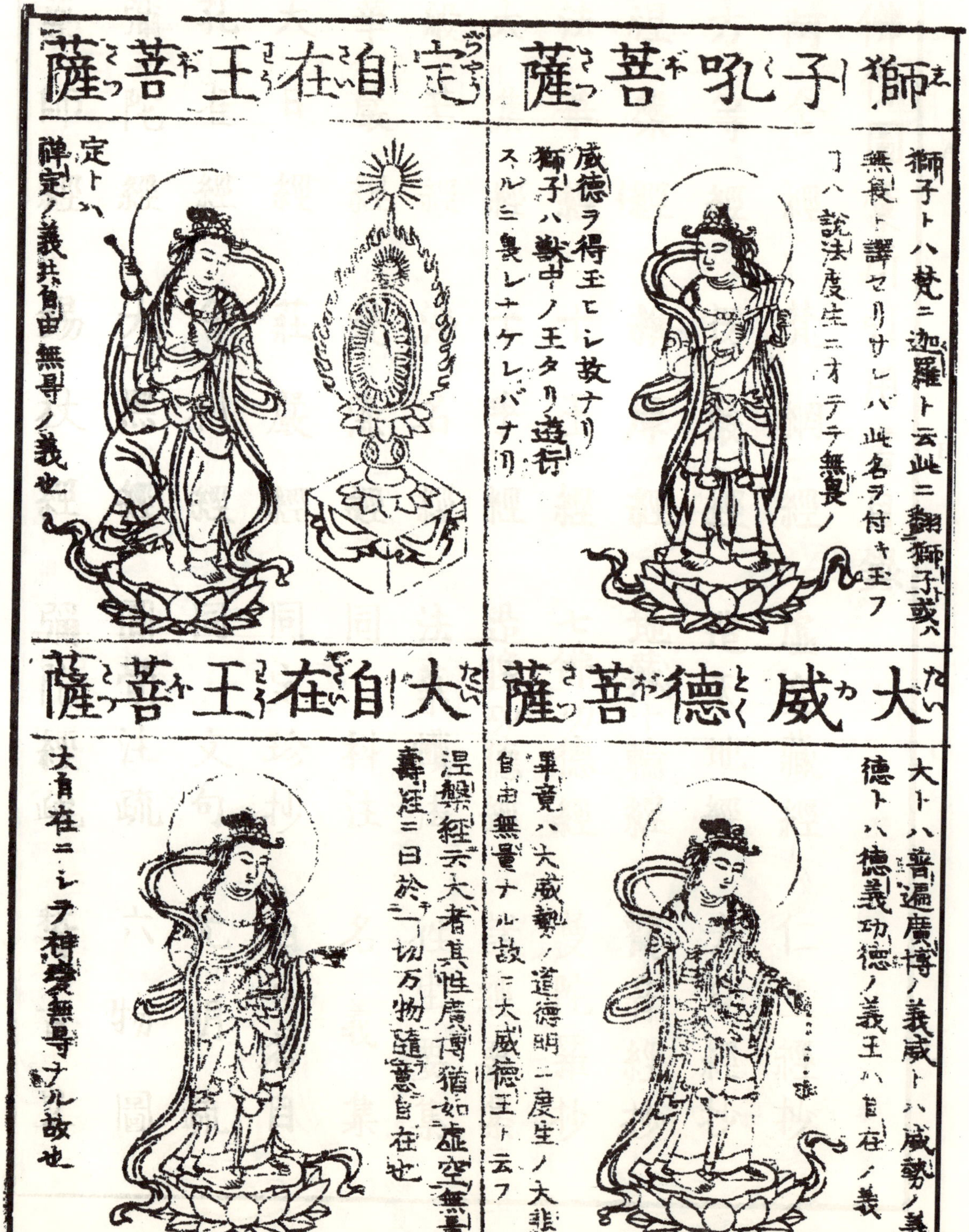

85. Daijizaiō Bosatsu
Maheśvararāja Bodhisattva

83. Taiitoku Bosatsu
Yamāntaka Bodhisattva

88. Myōon Bosatsu
Gadgadeśvara Bodhisattva

86. Muhenshin Bosatsu (25th)
Anantakāya Bodhisattva

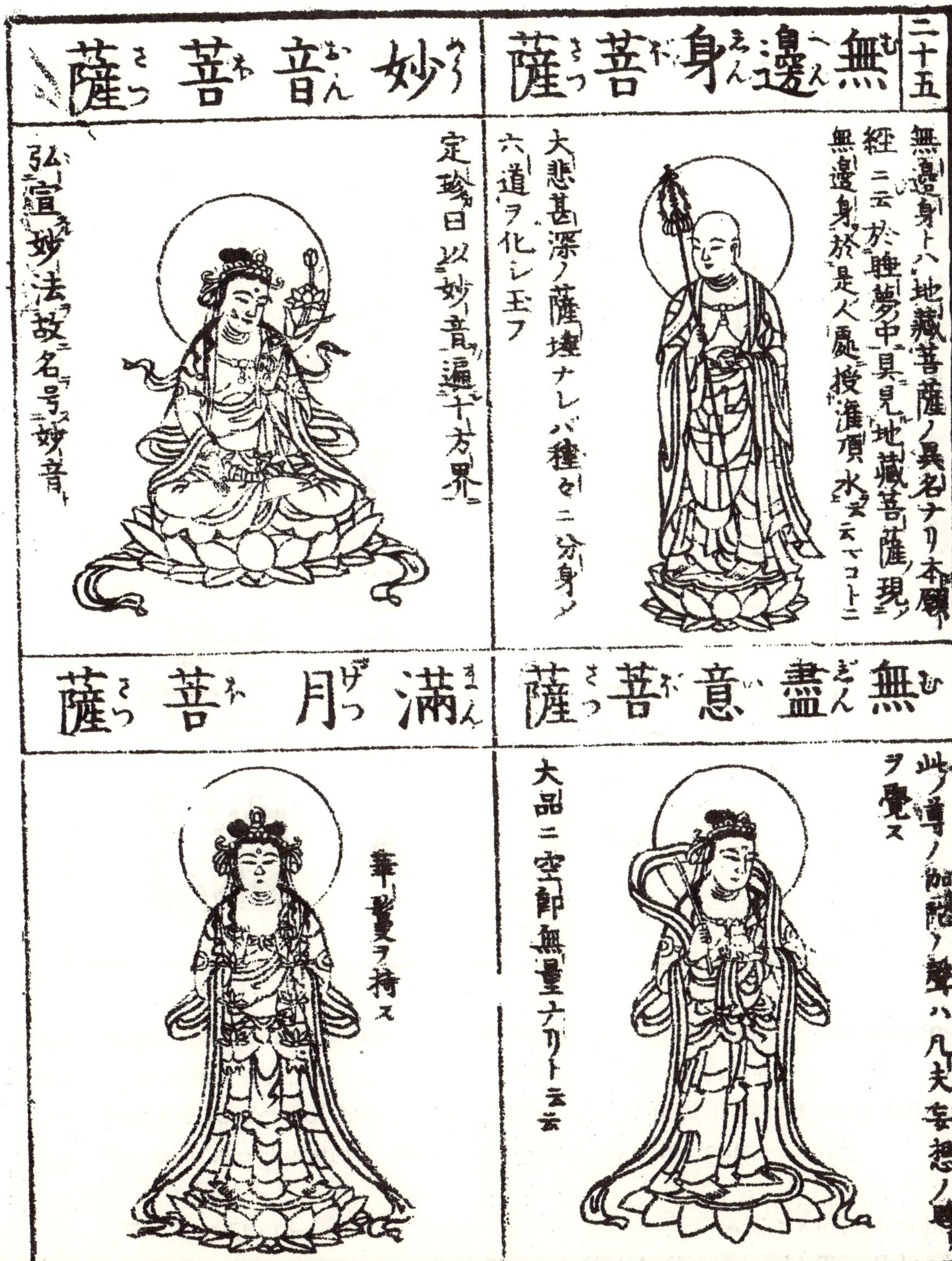

89. Mangetsu Bosatsu
Pūrṇacandra Bodhisattva

87. Mujini Bosatsu
Akṣayamati Bodhisattva

§ 8. Shichi Kannon
The Seven Avalokiteśvaras (90-97)

92. Jūichimen Kannon
Ekādaśamukha Avalokiteśvara

90. Senju Kannon
Sahasrabhuja Avalokiteśvara

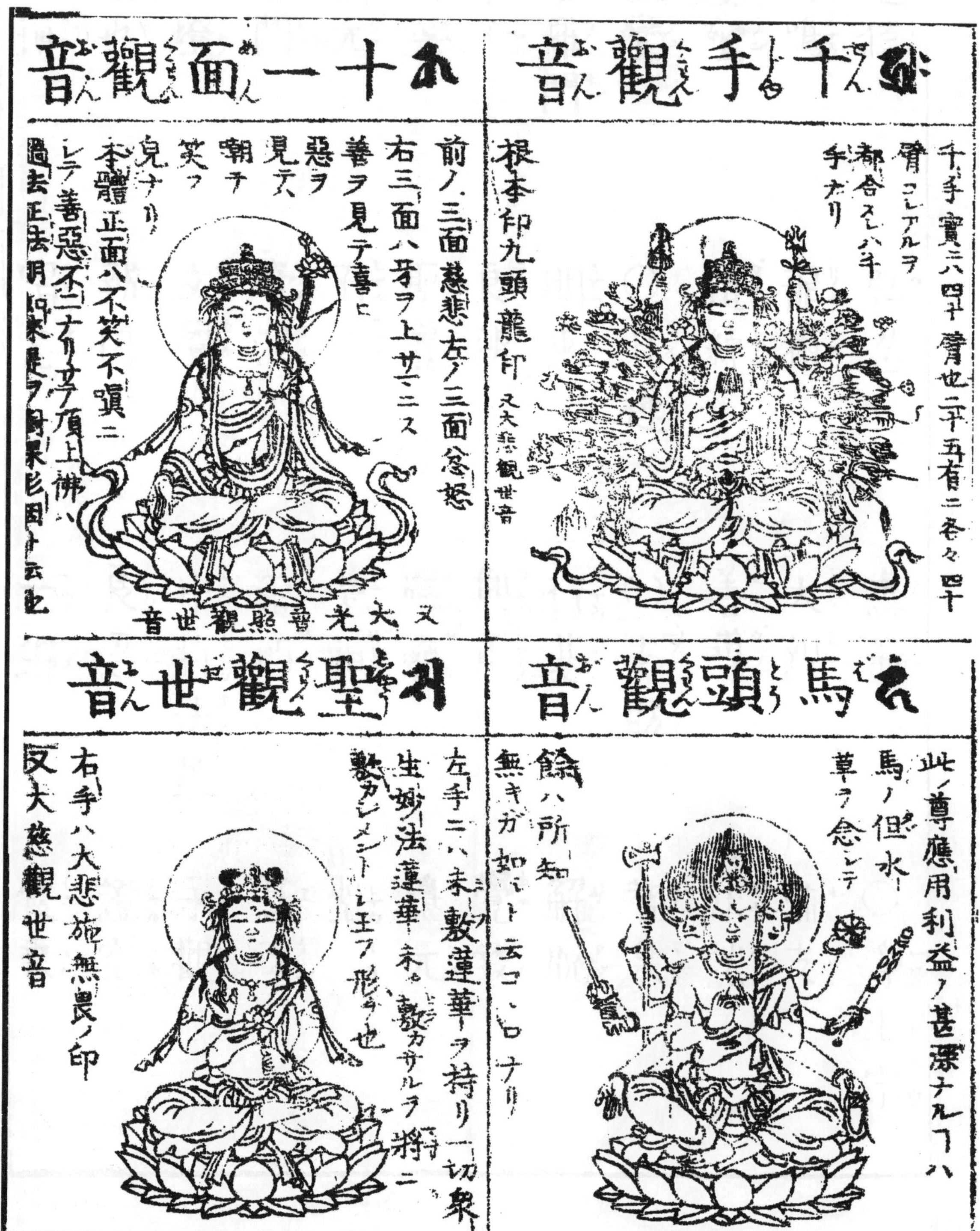

93. Shō Kanzeon
Ārya Avalokiteśvara

91. Batō Kannon
Hayagrīva Avalokiteśvara

96. Fukū Kensaku
Amoghapāśa Avalokiteśvara

94. Nyoirin Kannon
Cintāmaṇicakra Avalokiteśvara

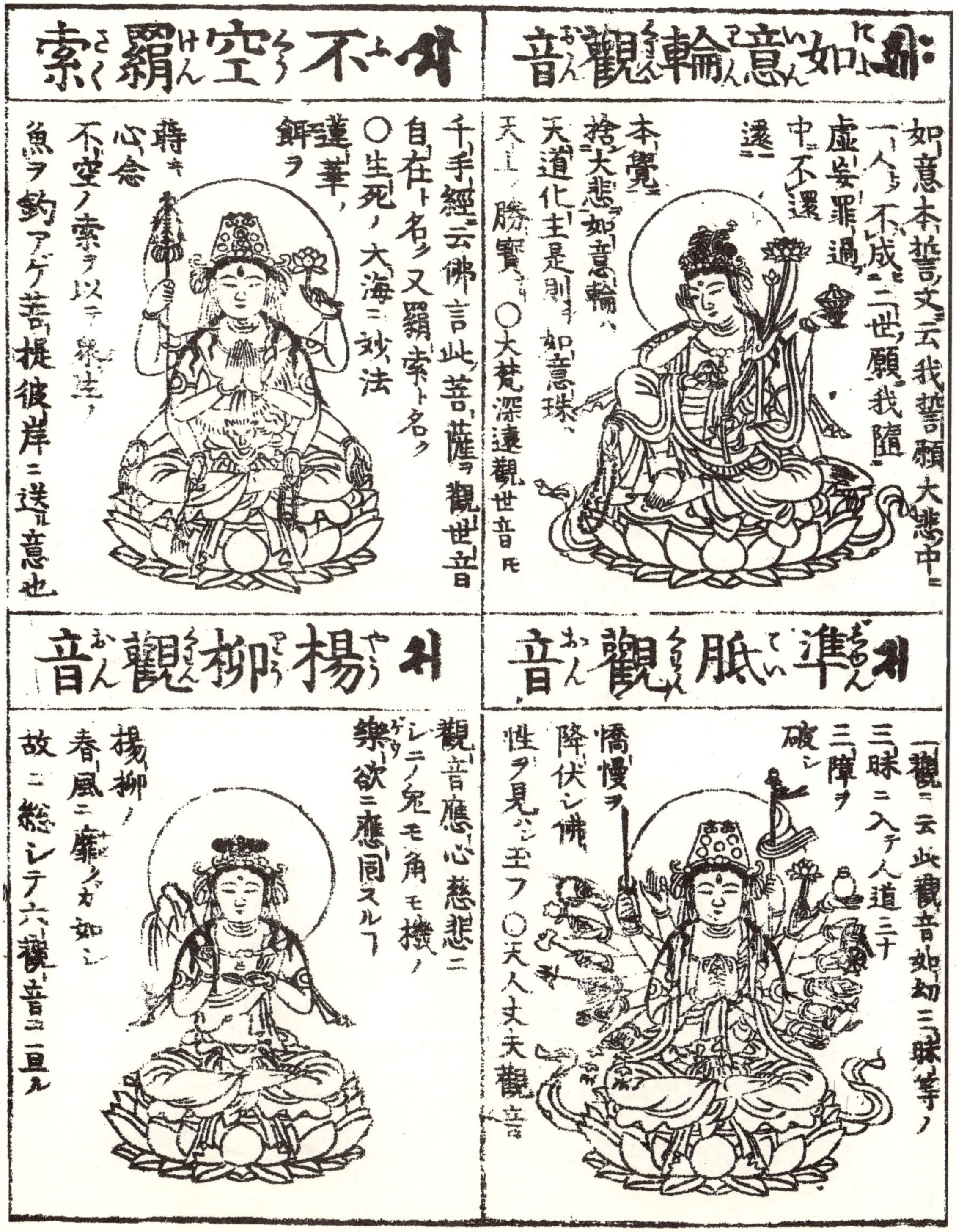

97. Yōryū Kannon
Willow Avalokiteśvara

95. Junitei Kannon
Caṇḍī Avalokiteśvara

§ 9. Sanjūsan-tai Kannon
The Thirty Three forms of Avalokiteśvara (98-129)

100. Enkō Kannon
Halo Avalokiteśvara

98. Ryūzu Kannon
Nāga-headed Avalokiteśvara

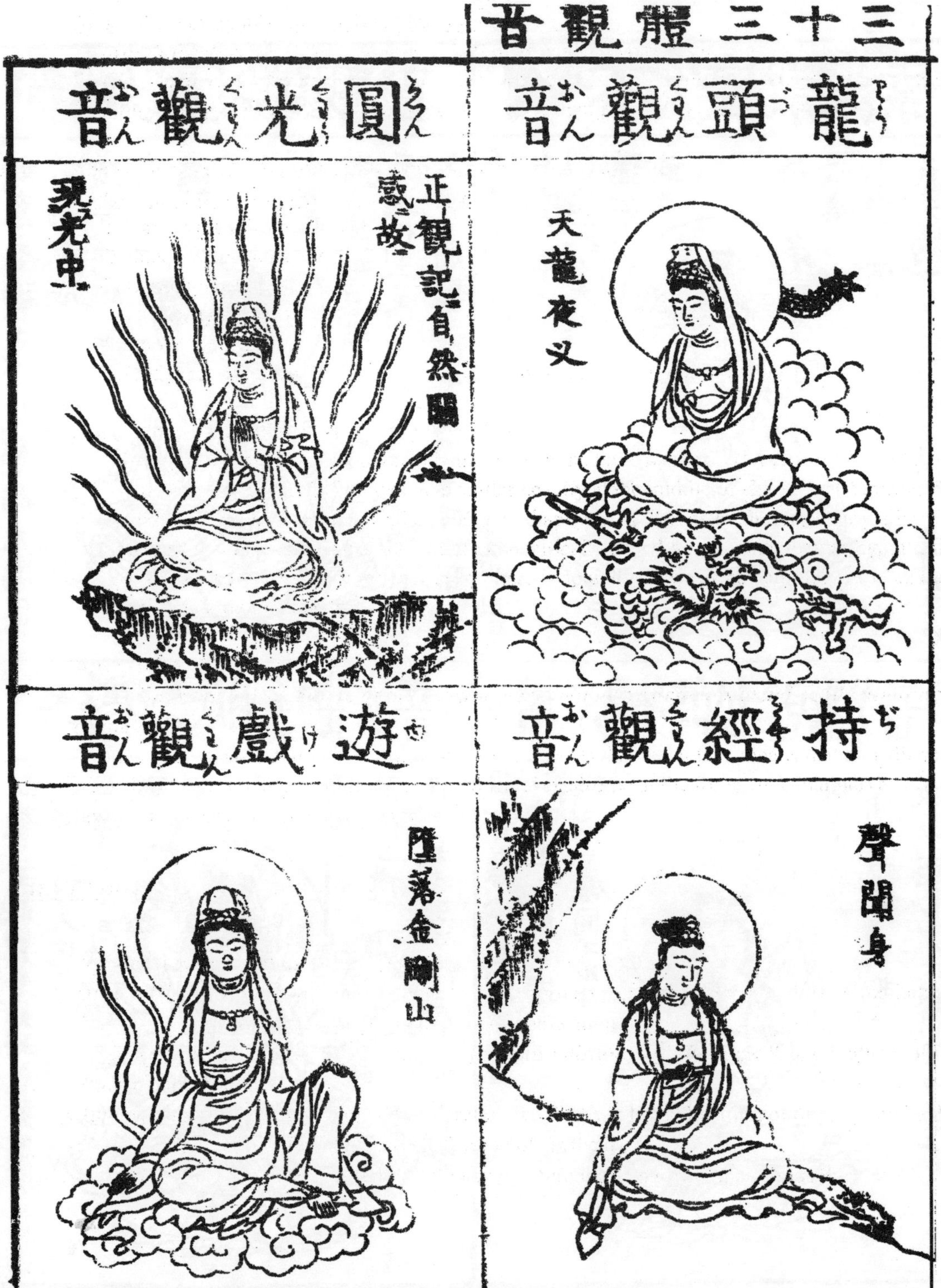

101. Yuge Kannon
Vikrīḍita Avalokiteśvara

99. Jikyō Kannon
Sūtra Avalokiteśvara

104. Takimi no Kannon
Avalokiteśvara gazing a Waterfall

102. Byakue Kannon
Pāṇḍara-vāsinī Avalokiteśvara

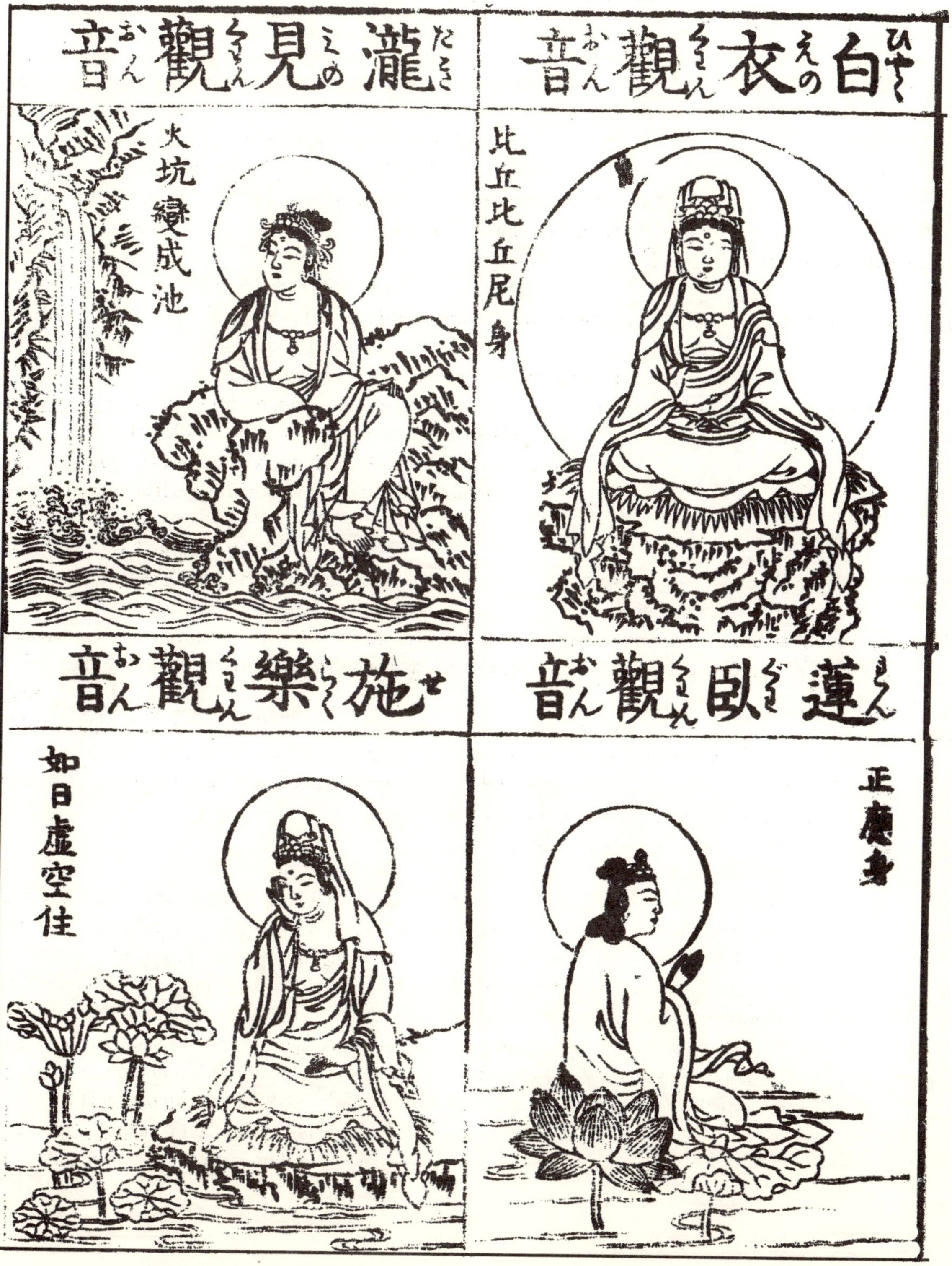

105. Seraku Kannon
Abhayaṁdada Avalokiteśvara

103. Renga Kannon
Avalokiteśvara Reclining on a Lotus

108. Suigetsu Kannon
Udakacandra Avalokiteśvara

106. Gyoran Kannon
Creel Avalokiteśvara

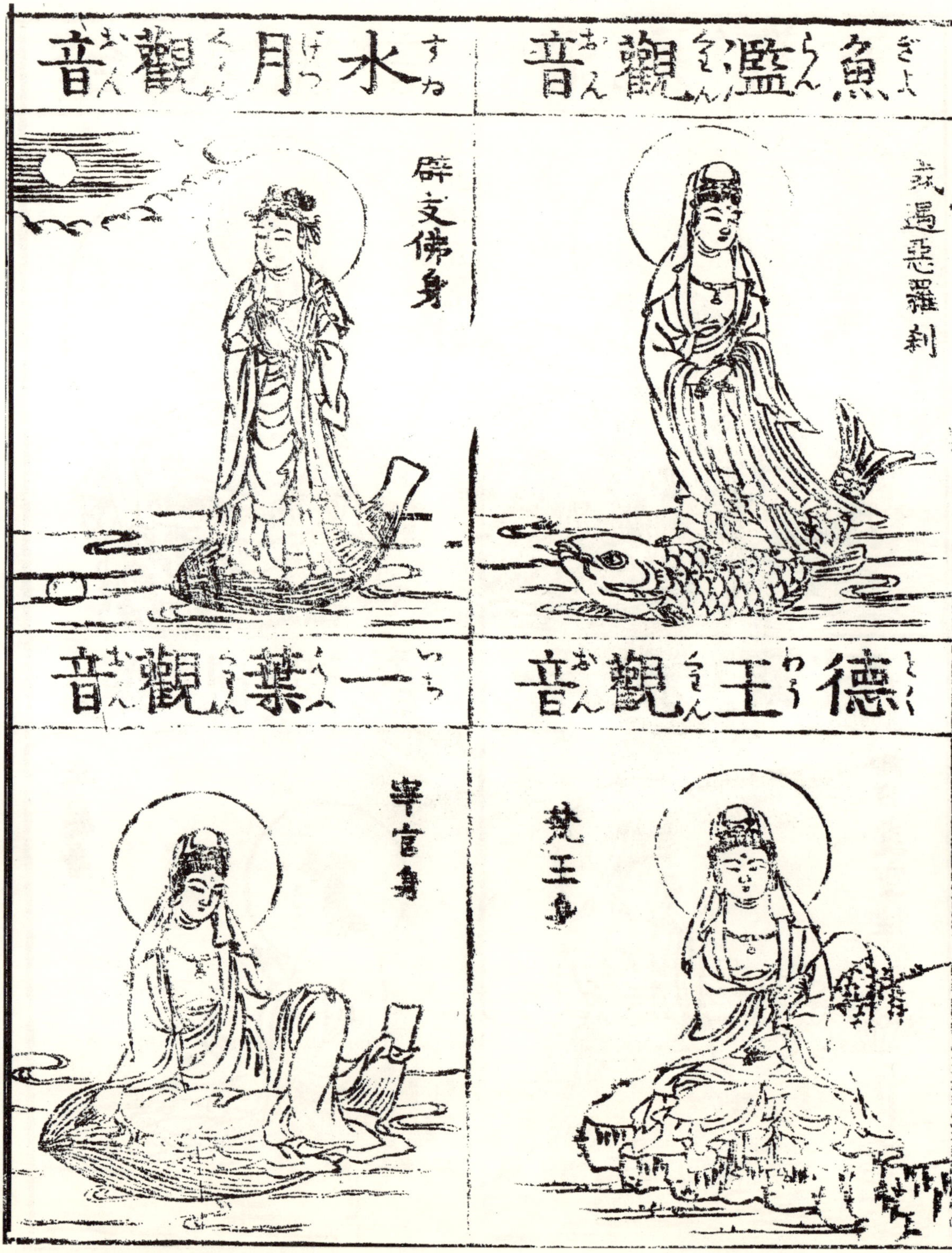

109. Ichiyō Kannon
Avalokiteśvara on a Lotus Leaf

107. Tokuō Kannon
Bhadanta Rāja Avalokiteśvara

112. Enmei Kannon
Avalokiteśvara of Longevity

110. Seizu Kannon
Nīlakaṇṭha Avalokiteśvara

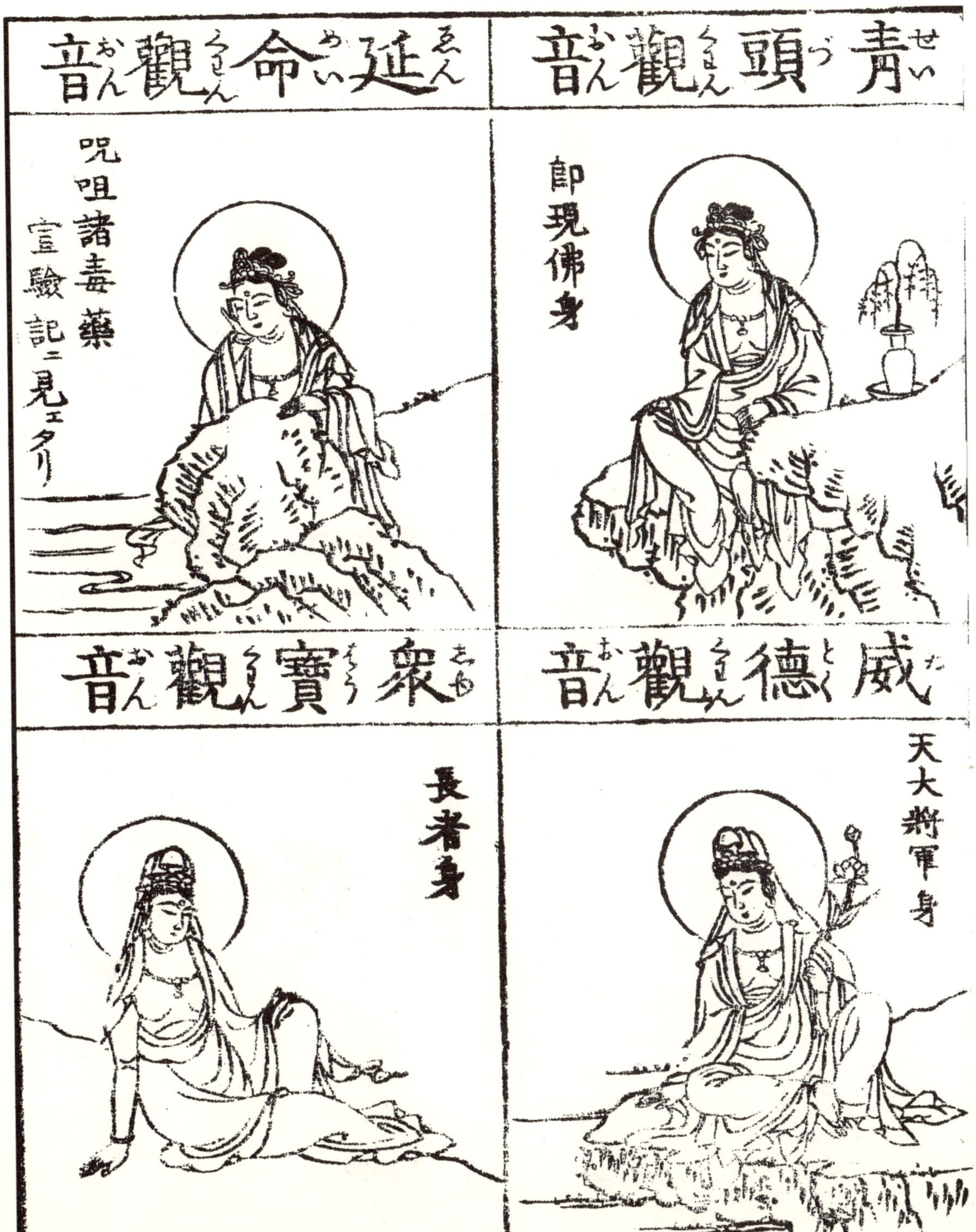

113. Shūhō Kannon
Sarvajña Ratna Avalokiteśvara

111. Itoku Kannon
Avalokiteśvara of Virtuous Authority

116. Anoku Kannon
Anuttara Avalokiteśvara

114. Iwato Kannon
Avalokiteśvara of Caverns

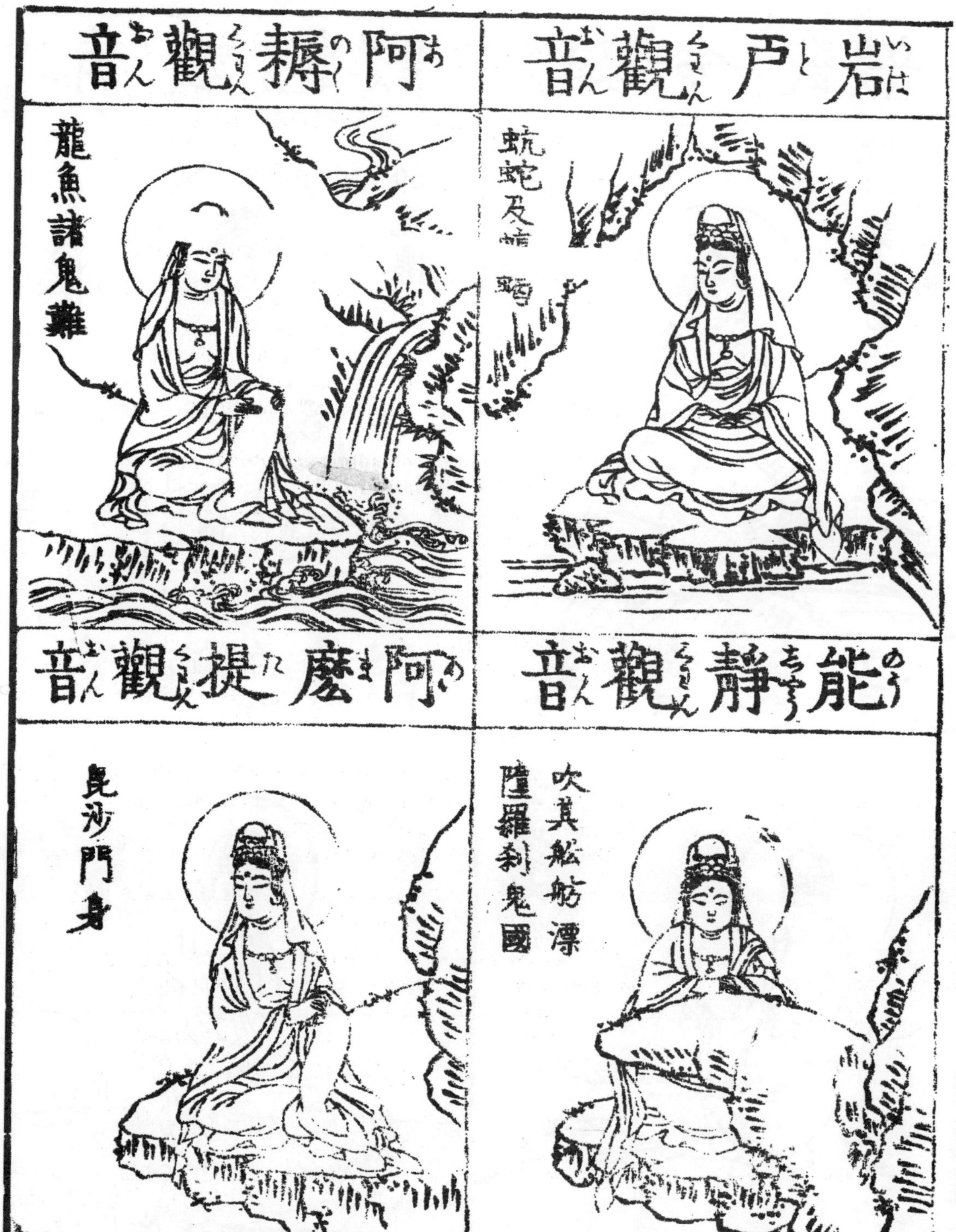

117. Amata Kannon
Āmodita Avalokiteśvara

115. Nōjō Kannon
Mystic Trance Avalokiteśvara

120. Tarason Kannon
Tārā Avalokiteśvara

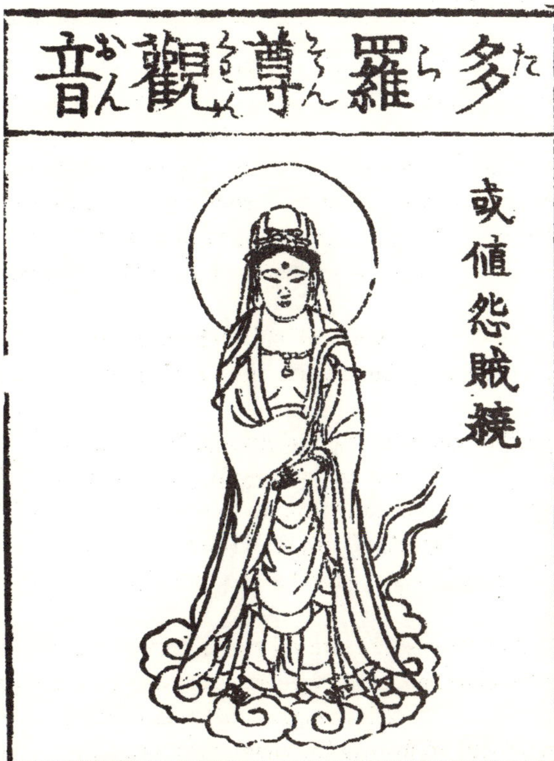

118. Yōe Kannon
Parṇaśabarī Avalokiteśvara

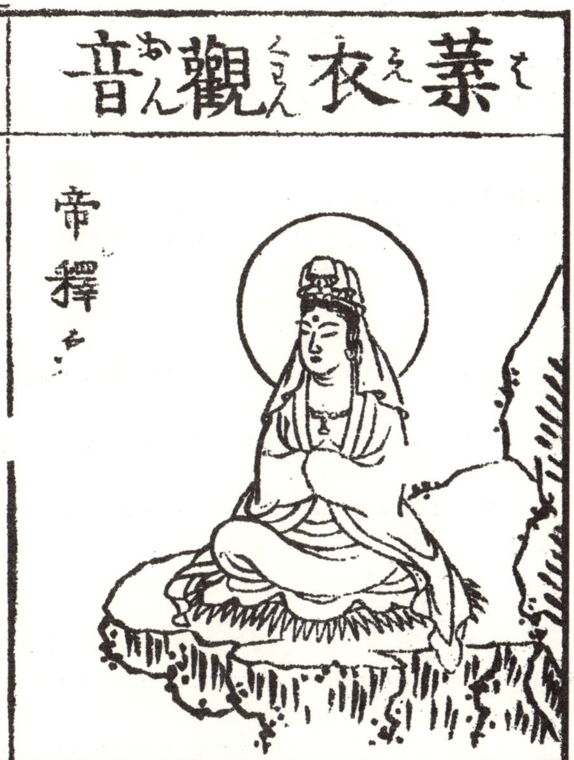

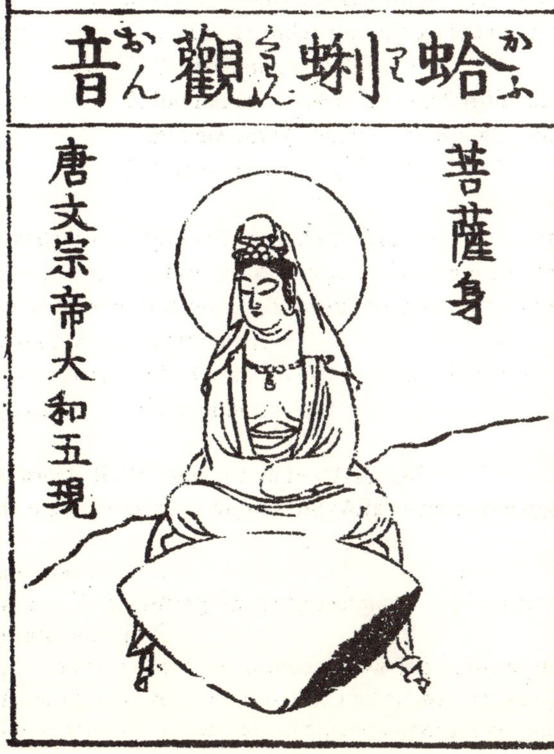

121. Kōri Kannon
Avalokiteśvara of shell

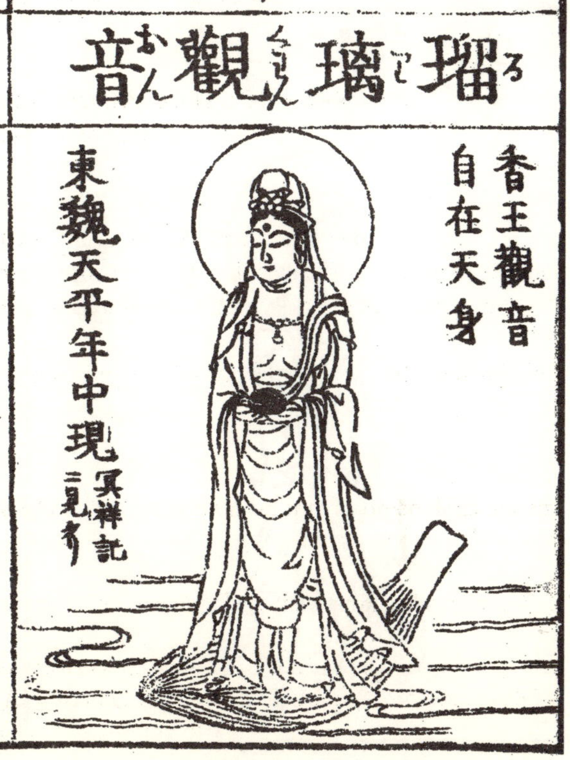

119. Ruri Kannon
Vaiḍūrya Avalokiteśvara

124. Barōfu Kannon
Hayagrīva Avalokiteśvara

122. Rokuji Kannon
Avalokiteśvara of six daily Meditations

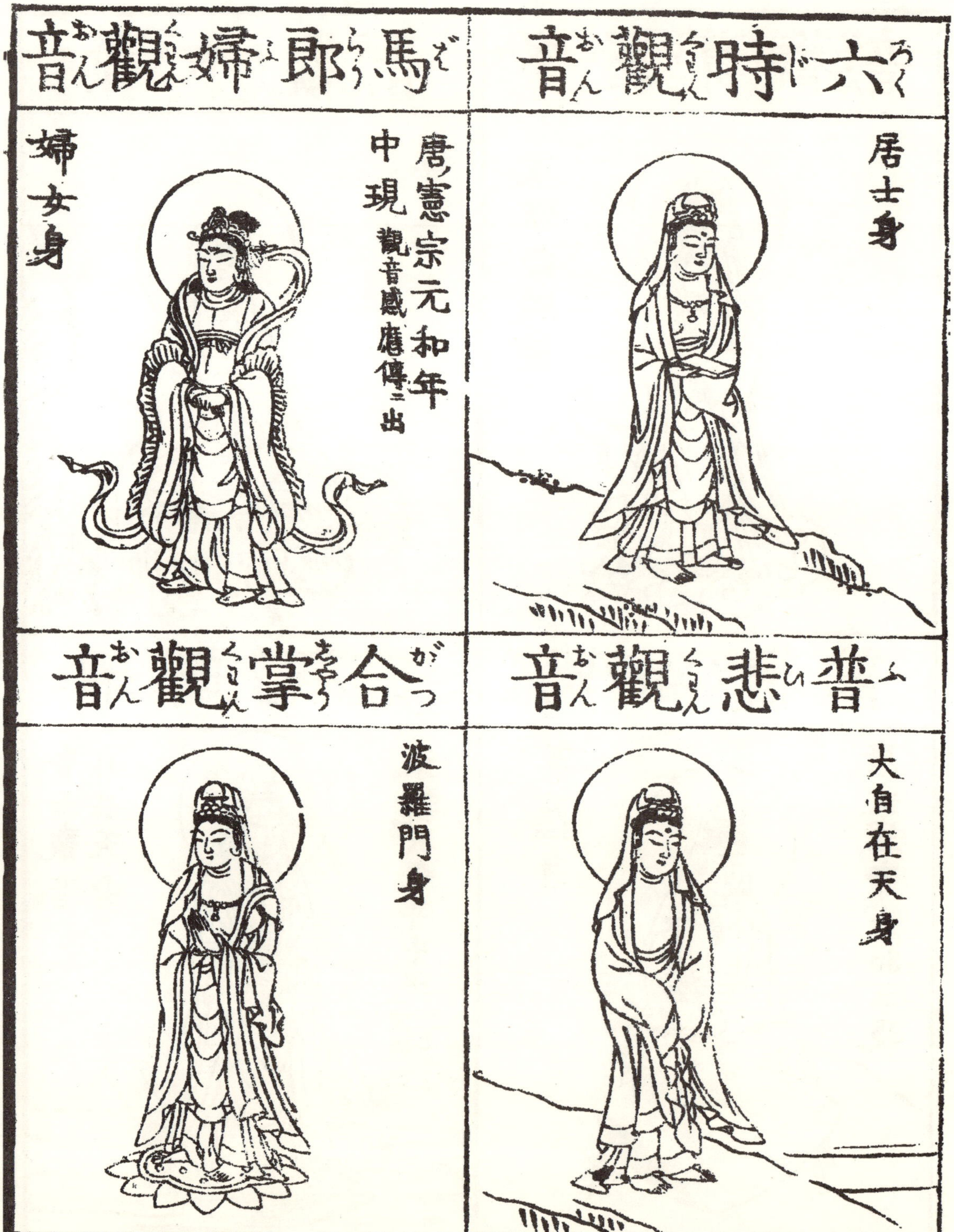

125. Gasshō Kannon
Añjali Avalokiteśvara

123. Fuhi Kannon
Avalokiteśvara of Universal Compassion

128. Jiren Kannon
Padmadhara Avalokiteśvara

126. Ichinyo Kannon
Ekatathatā Avalokiteśvara

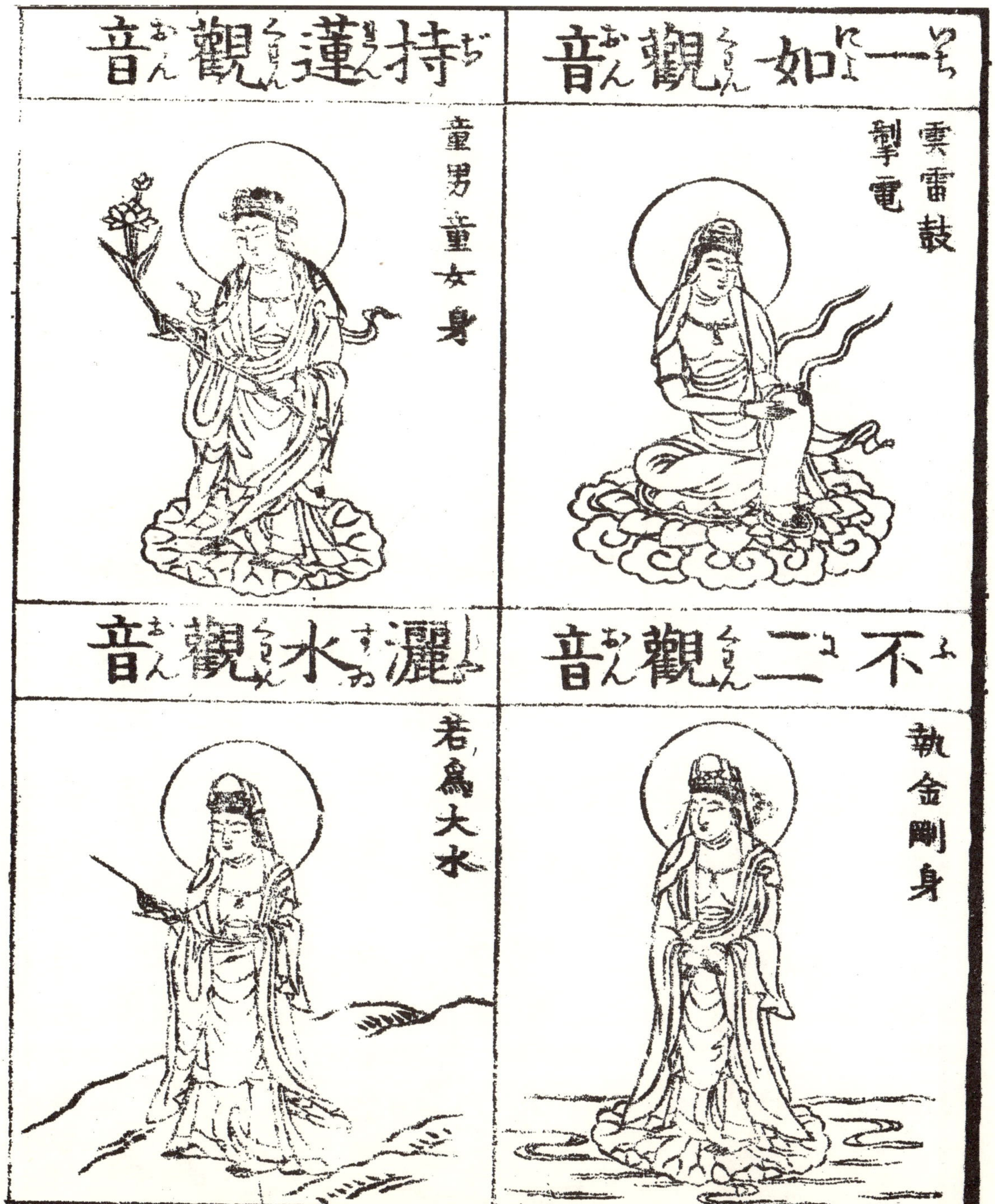

129. Shasui Kannon
Adhiṣṭhāna-Avalokiteśvara

127. Funi Kannon
Advaita Avalokiteśvara

§ 10. Roku Jizō
The Six Forms of Kṣitigarbha with Six other Kṣitigarbha (130-141)

134. Kongōtō Jizō	**132. Kongōgan Jizō**	**130. Yotenga Jizō**
Vajradhvaja Kṣitigarbha	Vajra-praṇidhāna Kṣitigarbha	Varada Kṣitigarbha

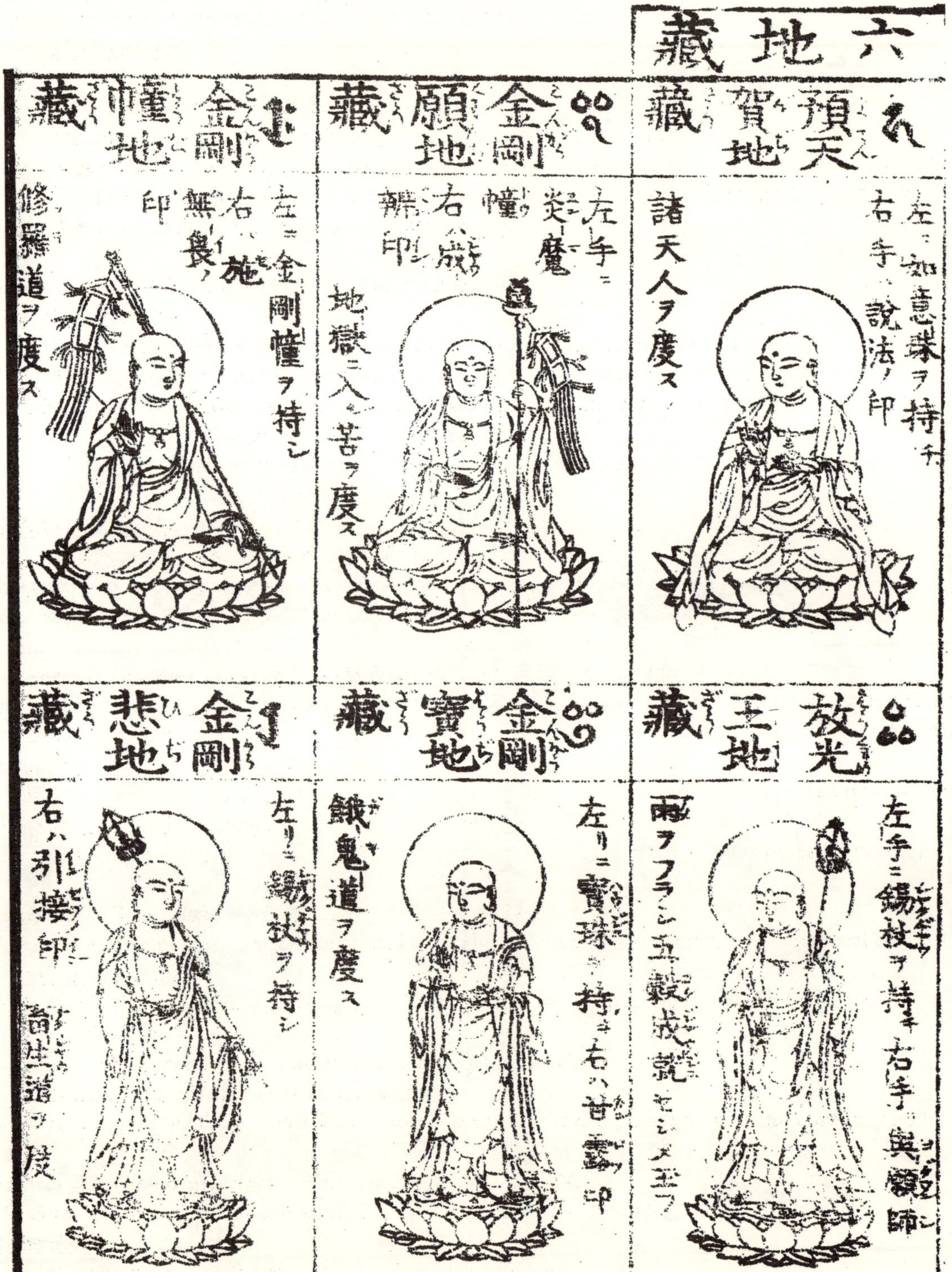

135. Kongōhi Jizō	**133. Kongōhō Jizō**	**131. Hōkōō Jizō**
Vajrakaruṇa Kṣitigarbha	Vajraratna Kṣitigarbha	Prabharāja Kṣitigarbha

140. Hosshō Jizō
Dharmatā Kṣitigarbha

138. Hōjō Jizō
Ratnākara Kṣitigarbha

136. Jichi Jizō
Dharaṇidhara Kṣitigarbha
(or Pṛthvī Kṣitigarbha)

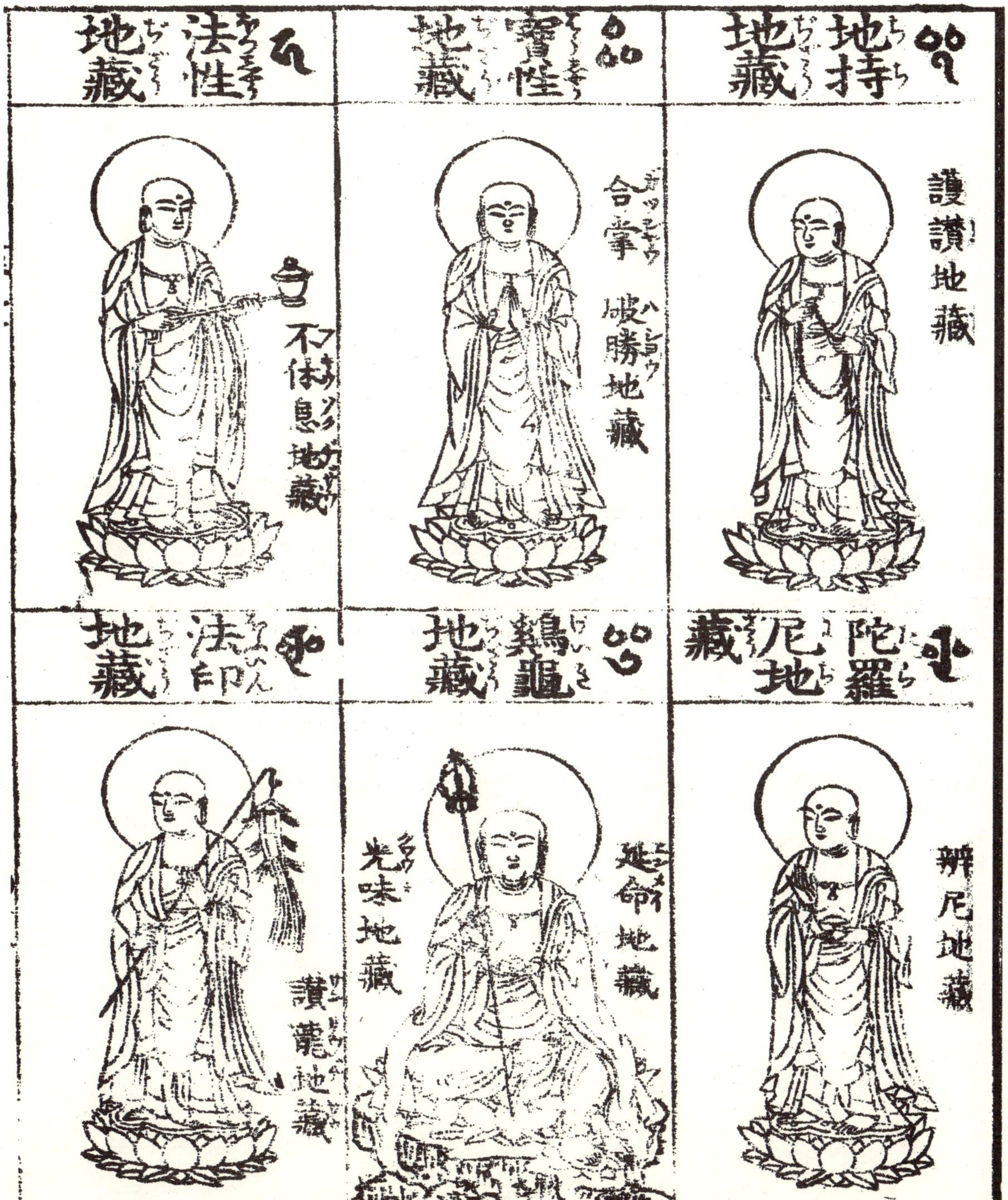

141. Hōin Jizō
Ratnamudrāpaṇi Kṣitigarbha

139. Keito Jizo
Ketu Kṣitigarbha

137. Darani Jizō
Dhāraṇī Kṣitigarbha

§ 11. The Hokke Shibosatsu
The Bodhisattvas in Lotus Sūtra (142-151)

146. Hōdange Bosatsu
Candanakusuma Bodhisattva

144. Darani Bosatsu
Dhāraṇī Bodhisattva

142. Metsu Akushu
Durgati-pariśodhana

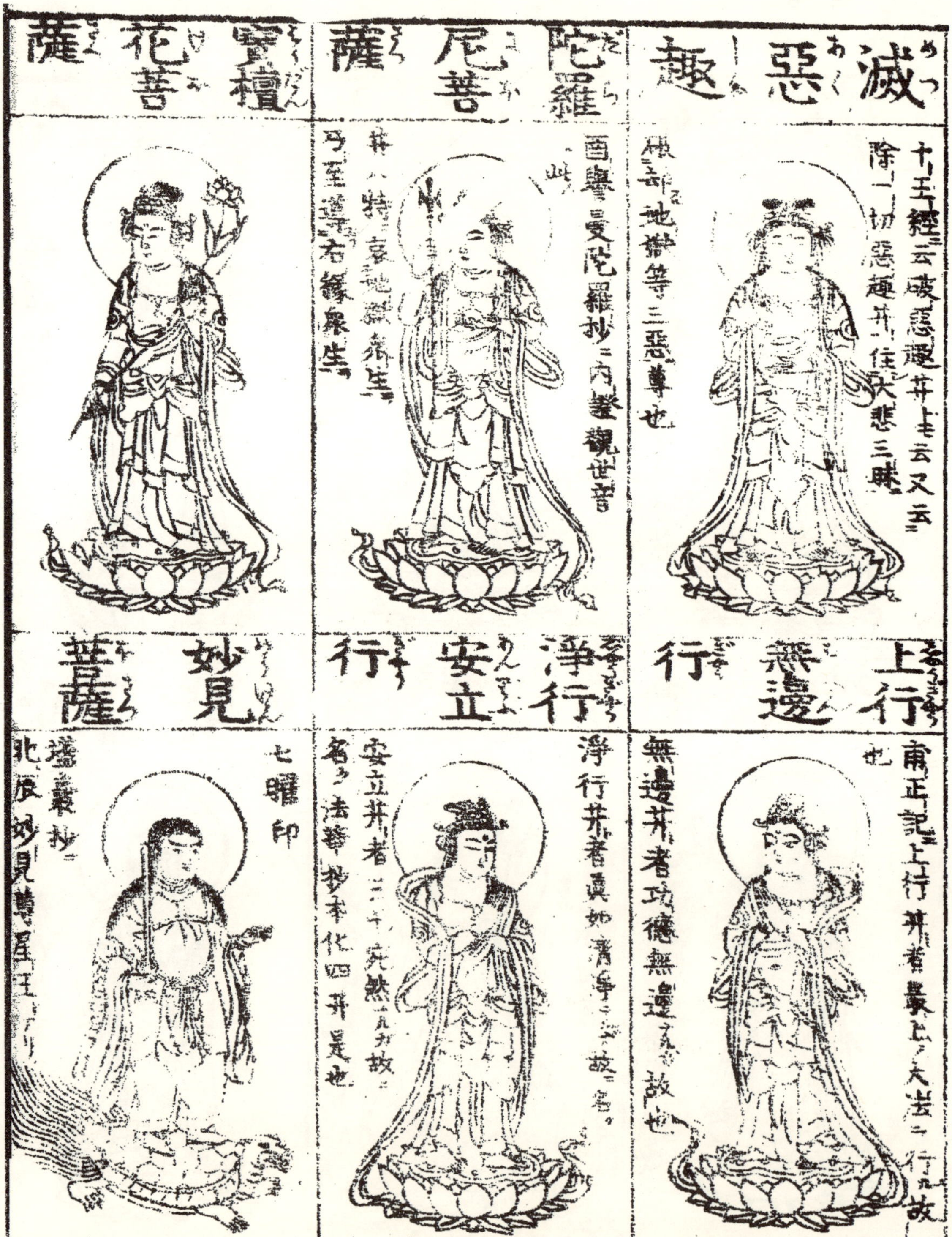

147. Myōken Bosatsu
Sudarśana Bodhisattva
(Ursa Major)

145. Jōgyō Anritsugyo
Pure Karma

143. Jōgyō Bishagyō
Viśiṣṭa Caritra

150. Kongōō
Vajrarāja

148. Kekō Bosatsu
Padmaprabhā Bodhisattva

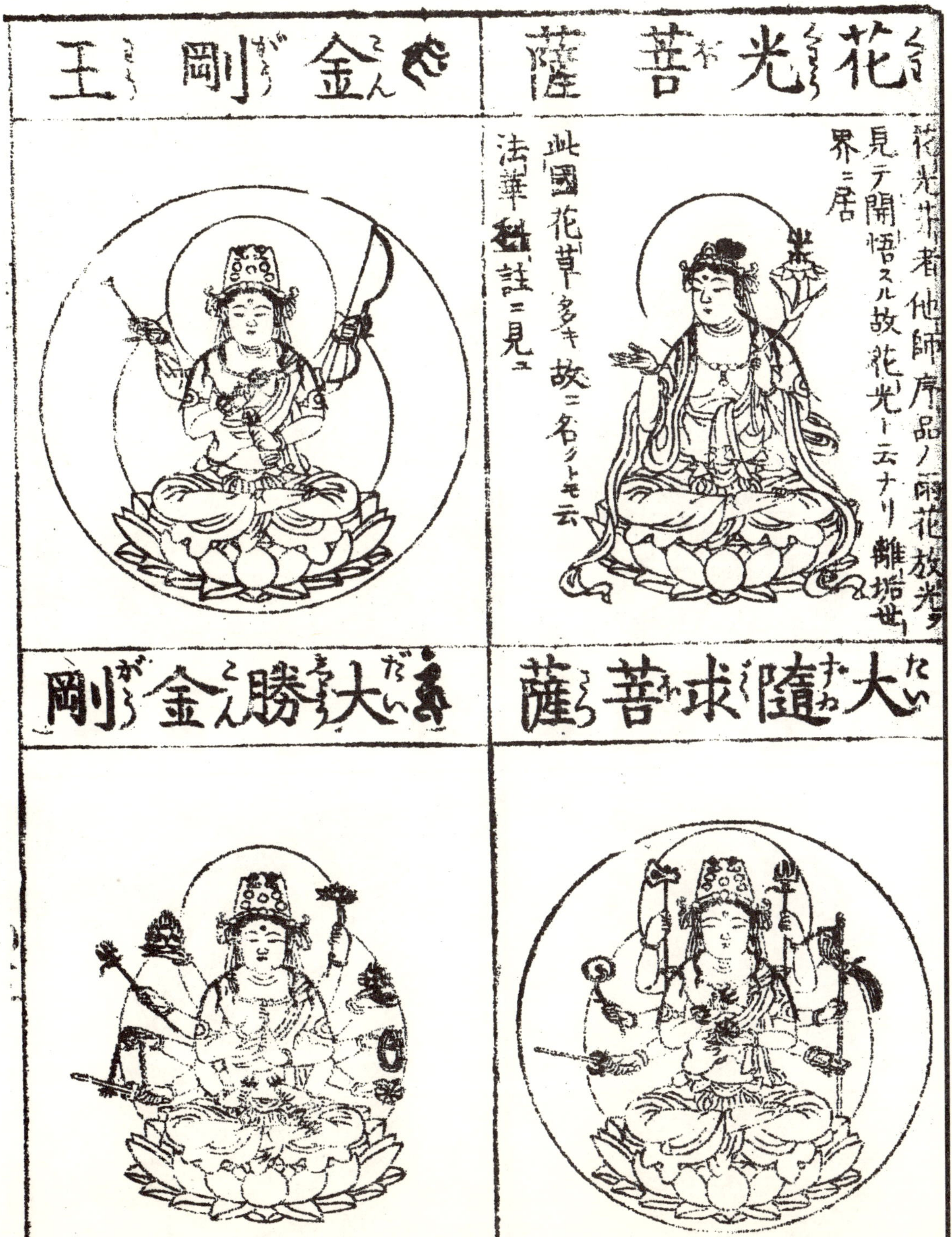

151. Daishōkongō
Mahāvajra

149. Daizuigu Bosatsu
Varada Bodhisattva

§ 12. Godairiki Bosatsu
The Five Mahābala Bodhisattvas and others (152-159)

154. Muihōku
Vaiśāradyanāda

152. Muryōrikiku
Anantanāda

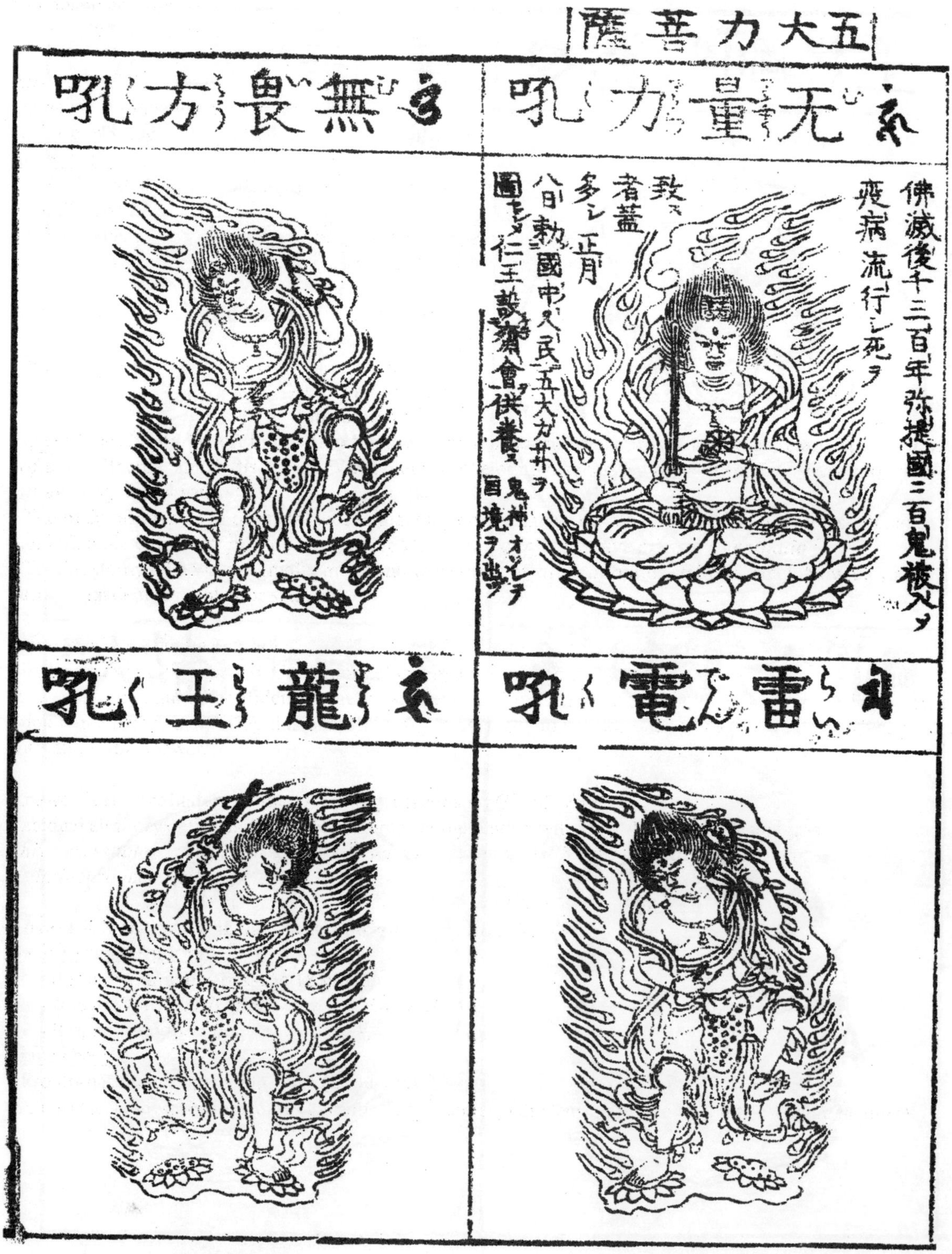

155. Ryūōku
Dragon-king Roar

153. Raidenku
Thunderbolt Roar

158. Aizen Myōō
Rāgarāja Vidyārāja

156. Kongōku
Vajranāda

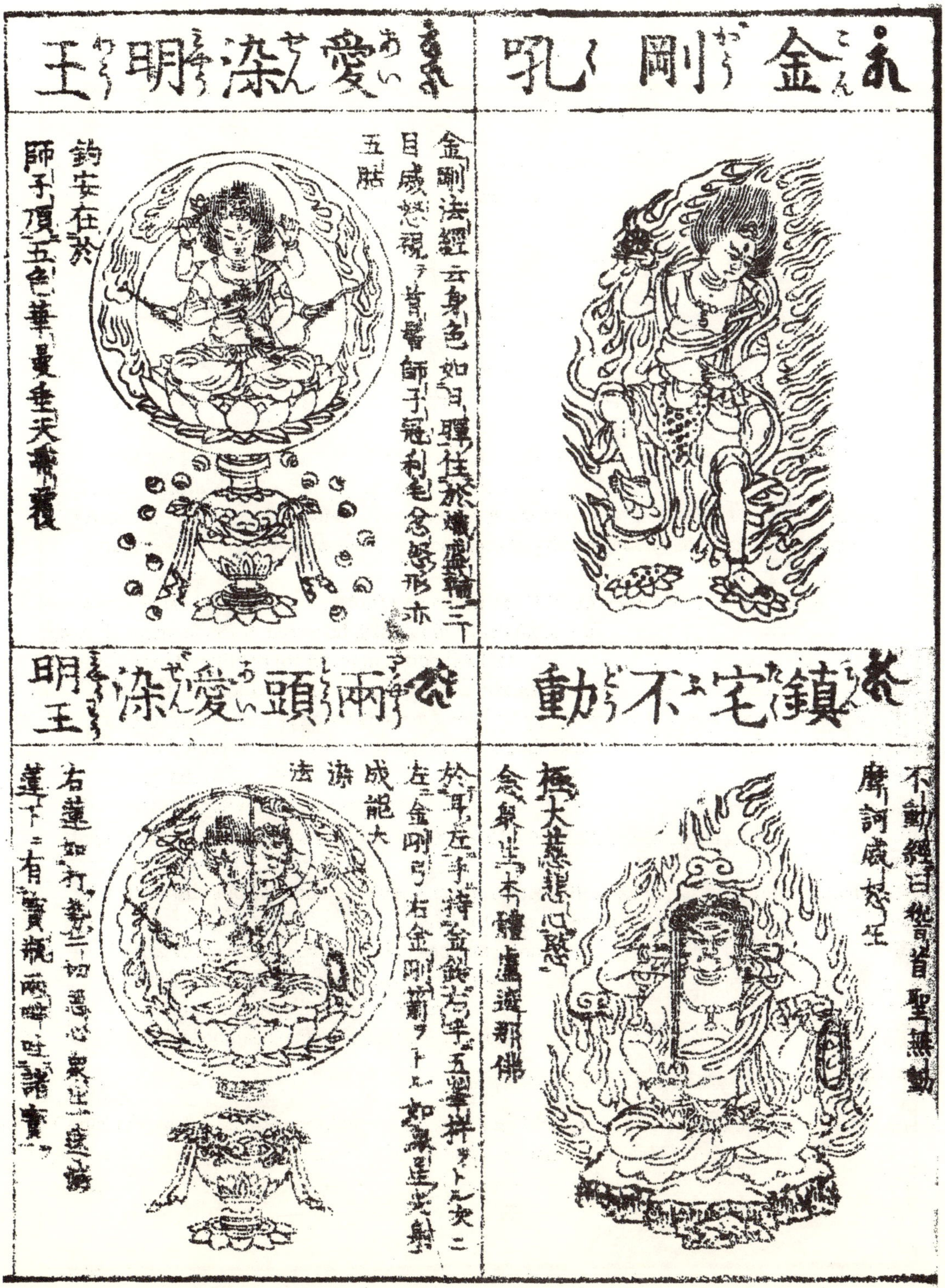

159. Ryōtō Aizen Myōō
Two-headed Rāgarāja Vidyārāja

157. Chintaku Fudō
Protector Acala

§ 13. Godaison Myōō
The Five Mahāvidyārājas (160-165)

162. Chūō; Daishō Fudō
Maharṣi Acala in the Center

160. Nanpō; Gundari
Kuṇḍalī in the South

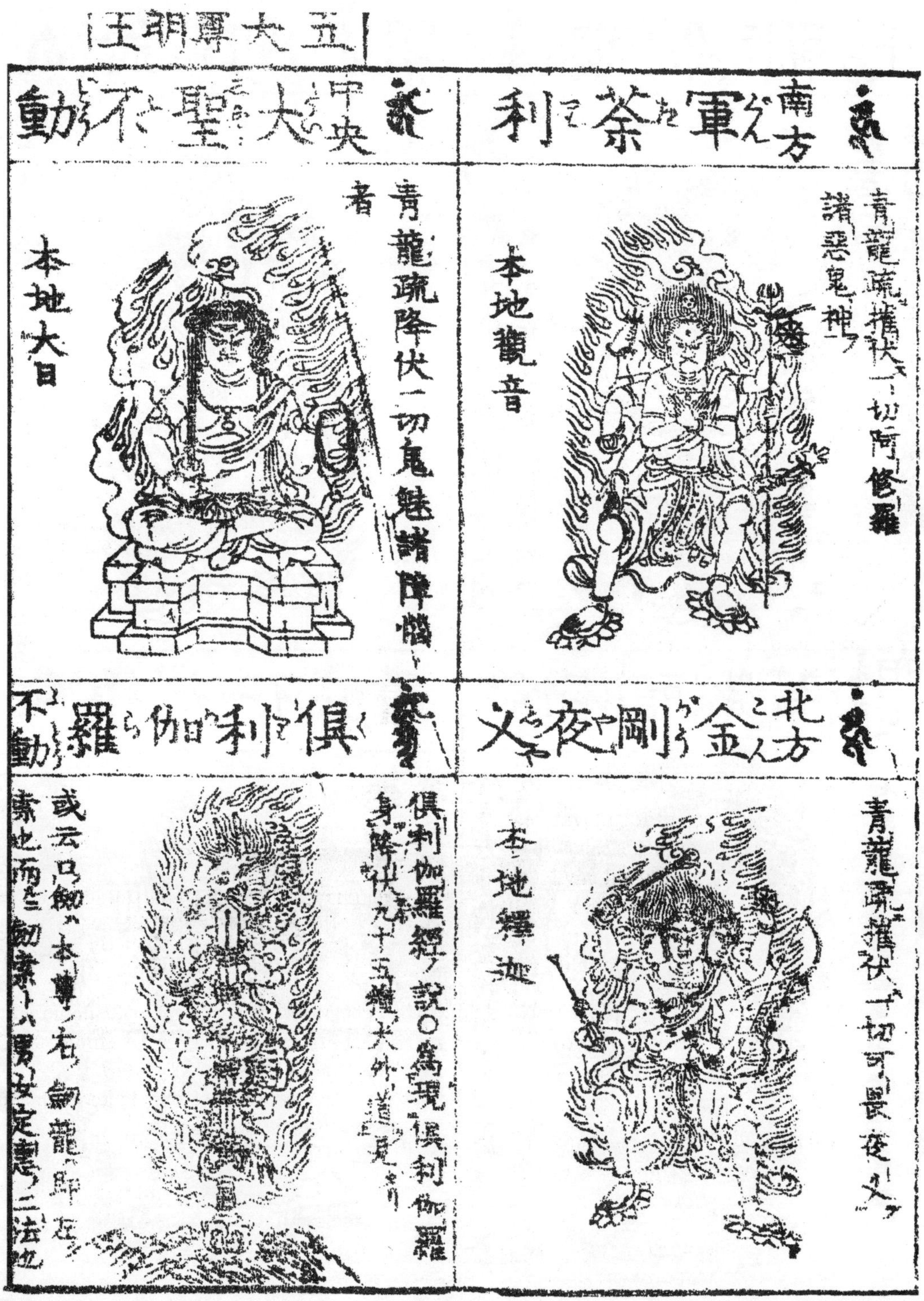

163. Kurikara Fudō
Kulika Acala

161. Hokuhō; Kongoyasha
Vajrayakṣa in the North

§ 14. Myōō Bu
The Vidyārājas (166-171)

166. Butsumo Daikujaku Myōō
Mahāmāyūrī Vidyārājñī

164. Tōhō; Kōsanze Myōō
Trailokyavijaya Vidyārāja in the East

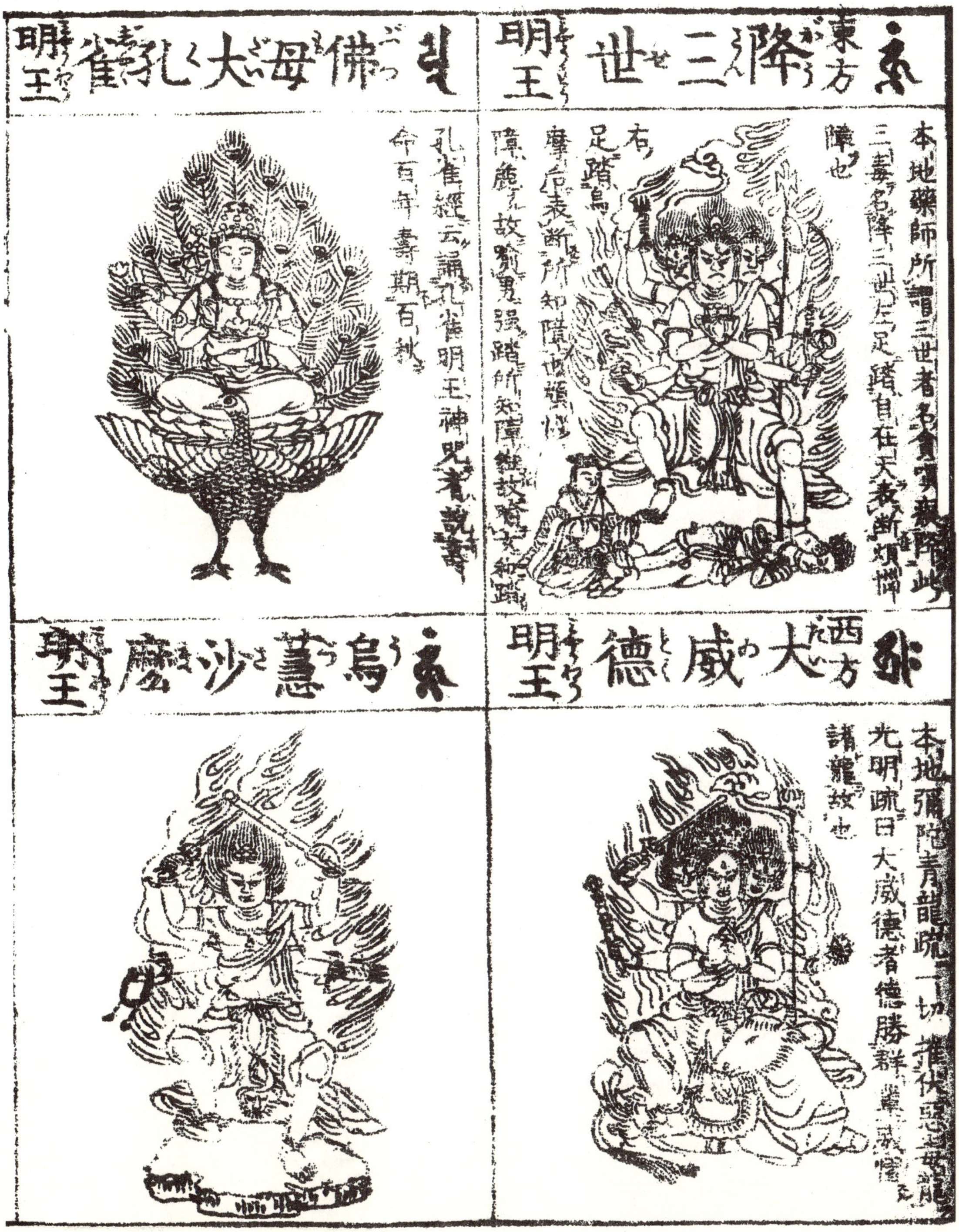

167. Ususama Myōō
Ucchuṣma Vidyārāja

165. Seihō; Daiitoku Myōō
Yamāntaka Vidyārāja in the West

170. Kongōdōji
Vajrakumāra

168. Rokuji Myōō
Ṣaḍakṣara Vidyārāja

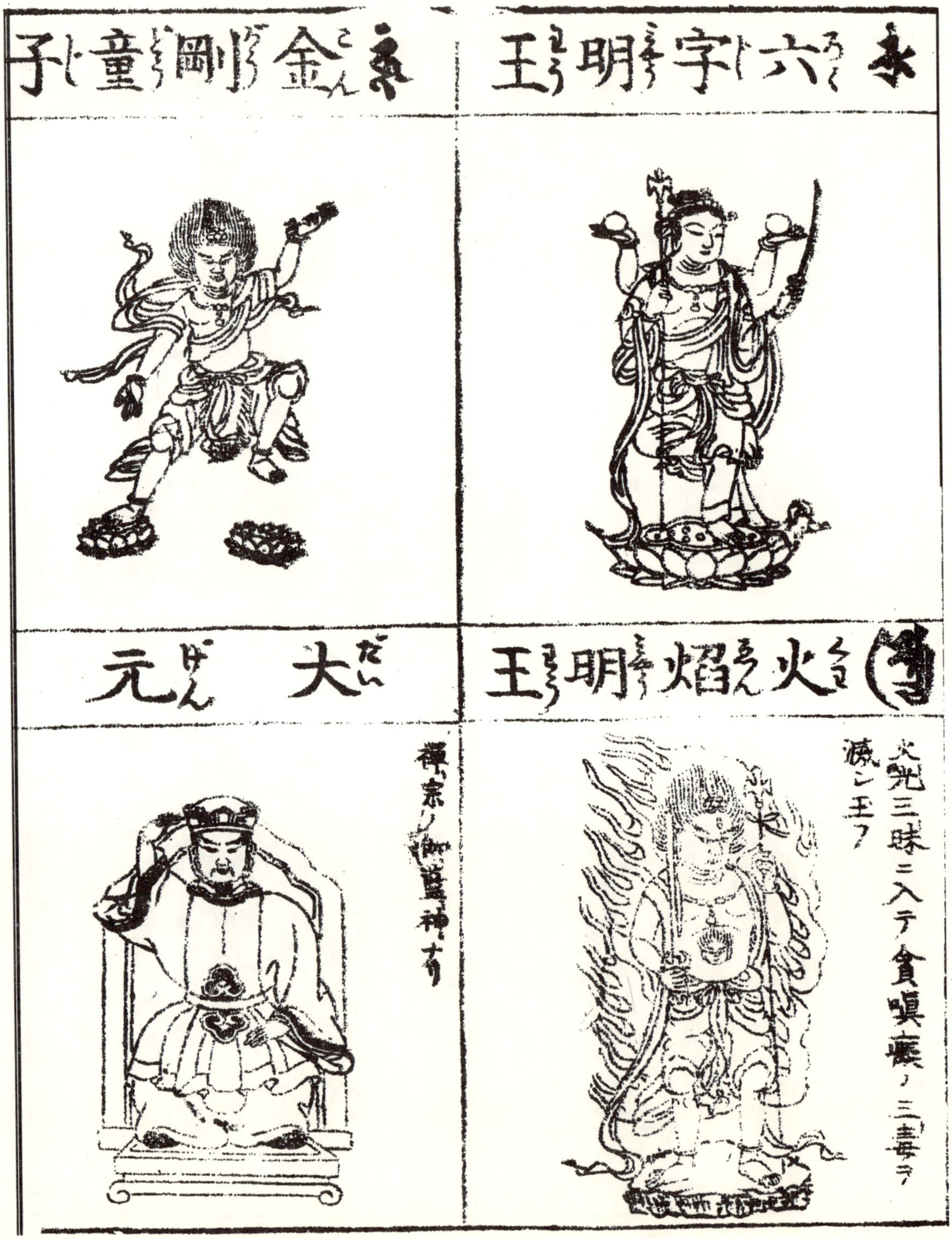

171. Daigen
Āṭavaka

169. Kaen Myōō
Vidyārāja of Flames

増補 諸宗

佛像圖彙

参ノ 3

Fascicle - III

§ 15. Sanjunichi Hibutsu Esoteric Buddhas of the Thirty Days (172-201)

§ 16. Sanjū Banjin Thirty Corresponding Vidyadevas (202-231)

172. Jōkō Butsu (1st day)
Buddha of Eternal Light

173. Tōmyō Butsu (2nd day)
Buddha of Illumination

174. Tahō Butsu (3rd day)
Prabhūtaratna Buddha

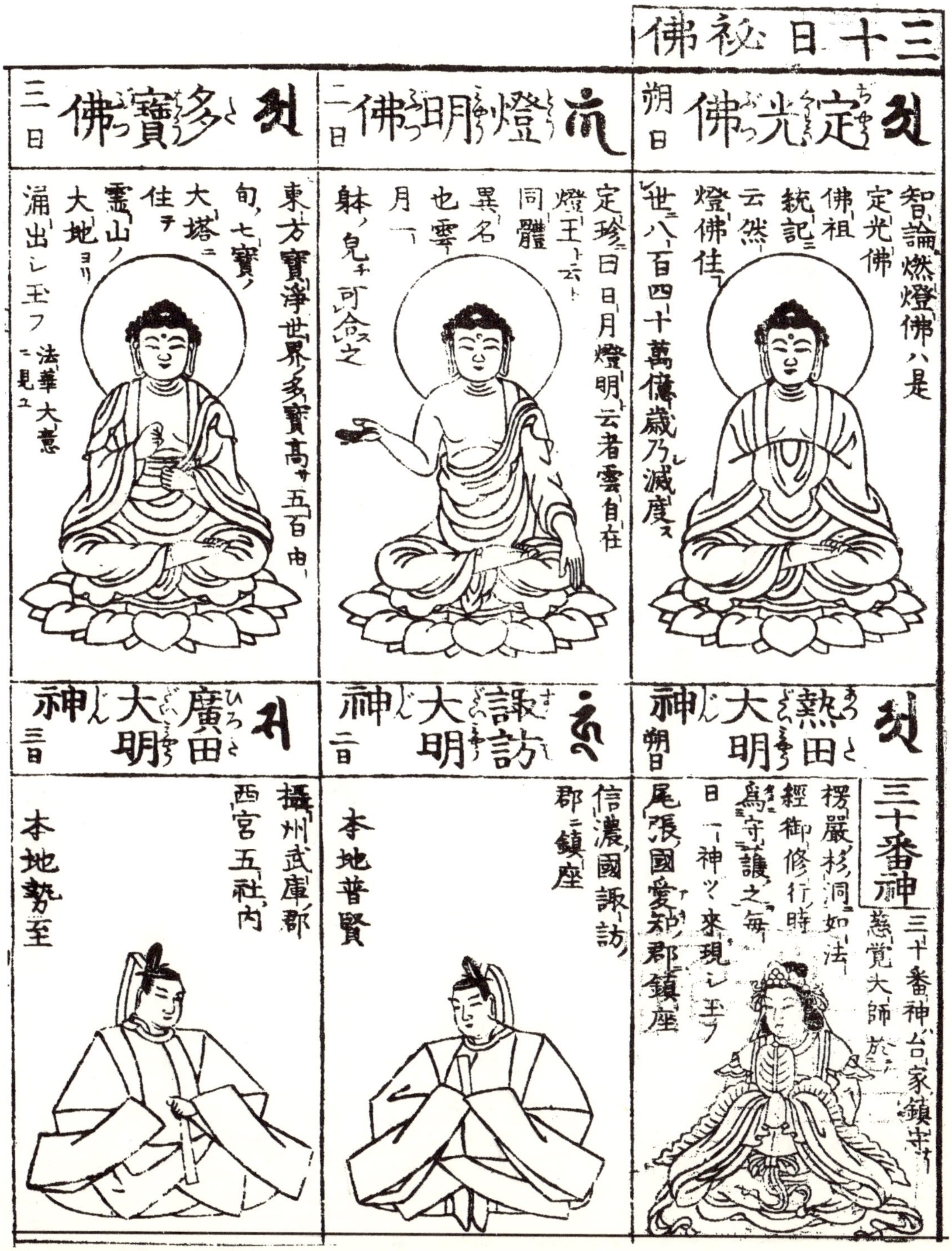

202. Atsuta Daimyōjin (1st day)
Vidyādeva of Atsuta

203. Suwa Daimyōjin (2nd day)
Vidyādeva of Suwa;
Emanation of Samantabhadra

204. Hirota Daimyōjin (3rd day)
Vidyādeva of Hirota;
Emanation of Mahāsthāmaprāpta

177. Nimantōmyō Butsu (6th day) Twenty Thousand Illuminations Buddha

176. Miroku Butsu (5th day) Maitreya Buddha

175. Ashuku Butsu (4th day) Akṣobhya Buddha

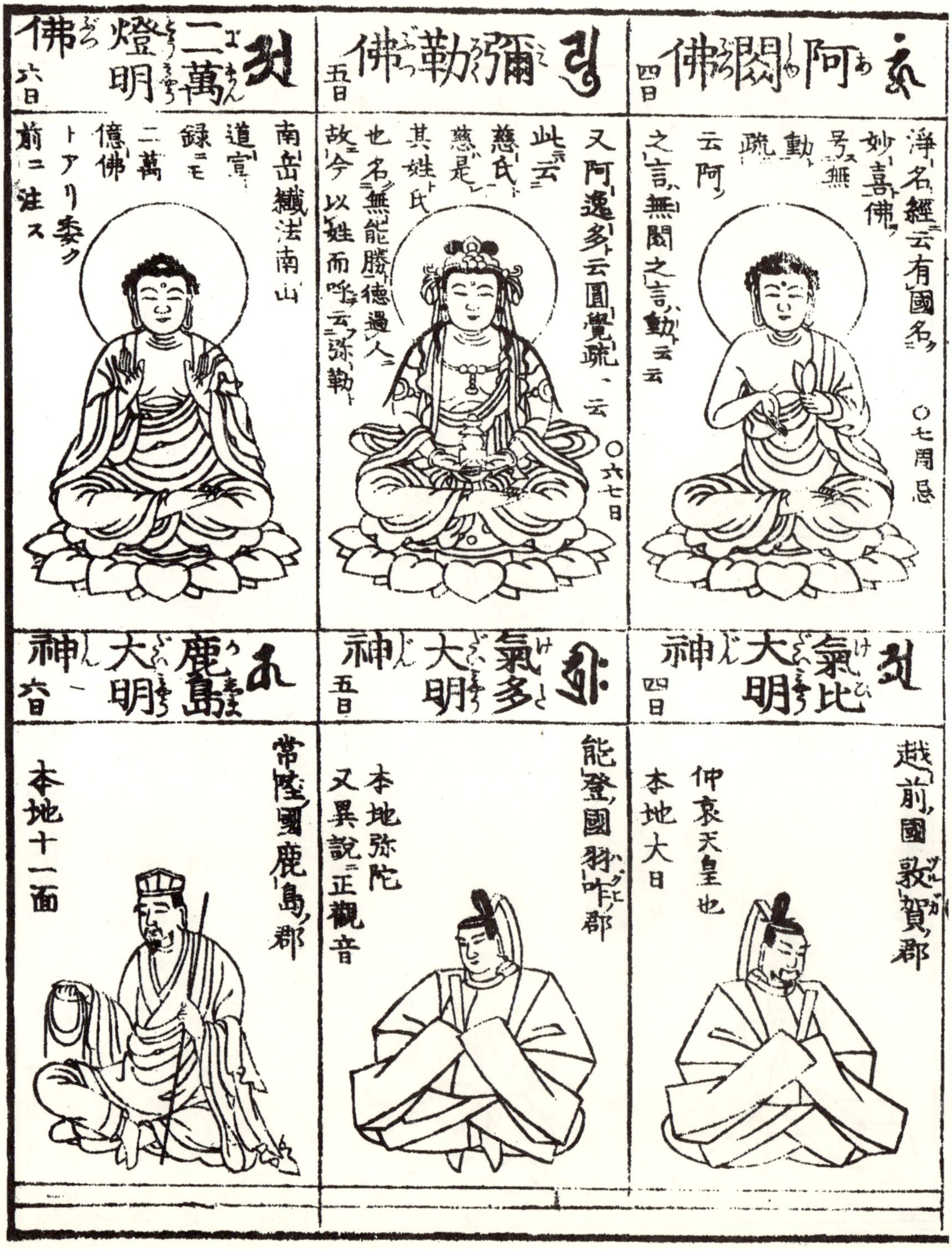

207. Kashima Daimyōjin (6th day) Vidyādeva of Kashima, Emanation of Ekādaśamukha

206. Keta Daimyōjin (5th day) Vidyādeva of Keta, Emanation of Amitābha

205. Kehi Daimyōjin (4th day) Vidyādeva of Kehi, Emanation of Mahāvairocana

180. Daitsūchishō Butsu (9th day) Mahābhijñābhibhū Buddha

179. Yakushi Nyorai (8th day) Bhaiṣajyaguru Tathāgata

178. Sanmantōmyō Butsu (7th day) Thirty-thousand Illumination Buddha

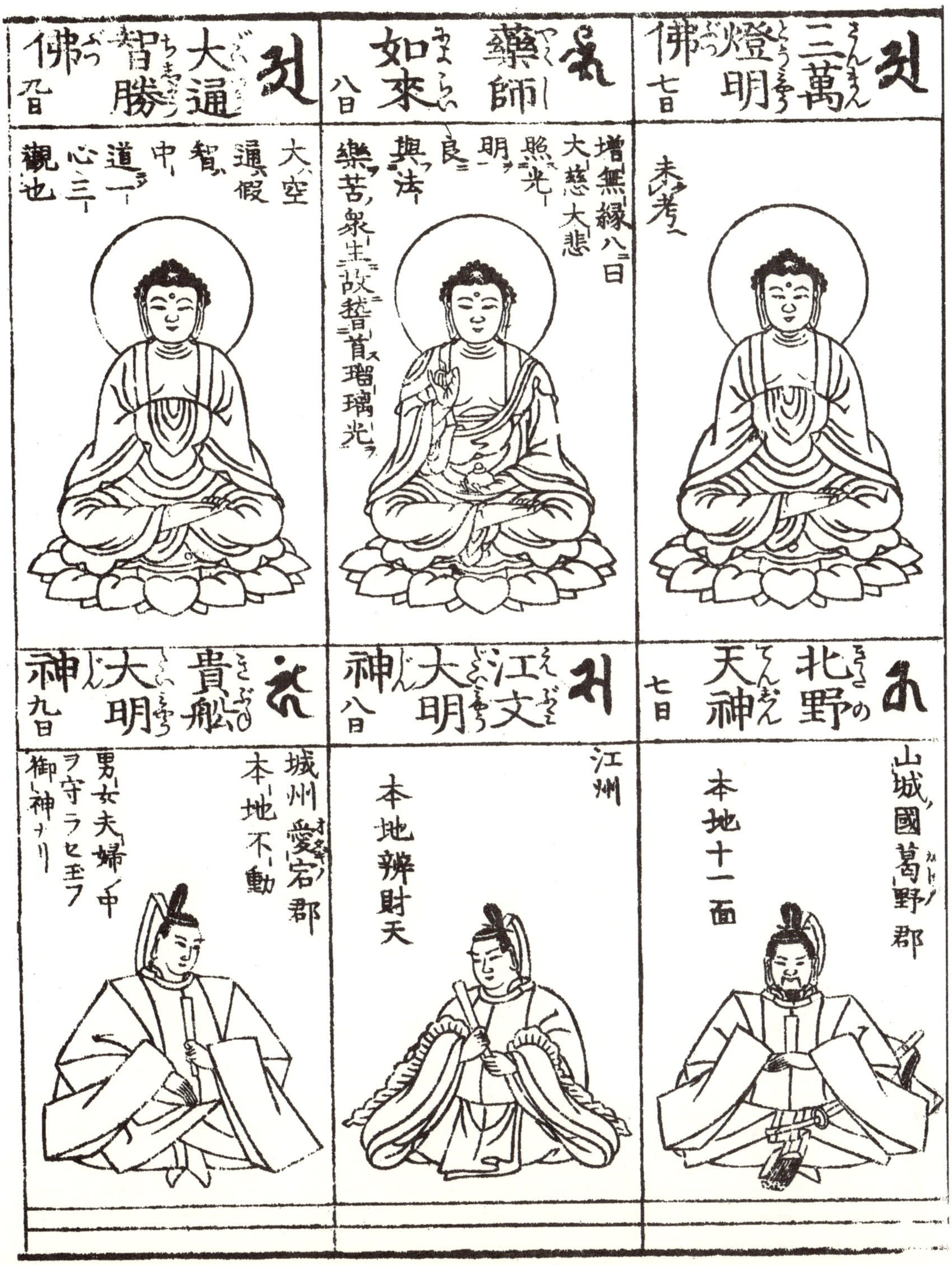

210. Kifune Daimyōjin (9th day) Vidyādeva of Kifune, Emanation of Acala

209. Ebumi Daimyōjin (8th day) Vidyādeva of Ebumi, Emanation of Sarasvatī

208. Kitano Tenjin (7th day) Deva of Kitano, Emanation of Ekādaśamukha

183. Nanshō Butsu (12th day)
Sudurjaya Buddha

182. Kangi Butsu (11th day)
Nandikeśvara Buddha

181. Nichigetsu Tōmyō -butsu (10th day)
Sūryacandraprabha Buddha

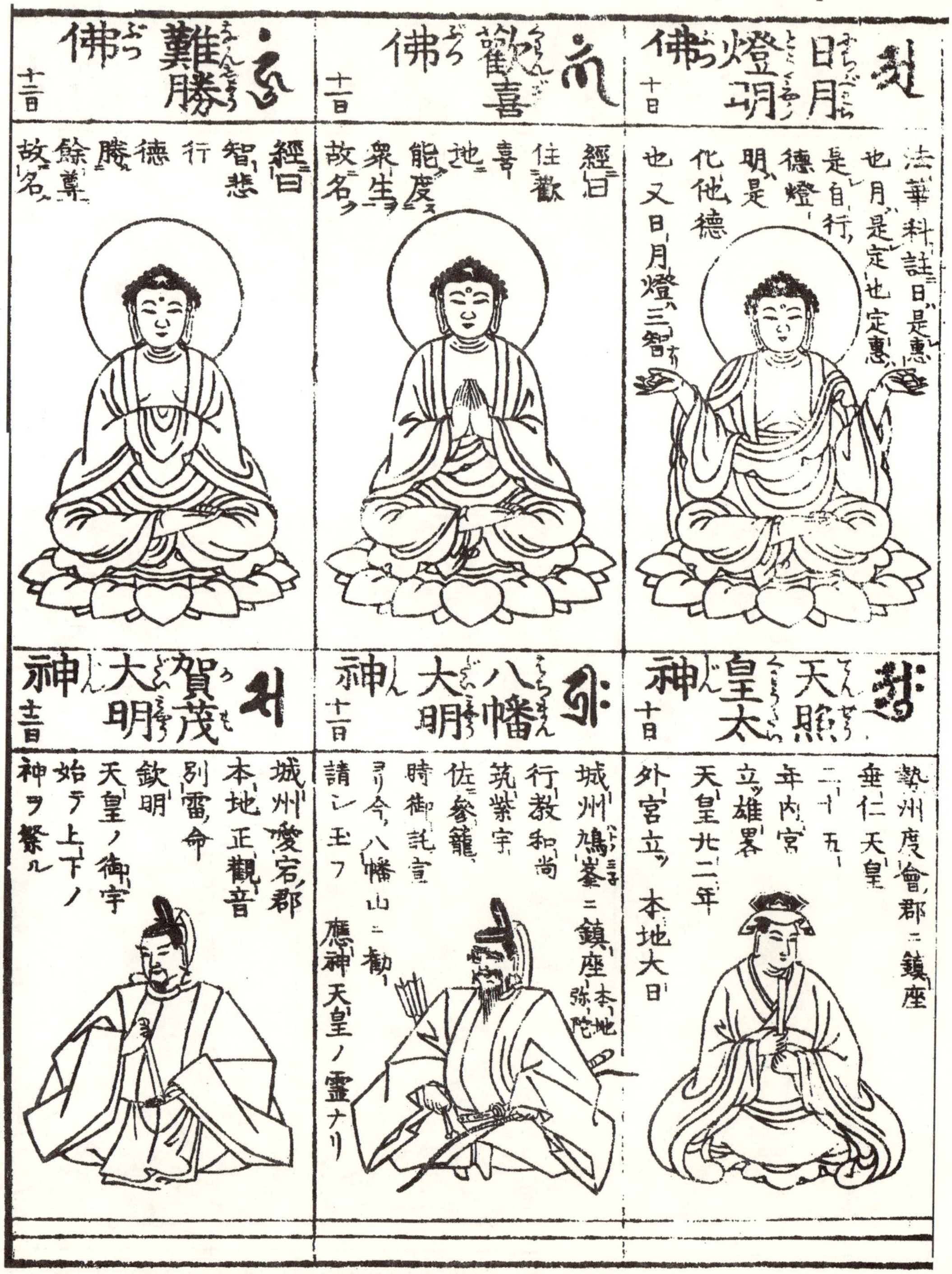

213. Kamo Daimyōjin (12th day) Vidyādeva of Kamo, Emanation of Āryāvalokiteśvara

212. Hachiman Daimyōjin (11th day) Vidyādeva of Hachiman, Emanation of Amitābha Spirit of Emperor Ojin

211. Amaterasu Ōmikami (10th day)
Goddess Amaterasu; Emanation of Mahāvairocana

186. Amida Butsu (15th day)
Amitābha Buddha

185. Fugen Bosatsu (14th day)
Sāmantabhadra Bodhisattva

184. Kokūzō Bosatsu (13th day)
Ākāśagarbha Bodhisattva

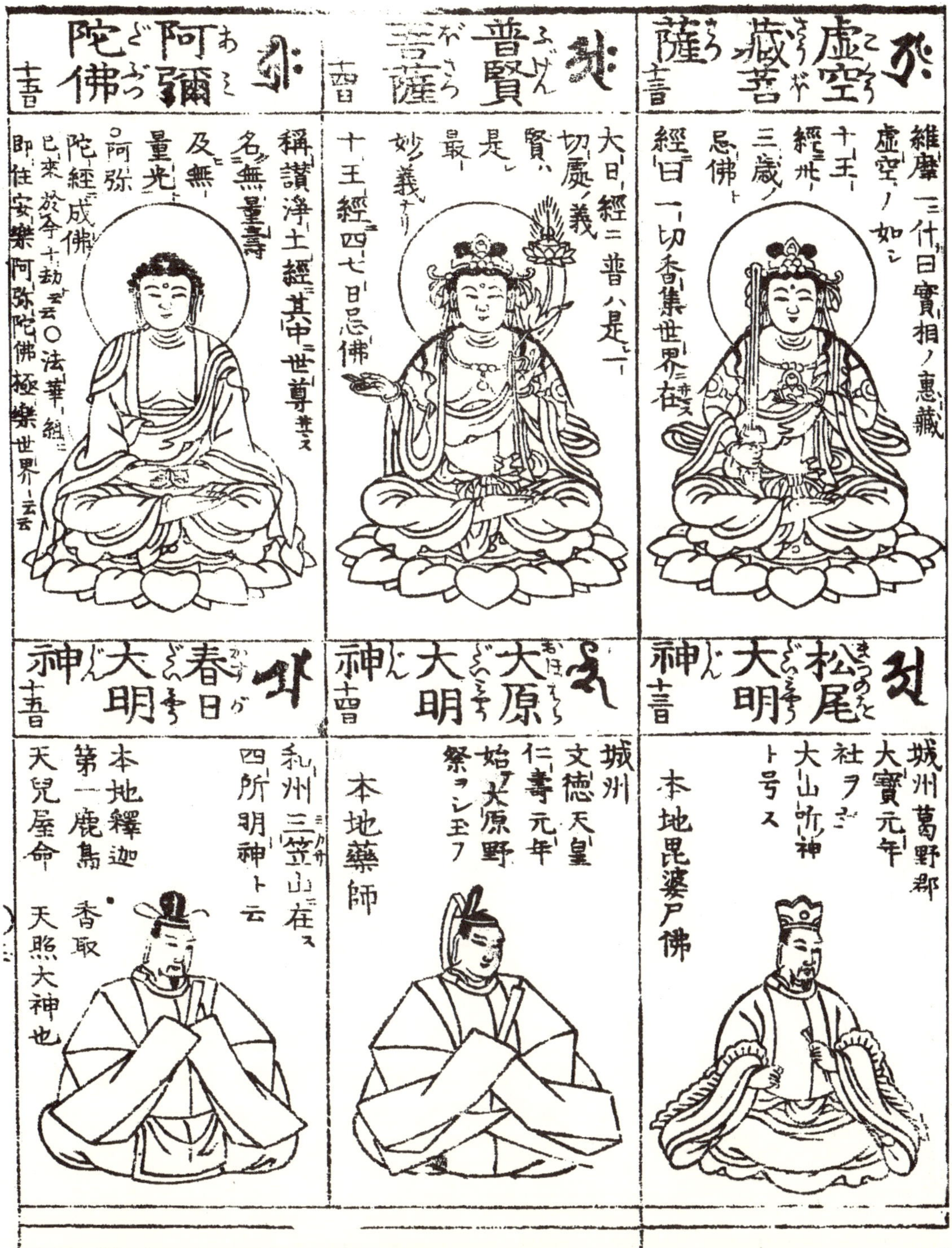

216. Kasuga Daimyōjin (15th day)
Vidyādeva of Kasuga, Emanation of Śākyamuni

215. Ōhara Daimyōjin (14th day)
Vidyādeva of Ōhara, Emanation of Bhaiṣajyaguru

214. Matsunō Daimyōjin (13th day)
Vidyādeva of Matsuno, Emanation of Vipaśyin

189. Kanzeon Bosatsu (18th day) Avalokiteśvara Bodhisattva

188. Ryūju Bosatsu (17th day) Nāgārjuna Bodhisattva

187. Darani Bosatsu (16th day) Dhāraṇī Bodhisattva

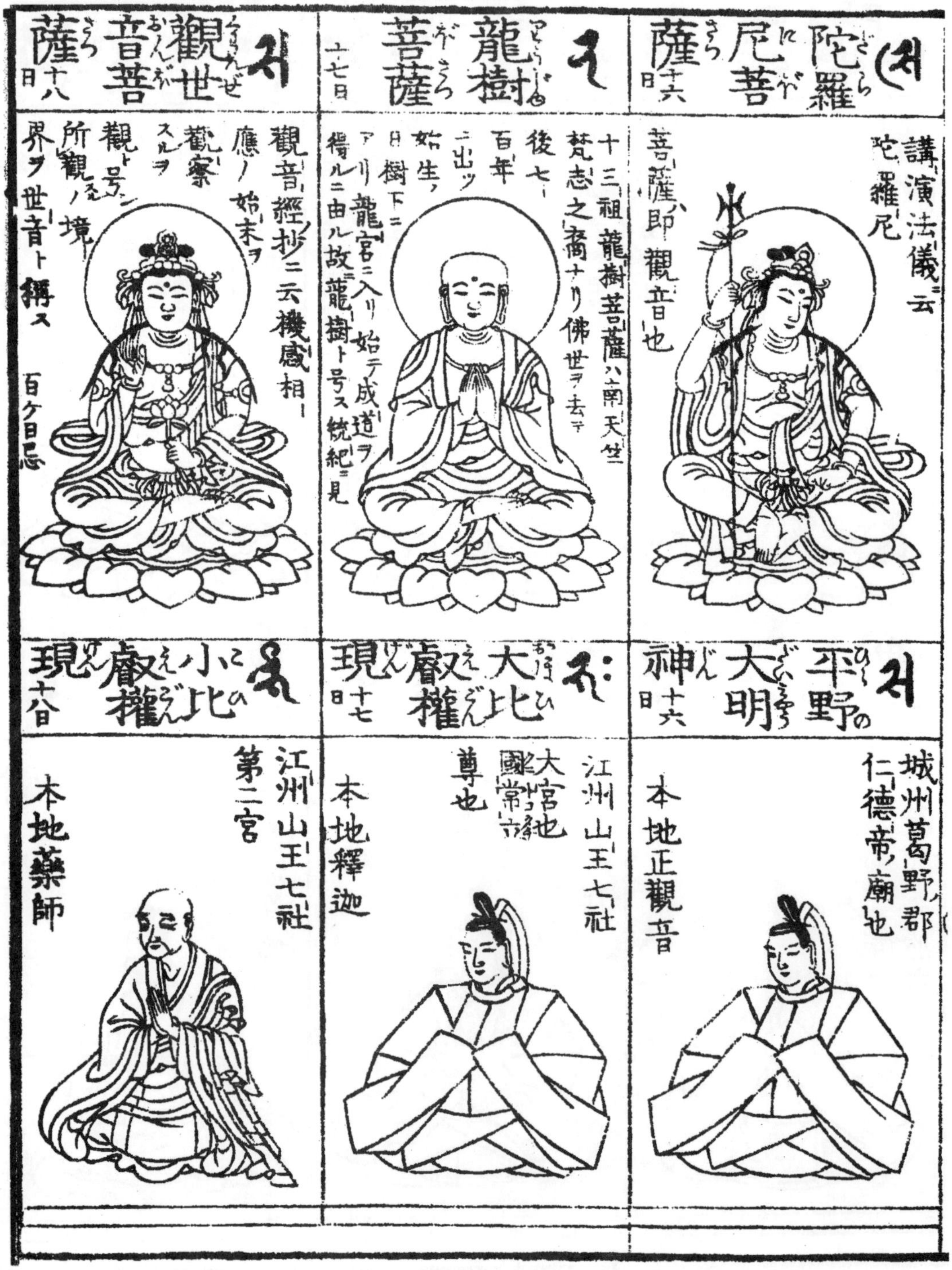

219. Ko-Hiei Gongen (18th day)
The Lesser Hiei Avatāra, Emanation of Bhaiṣajyaguru

218. Ō-Hie Gongen (17th day)
The Great Hie Avatāra Emanation of Śākyamuni

217. Hirano Daimyōjin (16th day)
Vidyādeva of Hirano, Emanation of Ārya Avalokiteśvara

192. Mujini Bosatsu (21st day) Akṣayamati Bodhisattva

191. Gekkō Bosatsu (20th day) Candraprabha Bodhisattva

190. Nikkō Bosatsu (19th day) Sūryaprabha Bodhisattva

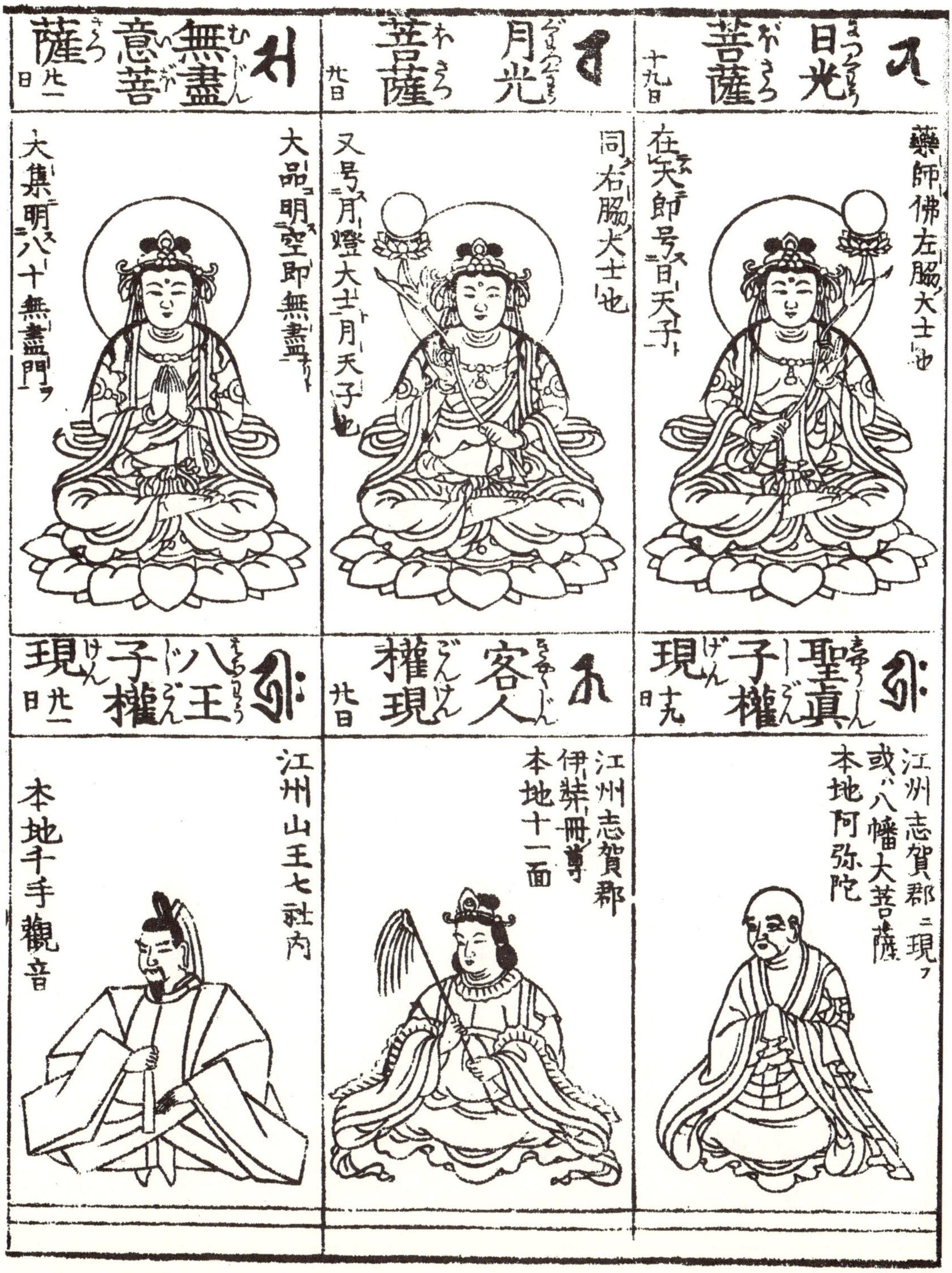

222. Hachiōji Gongen (21st day) Hachiōji Avatāra, Emanation of Sahasrabhuja Avalokiteśvara

221. Kyakujin Gongen (20th day) Kyakujin Avatāra, Emanation of Ekādaśamukha Avalokiteśvara

220. Shōshinshi Gongen (19th day) Shōshinshi Avatāra Emanation of Amitābha

195. Jizō Bosatsu (24th day)
Kṣitigarbha Bodhisattva

194. Daiseishi Bosatsu (23rd day)
Mahāsthāmaprāpta Bodhisattva

193. Semui Bosatsu (22nd day)
Abhayaṁdada Bodhisattva

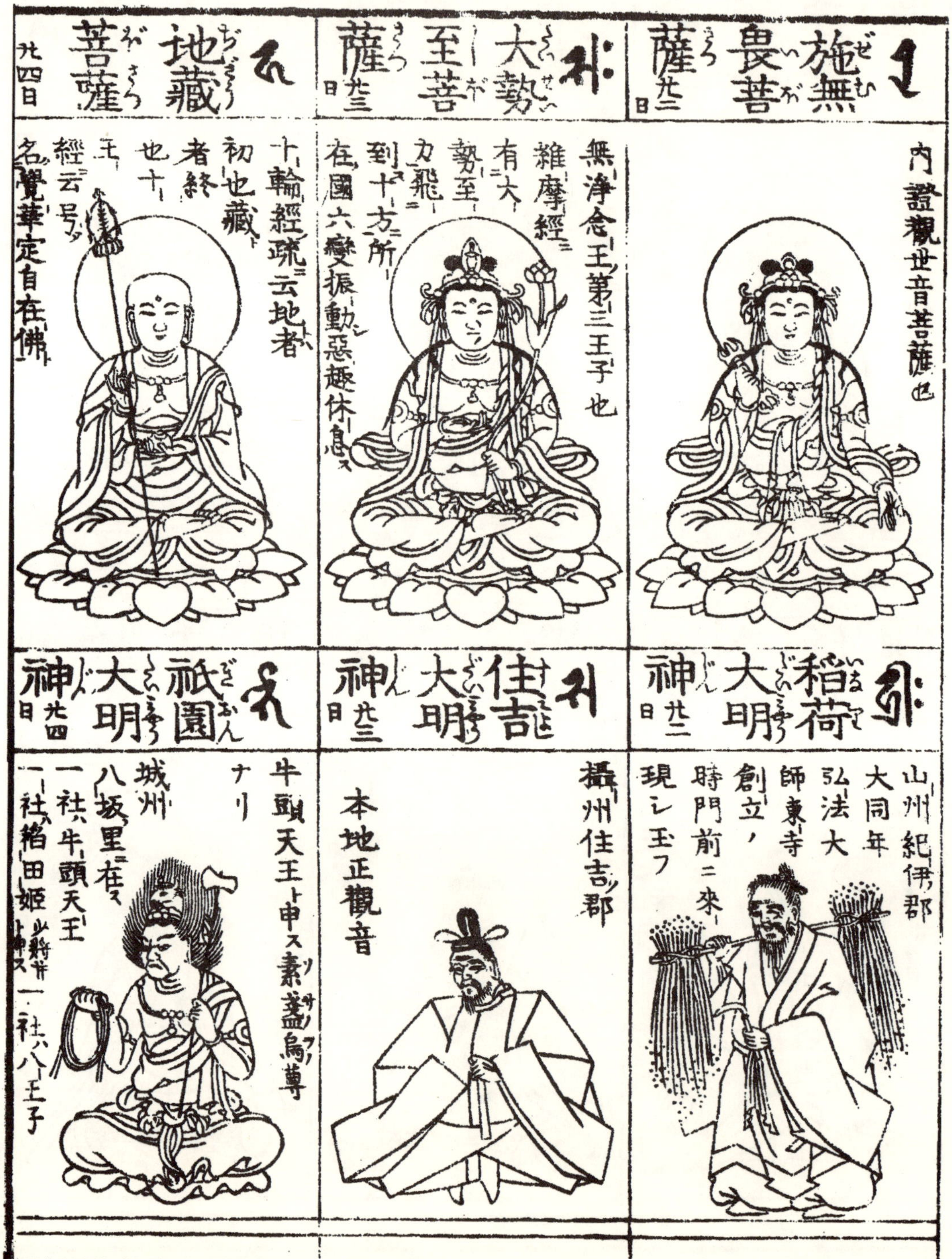

225. Gion Daimyōjin (24th day)
Gion Vidyādeva

224. Sumiyoshi Daimyōjin (23rd day) Sumiyoshi Vidyādeva, Emanation of Ārya Avalokiteśvara

223. Inari Daimyōjin (22nd day)
Inari Vidyādeva

198. Roshana Butsu
(27th day)
Rocana Buddha

197. Yakujō Bosatsu
(26th day)
Bhaiṣajyodgata Bodhisattva

196. Monju Bosatsu
(25th day)
Mañjuśrī Bodhisattva

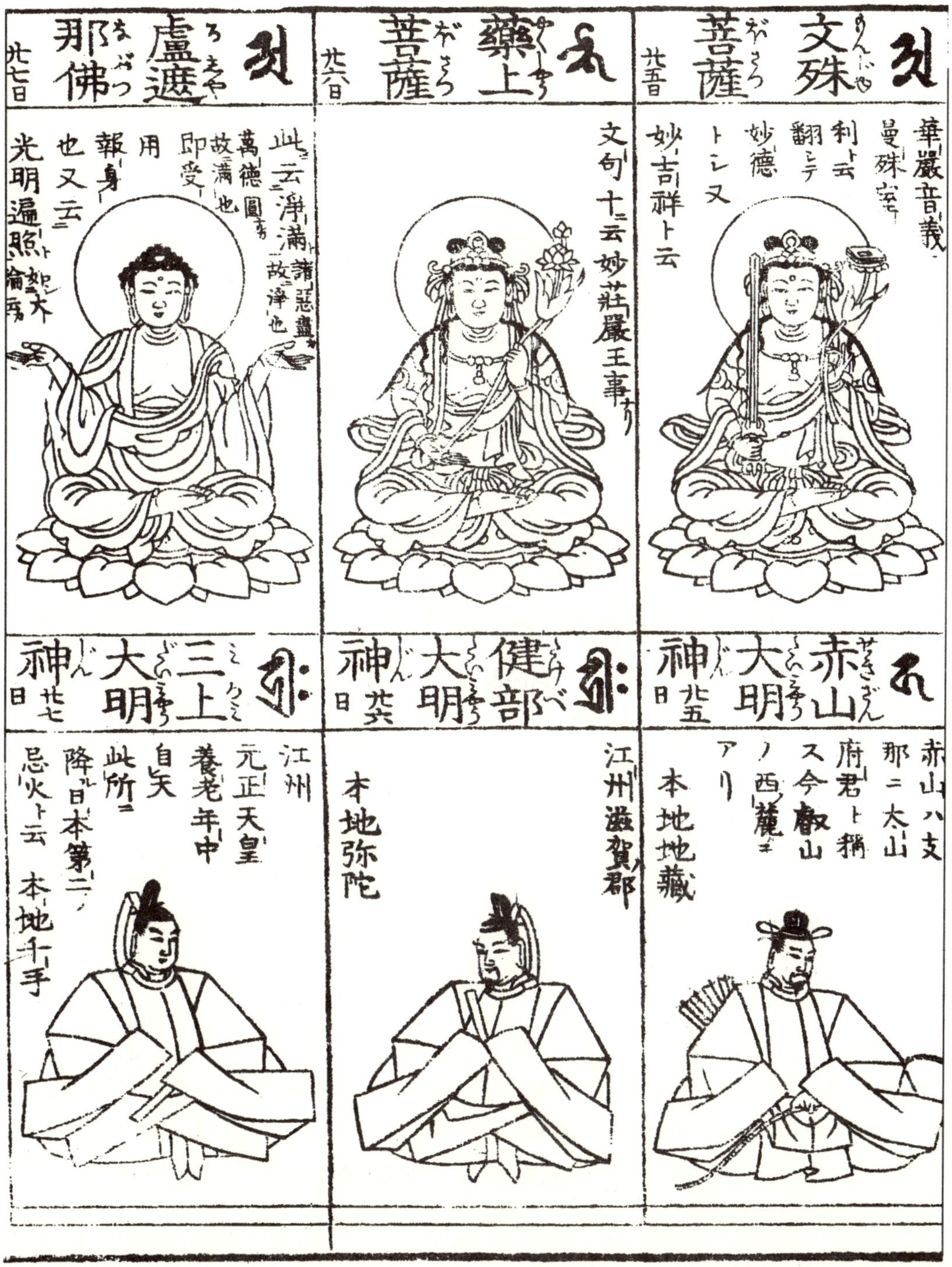

228. Mikami Daimyōjin
(27th day)
Mikami Vidyādeva
Emanation of Sahasrabhuja

227. Takebe Daimyōjin
(26th day)
Takebe Vidyādeva,
Emanation of Amitābha

226. Sekisan Daimyōjin
(25th day)
Sekisan Vidyādeva,
Emanation of Kṣitigarbha

201. Shaka Nyorai (30th day) Śākyamuni Tathāgata

200.Yakuō Bosatsu (29th day) Bhaiṣajyarāja Bodhisattva

199.Dainichi Nyorai (28th day) Mahāvairocana Tathāgata

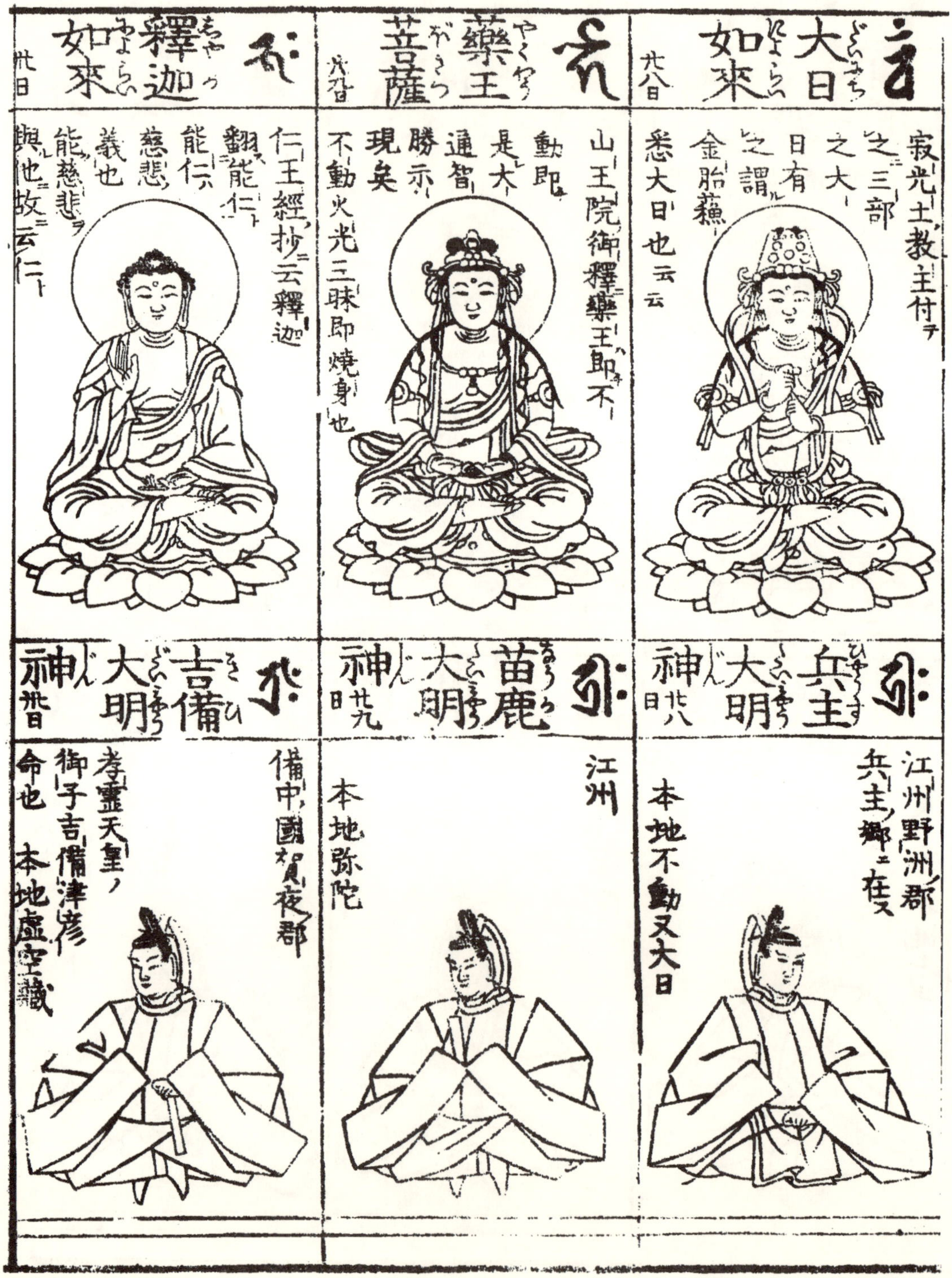

231. Kibi Daimyōjin (30th day)
Kibi Vidyādeva of Mt.Koya, Emanation of Ākāśagarbha

229. Nōka Daimyōjin (29th day)
Nōka Vidyādeva, Emanation of Amitābha

229.Hyōsu Daimyōjin (28th day)
Hyosu Vidyādeva Emanation of Acala or Mahāvairocana

§ 17. Sannōshichisha Gongen

Incarnates of the Seven Shrines of Sannō (232-238) and Other incarnates (239-251)

236. Shōshinji
Monk Shōshinji;
Emanation of Amitābha

234. Ōmiya Gongen
Incarnation of Ōmiya shrine
Emanation of Śākyamuni

232. Ninomiya Kobie
Ninomiya shrine of Kobie
Emanation of Bhaiṣajyaguru

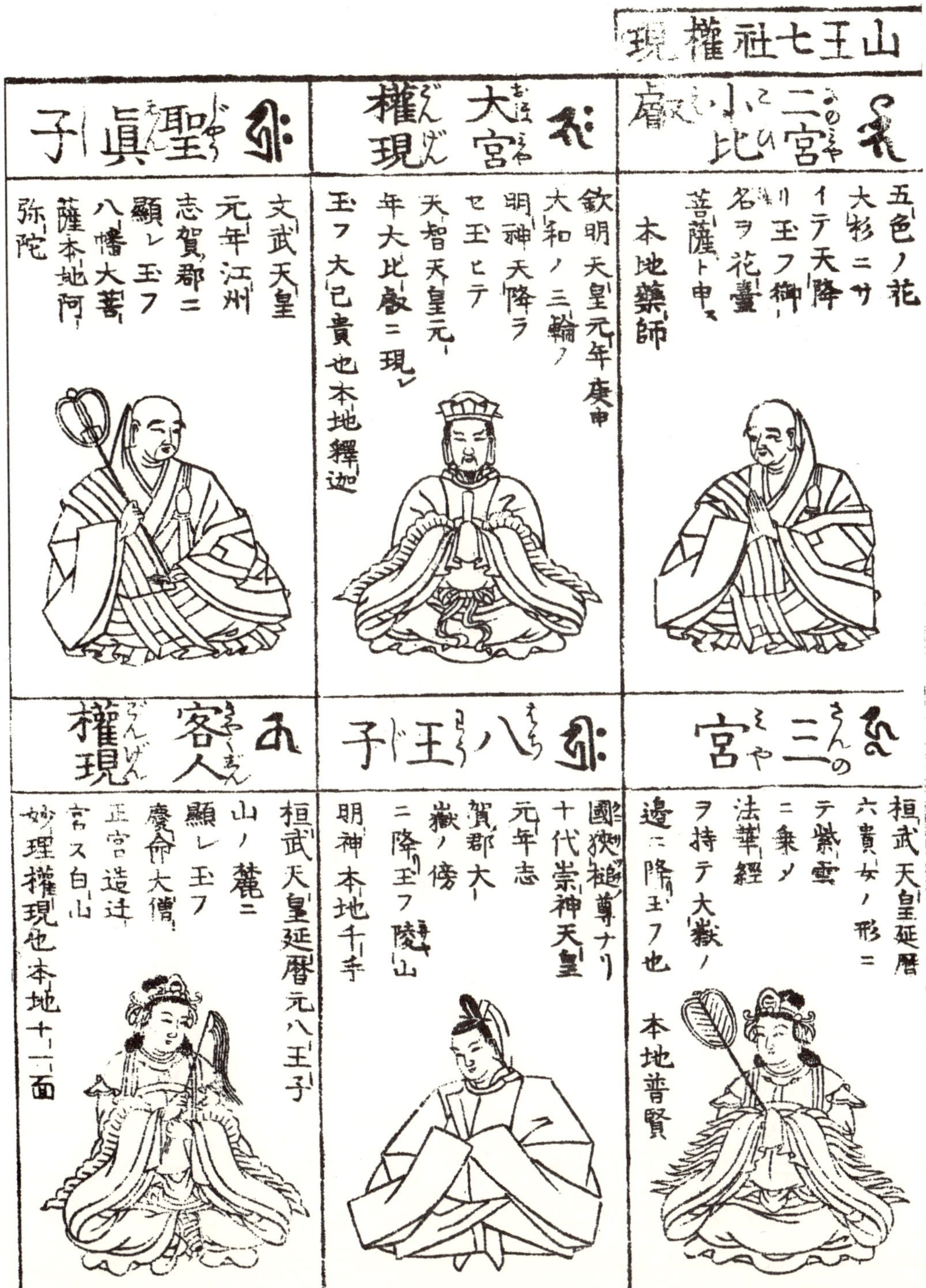

237. Kyakujin Gongen
Incarnation of Kyakujin
Emanation of Ekādaśamukha

235. Hachiōji
The Hachiōji
Emanation of Sahasrabhuja

233. Sanno Miya
Avatāra of Sannomiya shrine;
Emanation of Sāmantabhadra

242. Fuji Gongen
Avatāra of Fuji, Emanation of Mahāvairocana

240. Hakusan Myōtsuku Daigongen
Avatāra of Myotsuku of Mt. Hakusan

238. Jūzenji
Meditation-Master Jūzenji, Emanation of Kṣitigarbha

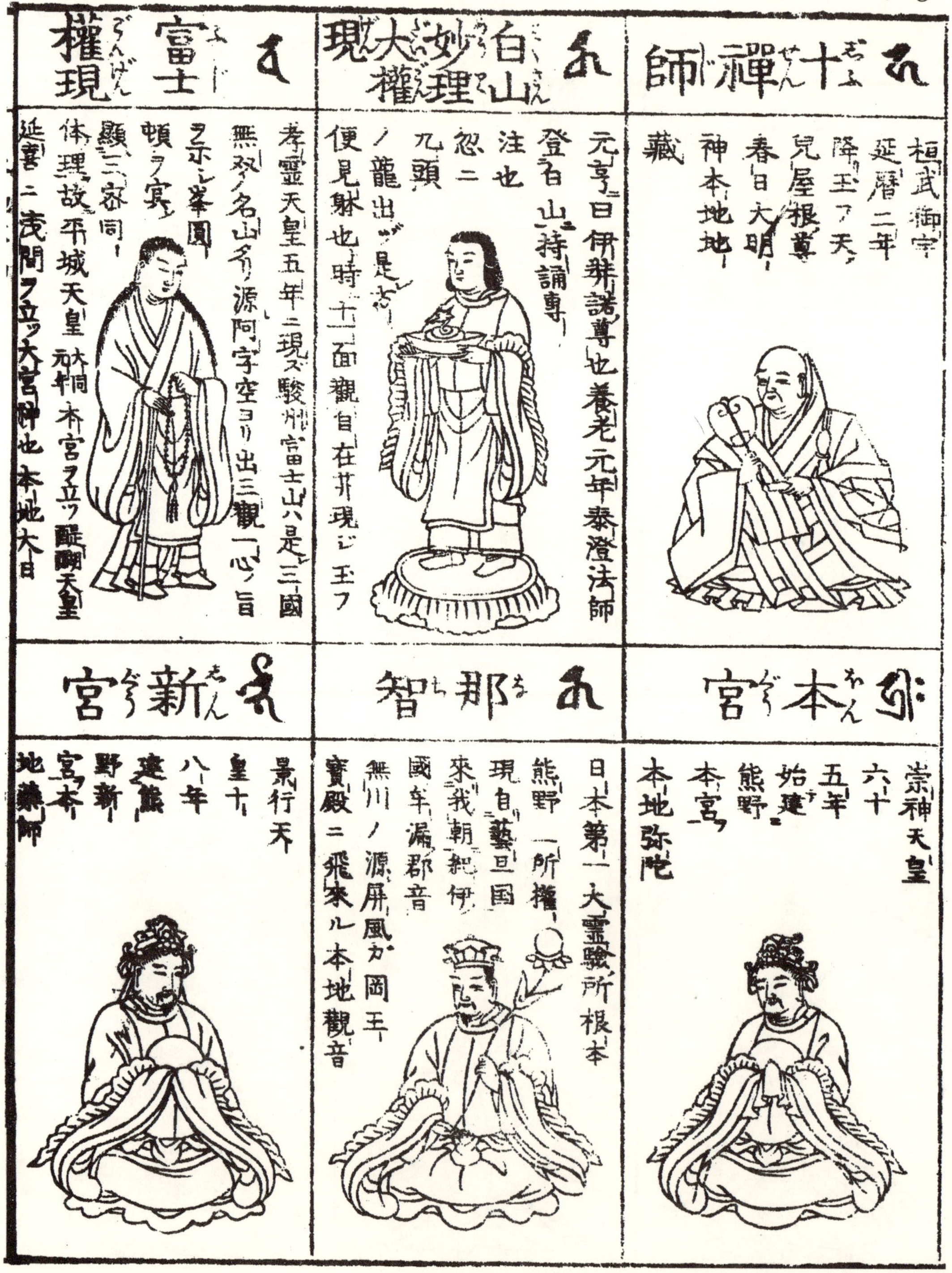

243. Shingū
Avatāra of New Shrine of Kumano, Emanation of Yakushi Buddha

241. Nachi
Avatāra of Nachi Emanation of Kannon

239. Hongū
Avatāra of Nimasu Shrine of Kumano; Emanation of Amitābha Buddha

248. Yoshinozōō Gongen
Incarnation of Yoshinō Āryarāja

246. Atago Gongen
Atago Incarnation

244. Izuna Gongen
Avatāra of Izunaat Mt. Takao;
Emanation of Acala

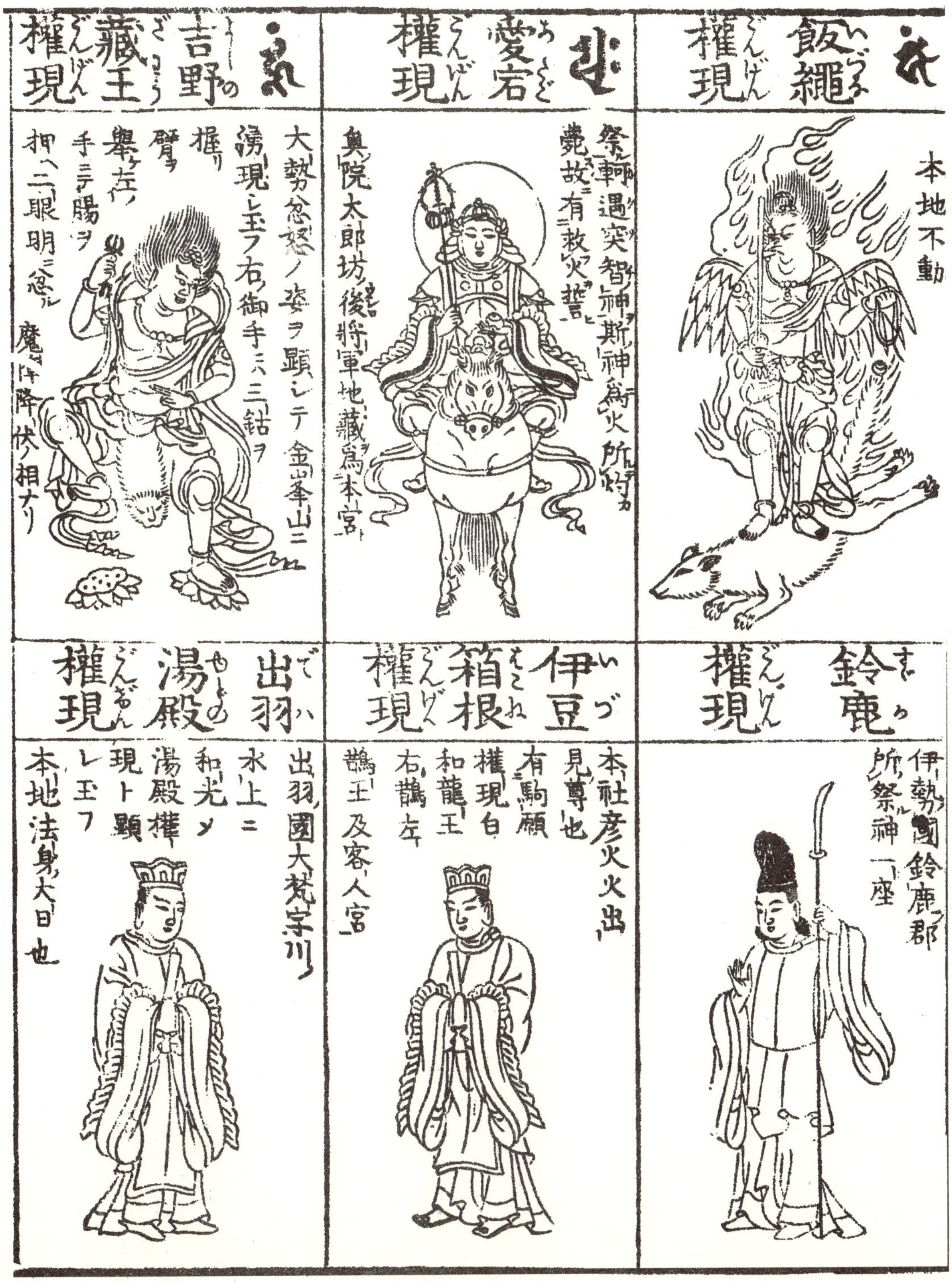

249. Debayudono Gongen
Yudono Avatāra,
Dharmakāya of Mahāvairocana

247. Izu Hakone Gongen
Izu Hakone Incarnation

245.Suzuro Gongen
Suzuro Incarnation

§18. Kōyasan Shisha Myōjin
Vidyadevas of the four shrines at Mt. Kōya (252-256)

253. Koya Daimyōjin
Deity Koya Myōjin

252. Niu Daimyōjin
Mahādevī of Niu

250. Nachi Hiryu Gongen
Incarnation of Nachi Hiryu,
Emanation of Nāgarāja

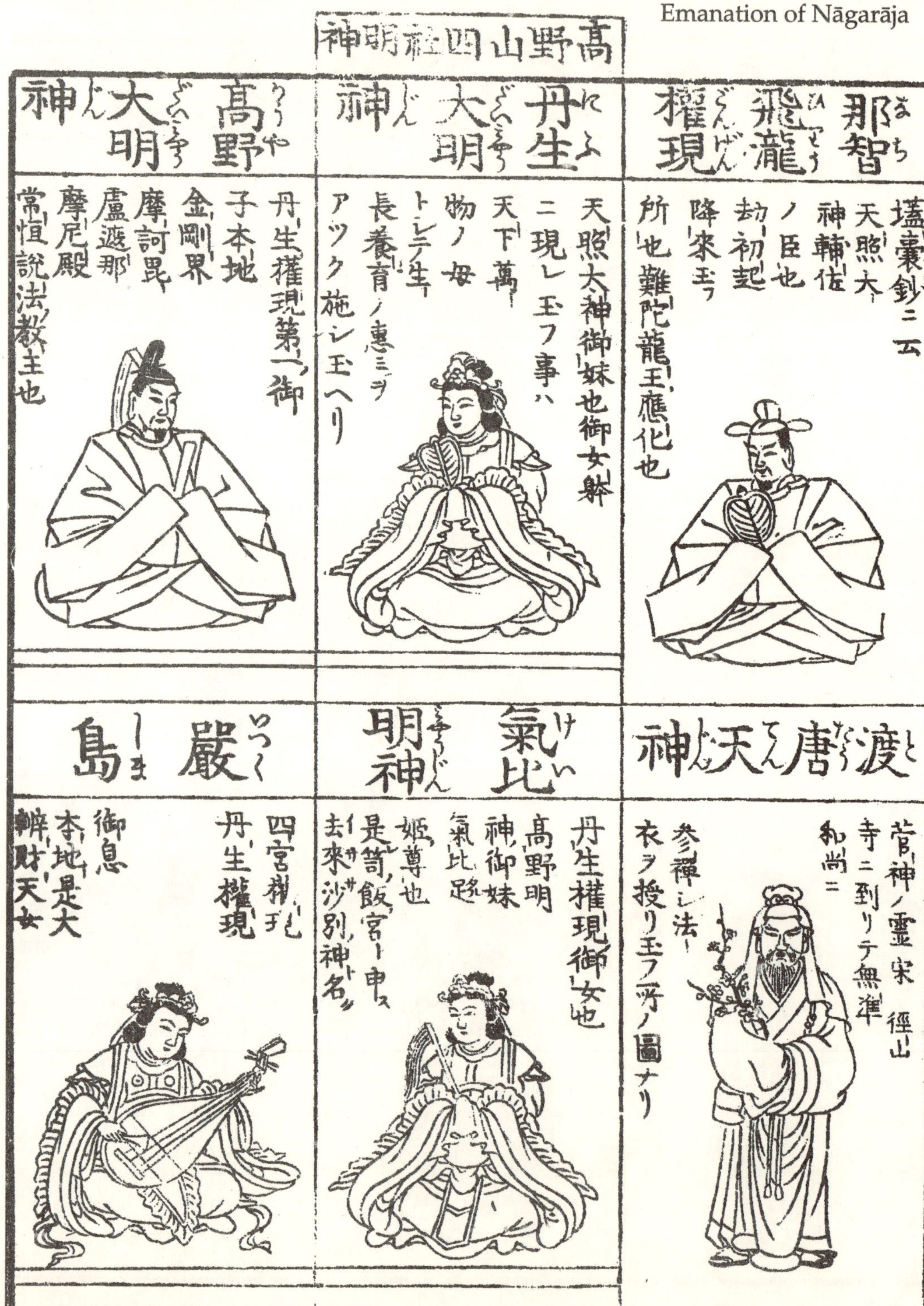

255. Itsuku Shima
Avatāra of Miyajima

254. Kei Myōjin
Deity Kei-Myōjin

251. Totō Tenjin
Deity of Totō

§ 19. Dōji no Bu
Kumāras (257-264) and 4 Dogmas (265-268)

258. Aka Dōji
Red Kumāra

257. Uhō Dōji
Ratna Varṣa Kumāra

256. Hachiman
Hachiman, the God of War

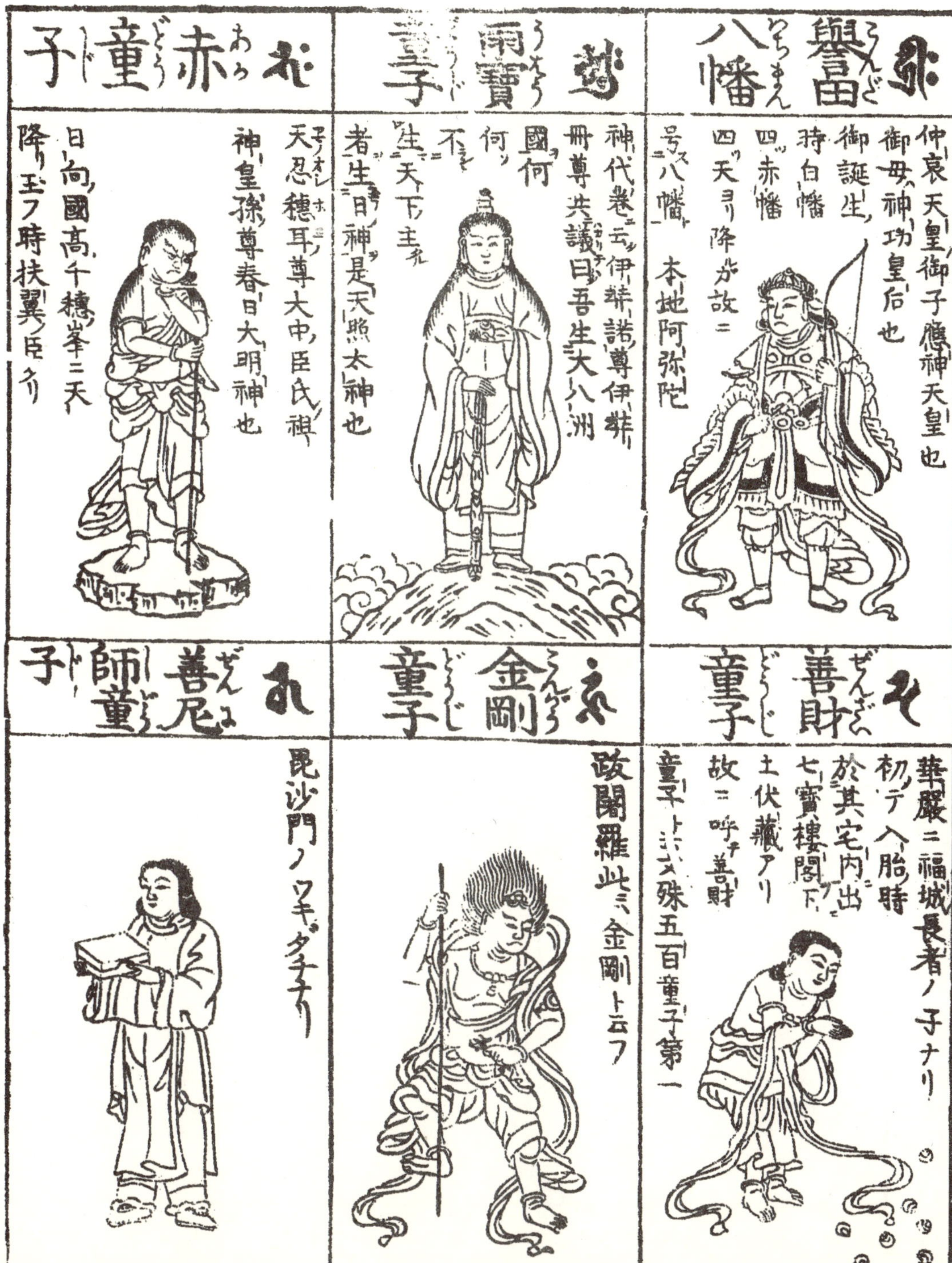

261. Zennishi Dōji
Virtuous Kumāra as an Abbess, stands besides Vaiśravaṇa

260. Kongō Dōji
Vajrakumāra

259. Zenzai Dōji
Sudhana Śreṣthidāraka Kumāra

264.Sahō Dōji
Kumāra of the Left Side

263. Koshin Shōmen Kongō
Nīlamukha Vajra (Worshipped on the unlucky day of Koshin (monkey) with both Kumāras

262. Uhō Dji
Kumāra on right

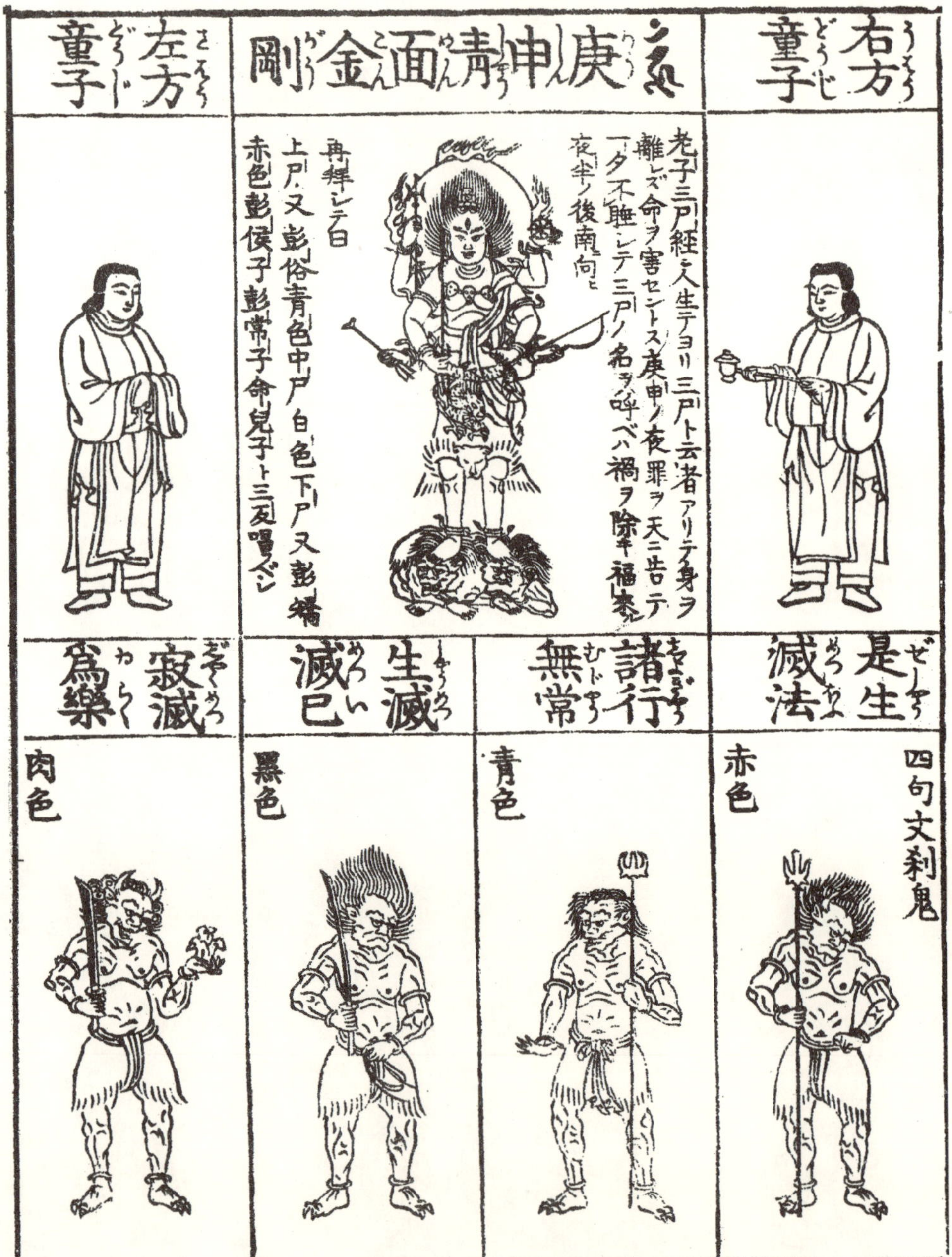

268. Jakumetsu Iraku
"Nirvāṇa alone is tranquil", represented by skin color Rākṣasa

267. Shōmetṣu Metsui
"There is constant Birth & extinction" represented by black Rākṣasa

266. Shogyō Mujō
"All things are impermanent", represented by blue Rākṣasa

265. Zesshō Meppō
(four letter dogmas)
All that is born is destined to destruction, represented by red Rākṣasa

§ 20. Benzaiten Jūroku Dōji
The Sixteen Kumāras of Sarasvatī (269-284)

273. Tawara Dōji, 5th	**271. Hikken Dōji, 3rd**	**269. Inkan Dōji, Ist**
Kumāra with straw	Kumāra with brush and ink	Kumāra with seal

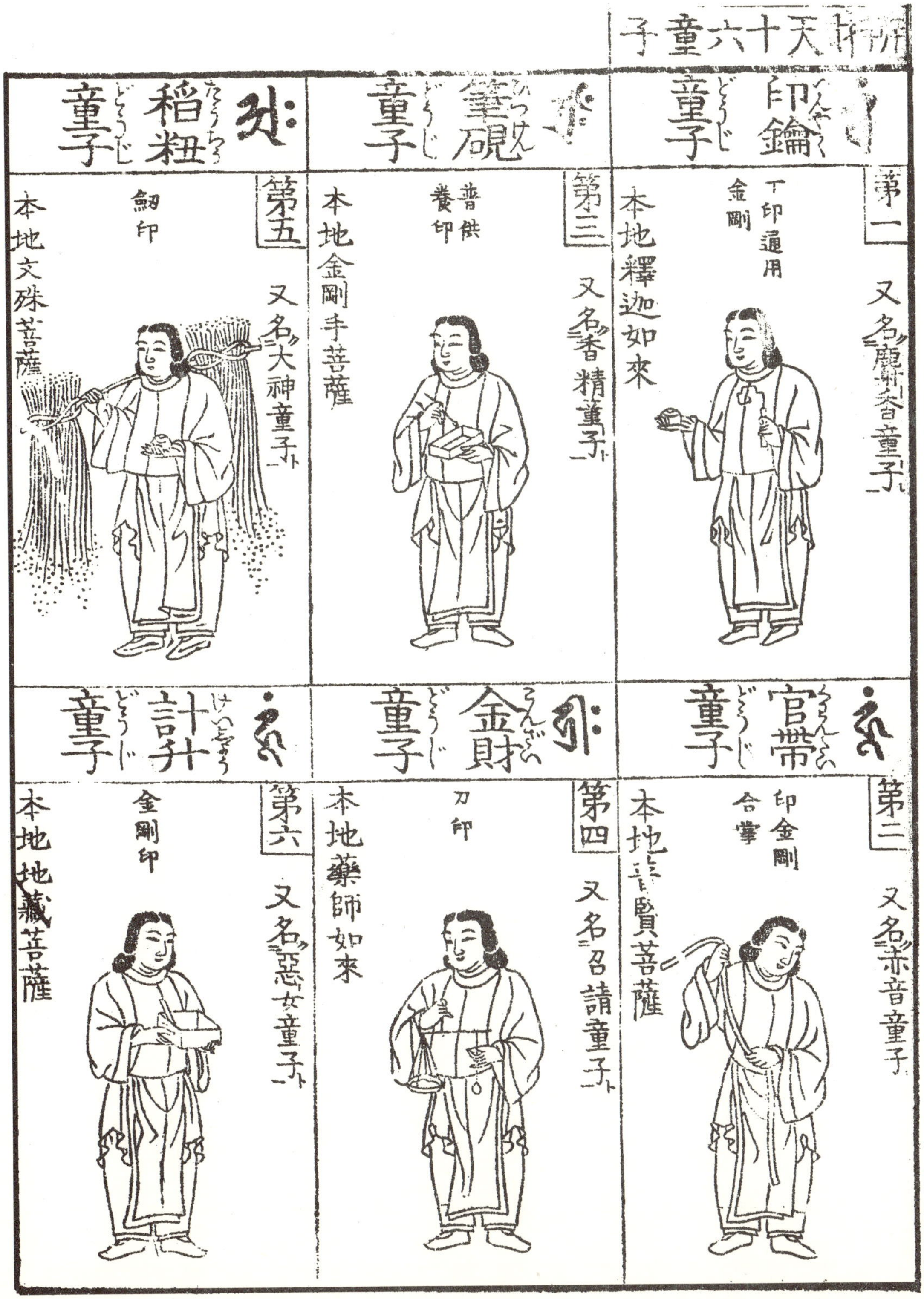

274. Keisho Dōji, 6th	**272. Konzai Dōji, 4th**	**270. Kantai Dōji, 2nd**
Kumāra with measuring box	Mudrā Kumāra	Red-Kumāra with belt

279. Aikyō Dōji, 11th
Kumāra of affection, Emanation of Avalokiteśvara Bodhisattva

277. Sanyō Dōji, 9th
Kumāra rearing silk worms

275. Meshibitsu Dōji, 7th
Kumāra with cooked-rice tub

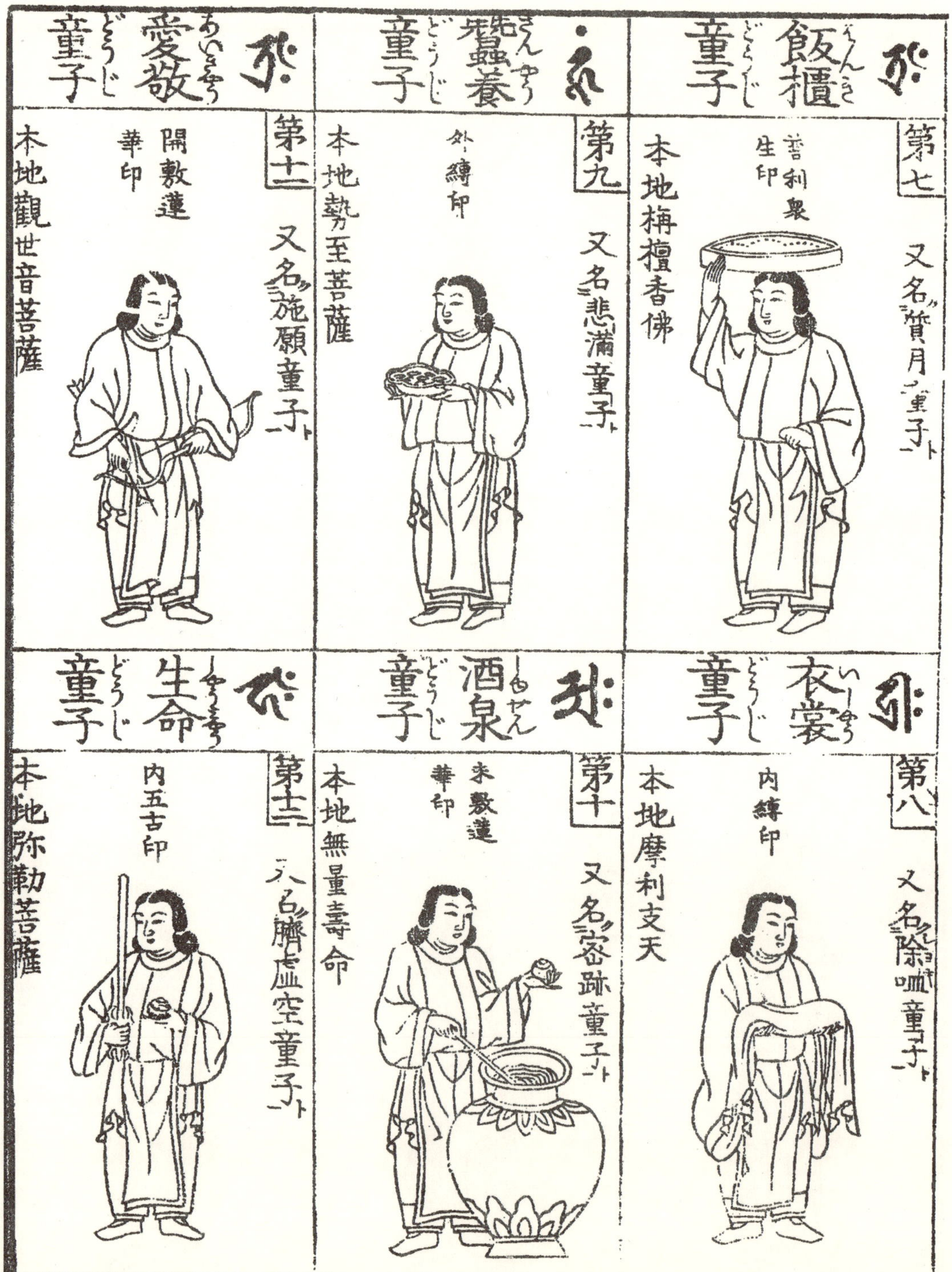

280. Shōmyō Dōji, 12th
Āyuḥ Kumāra

278. Shusen Dōji, 10th
Kumāra with spring of sake wine

276. Ishō Dōji, 8th
Kumāra with garment

§ 21. Fudō Hachidaidōji
The Eight Mahākumāras of Acala (285-292)

285. Ekō Dōji
Divine Light Kumāra

283. Sensha Dōji, 15th
Kumāra with cart

281. Jūsha Dōji, 13th
Anugami (Attendant) Kumāra

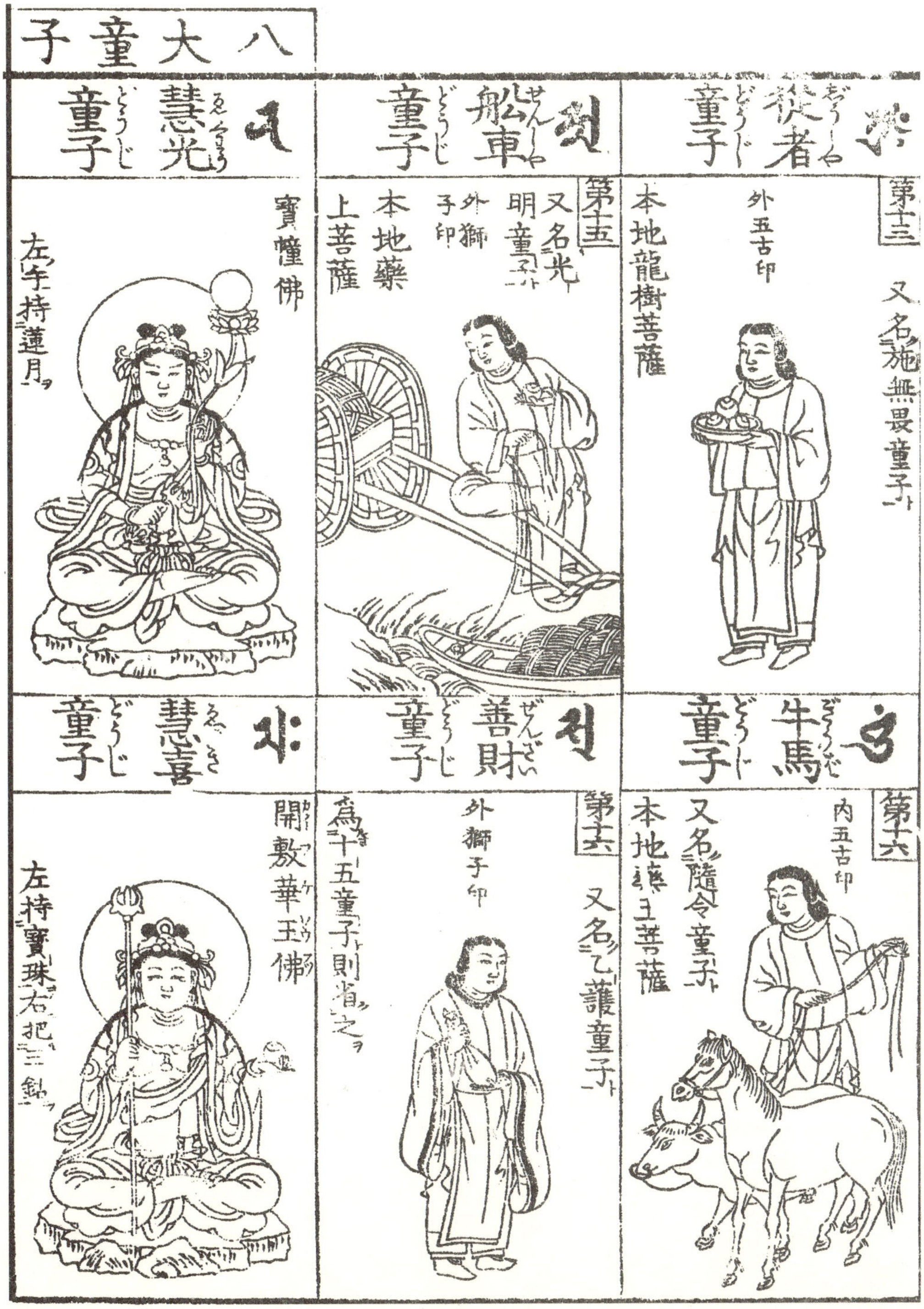

286. Eki Dōji
Kumāra of Bliss

284. Zenzai Dōji, 16th
Sudhana Śreṣṭhidāraka
(Avataṁsaka sūtra)

282. Gyūba Dōji, 14th
Ox-Horse Kumāra

291. Konkara Dōji
Kiṁkara Kumāra

289. Ukubaga Dōji
Ugra-bhaga Kumāra

287. Anokudatsu Dōji
Anavatapta Kumāra

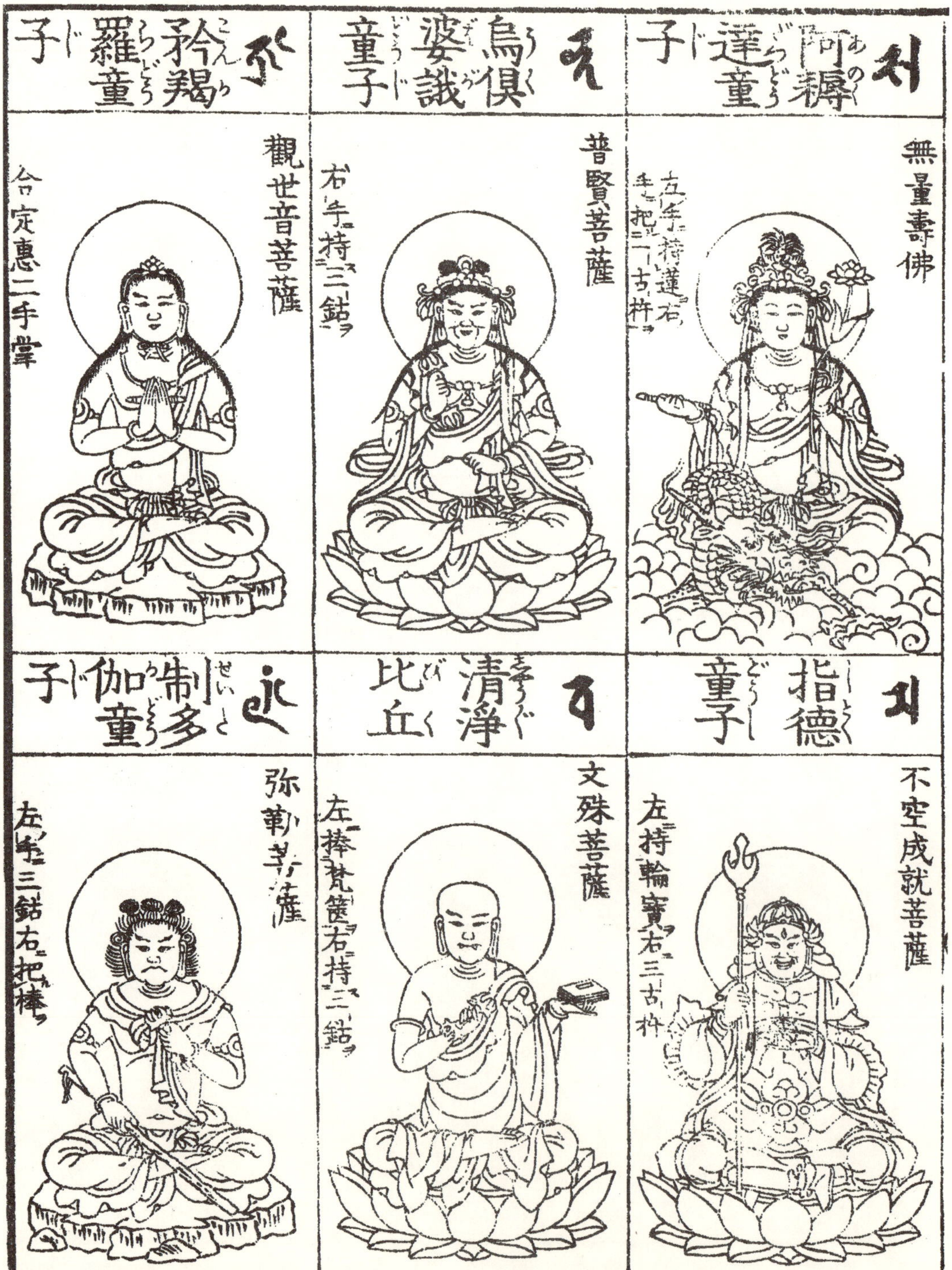

292. Seitaka Dōji
Ceṭaka Kumāra

290. Shōjō Bikku
Vimala Bhikṣu

288. Shitoku Dōji
Kumāra of Virtue

§ 22. Jū Rasetsn
The Ten Rākṣasīs & Parents (293-304)

297. Koku Shi, 3rd
Kūṭadantī

295. Ranba, Ist
Ramba

293. Godō Ten
Father of the retinue of the Ten Kings of Hades

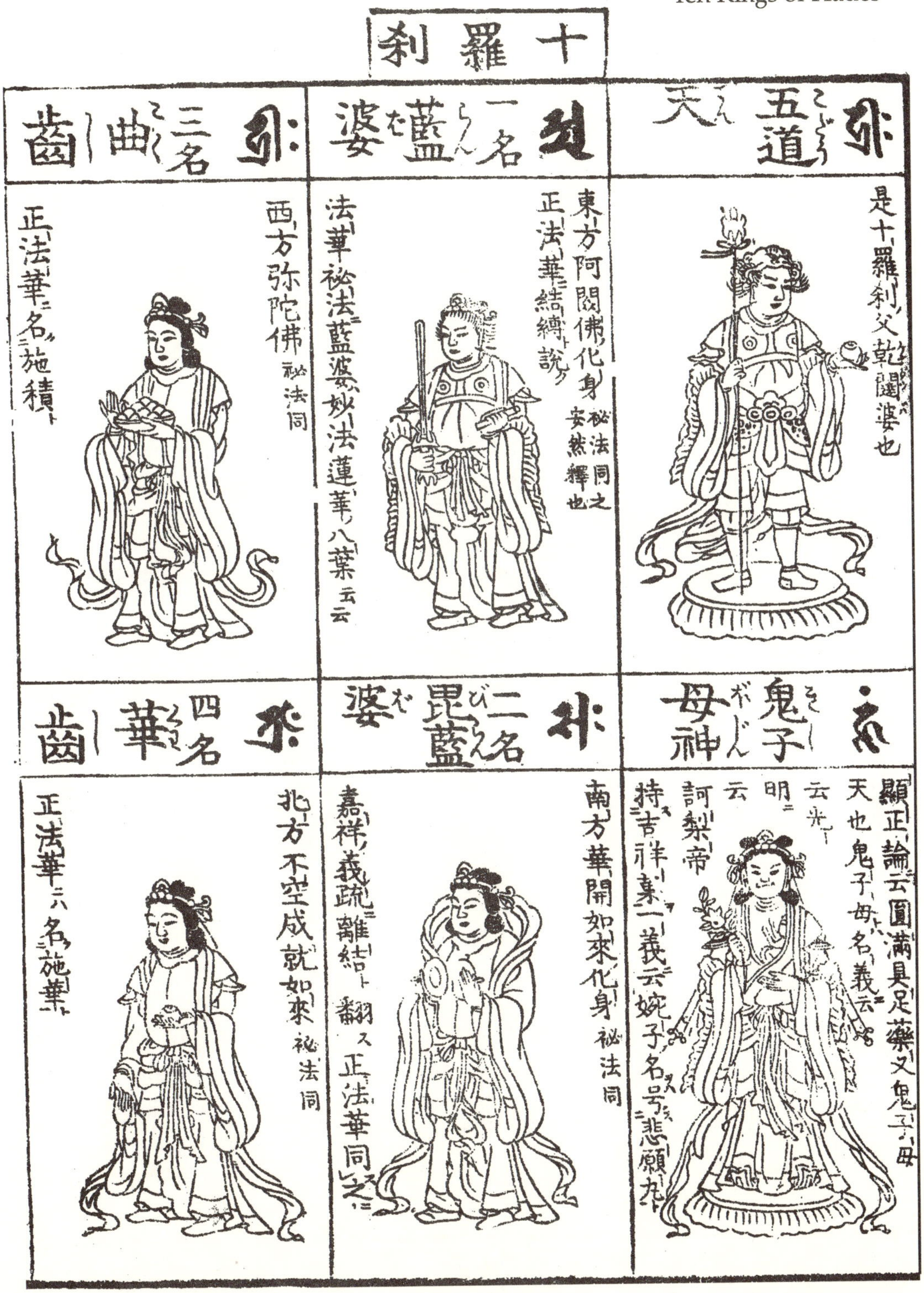

298. Kashi, 4th
Puṣpadantī

296. Biranba, 2nd
Vilambā

294. Kishibojin
Hārītī

303. Ko tei, 9th
Rākṣasī Kuntī

301. Muen soku, 7th
Insatiable Rākṣasī

299. Koku Shi, 5th
Maṭutacaṇḍī

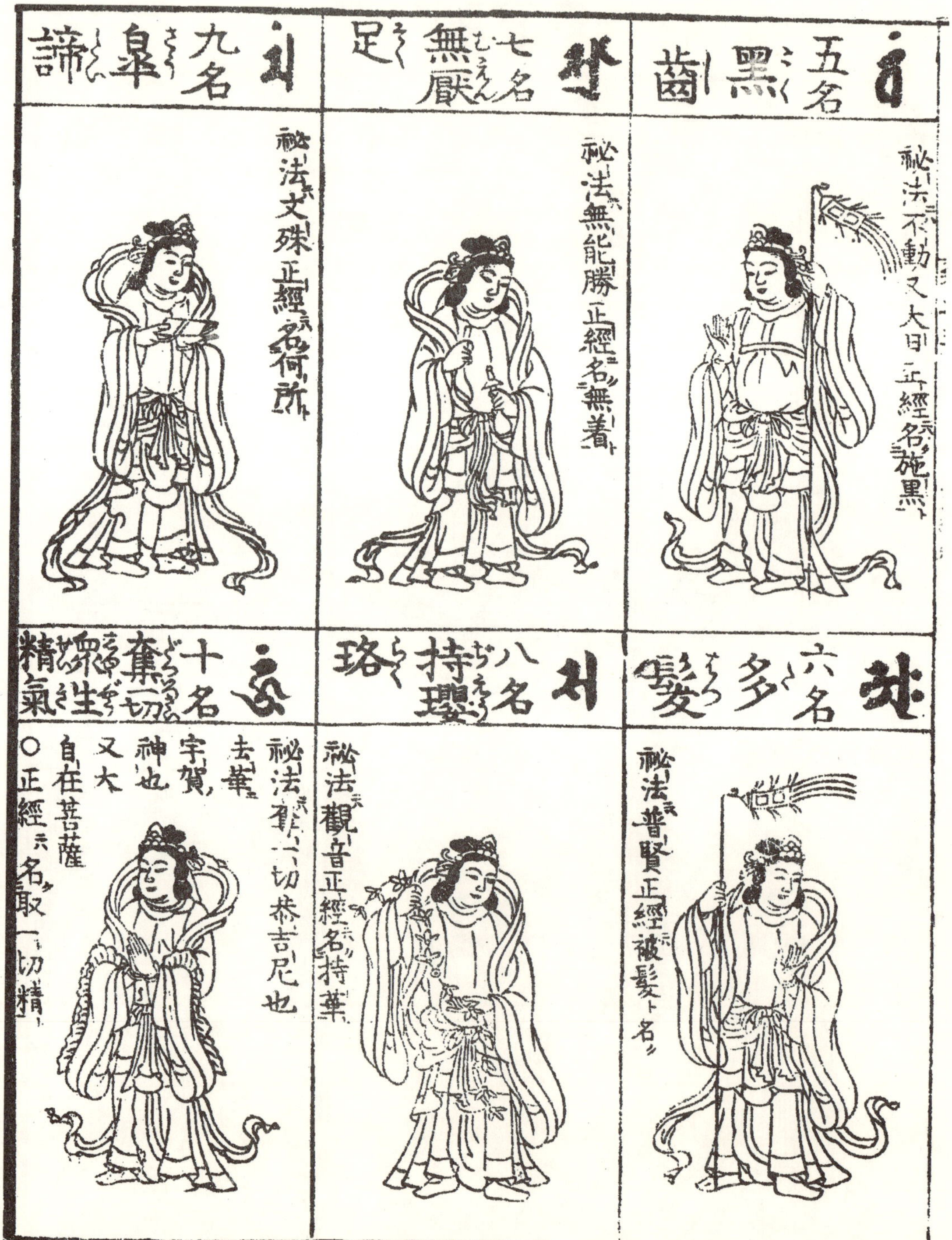

304. Datsuissai Shūjō Seiki, 10th
Rākṣasī that carries off
the vital breath of the dying

302. Jiyōraku, 8th
Mālādhāriṇī

300. Tahatsu, 6th
Keśinī

§ 23.Shoten
Various Devas (305-308)

§ 24. Nanayō Shō
Saptarṣi, Star of the Seven Days (309-315)

309. Tonro Shō, 1st
Wolf Star
Āditya Bodhisattva

307. Hokuto
Ursa Major
The Northern Bushel
with seven stars

305. Nichi Rin
Sun's Halo (Sphaṭika crystals)

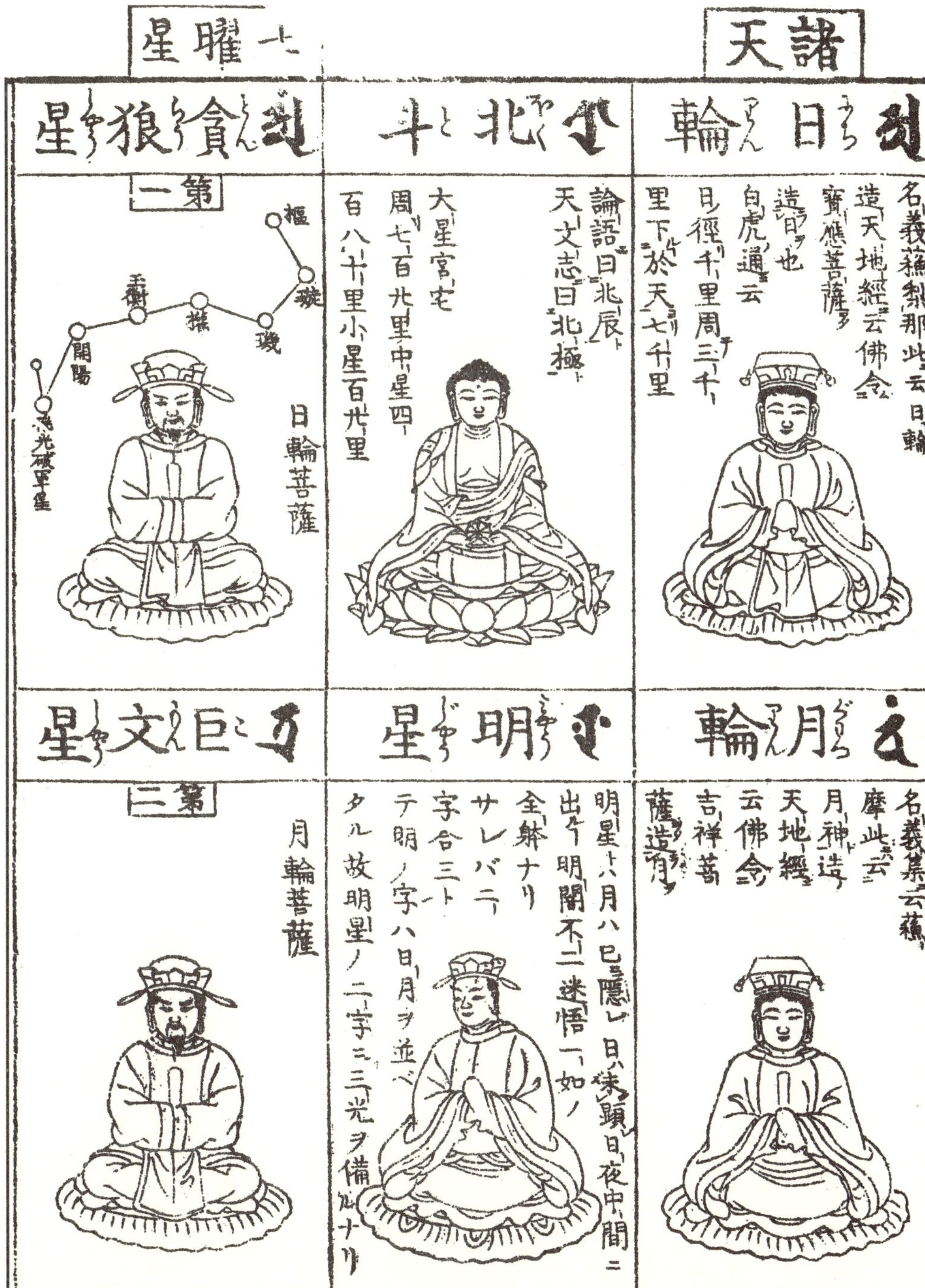

310. Kobun Sei, 2nd
Giant Star
Soma Bodhisattva

308. Myōjō
Aruṇa

306. Getsu Rin
Moon's Halo (Soma)

315. Hagun Shō, 7th
Bhrigu

313. Rentei Shō, 5th
Aṅgiras

311. Rokuzon Shō, 3rd
Pulastya

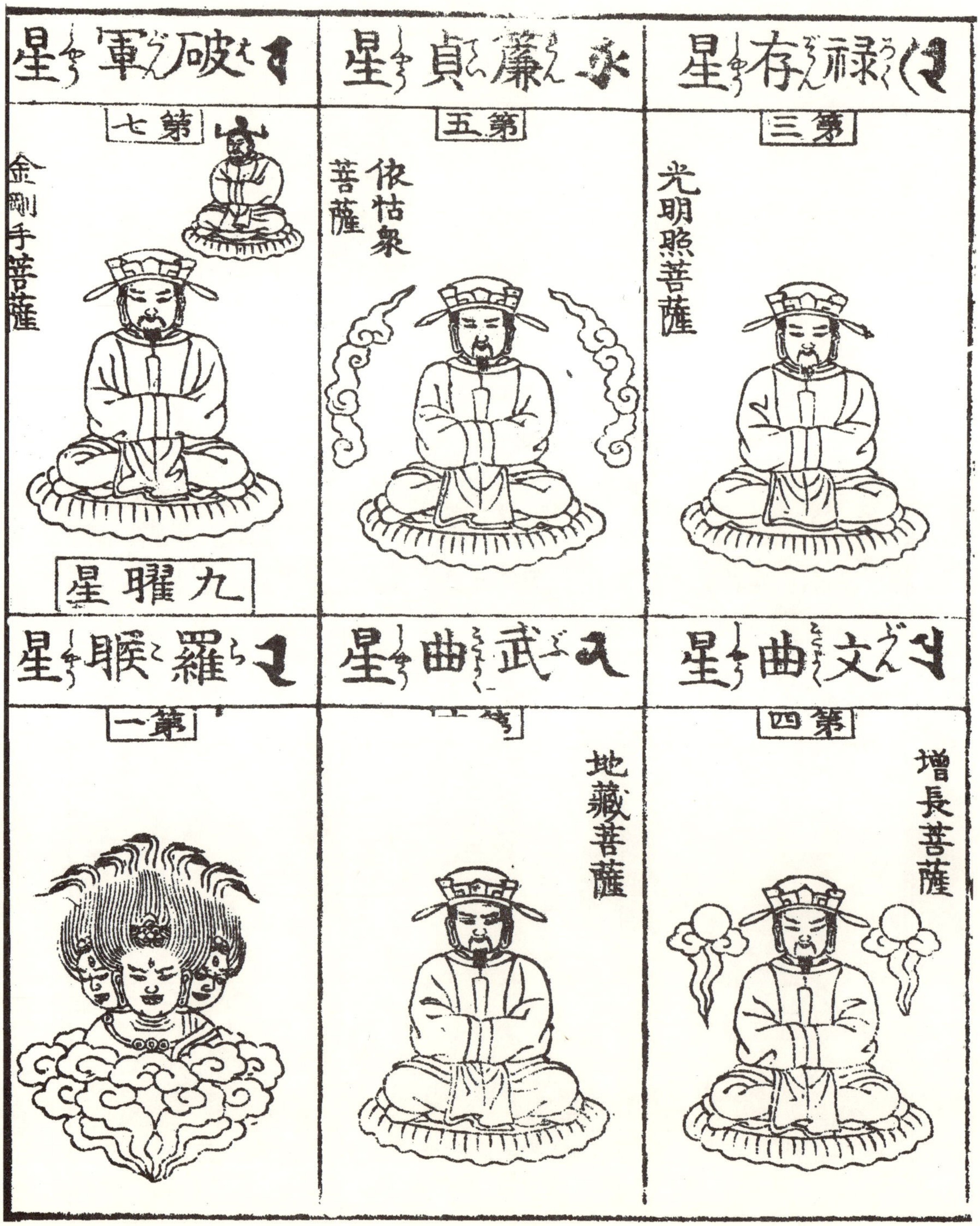

316. Rako Shō, 1st
Rāhu

314. Bukyoku Shō, 6th
Vasiṣṭha

312. Monkyoku Shō, 4th
Atri

§ 25. Kuyō Shō
The Nine Planets (Navagraha)(316-324)

321. Kayō Shō, 6th
Aṅgāraka graha, Yakushi Butsu,
Bhaiṣajayaguru Buddha

319. Konyō Shō, 4th
Śukra graha, Seshi Bosatsu,
Mahāsthāmaprāpta Bodhisattva

317. Doyō Shō, 2nd
Śanaiścara graha
Bishamon, Vaiśravaṇa

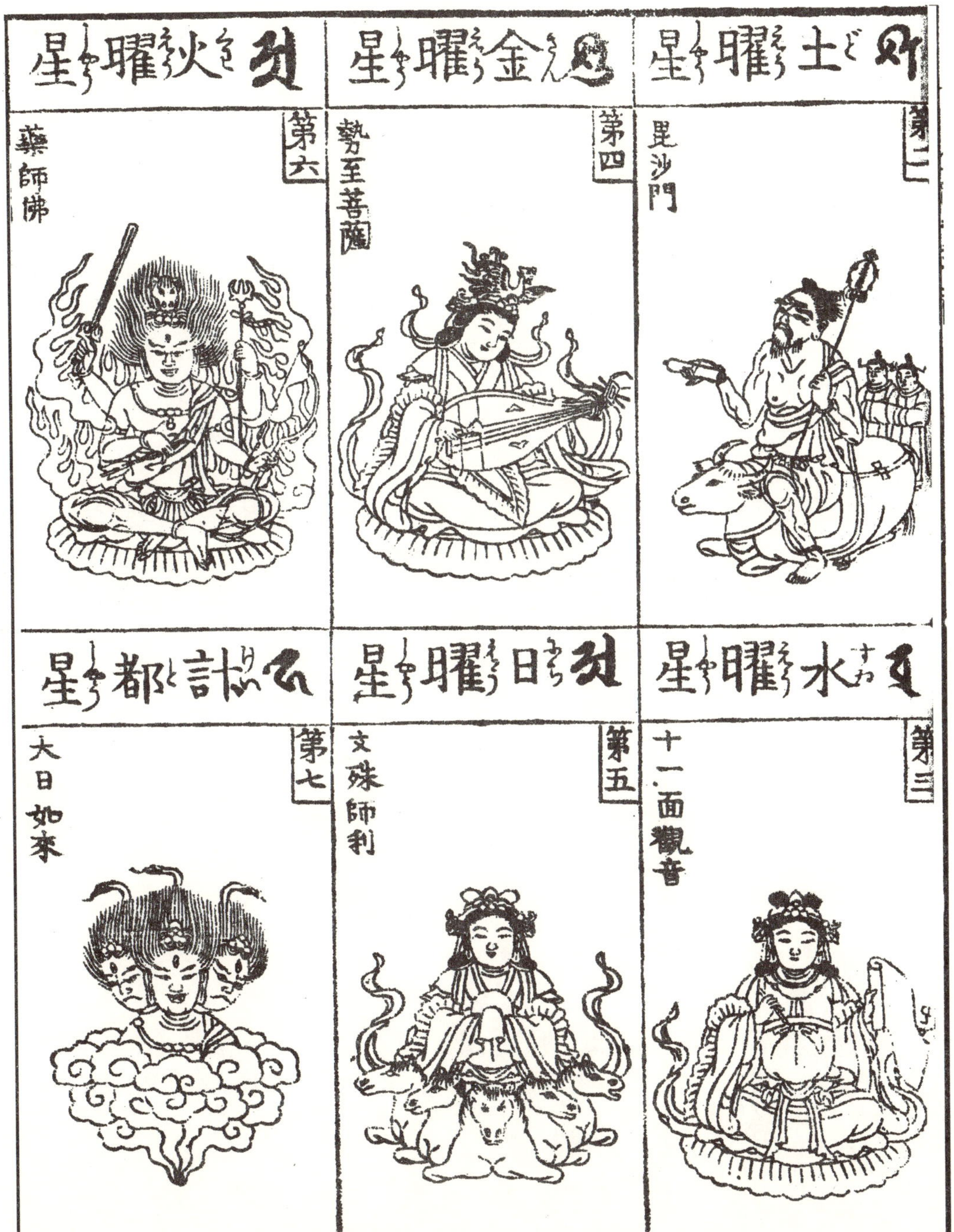

322. Keito Shō, 7th
Ketu graha, Dainichi Nyorai,
Vairocana Tathāgata

320. Nichiyō Shō, 5th
Āditya graha
Mañjuśrī

318. Suiyō Shō, 3rd
Budha graha, Jūichimen Kannon,
Ekādaśamukha Avalokiteśvara

§ 26. Nijūhatsu Shuku
The Twenty-eight Nakṣatras (325-352)

327. Tei-shuku, 3rd
Viśākhā Nakṣatra

325. Kaku-shuku, 1st
Citrā Nakṣatra

323. Getsuyō Shō
Soma graha,
Amida, Amitābha

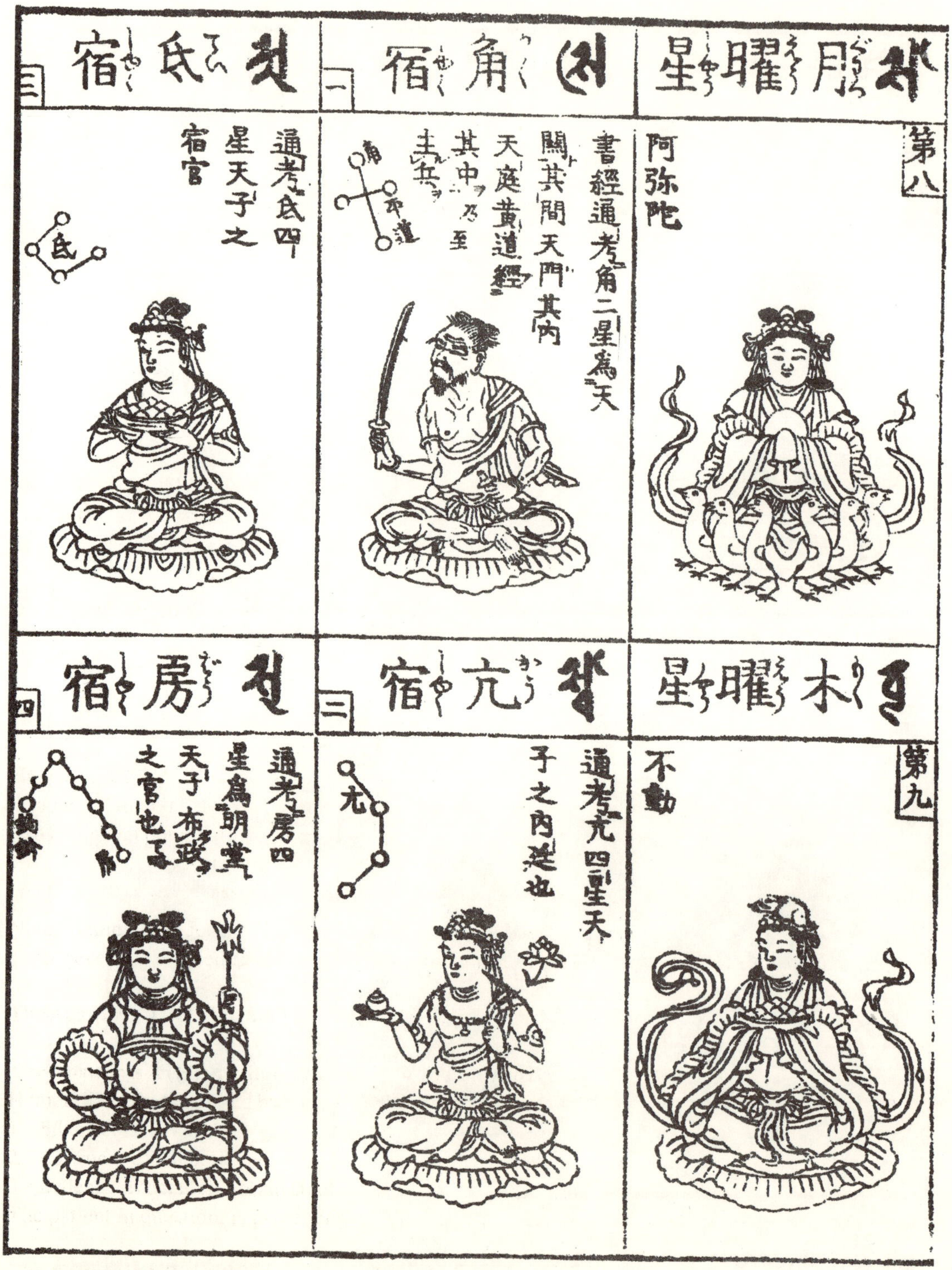

328. Bō-shuku, 4th
Anurādhā Nakṣatra

326. Kō-shuku, 2nd
Svāti Nakṣatra

324. Mokuyō Shō, 9th
Bṛhaspati graha, Fudō, Acala

333. Gyū-shuku, 9th
Abhijit Nakṣatra

331. Ki-shuku, 7th
Pūrva-Āṣāḍhā Nakṣatra

329. Shin-shuku, 5th
Jyeṣṭhā Nakṣatra

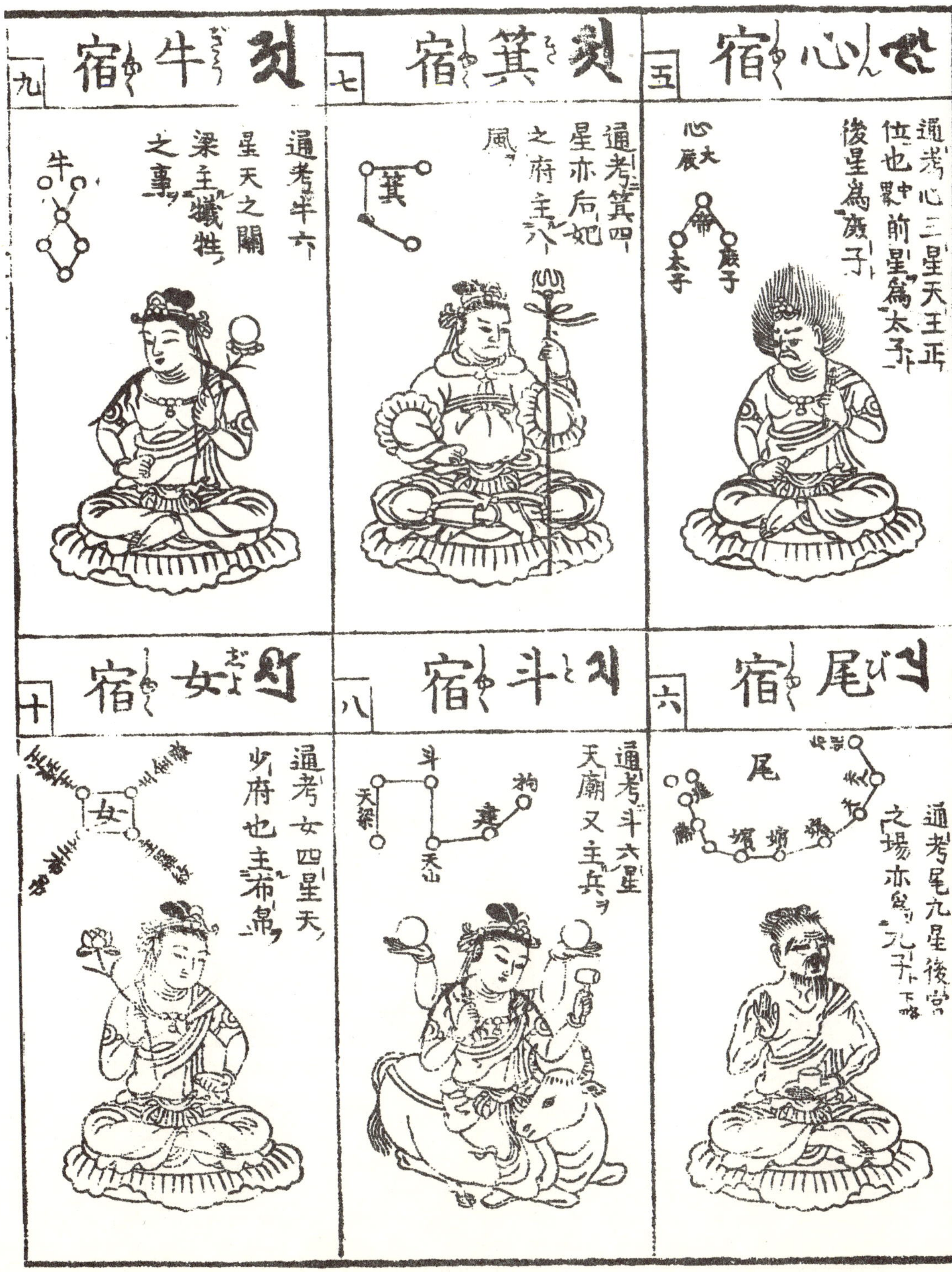

334. Jo-shuku
Śravaṇā Nakṣatra

332.To-shuku
Uttra-Āṣāḍhā Nakṣatra

330. Bi-shuku
Mūla Nakṣatra

339. Kei Shuku, 15th
Revatī Nakṣatra

337. Shitsu Shuku, 13th
Pūrvap-proṣṭhapadā

335. Gyo Shuku, 11th
Śraviṣṭhā Nakṣatra

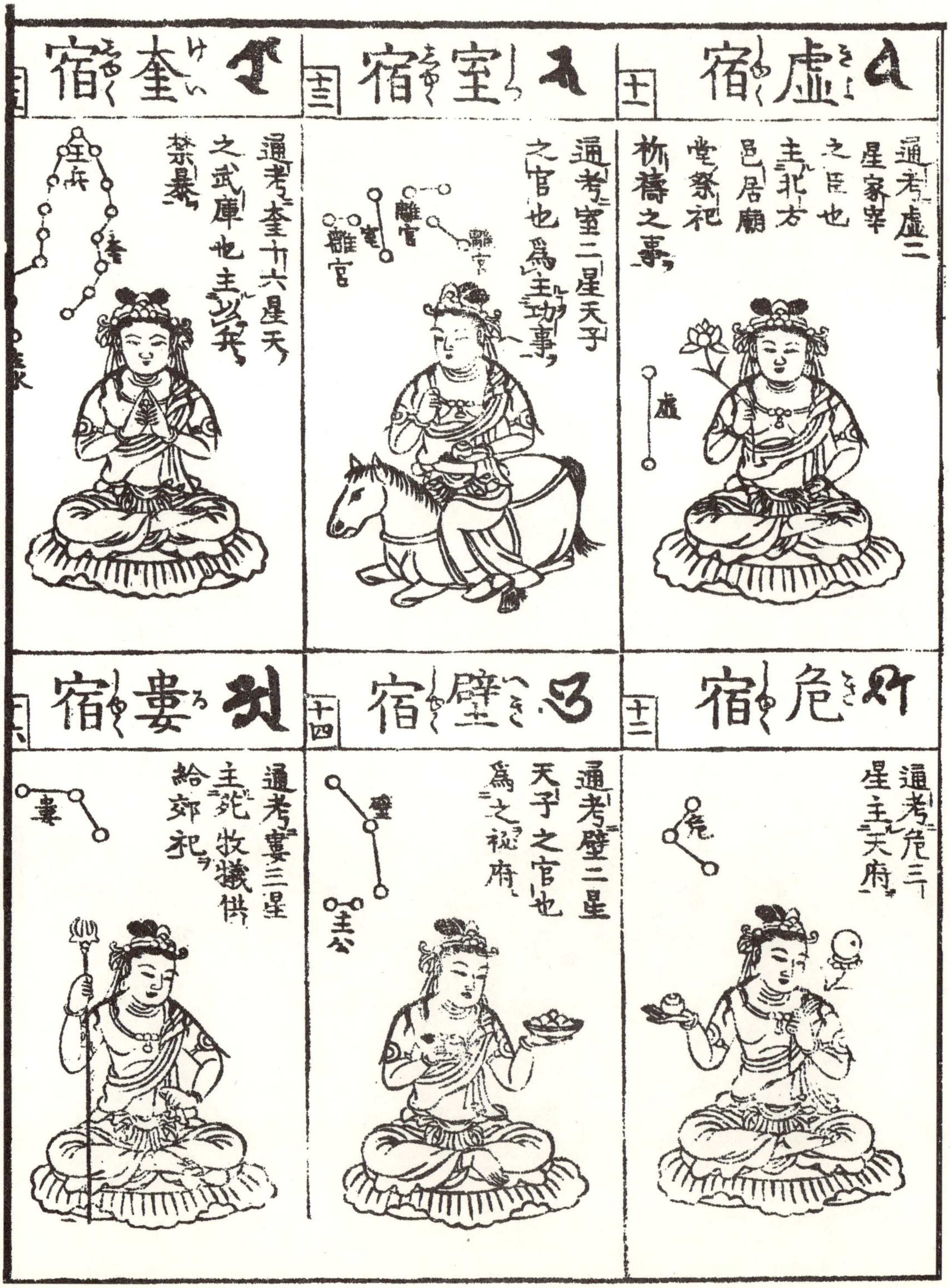

340. Rō Shuku, 16th
Aśvayuj Nakṣatra

338. Heki Shuku, 14th
Uttaraproṣṭhapadā

336. Ki Shuku, 12th
Śatabhiṣā

345. Shin Shuku, 21st
Bāhu Nakṣatra

343. Hitsu Shuku, 19th
Rohiṇī Nakṣatra

341. Ishuku, 17th
Bharaṇī Nakṣatra

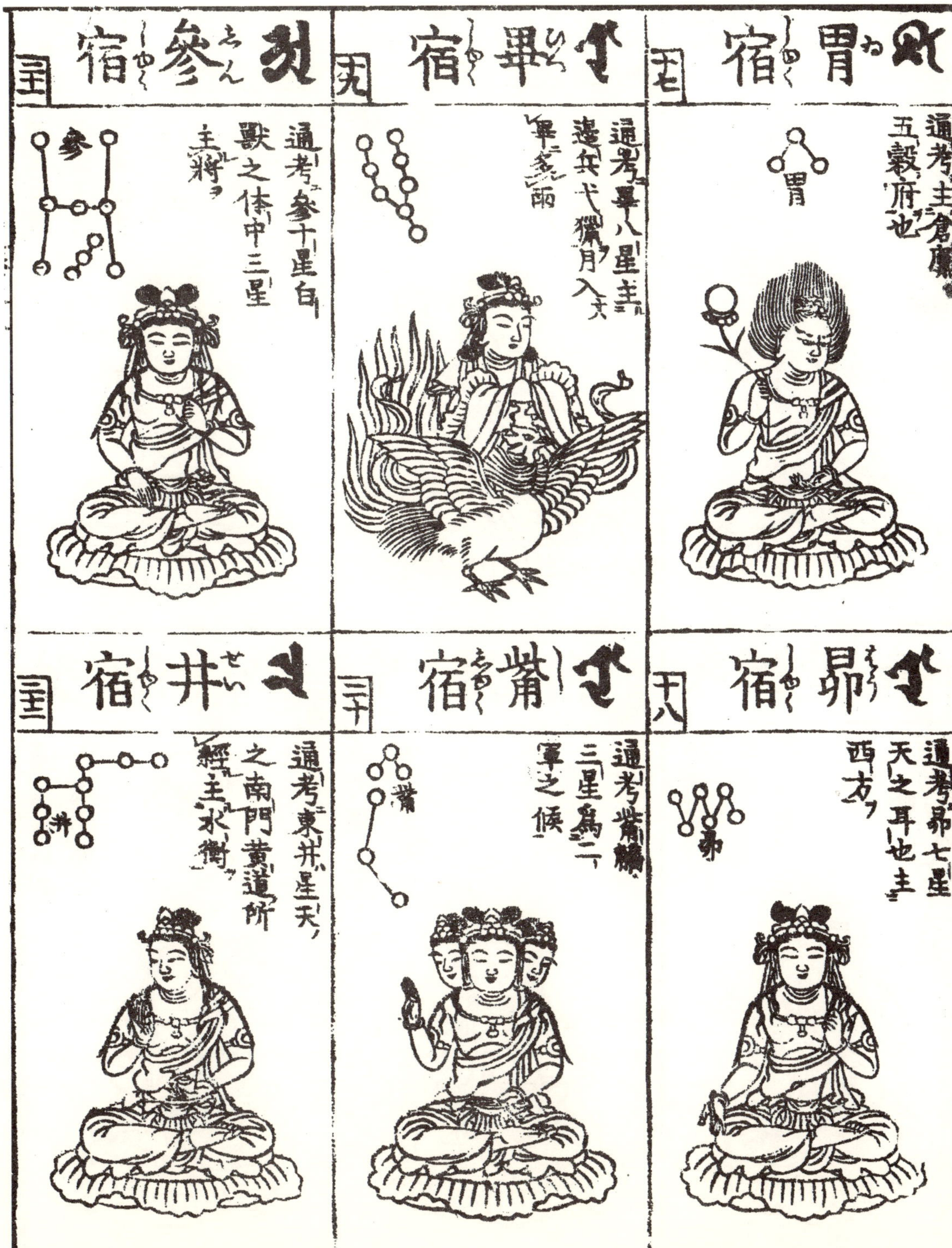

346. Sei Shuku, 22nd
Punarvasu Nakṣatra

344. Shi Shuku, 20th
Invakā Nakṣatra

342. Kō Shuku, 18th
Kṛttikā Nakṣatra

351. Yoku Shuku, 27th
Uttra-Phālgunī Nakṣatra

349. Sei Shuku, 25th
Maghā Nakṣatra

347. Ki Shuku, 23rd
Tiṣya Nakṣatra

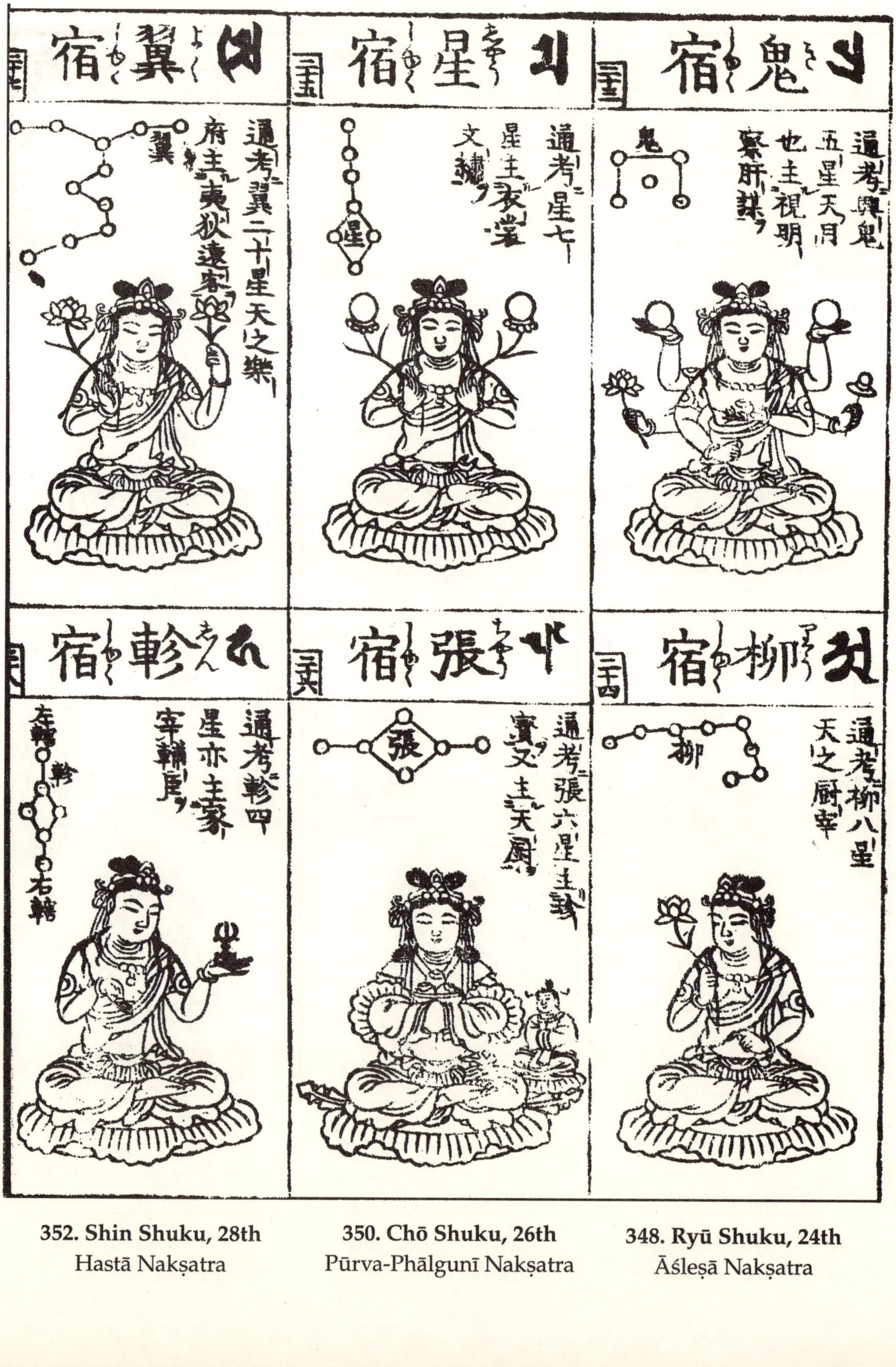

352. Shin Shuku, 28th
Hastā Nakṣatra

350. Chō Shuku, 26th
Pūrva-Phālgunī Nakṣatra

348. Ryū Shuku, 24th
Āśleṣā Nakṣatra

§ 27. Jūni Kyū
The Twelve Zodiacal Mansions (353-364)

357. Gomitsu-kyū
Taurus (Vṛṣa)

355. Kumogani-kyū
North: Cancer (Karka)

353. Sōnyo-kyū
Kanyā (Virgo)

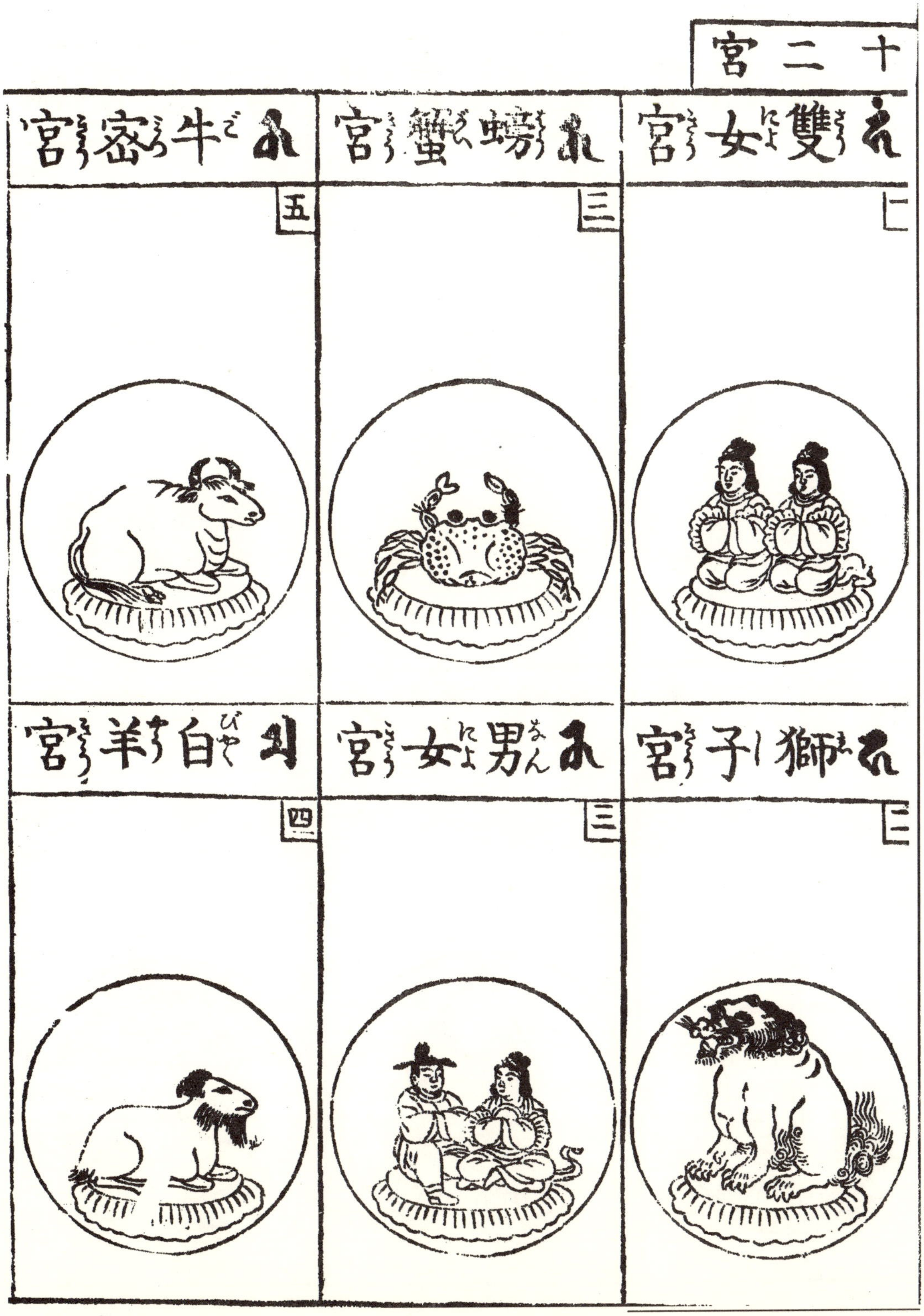

358. Byakuyō-kyū
Aries (Meṣa)

356. Nannyo-kyū
East: Gemini (Mithuna)

354. Shishi-kyū
Leo (Siṁha)

363. Ḳatsu-chu-kyū
Scorpio (Vr̥ścika)

361. Hohei-kyū
South: Aquarius (Kumbha)

359. Sōgyo-kyū
Twin:Pisces (Mīna)

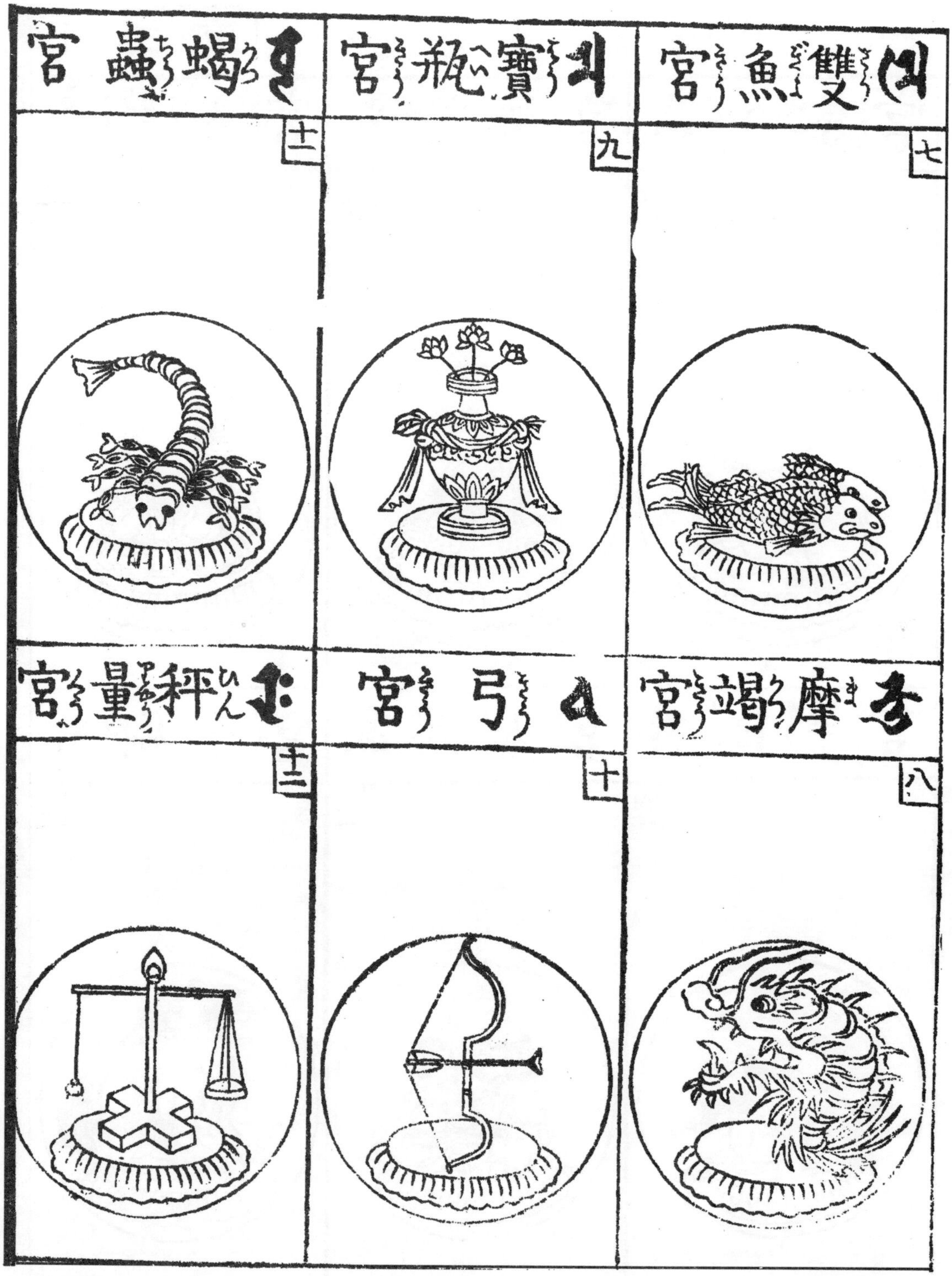

364. Hinryō-kyū
West: Libra (Tulā)

362. Kyū-kyū
Sagittarius (Dhanuṣa)

360. Makatsu-kyū
Capricorn (Makara)

§ 28. Sanjūroku Kinkeizō
The Thirty-six Animal Figures (366-401)

369. Kani
Crab (4th, North)

366. Nezumi
Rat (1st, North)

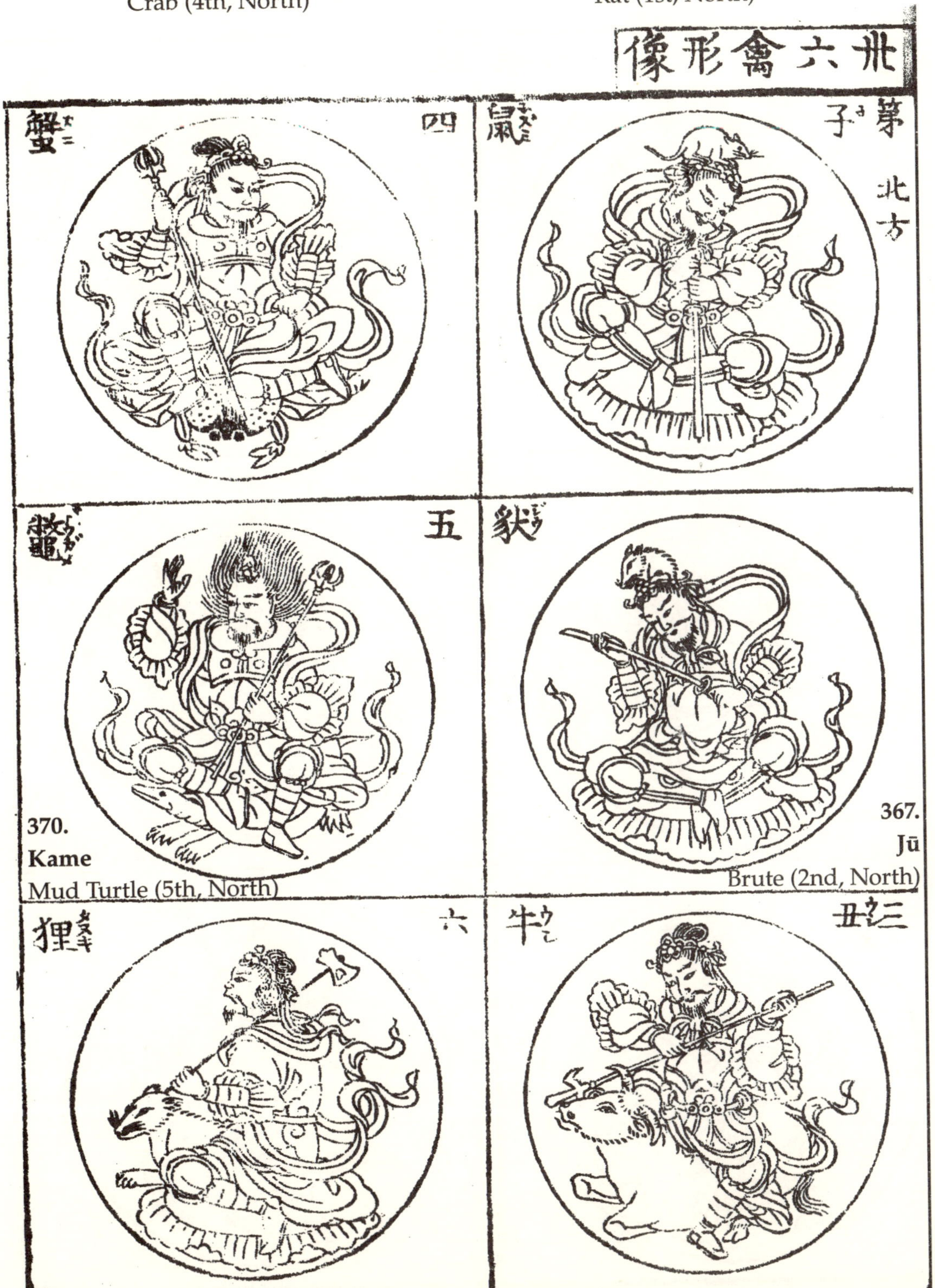

370. Kame
Mud Turtle (5th, North)

367. Jū
Brute (2nd, North)

371. Tanuki
Badger (6th, North)

368. Ushi
Cow (3rd, North)

375. Usagi
Rabbit (10th, East)

372. Hyō
Leopard (7th, North)

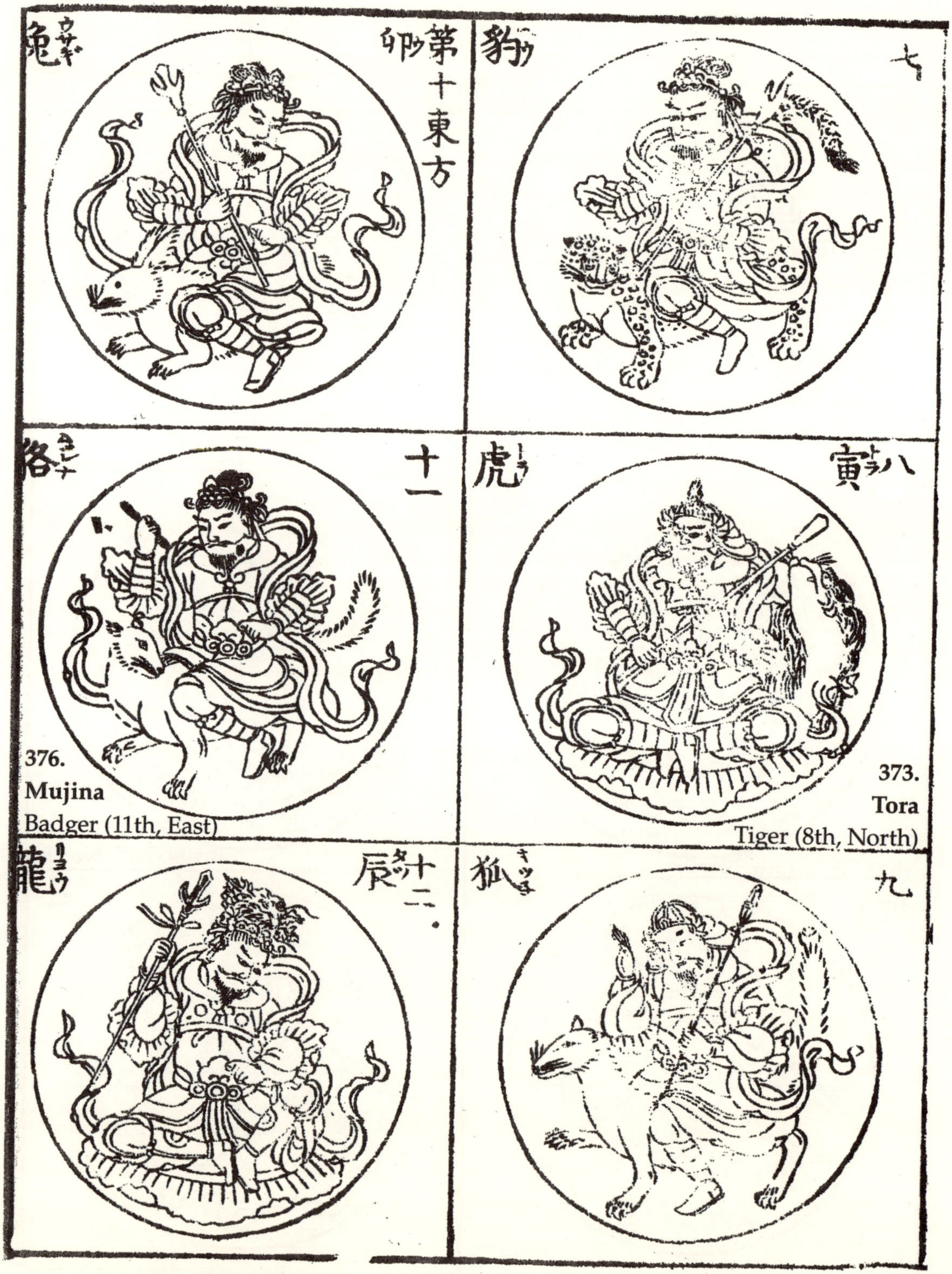

376. Mujina
Badger (11th, East)

373. Tora
Tiger (8th, North)

377. Ryū/Tatsū
Dragon (12th, East)

374. Kitsune
Fox (9th, North)

381. Mukade
Centipede (16th, East)

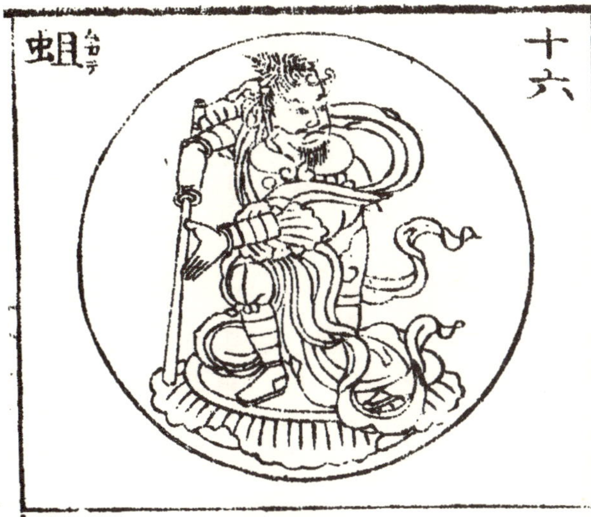

378. Same
Shark (13th, East)

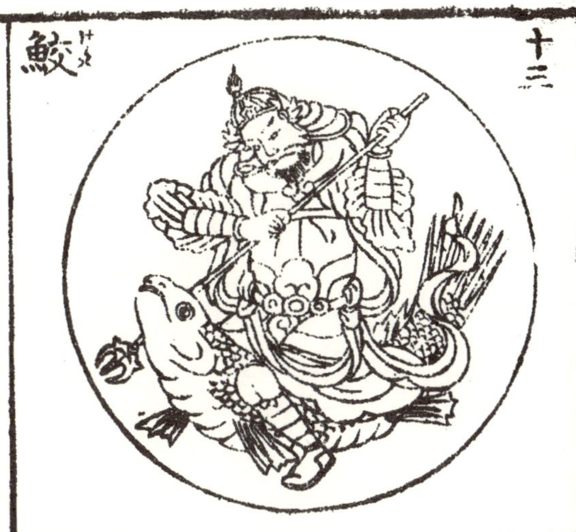

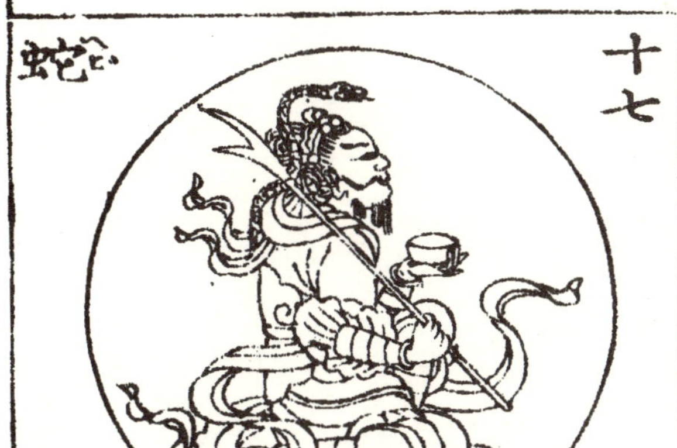

382. Hebi
Snake (17th, East)

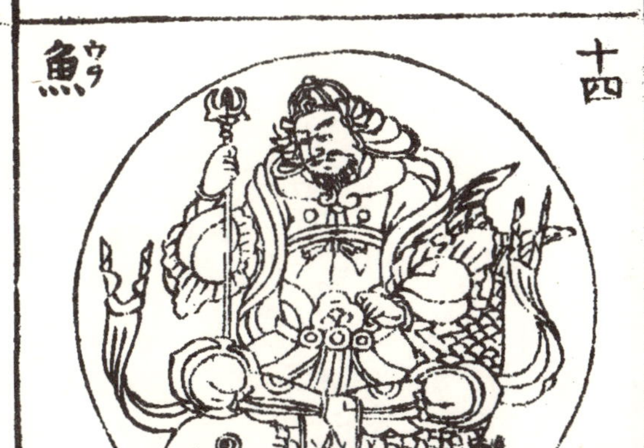

379. Uo
Fish (14th, East)

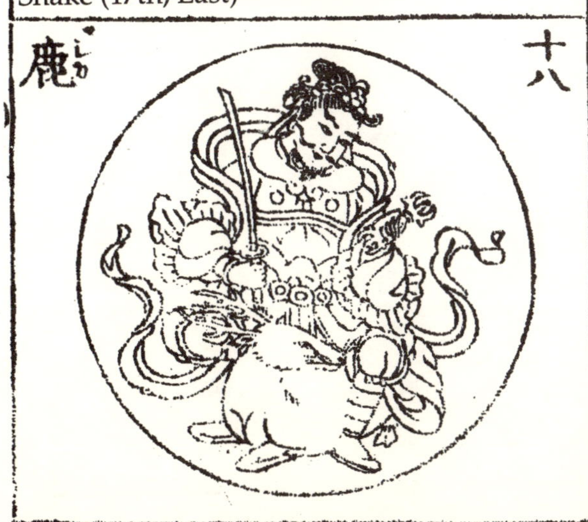

383.Shika
Deer (18th, East)

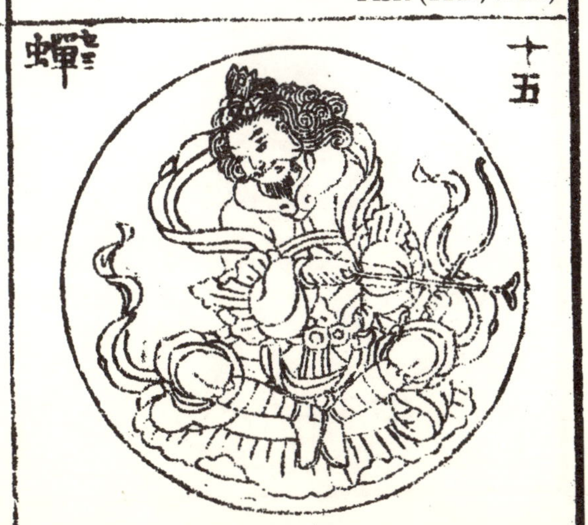

380. Semi
Cicada (15th, East)

387. Gan
Goose (22nd, South)

384. Uma
Horse (19th, Frontal-South)

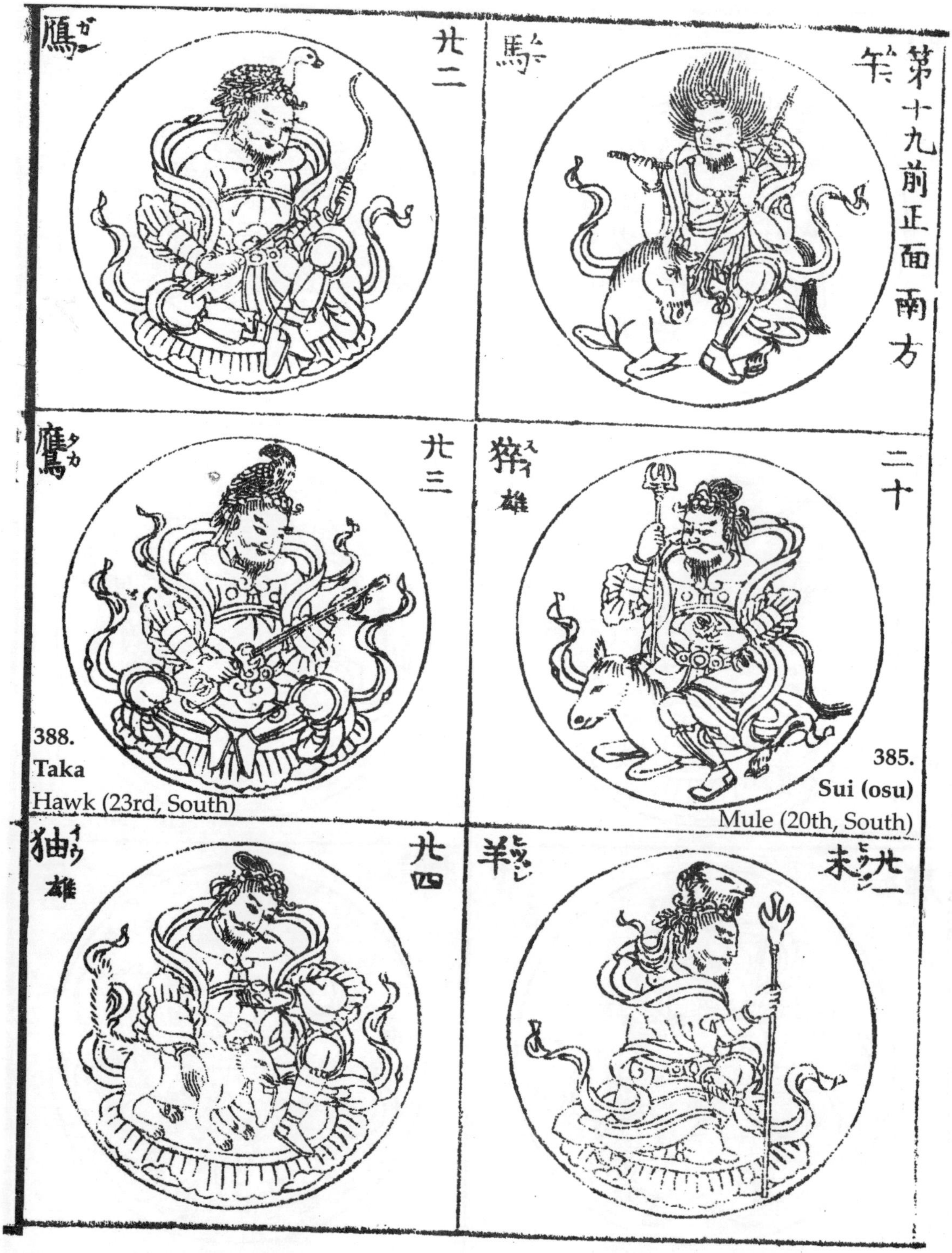

388. Taka
Hawk (23rd, South)

385. Sui (osu)
Mule (20th, South)

389. Iu (Mesu)
Cat male, (24th, South)

386. Hitsuji
Sheep (21st, South)

393. Niwatori (Tori)
Cock (28th, West)

390. Saru
Monkey (25th, South)

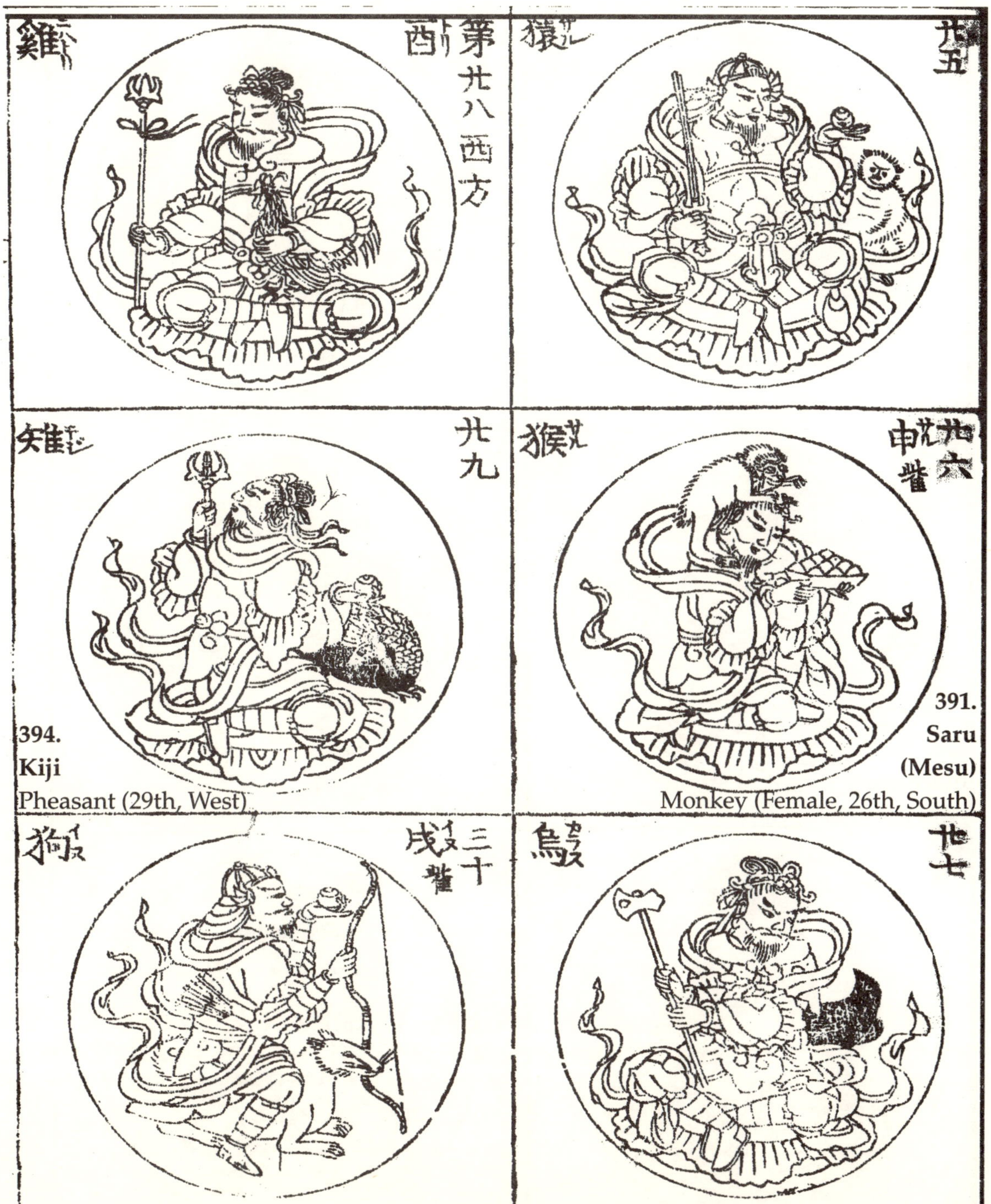

394. Kiji
Pheasant (29th, West)

391. Saru (Mesu)
Monkey (Female, 26th, South)

395. Inu (Mesu)
Bitch (30th, West)

392. Karasu
Crow (27th, South)

399. Iyu
A mythical beast

396. Ōkami (Osu)
Wolf (Male 31st, West)

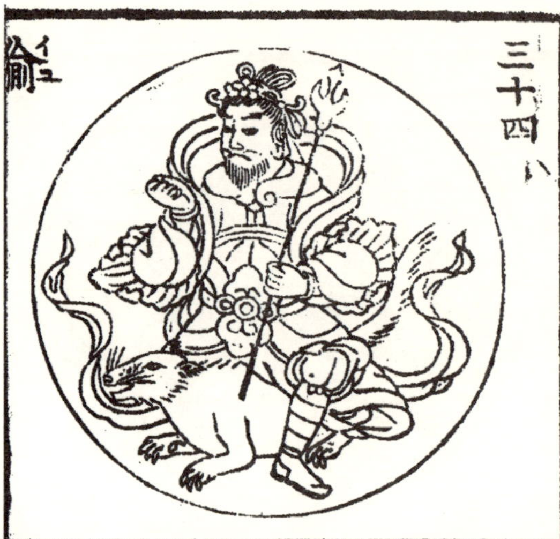

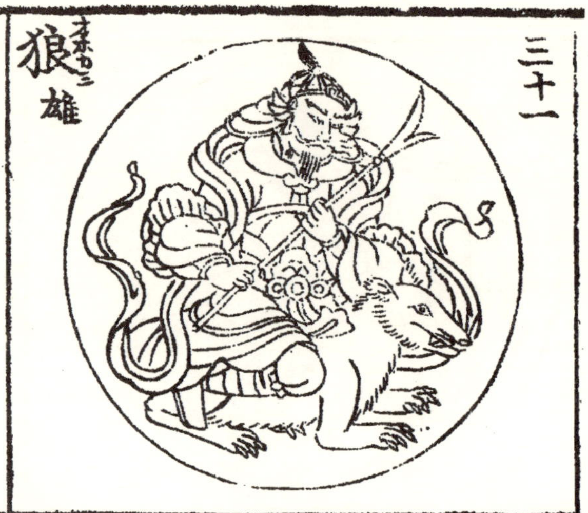

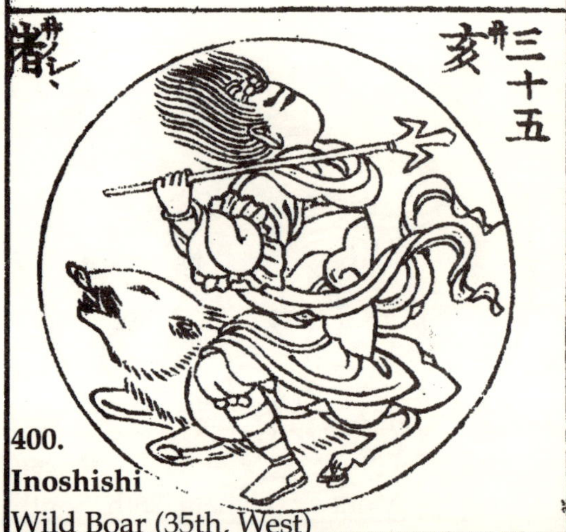

400. Inoshishi
Wild Boar (35th, West)

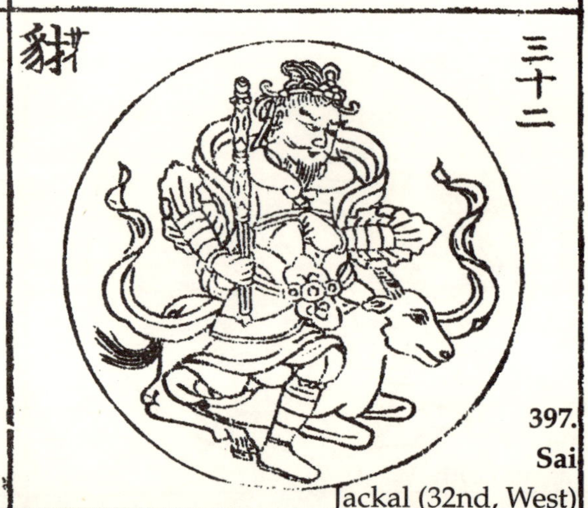

397. Sai
Jackal (32nd, West)

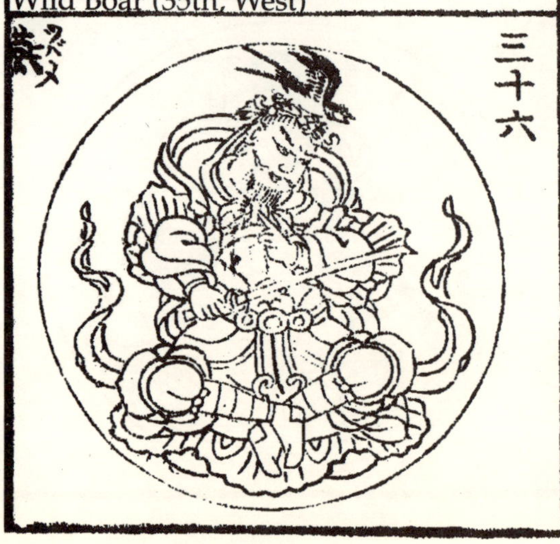

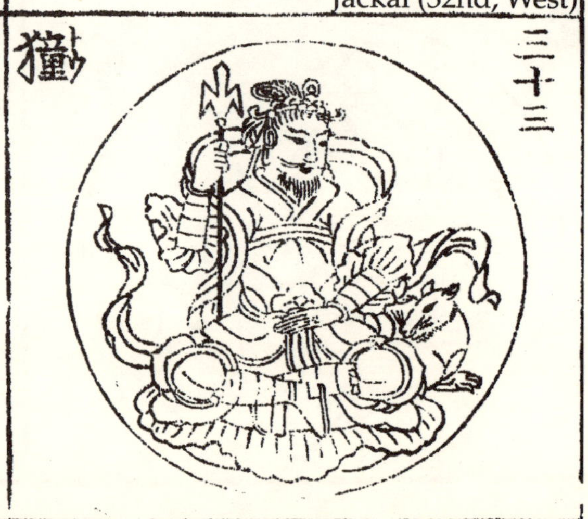

401. Tsubame,
Swallow (36th, West)

398. Tō
Dog (33rd, West)

§ 29. Jūni Ten
The Twelve Devas (402-413)

406. Suiten
Varuṇa

404. Bishamonten
Vaiśravaṇa

402. Chiten
Pṛthivī

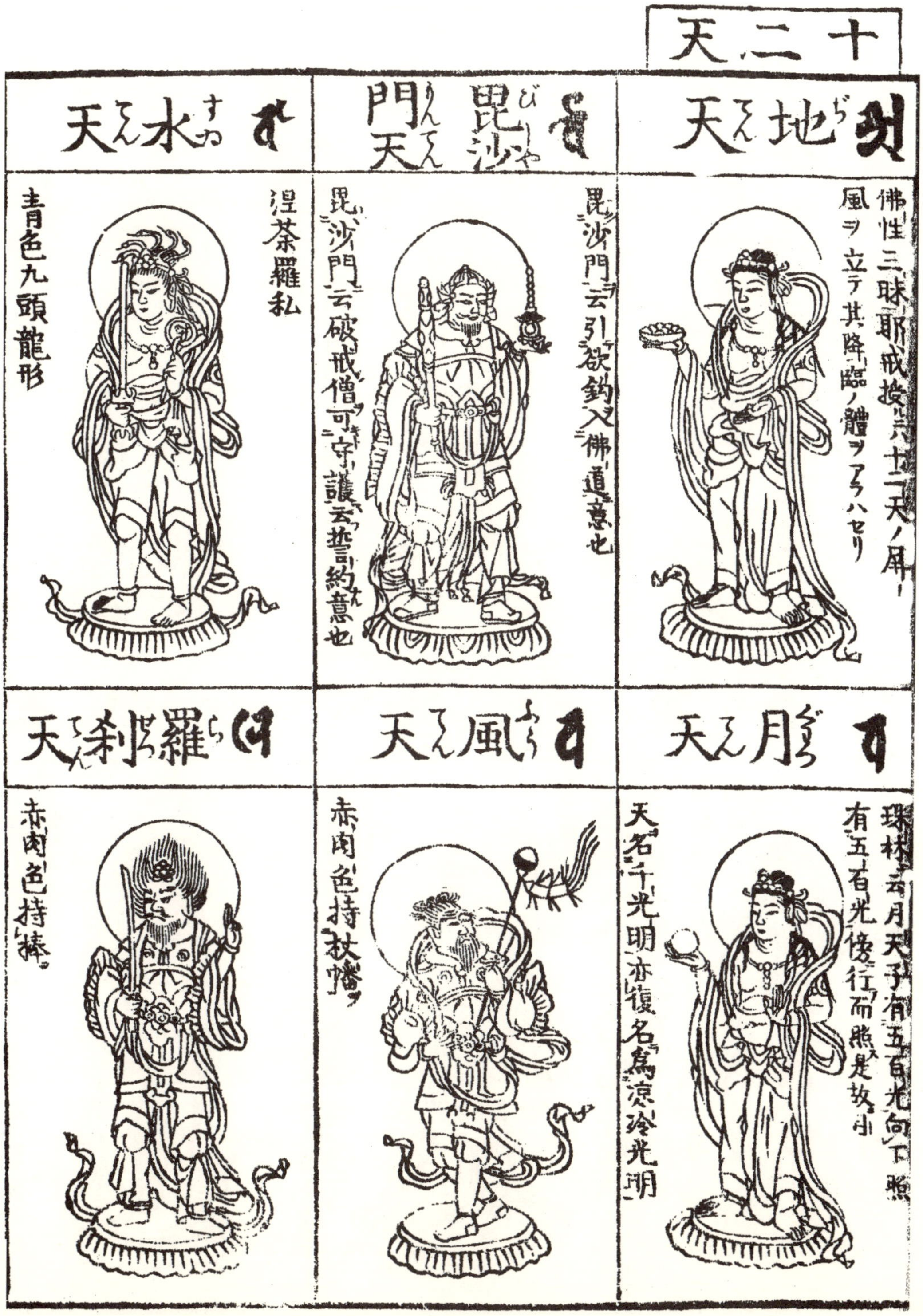

407. Rasetsuten
Nairṛtirāj Rākṣasa

405. Fūten
Vāyu

403. Gatten
Candra

412. Katen
Agni

410. Ishanaten
Īśāṇa

408. Bonten-ō
Brahmā

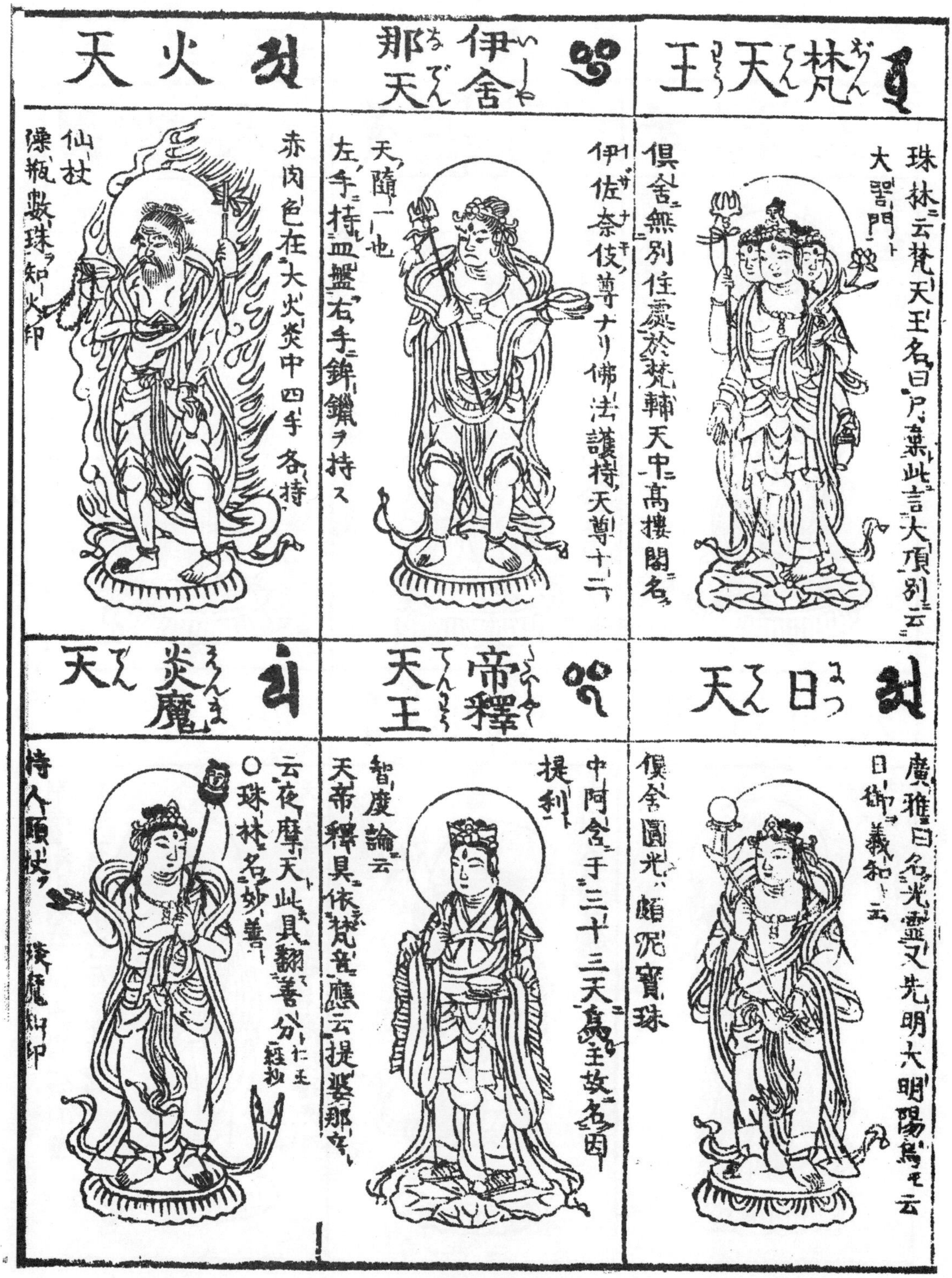

413. Enmaten
Yama

411. Taishakutenō
Indra Devarāja

409. Nitten
Āditya

§ 30. Shoten Bu
Various Guardians (414-437)

418. Marishi-ten	416. Kōmoku Tennō	414. Tamon Taro
Mārīcī goddess	Virūpākṣa Devarāja	Vaiśravaṇa Devarāja

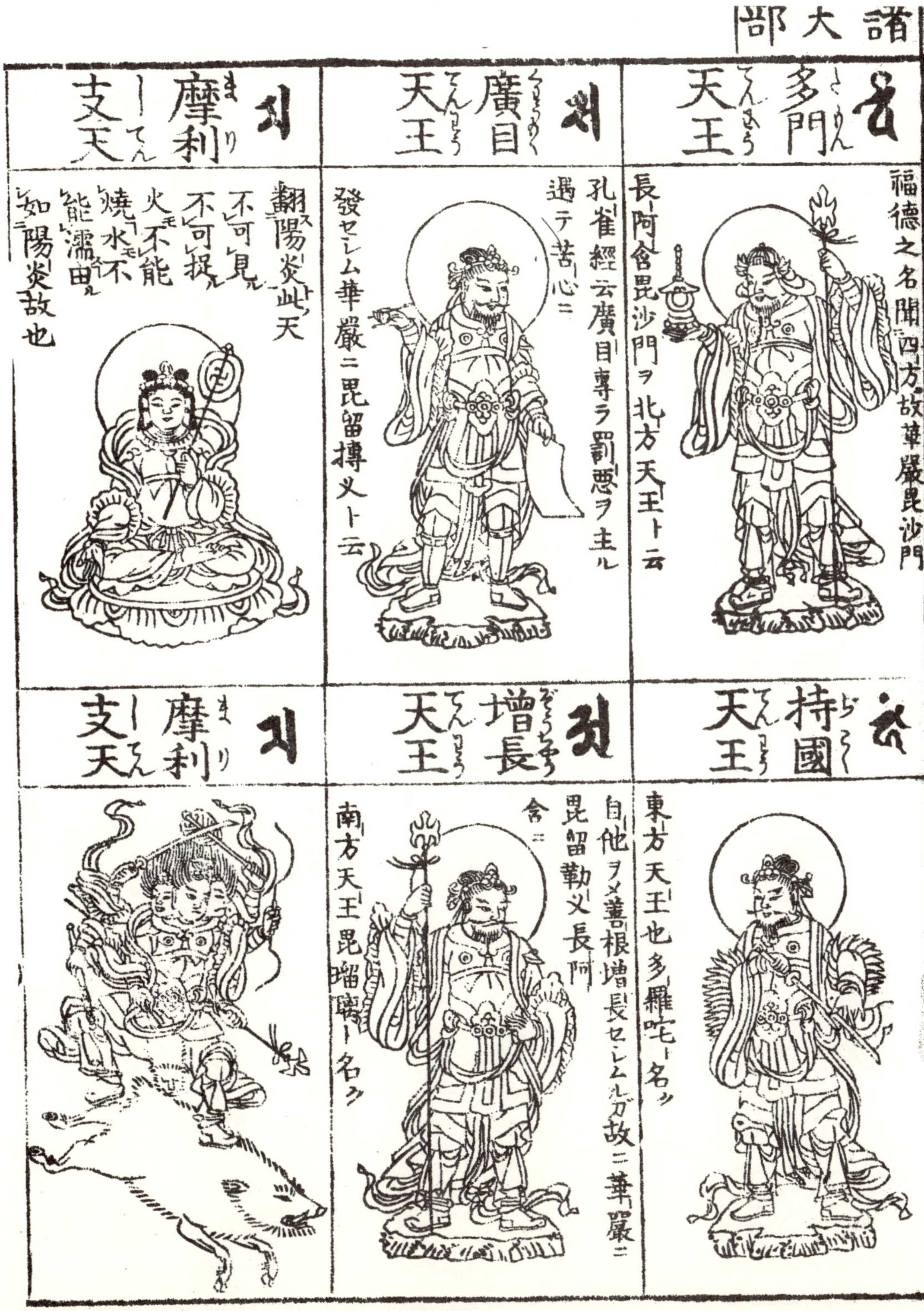

419. Marishi-ten	417. Zōchō Tennō	415. Jikoku Tennō
Mārīcī Prajāpati	Virūḍhaka Devarāja	Dhṛtarāṣṭra Devarāja

424. Kenrōjishin
Dhāranī dhāra

422. TakeJizaiten
Paranirmita-vaśavartin

420. Daishō Kangi-ten
Nandikeśvara (Gaṇeśa)

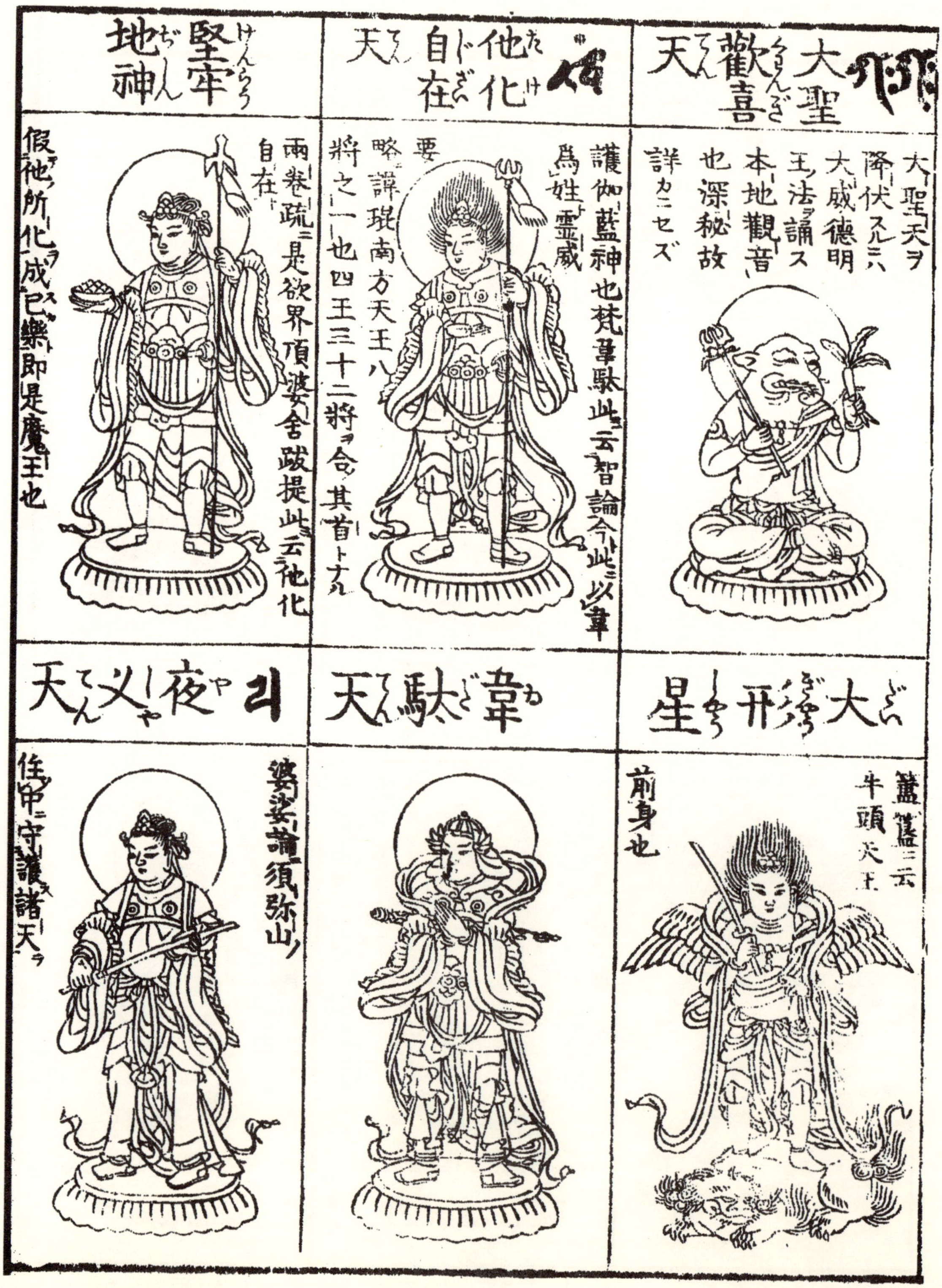

425. Yashaten
Yakṣa Deva

423. Idaten
Skanda Deva

421. Daigyō Shō
Giant Star

430. Bodaijū Shinten
Deva of Bodhi-vṛkṣa

428. Nyorai Kōjin
Tathāgata Kōjin

426. Sambō Kōjin
Deity of fireplace or kitchen

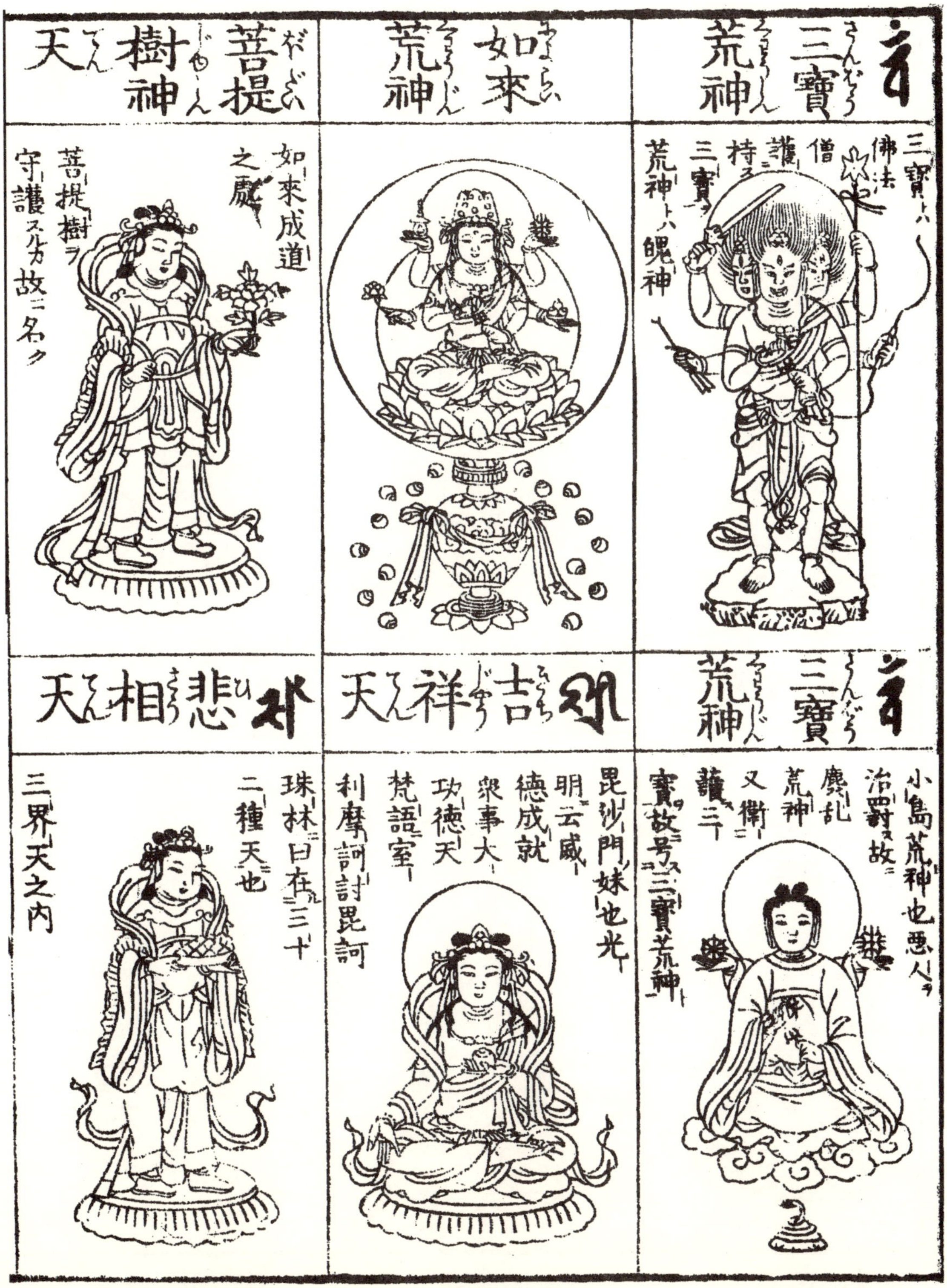

431. Hisō Ten
Deva of Arūpadhātu

429. Kichijōten
Śrī Mahādevī

427. Sambō Kōjin
Kitchen deity of Kojima

436. Konkōmyō Benten
Suvarṇaprabhāsa Sarasvatī

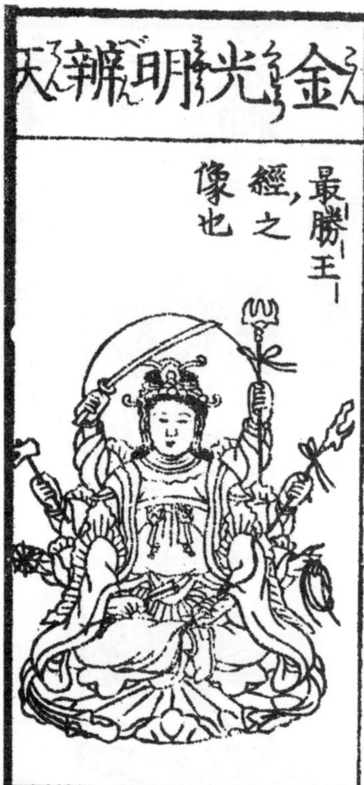

434. Happi Benzaiten
Eight-armed Sarasvatī

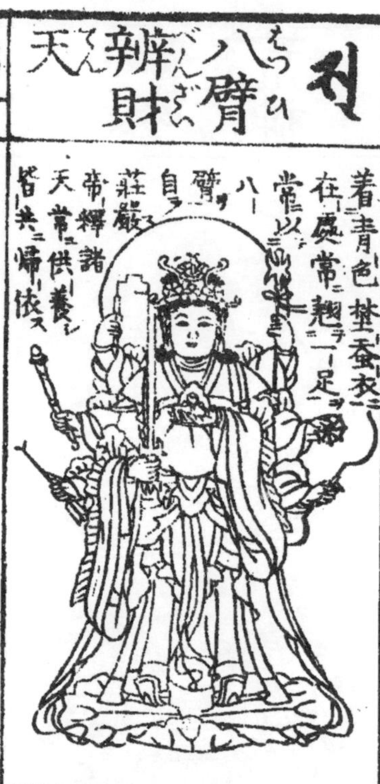

432. Tohatsu Bishamon
Vaiśravaṇa with eight swords

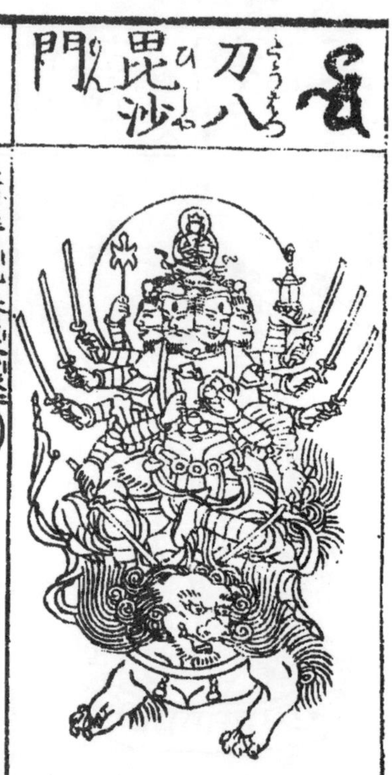

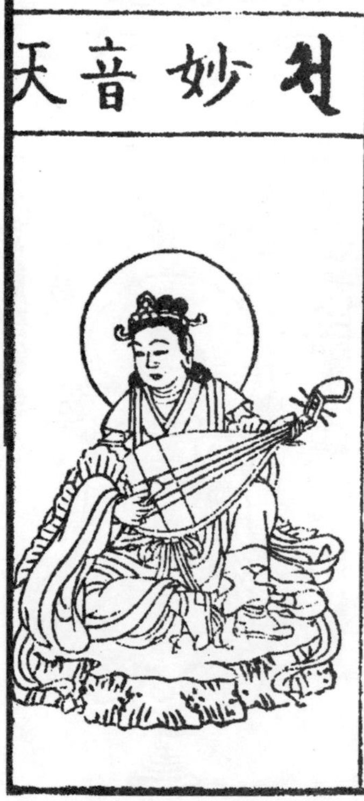

437. Myōonten
Divyabhāṣiṇī (Sarasvatī)

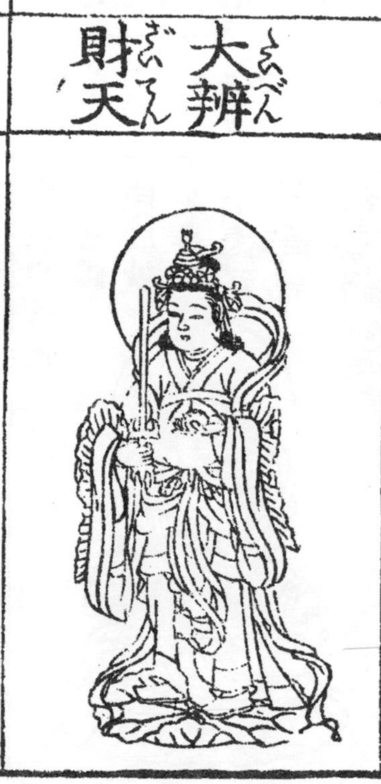

435. Daibenzaiten
Sarasvatī

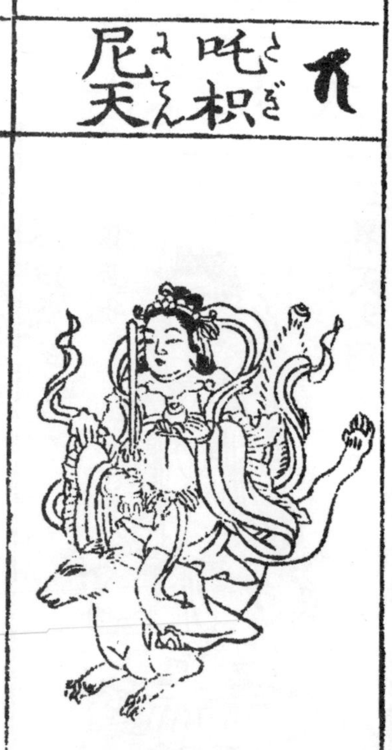

433. Dakinī Ten
Ḍākinī Devī
(Shinto goddess of Inari)

§ 31. Roku Daikoku
The Six forms of Mahākāla (438-443) and Others (444-451)

442. Yasha Daikoku
Yakṣa Mahākāla

440. Ōjikara Daikoku
Mahākāla as Prince

438. Bikku Daikoku
Bhikṣu Mahākāla, guardian of the refectory.

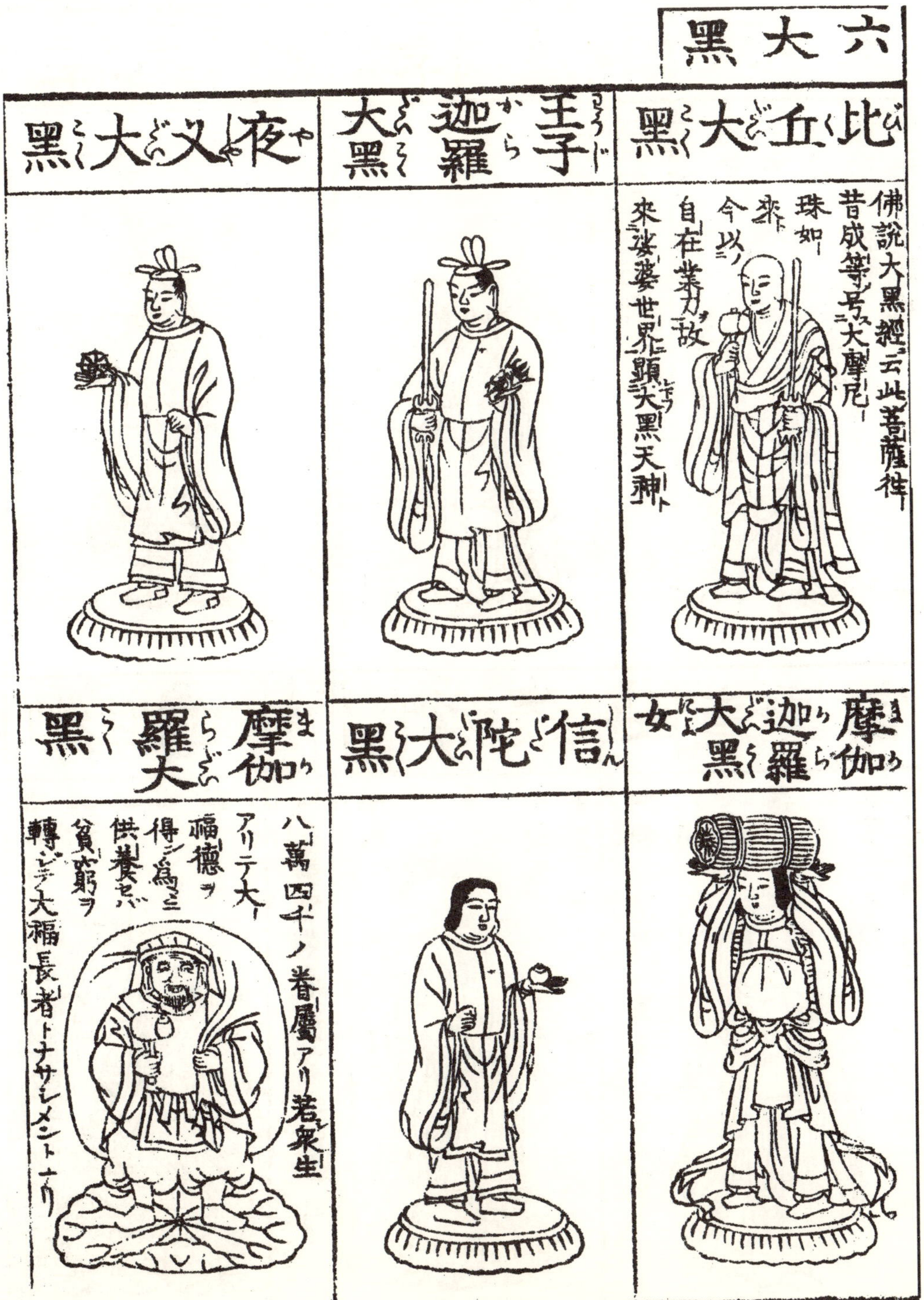

443. Makara Daikoku
Mahākāla, with a bag on back and a hammer in right hand

441. Shinda Daikoku
Mahākāla as boy with cintāmaṇi

439. Makakara Daikokunyo
Mahākāla as a lady with bale of rice

448. Uten Ō
Udayana, the King of Kauśāmbī

446. Hōzō Tennyō
Ratnāvalī Devī

444. Sanmen Daikoku-ten
Three-faced Mahākāla

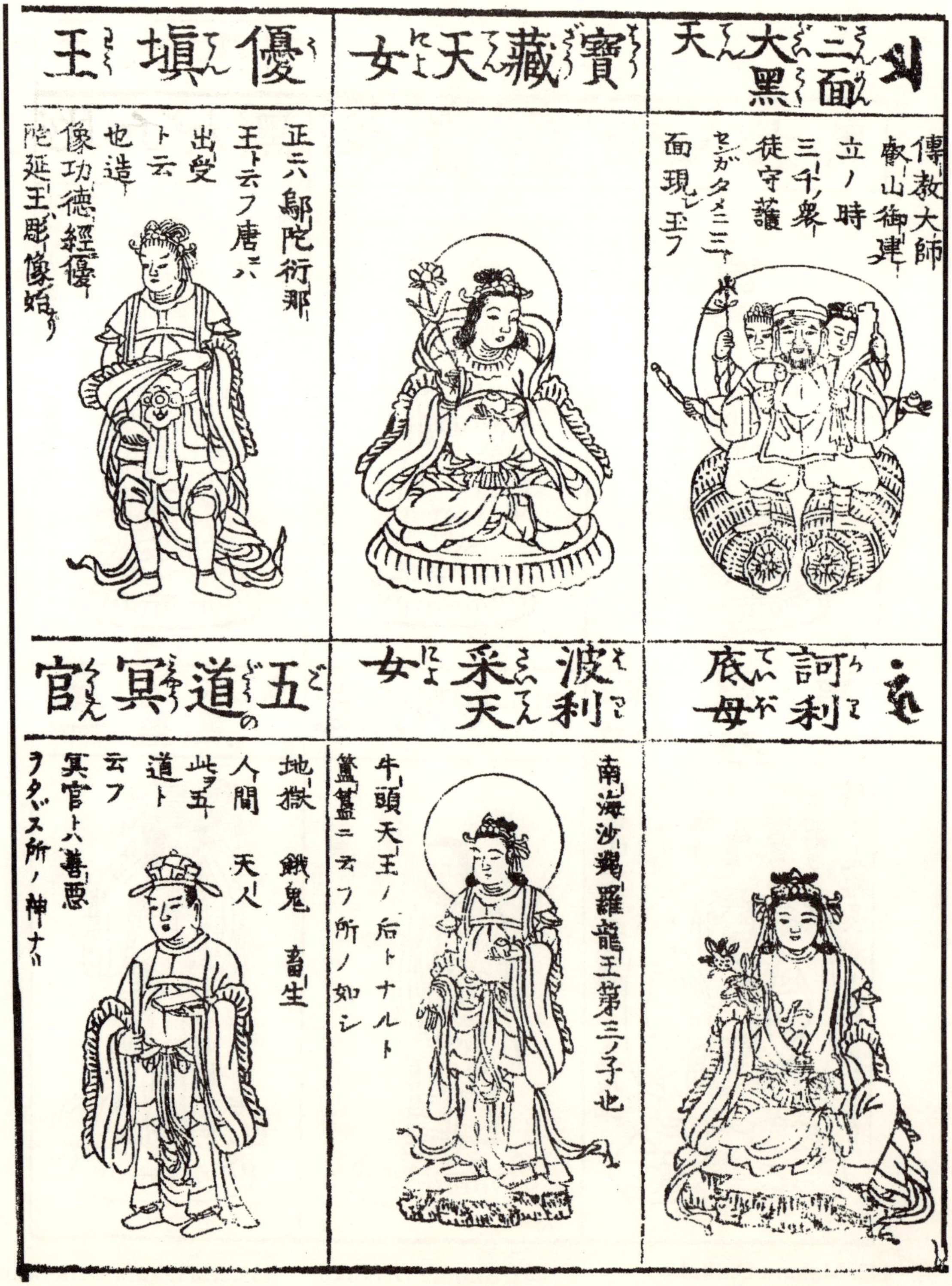

449. Godō Myokan
Dharmarāja of Pañcagati Hell

447. Harisai Tennyō
Pṛthvī Devī

445. Kariteimo
Hārīti, the consort of Pañcika

§ 32. Jū ō
The Ten Kings of Hell (452-461)

454. Sōtei-ō (21st Day)
Emanation of Mañjuśrī

452. Shinkō-ō (7th Day of Funeral)
Emanation of Acala

450. Kushō Jin
Ālayavijñānarāja the spirit that records the deeds of men and reports to Yama

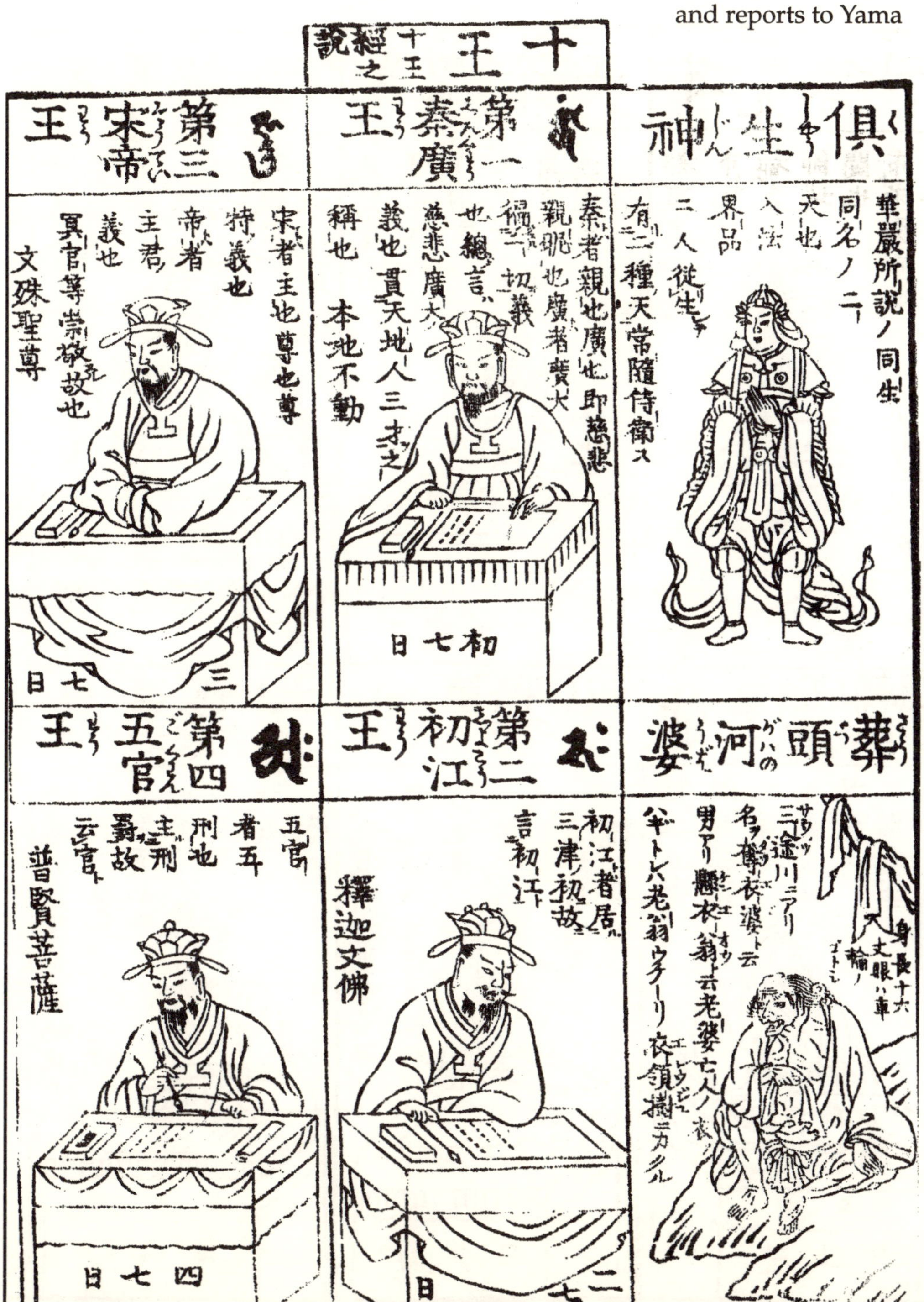

455. Gokan-ō (28th Day)
Emanation of Samantabhadra Bodhisattva

453. Shokō-ō (14th Day)
Emanation of Śākya-Buddha.

451. Sōzugawa no Baba
The old woman of the Sanzu River

460. Tsushi-ō (Ist mass of one year) Emanation of Mahāsthāmaprāpta

458. Taizan-ō (49th Day) (King of Mt. Taizan) Emanation of Bhaiṣajyaguru

456. Enma-ō Yama-Rāja (35th Day) Emanation of Kṣitigarbha

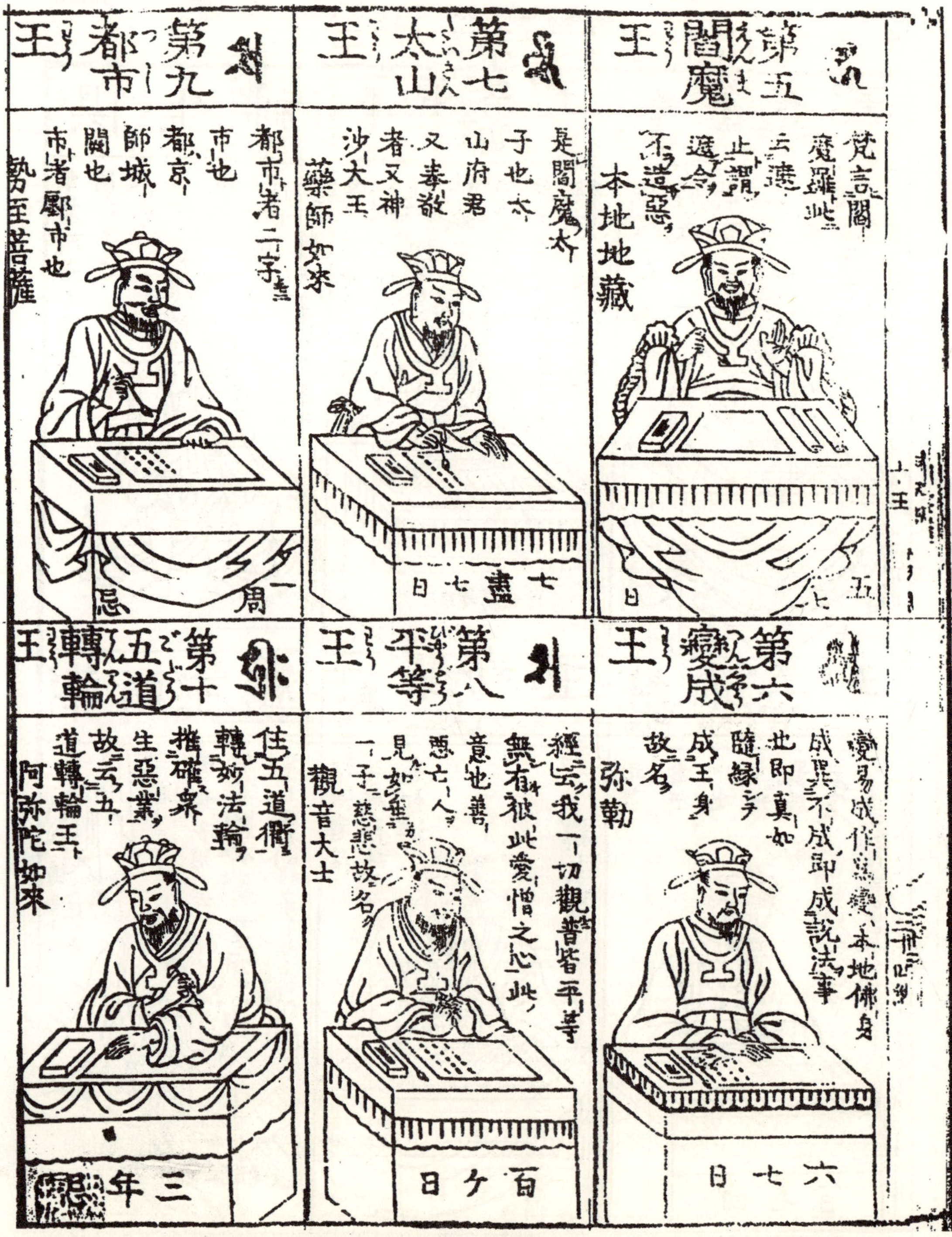

461. Gotōtenrin-ō (3rd mass of second year) Emanation of Amitābha Tathāgata

459. Byōdō Ō (100th Day) Emanation of Mahāsattva

457. Henjō-ō (42nd Day) Emanation of Maitreya

增補諸宗

佛像圖彙

肆

4

Fascicle - IV

§ 33. Yakushi Jūnishinsho
Twelve Marshals of Bhaiṣajyaguru (462-473)

466. Haira Taishō
Pajira (guardian spirit of the hour of dragon), Emanation of Mañjuśrī

464. Shindara Taishō
Sindūra (guardian spirit of hour of tiger)

462. Bikara Taishō
Vikarāla (guardian spirit of the hour of rat), Emanation of Śākyamuni

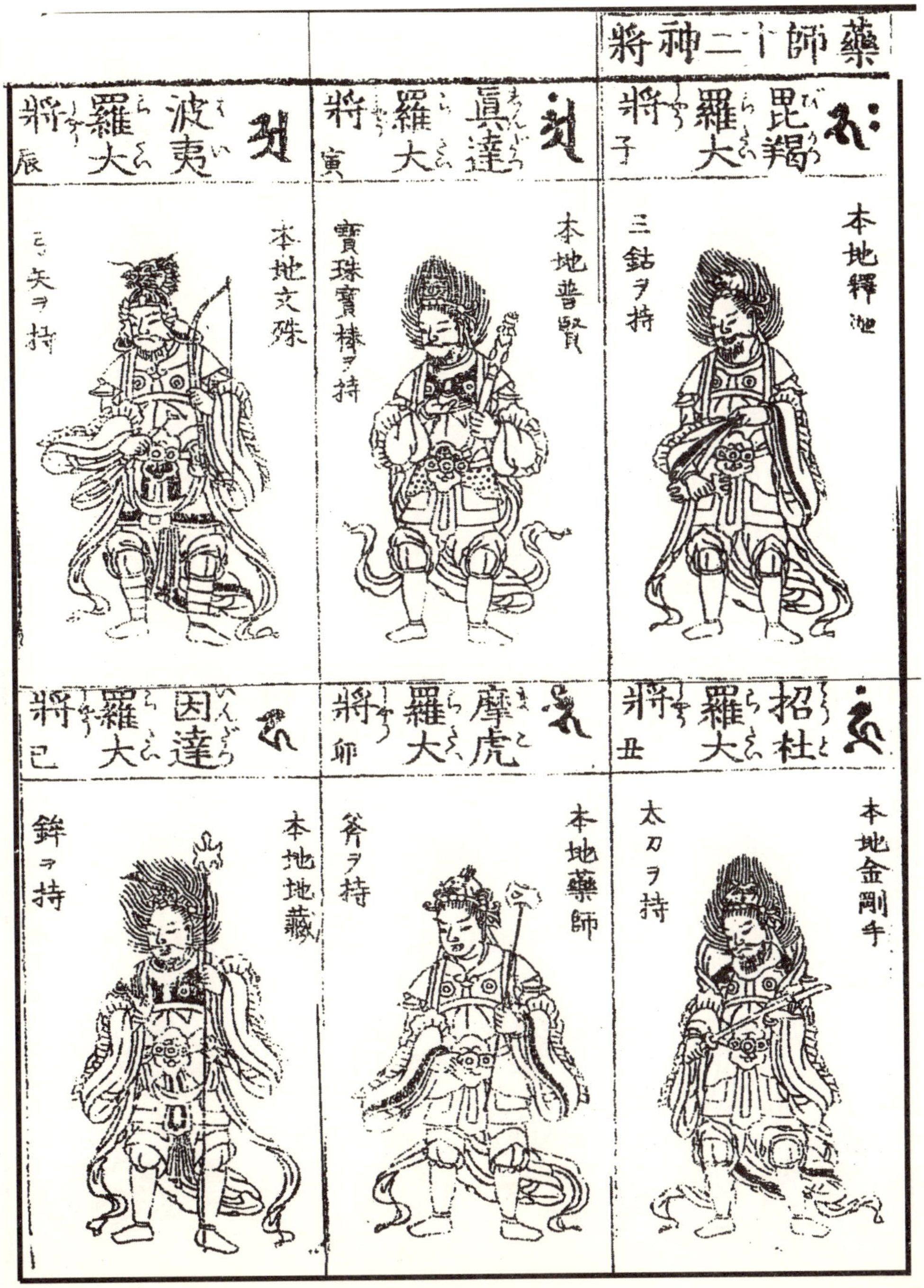

467. Indaṭṣura Taishō
Indala (guardian spirit of the hour of snake), Emanation of Kṣitigarbha

465. Makora Taishō
Mahoraga (guardian spirit of hour of rabbit), Emanation of Bhaiṣajyaguru

463. Shōtōra Taishō
Catura (guardian spirit of the hour of cow), Emanation of Vajrapāṇi

472. Basara Taisho
Vajra (guardian spirit of the hour of dog), Mahāsthamaprāpta

470. Anchira Taishō
Andira (guardian spirit of hour of monkey), Emnation of Avalokiteśvara

468. Santeira Taishō
Sandila (guardian spirit of the hour of horse), Emanation of Ākāśa-garbha

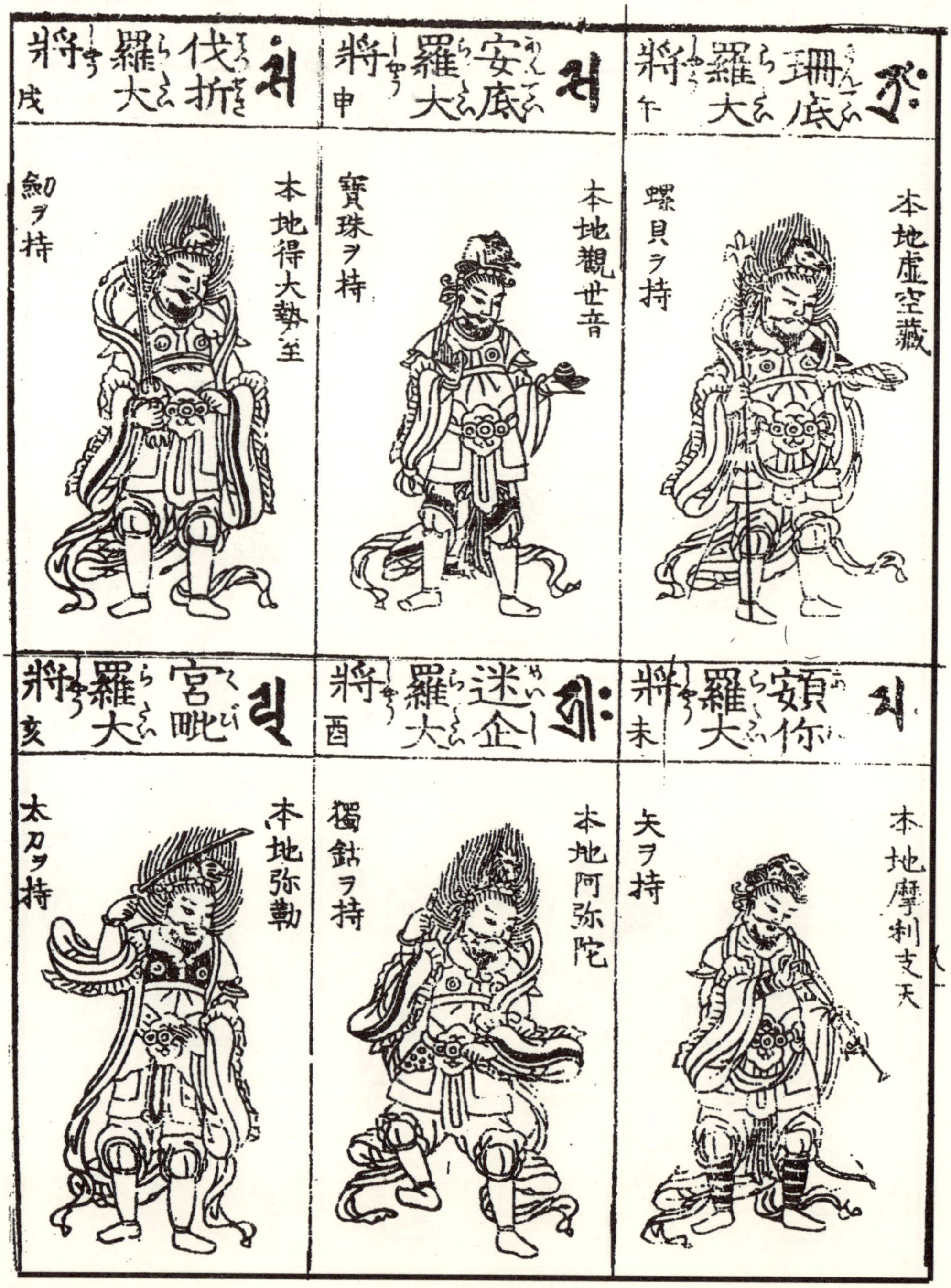

473. Kubira Taishō
Kubera (guardian spirit of the hour of boar), Emnation of Maitreya

471. Mekira Taishō
Mekhila (guardian spirit of hour of cock), Emnation of Amitābha Tathāgata

469. Anira Taishō
Anīla (guardian spirit of hour of sheep), Emnation of Mārīchi

§ 34. Daihanya shugo Jūroku Zenshin
The Sixteen Protectors of Mahāprajñāpāramitā (474-493)

478. Yūmōshinchi Zenshin	**476. Jinja Jin**	**474. Genjō Sanzō**
Virachita Yaksha	Vaiśravaṇa- Deva	Hsüan tsang

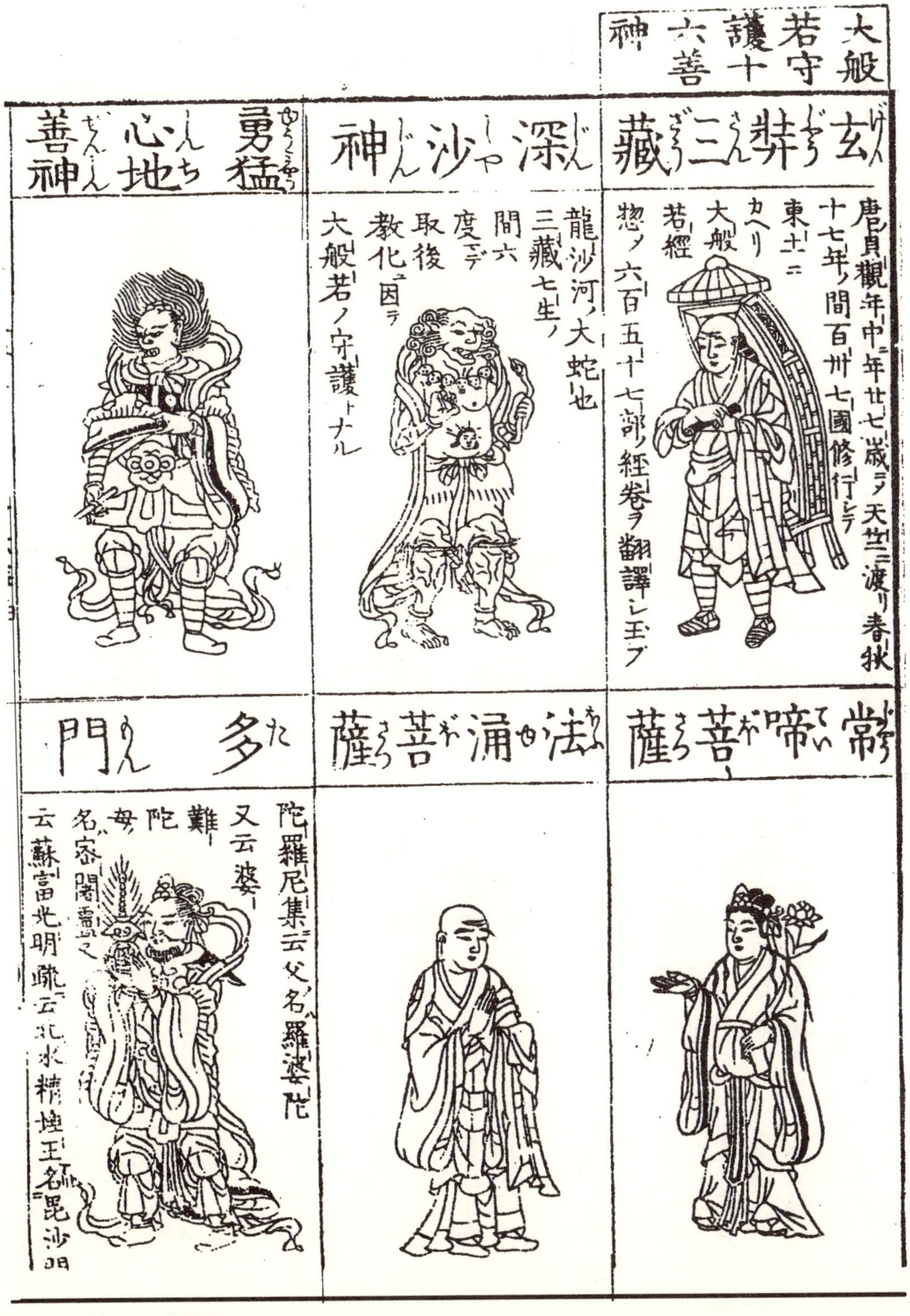

479. Tamon	**477. Hōyu Bosatsu**	**475. Jōtei Bosatsu**
Vaiśravaṇa	Fa-Jung Bodhisattva	Sadāprarudita Bodhisattva

484. Hirohakusha Zenshin
Virūpākṣa

482. Shiimō Zenshin
Majestic Master

480. Birubakunin Zenshin
Virūpāksī

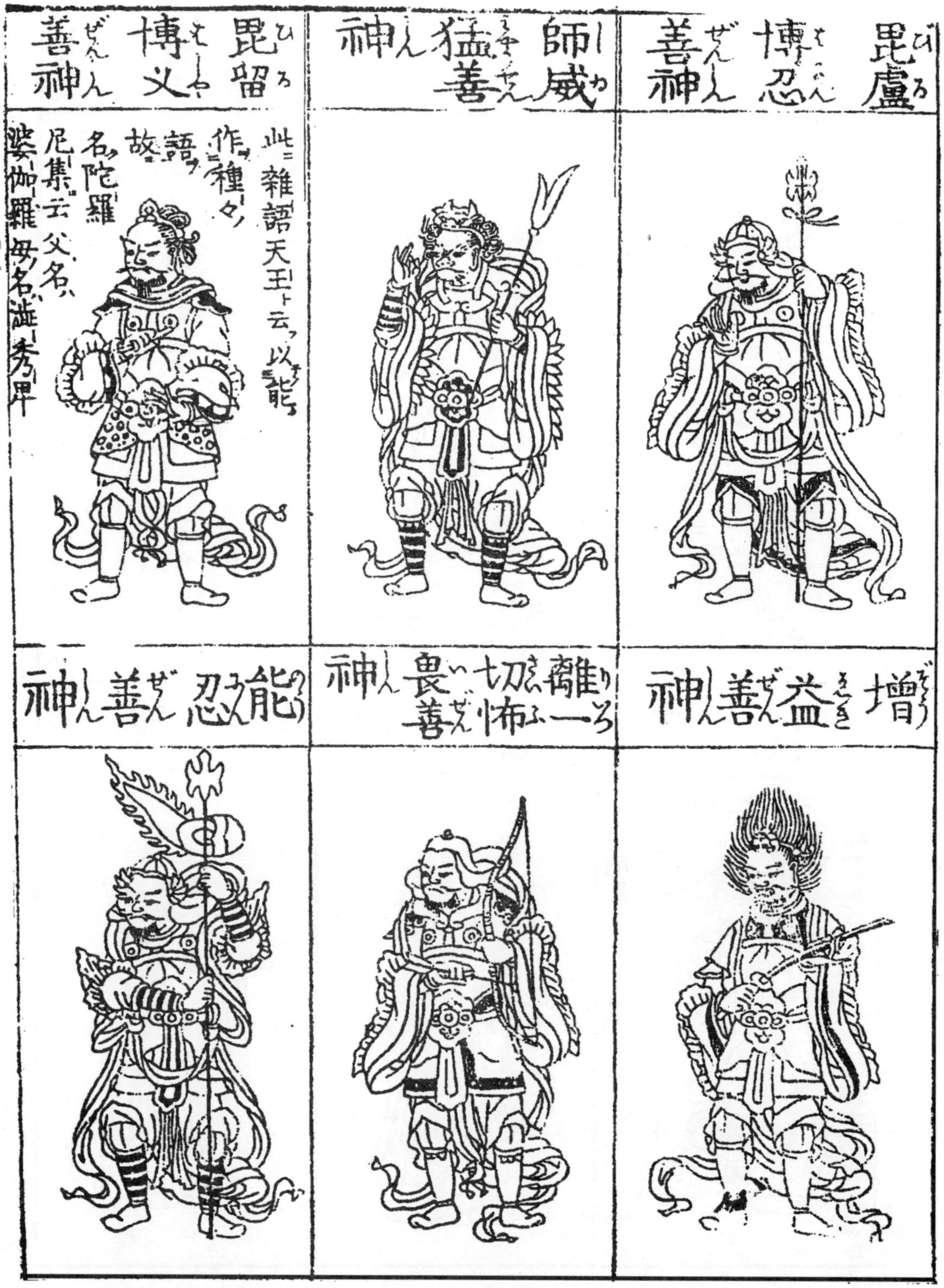

485. Nōnin Zenshin
Śākya Deva

483. Riissaifui Zenshin
Sarvabhaya-Nivaran

481. Zōeki Zenshin
Pauṣtika

490. Beiroraro Zenshin Vaiśravaṇa

488. Joissaishōnan Zenshin Sarvabadha Haran

486. Daitorada Zenshin Dhṛtarāṣṭra

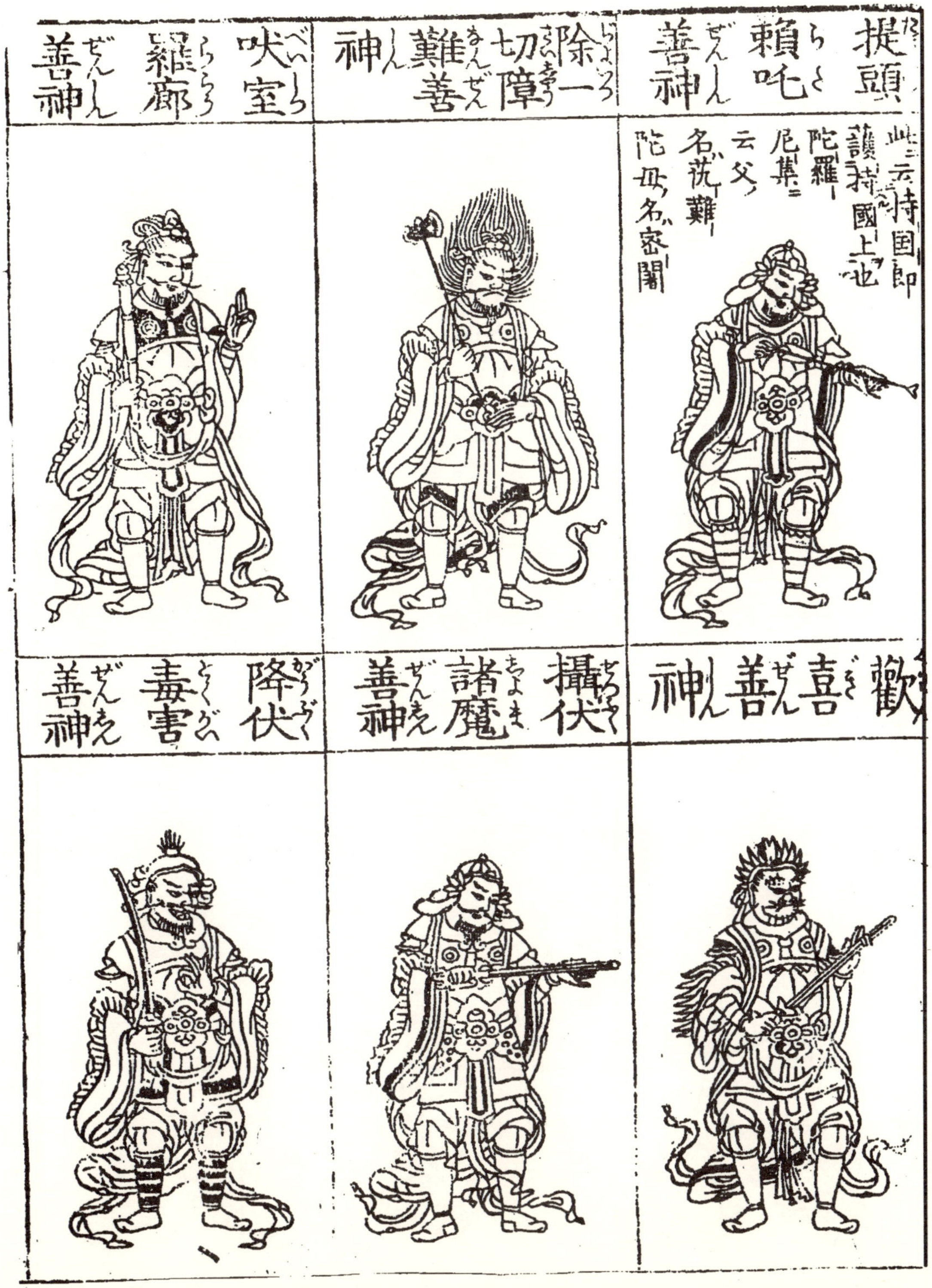

491. Gofuku Dokugai Zenshin Ābhicāruka

489. Shōfukushoma Zenshin Mātaṅga

487. Kanki Zenshin Nandikeśvara

§ 35. Kannon Nijūhachi Bushū
The Twenty-eight Marshals of Avalokiteśvara (494-527)

496. Daiben Kudoku-ten
Devī of good fortune

494. Baso Sennin
Old Ascetic (guides travellers)

492. Birurokusha Zenshin
Virūḍhaka Deva

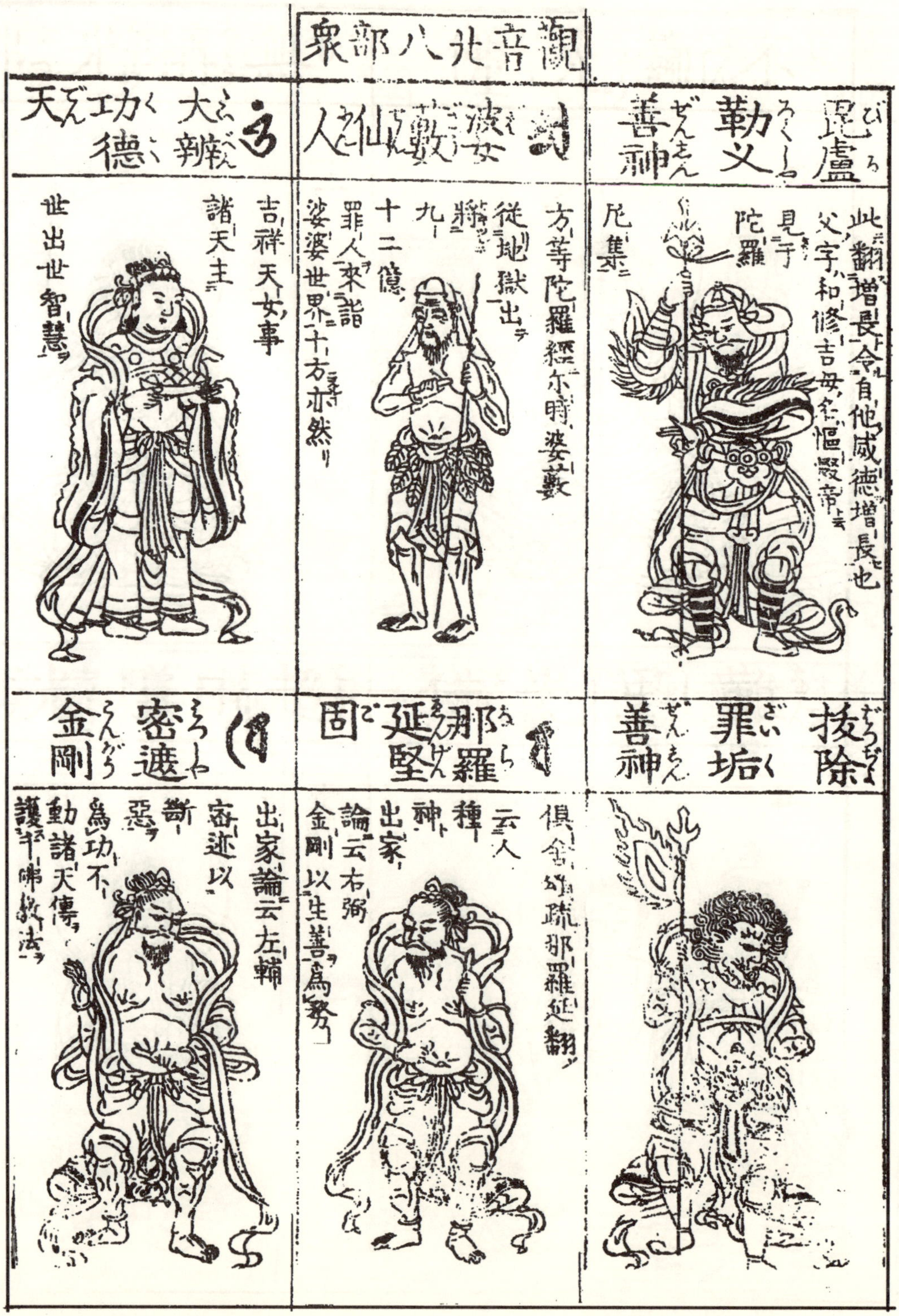

497. Misshaku-Kongō
Guhyavajra

495. Naraen Kengo
Nārāyaṇa

493. Batsujozaiku Zenshin
Remover of obstacles & impurity

502. Konjiki Kujaku Ō
Svarṇa-varṇa Mahāmayūrī

500. Taishakuten Ō
Śakra Devarāja

498. Daibonten Ō
Mahābrahmā

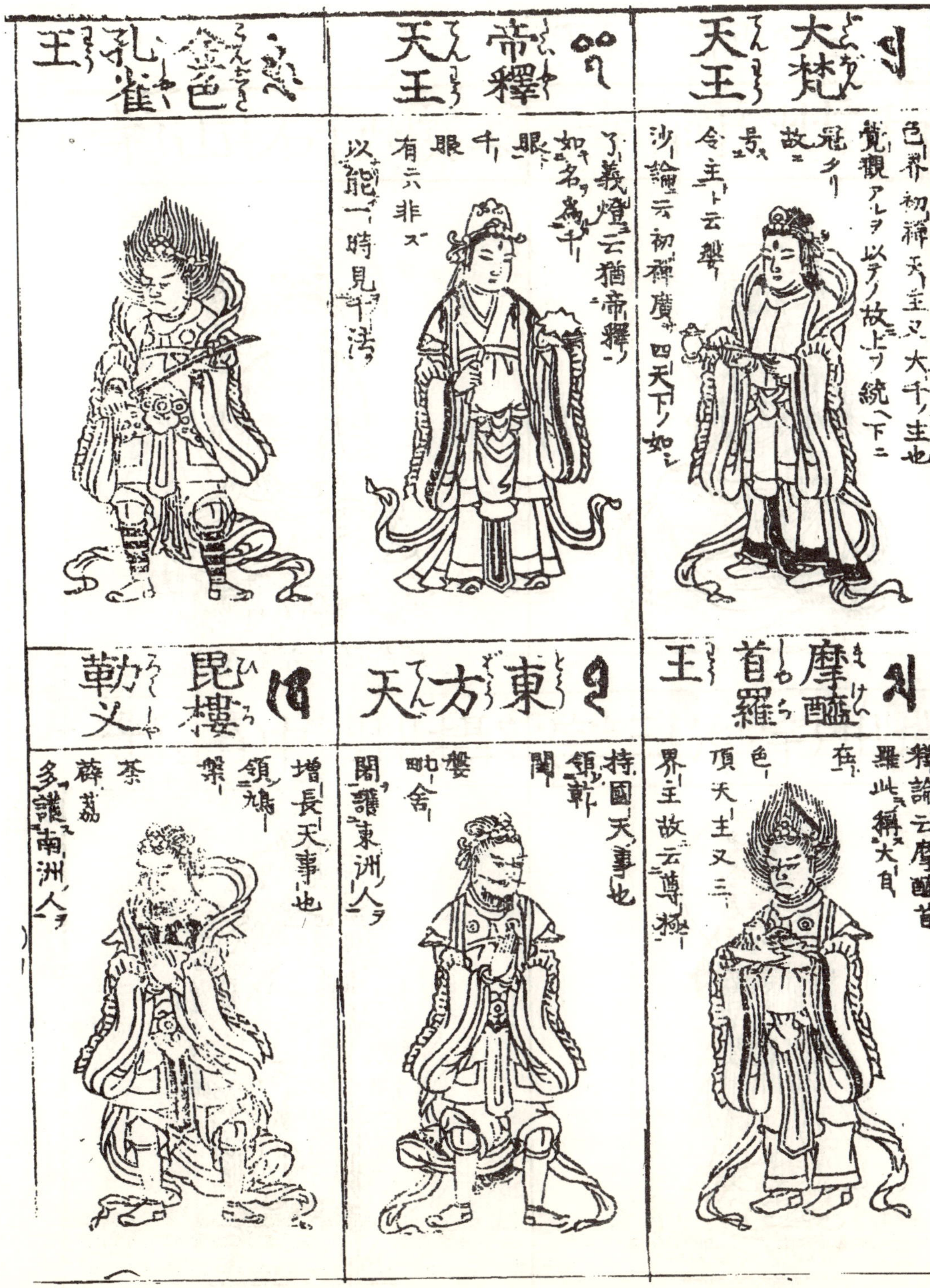

503. Birurokusha
Virūḍhaka

501. Tōhōten
Dhṛtarāṣṭra

499. Makeishura Ō
Maheśvara

508. Jinmoten
Hāriti

506. Birubakusha
Virūpākṣa

504. Mawara Nyo
Mahābala,the female general

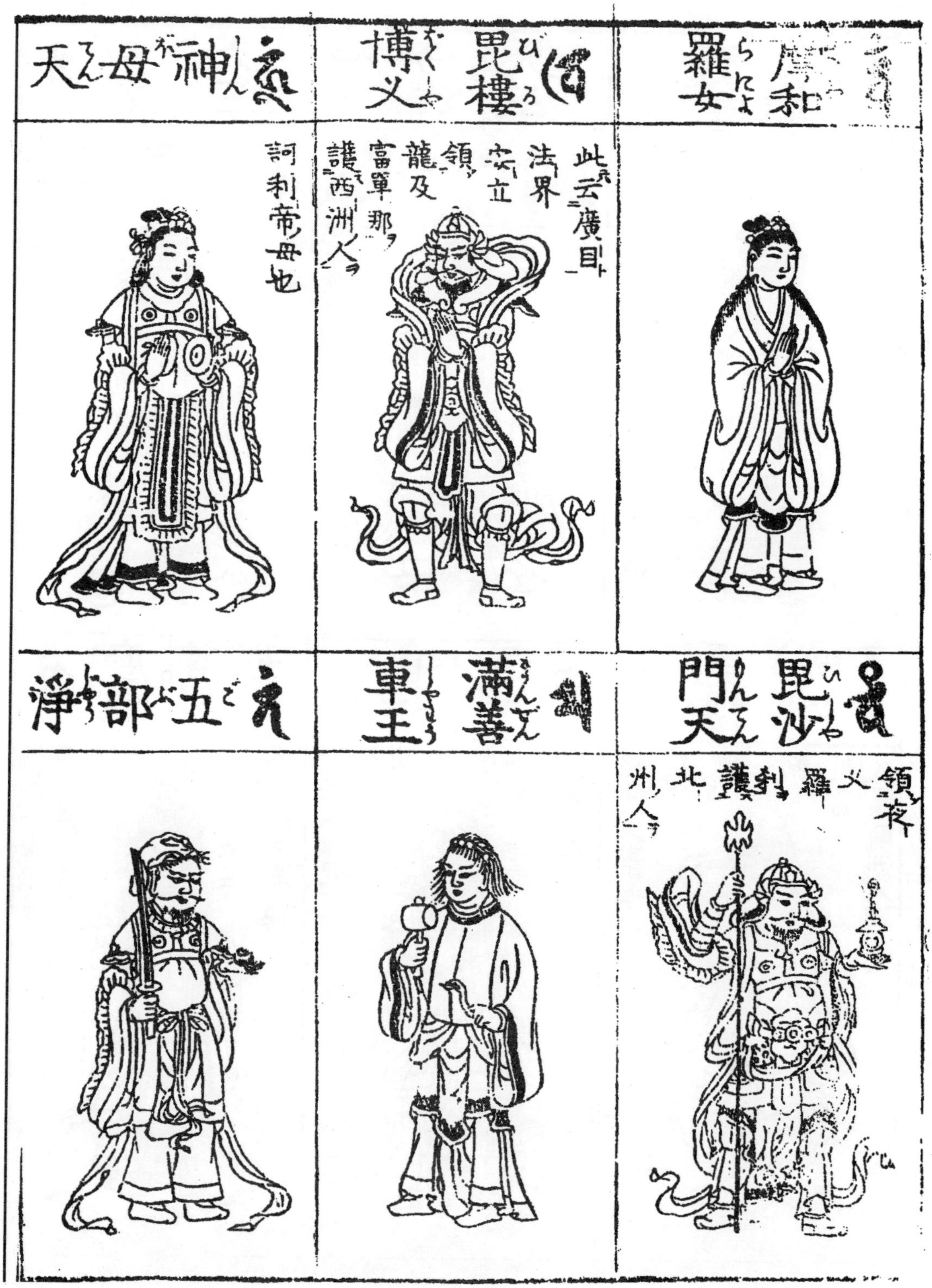

509. GobuJō
Yama as proctector

507. Manzensha-Ō
Sarvamaṅgala Vehicle king

505. Bishamon ten
Vaiśravaṇa

514. Kondai Ō
The Protector of Travellers

512. Kinnara ō
Kinnara-rāja

510. Nanda Ryūō
Nāgarāja Nanda

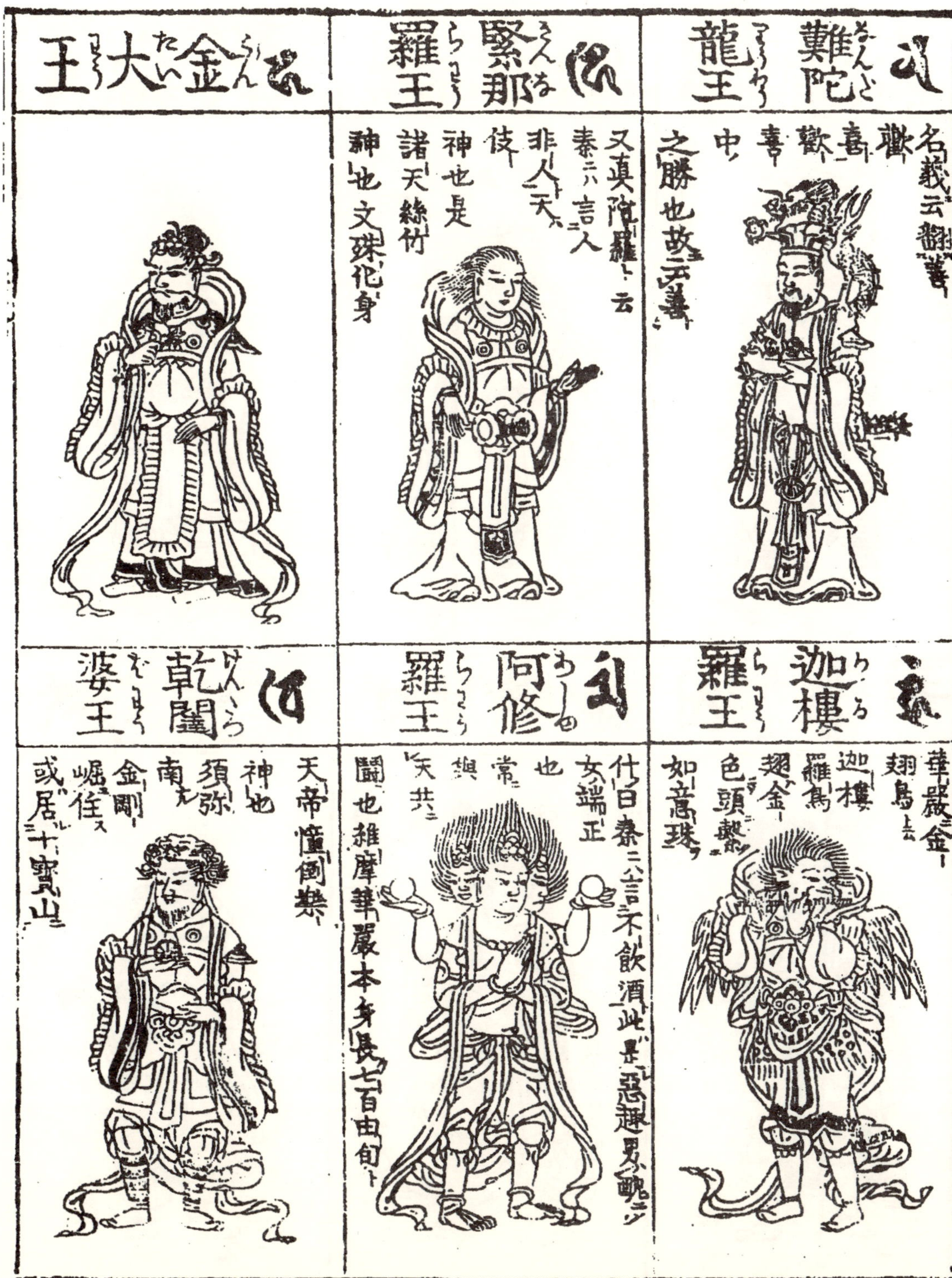

515. Kendatsuba Ō
Gandaharva-rāja

513. Ashura Ō
Asura-rāja (the Demon King)

511. Karura Ō
Garuḍa-rāja

520. Sanshi Taisho
Pañcika

518. Man Senō
Ascetic Maṇa

516. Sakararyū Ō
Nāgarāja-Sagara

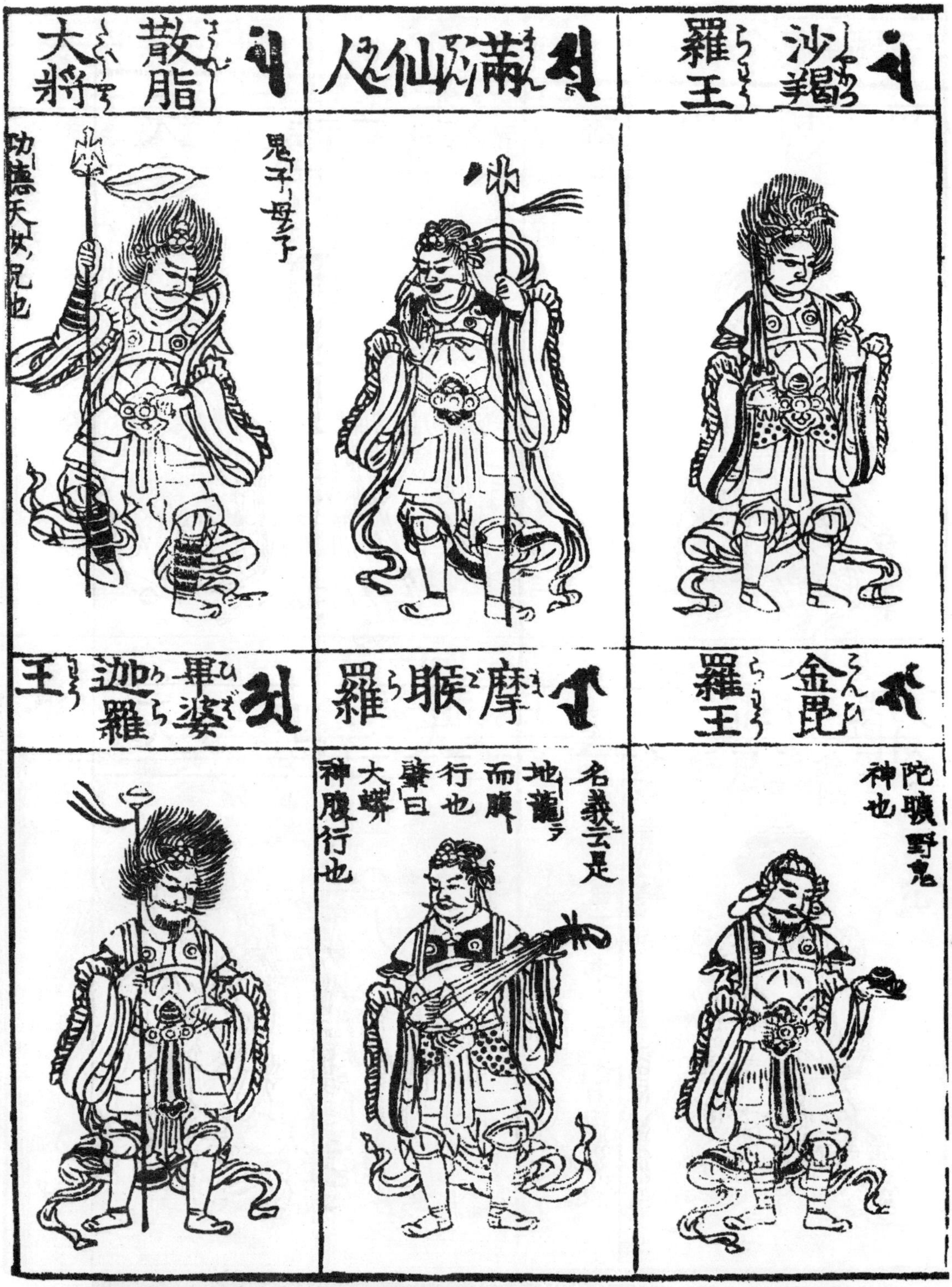

521. Hibbakaraō
Vibhākara-vajrāja

519. Magoraka
Mahorāga

517. Konpira Ō
Kumbhīra-rāja

526. Shōaku Doji
Akuśala Kumara

524. Shōzen Dōji
Kuśhala Kumara

522. Fūten
Vāyu

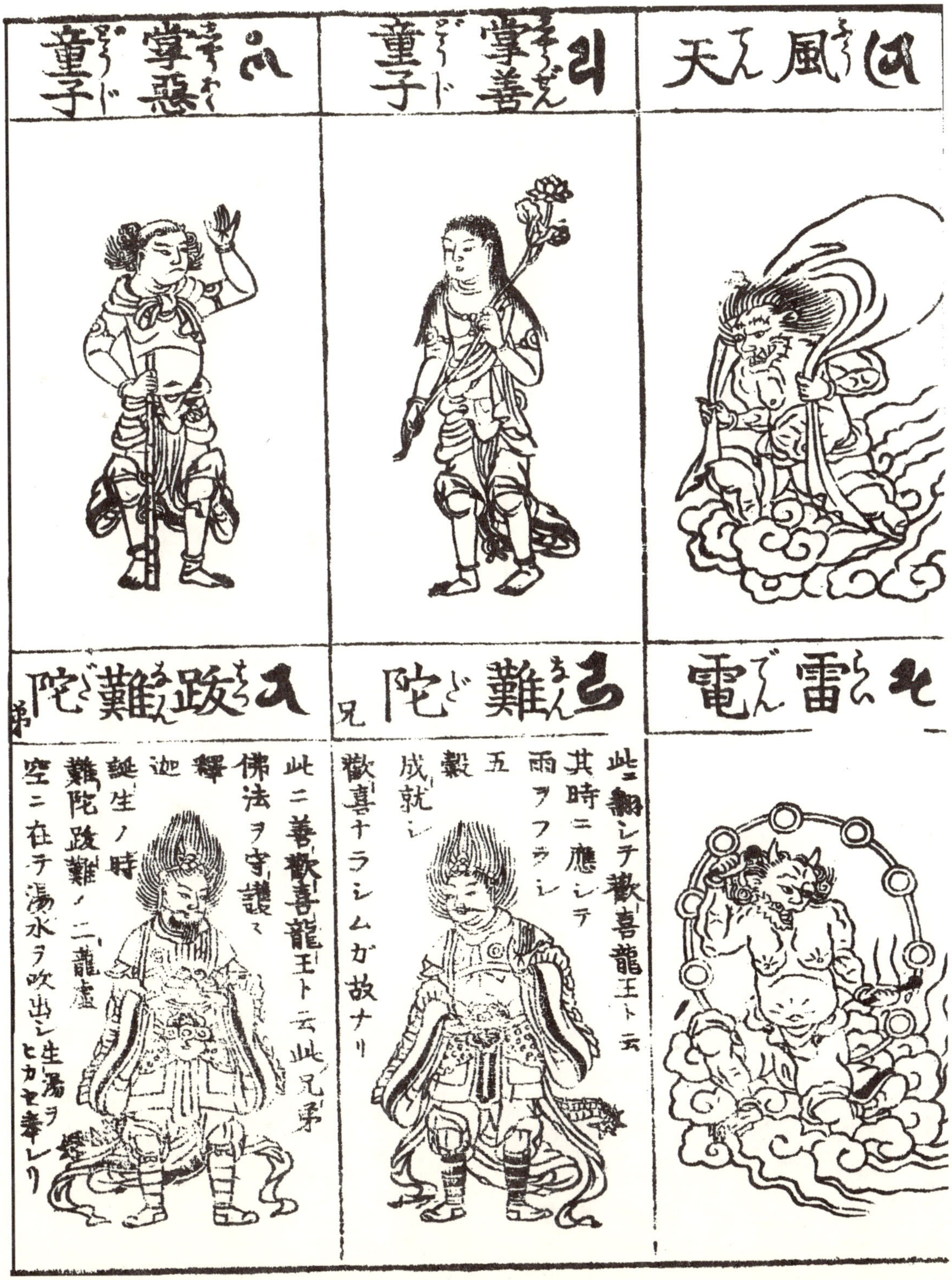

527. Batsunanda
Bhadra Nanda, the younger Brother

525. Nanda
Nanda, the elder Brother

523. Raiden
Vajra (Thunder)

§ 36. Ichidai Mamori Honzon
Main Deities Enshrined in Temples (528-535)

530. Monjūran, Chūdan
Mañjuśrī; middle altar

528. Senjukan, Chūren
Thousand-armed Avalokiteśvara; middle altar

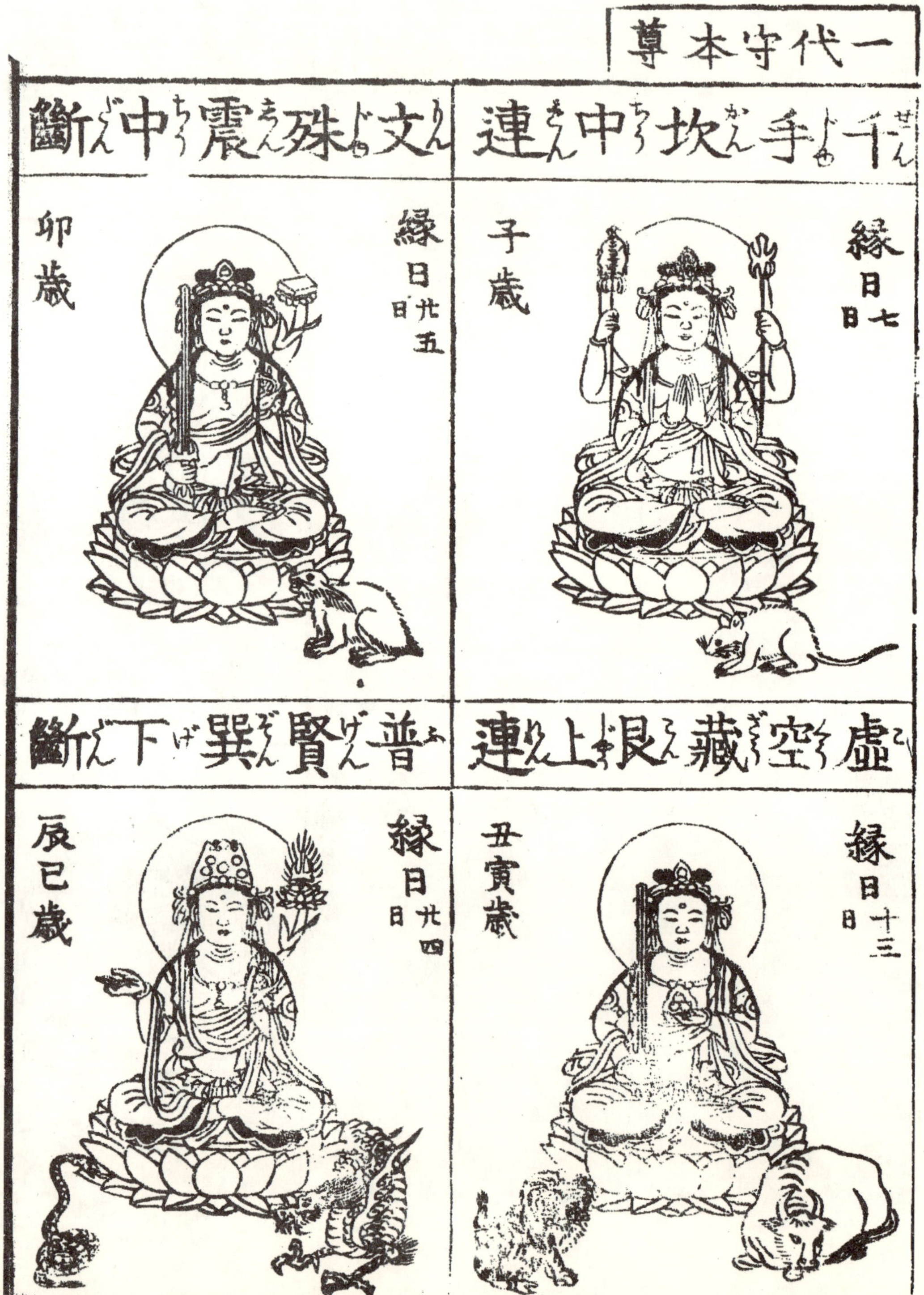

531. Fugenzon Gedan
Samantabhadra; lower altar

529. Kokūzō Jōren
Ākāśagarbha; upper altar

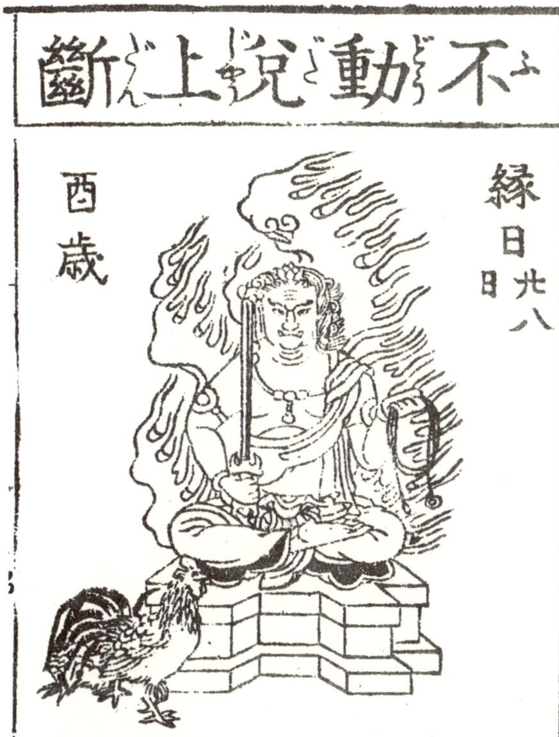

534. Fudō, Jōdan
Acala; Upper altar

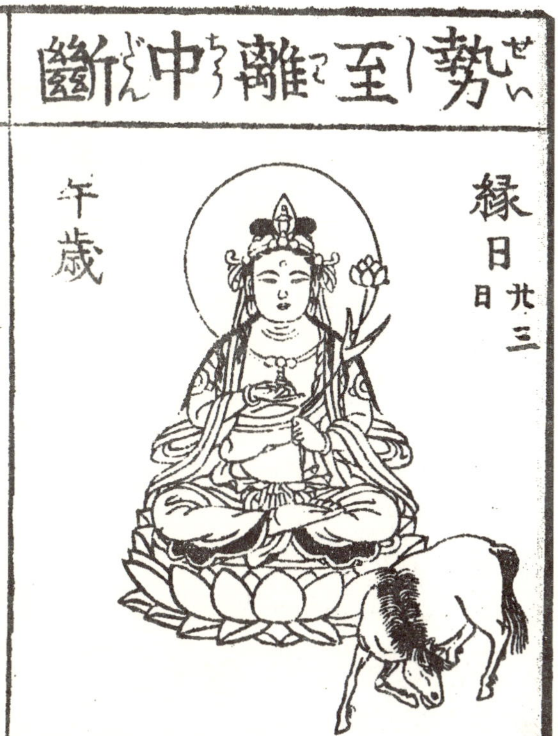

532. Seishi, Chūdan
Mahāsthāmaprāpta; Middle altar

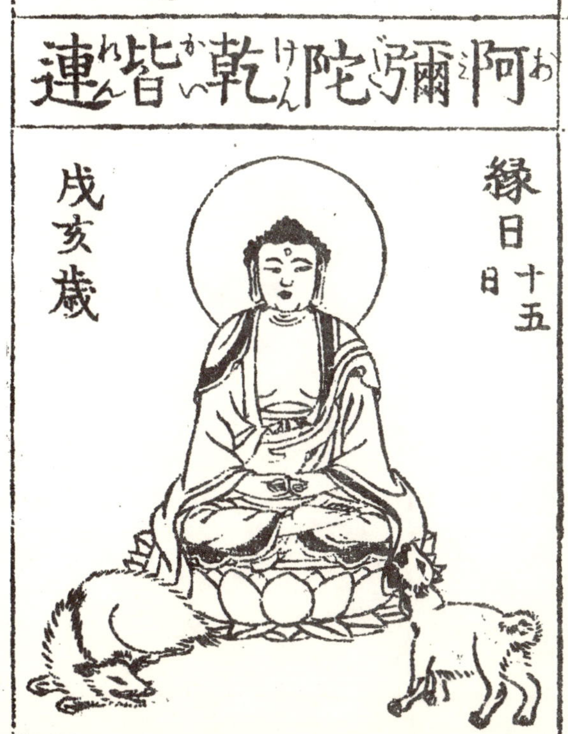

535. Amida-ken, Kairen
Amitābha; Main altar

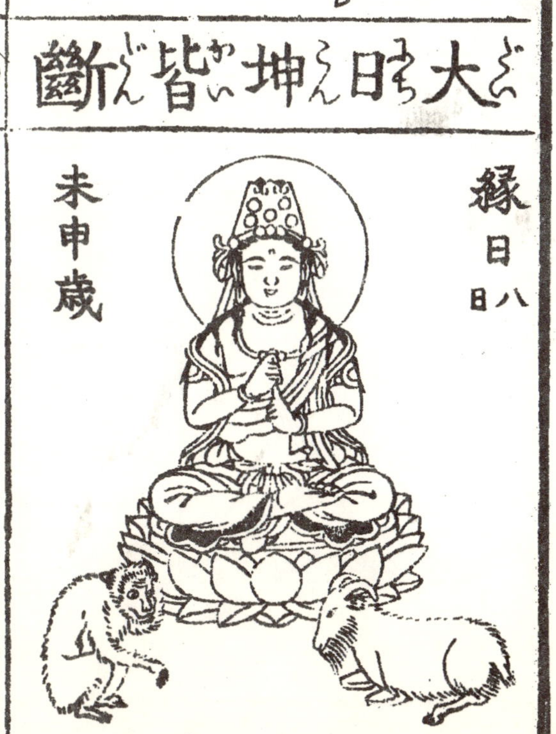

533. Dainichiran, Kaidan
Mahāvairocana; Main altar

§ 37. Jūsan Butsu
TheThirteen Buddhas (536-548)

540. Jizō, 5
Kṣitigarbha, 35th day since death

538. Monjū, 3
Mañjuśrī, 21st day since death

536. Fudō, 1
Acala, 7th day since death

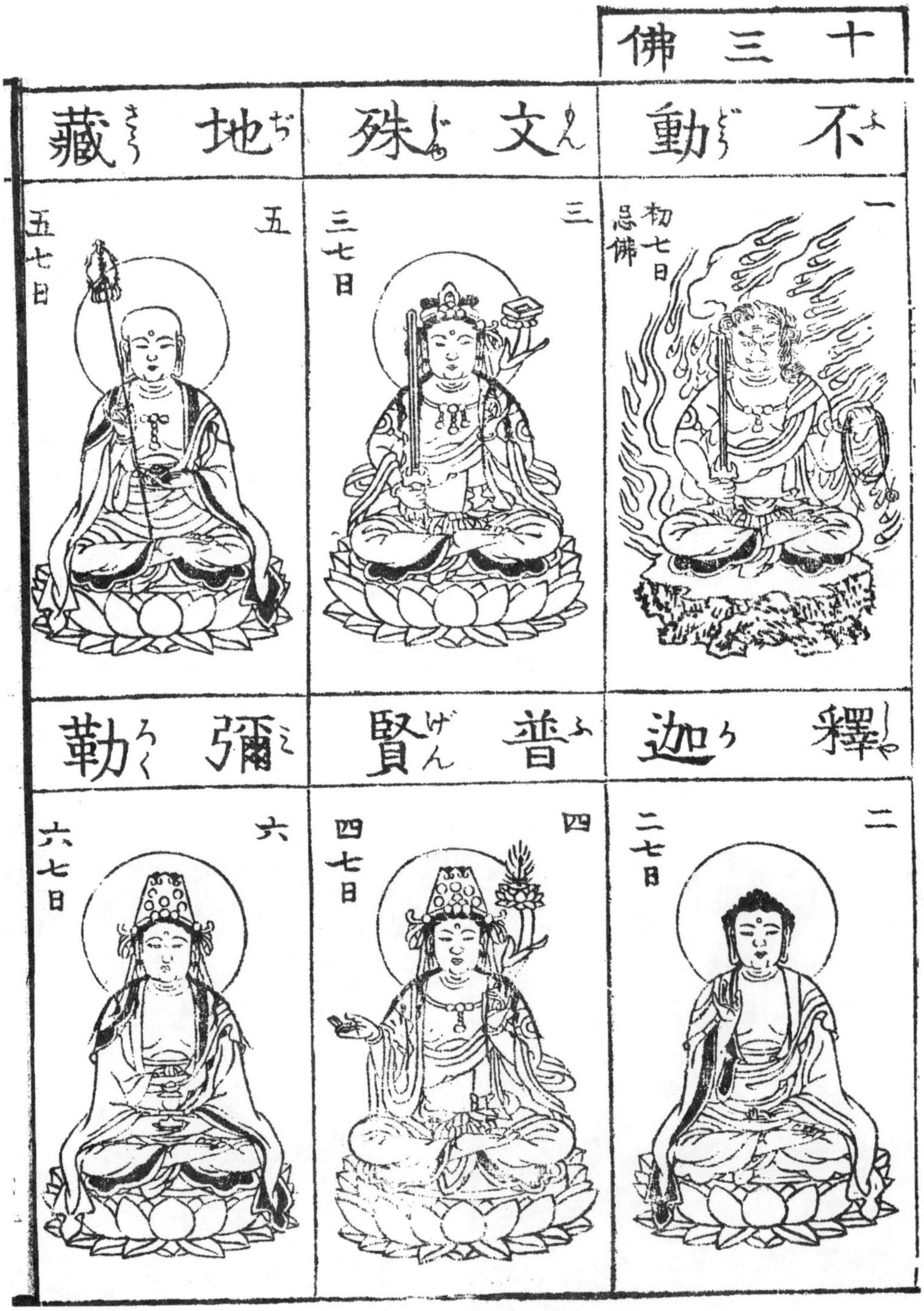

541. Miroku, 6
Maitreya, 42nd day since death

539. Fugen, 4
Samantabhadra, 28th day since death

537. Shaka, 2
Śākyamuni, 14th day since death

546. Ashuku, 11
Akṣobhya
(Seventh death anniversary)

544. Seishi, 9
Mahāsthāmaprāpta
(first death anniversary)

542. Yakushi, 7
Bhaiṣajyaguru,
49th day since death

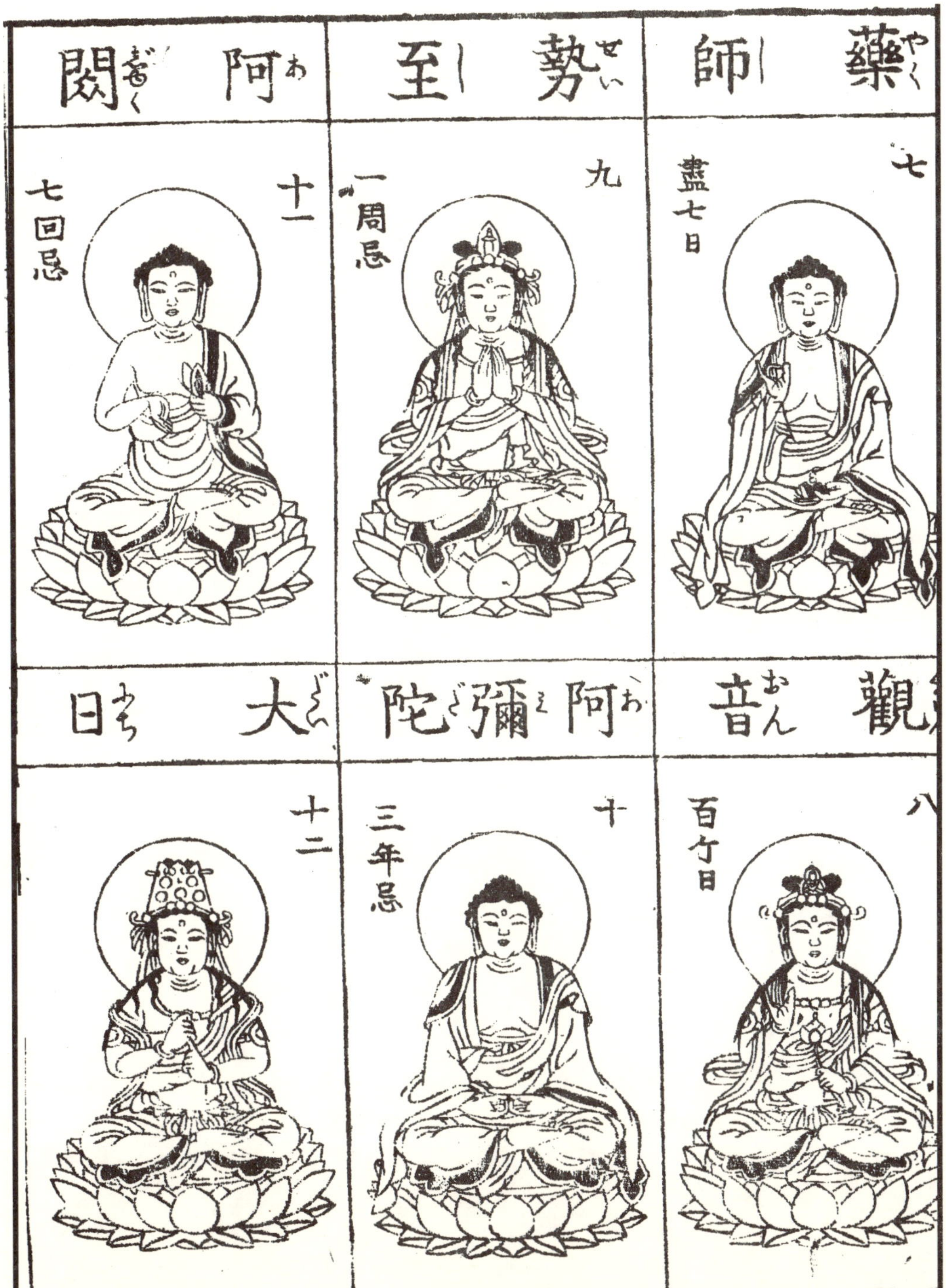

547. Dainichi, 12
Vairocana
(13th death anniversary)

545. Amida, 10
Amitābha
(Second death anniversary)

543. Kannon, 8
Avalokiteśvara, 100th day
since death

§ 38. Ryūjū Bosatsu
Nāgārjuna & Other Bodhisattvas (549-553)

552. Enmei Son Ksitigarbha of longevity | **550. Jizō Bosatsu** Kṣitigarbha Bodhisattva | **548. Kokū-zō, 13** Ākāśagarbha (33rd death anniversary)

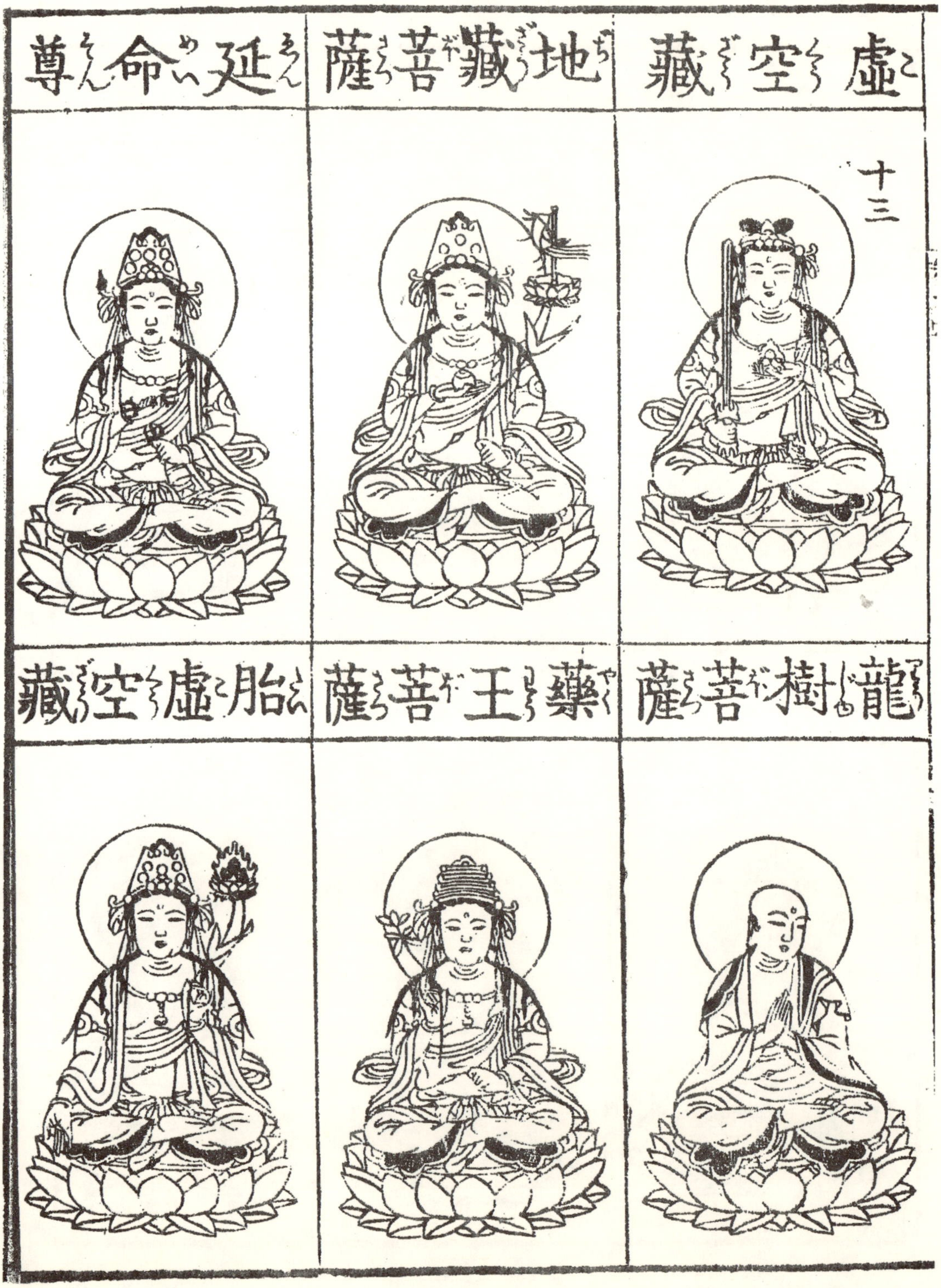

553.Taikokū zō Ākāśagarbha of the Garbhadhātu | **551. Yakuō Bosatsu** Baisajyarāja Bodhisattva | **549. Ryūjū Bosatsu** Nāgārjuna Bodhisattva

§ 39. Godai Kokūzō
The Five Manifestations of Ākāśagarbha and Others (554-558)

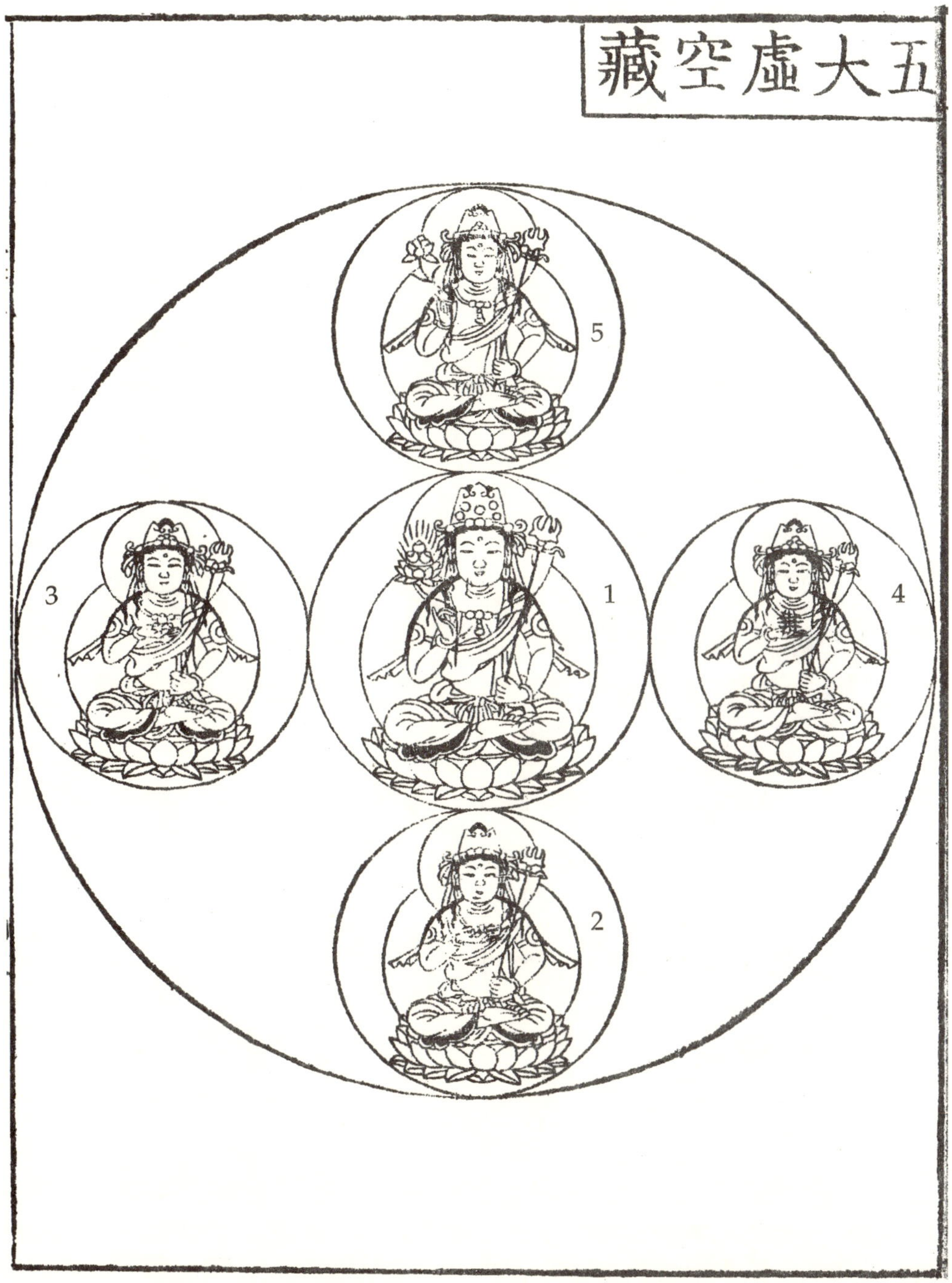

554. Five Ākāśagarbha according to Kōzen (AD 1120-1203)

1. Holds *cintāmaṇi* on a lotus in his right hand.
2. Holds a *vajra* in his right hand.
3. Holds three jewels on a lotus in his right hand.
4. Holds a *cintāmaṇi* on a lotus in his right hand.
5. Holds a *viśvajra* in his right hand.

557. Fugen Enmei
Sāmantabhadra of Long Life

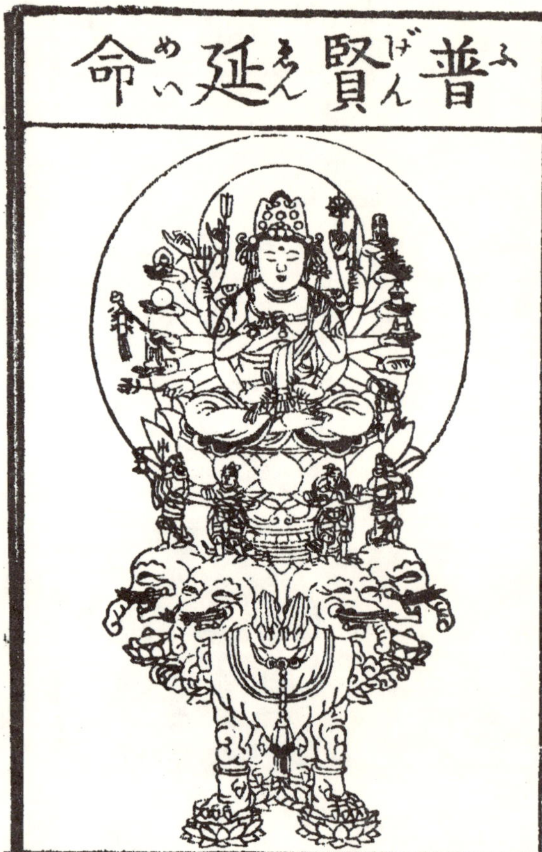

555. Gumonji Kokūzo
Ākāśagarbha of Gumonji

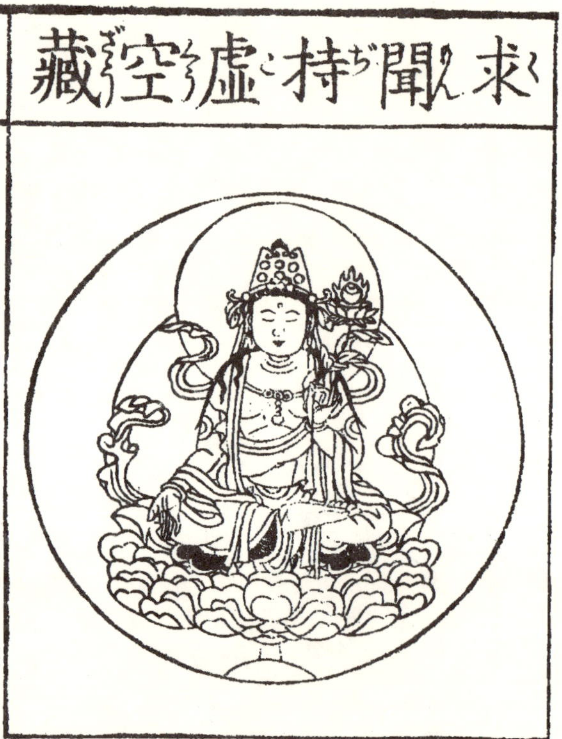

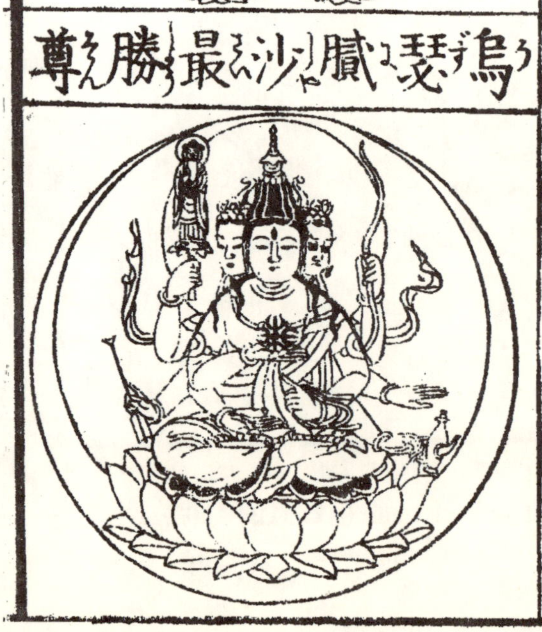

558. Uzunisha Saiahōson
Uṣṇīṣa of the Reverend

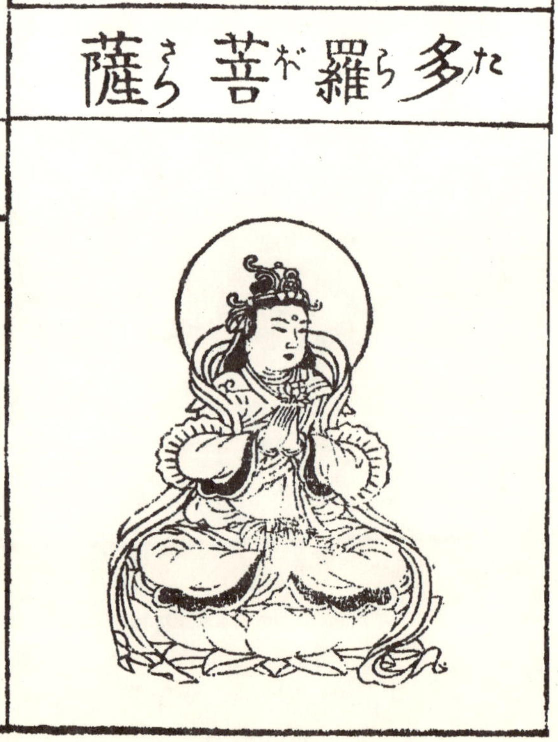

556. Tara Bosatsu
Tārā Bodhisattva

§ 40. The Oldest Statues of Buddha in Japan (559-562)

561. Saga Shaka Nyōrai
Śākyamuni Tathāgata of Saga temple

559. Zenkōji Nyorai
Tathāgata of the Zenkōji Temple

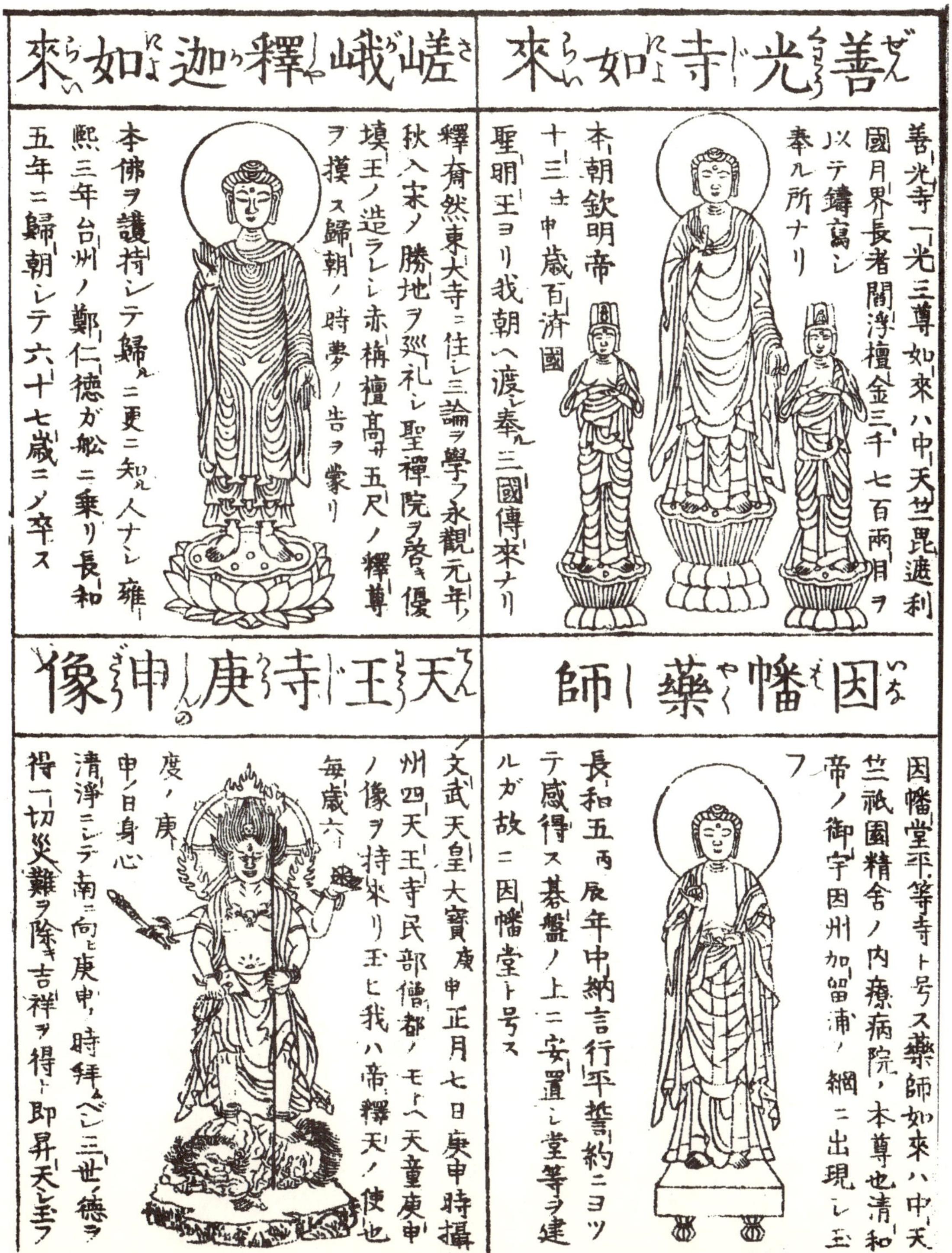

562. Tennōji Kōshinzō
Blue-faced Vajrarāja of
Tennōji Temple (see fig. 262)

560. Inaba Yakushi
Bhaiṣajyaguru of Inaba

§ 41. Jūni kōbutsu
The Twelve Titles of Amitābha (563-574)

565. Mugekō Butsu, 3
Buddha of Irresistible Light

563. Muryōkō Butsu
Buddha of Immeasurable Light

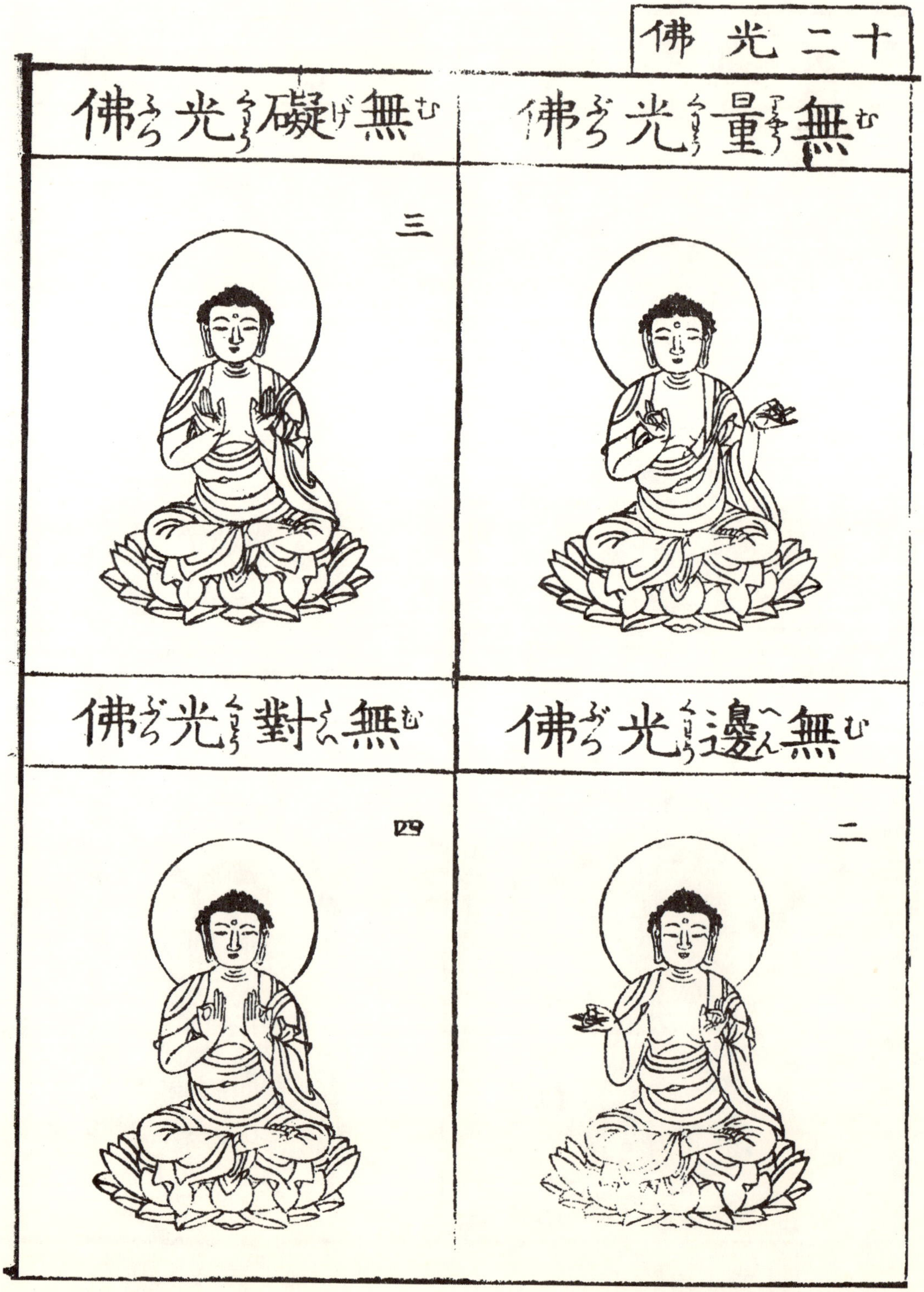

566. Mutaikō Butsu, 4
Buddha of Incomparable Light

564. Muhenkō Butsu, 2
Buddha of Boundless Light

569. Kankikō Butsu, 7
Buddha of Joyous Light

567. Enōkō Butsu, 5
Buddha of Flaming Light

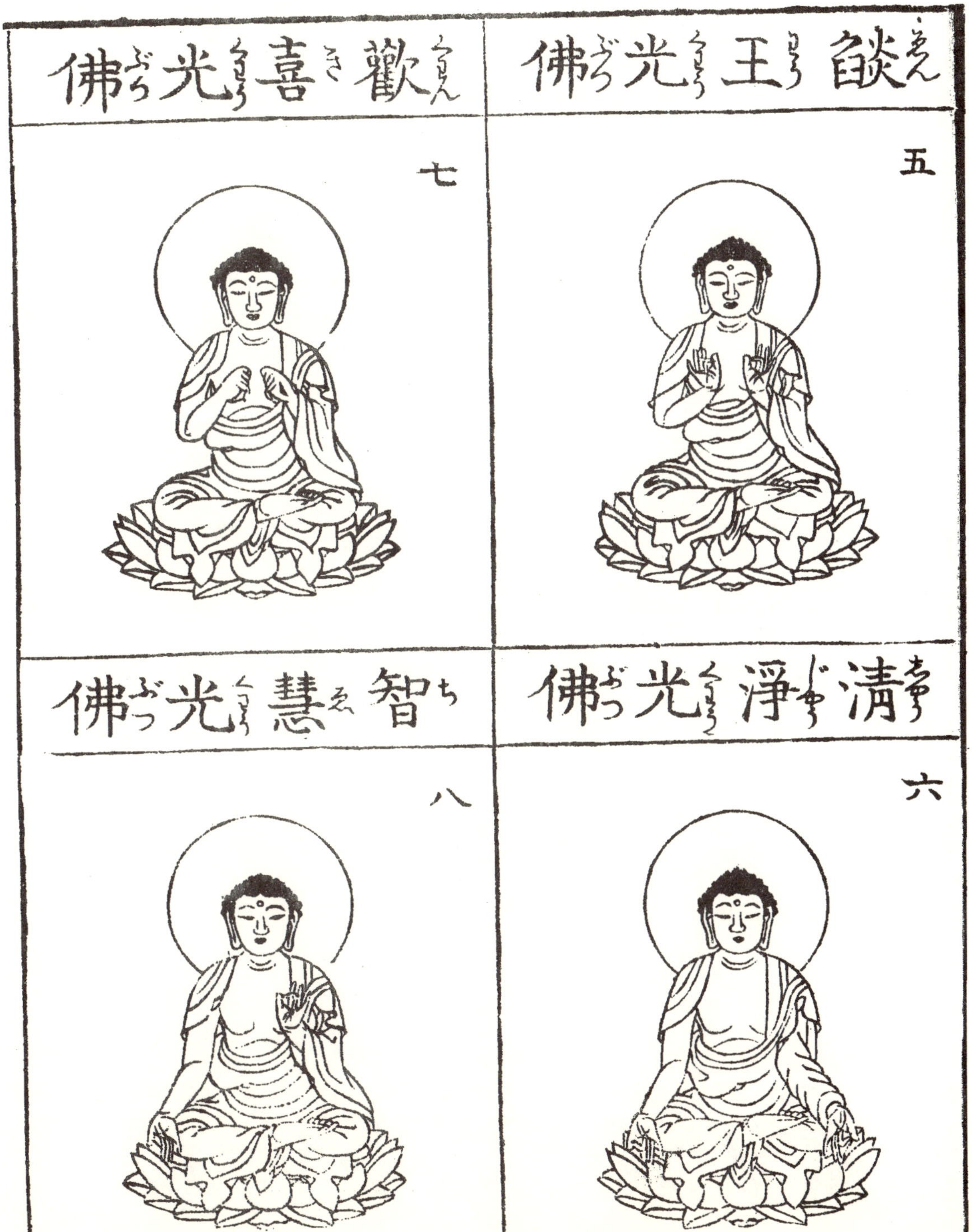

570. Chiekō Butsu, 8
Buddha of Light of Wisdom

568. Shōjōkō Butsu, 6
Buddha of Pure Light

573. Mukō Butsu, 11
Buddha of Ineffable Light

571. Fudankō Butsu, 9
Buddha of Incessant Light

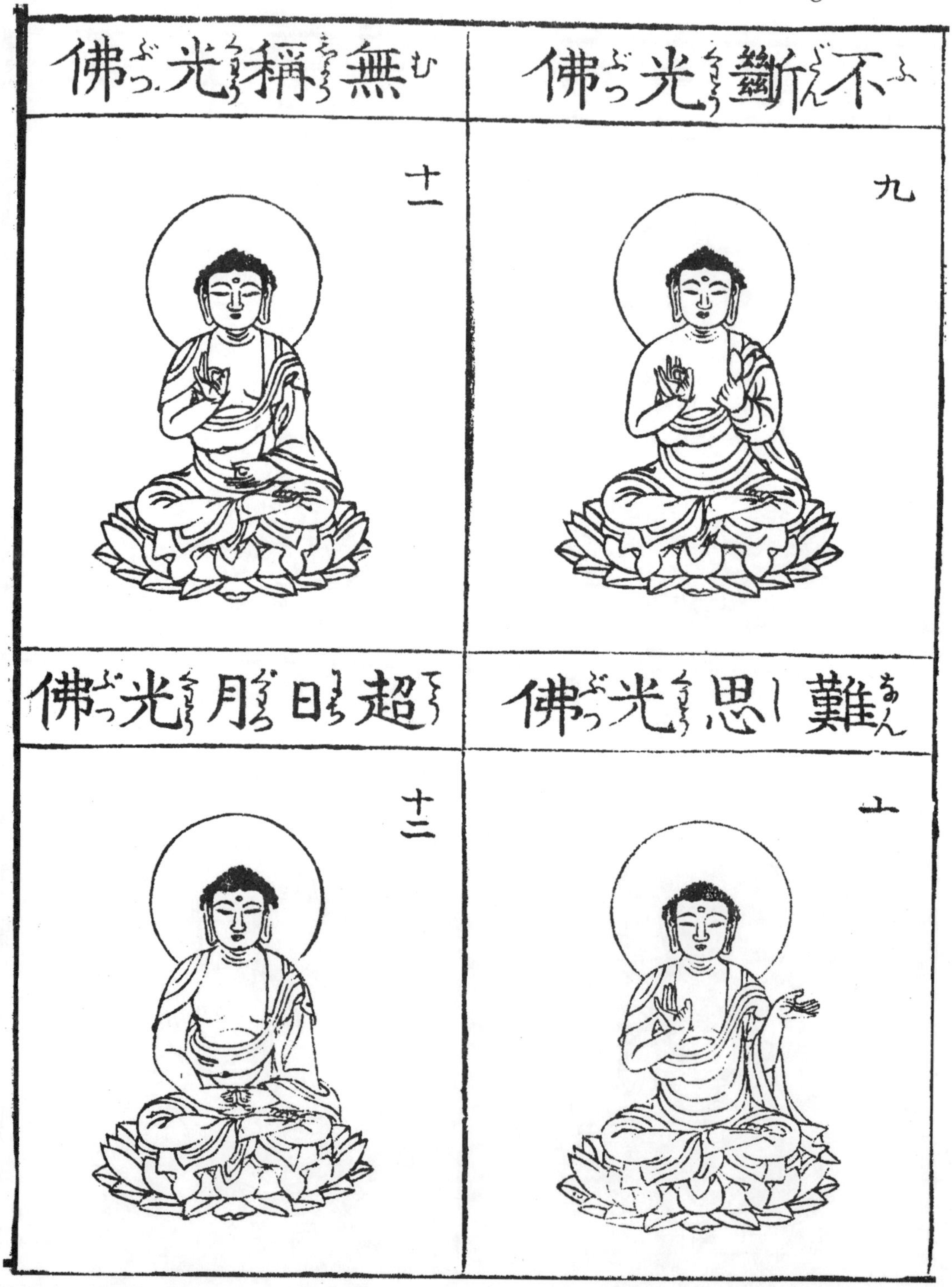

574. Chōnichi-getsukō Butsu, 12
Buddha of Light that surpass
the Sun and Moon

572. Nanshikō Butsu, 10
Buddha of Light of
Surpassing Thought

§ 42. Sanjūsan Shonai Kanonzō
The Idols of 33 Avalokiteśvara Temples in Japan (575-580)

577. Eshū Ishiyamadera
Ishiyamadera temple of Eshū

575. Washū Okadera
Okadera Temple in Yamato province

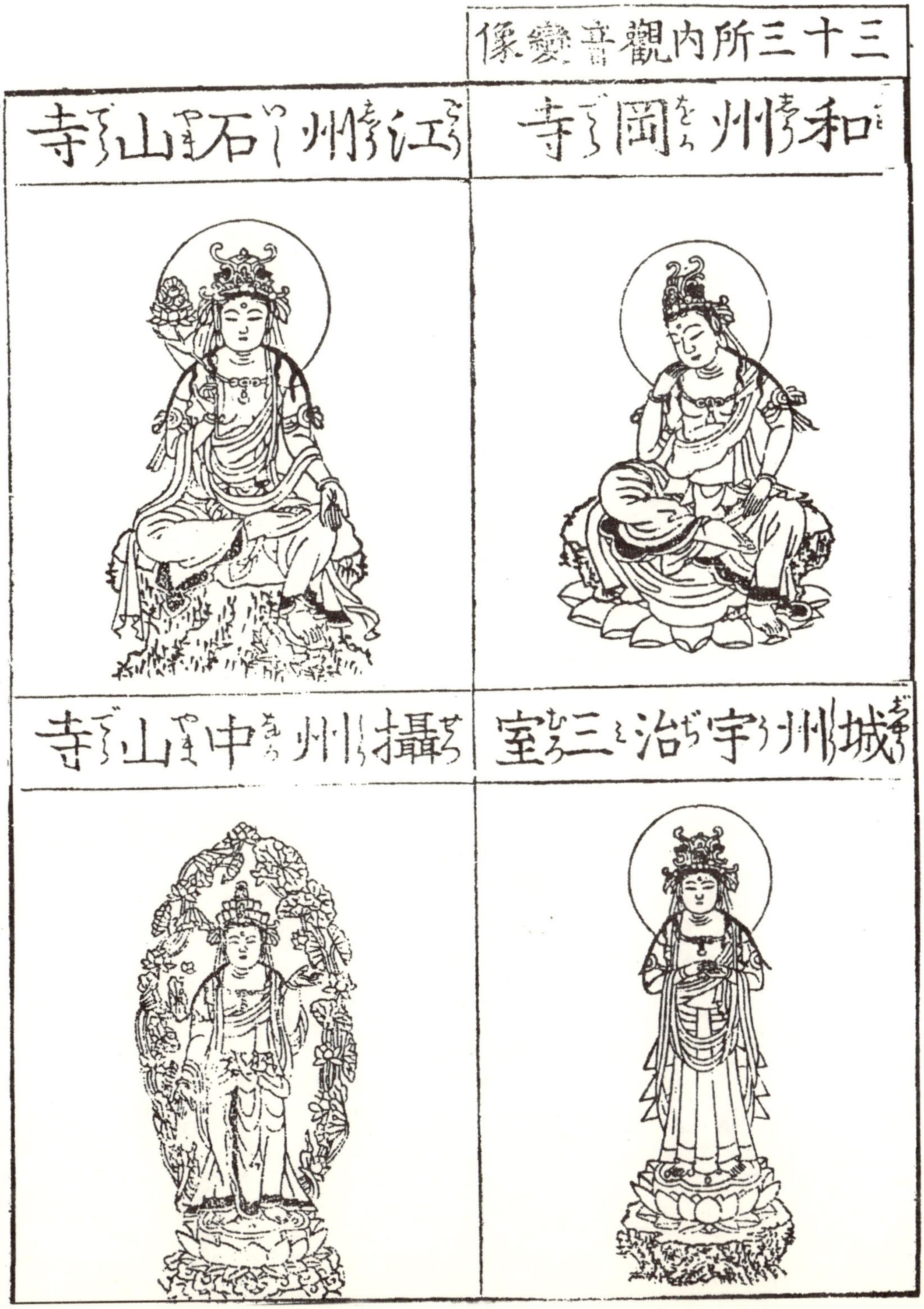

578. Sesshū-Nakayamadera
Nakayama dera Temple in Sesshū

576. Joshū Uji Mimuro
Mimuro Temple in Uji at Joshū

§ 43.Roku Saī jitsu Honzon
Deities of the Six days of Upoṣadha (581-586)

581. Yakushi Nyorai (8th day)
Bhaiṣajyaguru Tathāgata (see fig. 179)

579. Banshū Hokkesan
Hokkesan in Banshū

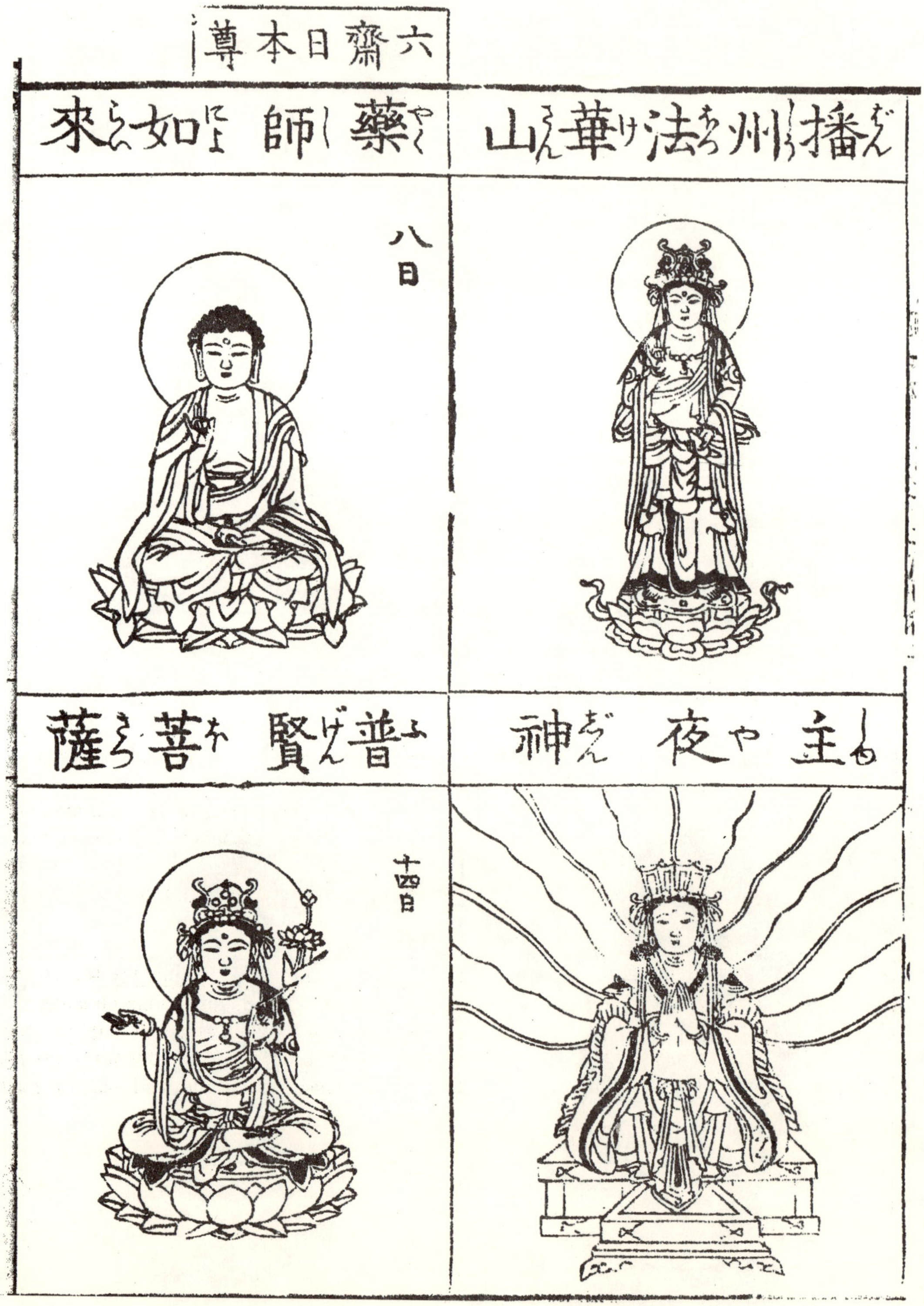

582. Fugen Bosatsu (14th day)
Samantabhadra Bodhisattva

580. Shuya Jin
Suiya Devi

586. Shaka Nyorai (30th day)
Śākyamuni Tathāgata

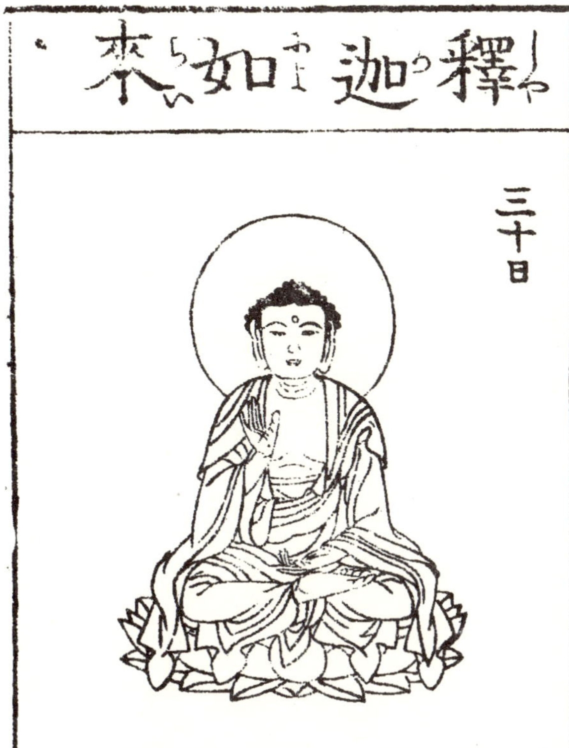

583. Amida Nyorai (15th day)
Amitābha Tathāgata

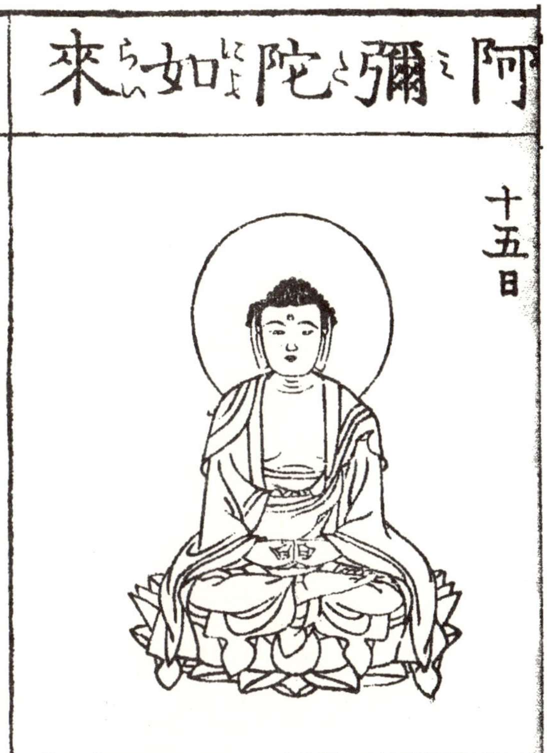

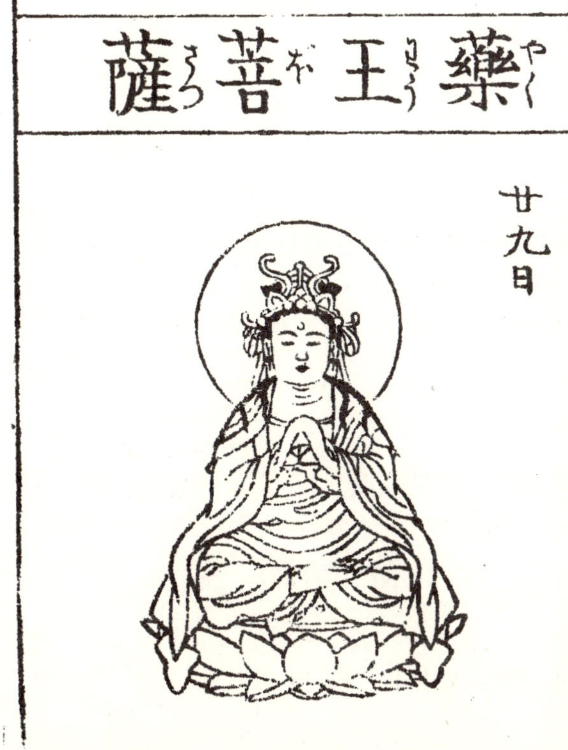

585. Yakuō Bosatsu (29th day)
Bhaiṣajyarāja Bodhisattva

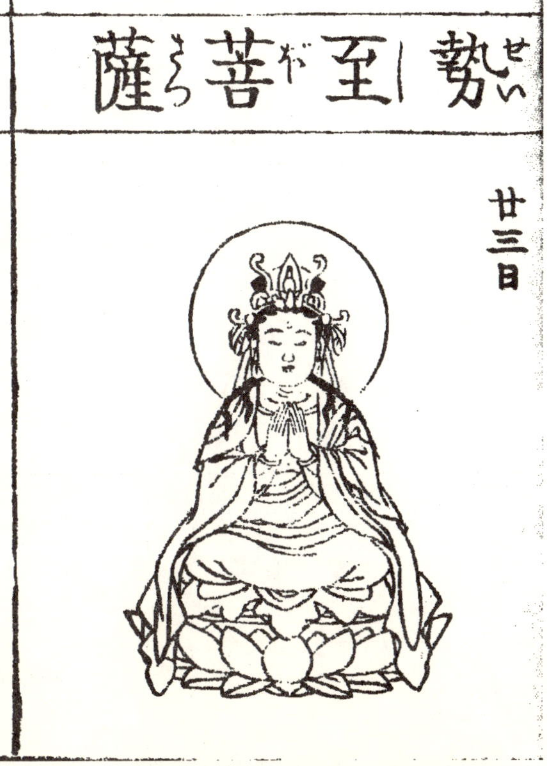

584. Seishi Bosatsu (23rd day)
Mahāsthāmaprāpta Bodhisattva

§ 44. Shichi Fukujin
The Seven Deities of Fortune (587-593)

589. Kisshō-ten
Śrī Mahādevī

587. Bishamon-ten
Vaiśravaṇa

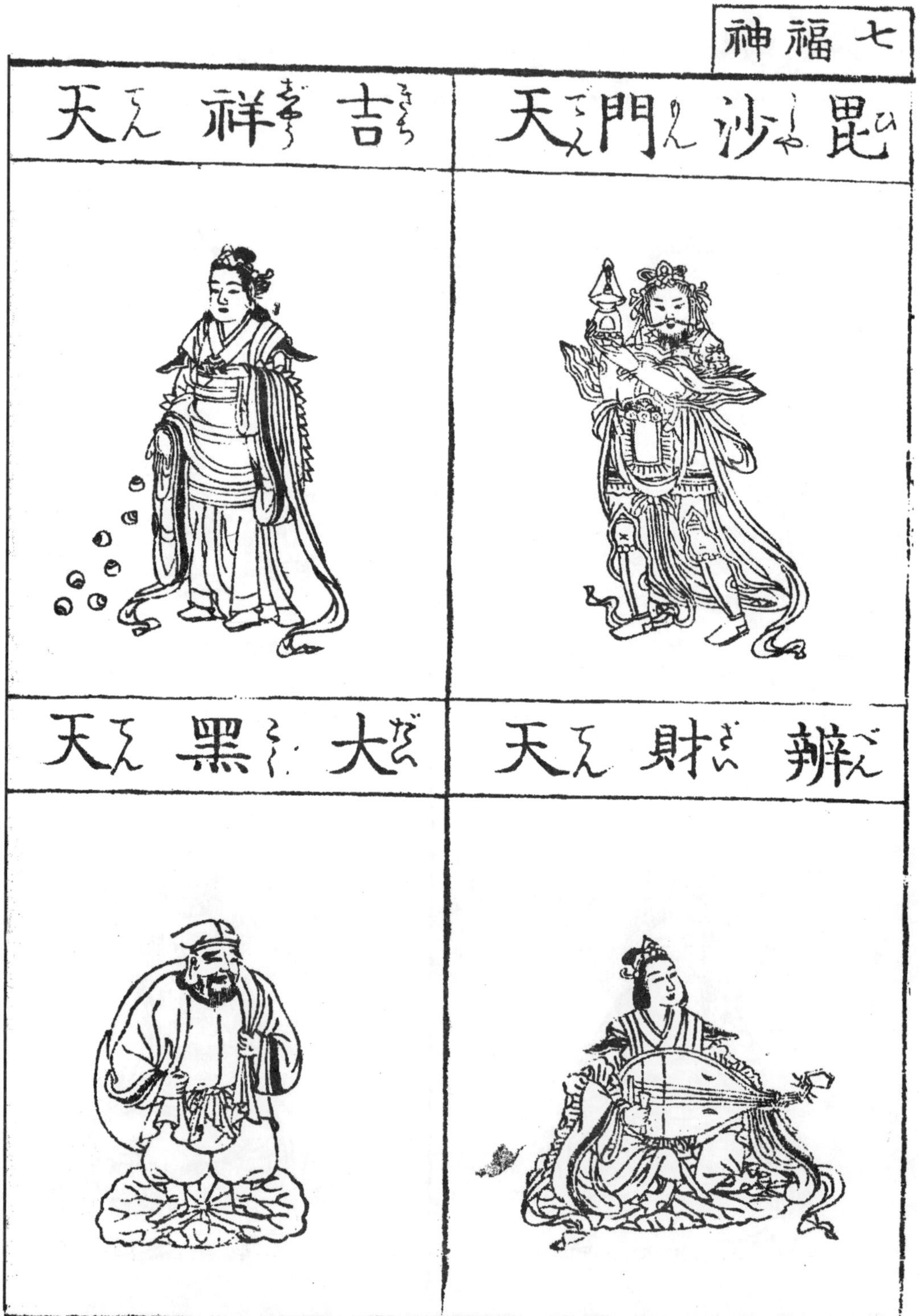

590. Dai koku-ten
Mahākāla, God of Good Luck

588. Benzai-ten
Sarasvatī

§ 45. Funadama Kyū
The Goddess of Sailors and Other Beings (594-606)

593. Jurō
God of Longevity

591. Ebisu
God of Wealth

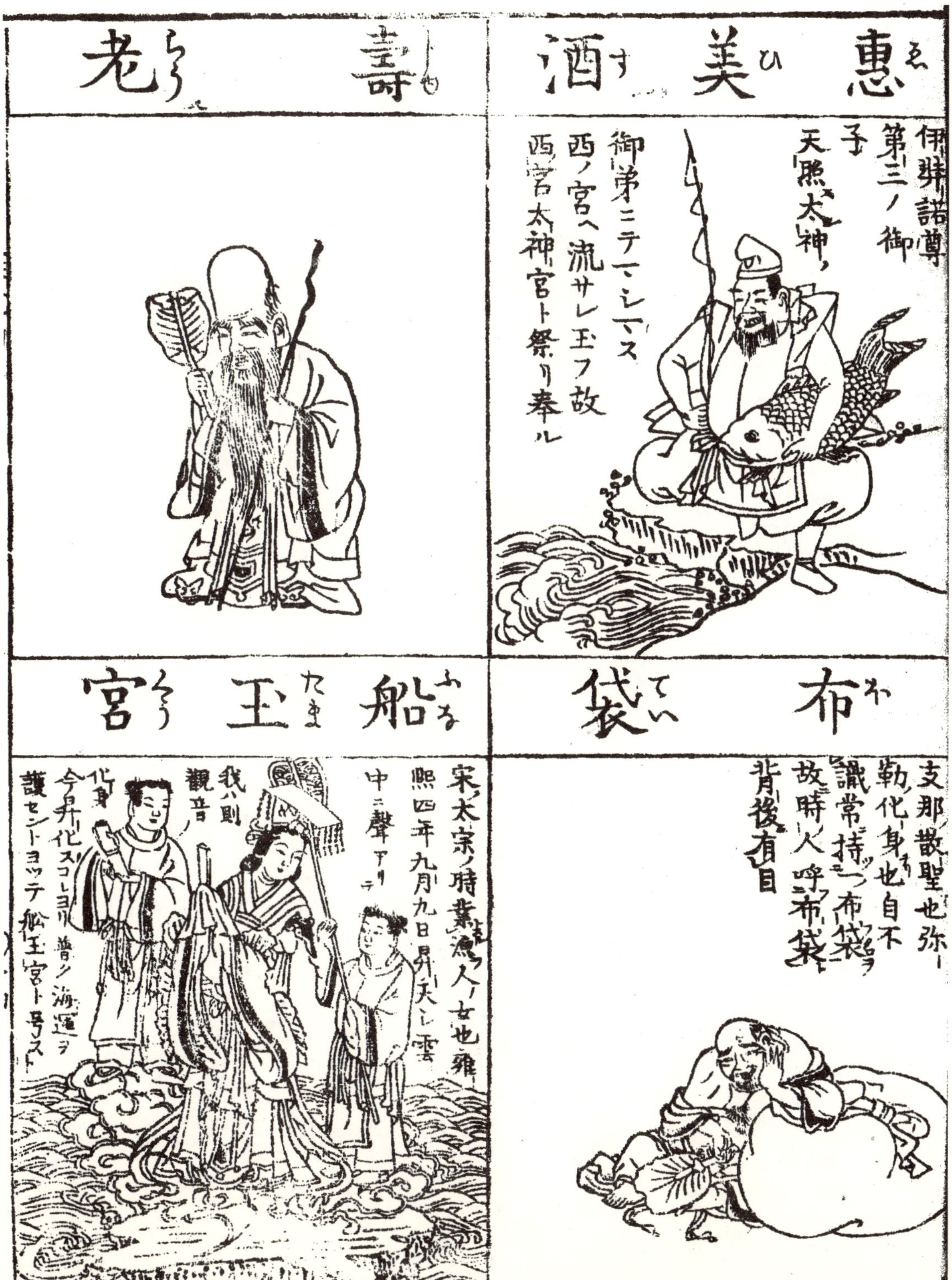

594. Funadama Kyū
The goddess of Sailors

592. Ho Tei
God of Good Fortune

597. Makatsu, Kekatsu
Rahu and Ketu

595. Shōjō
Hanumān

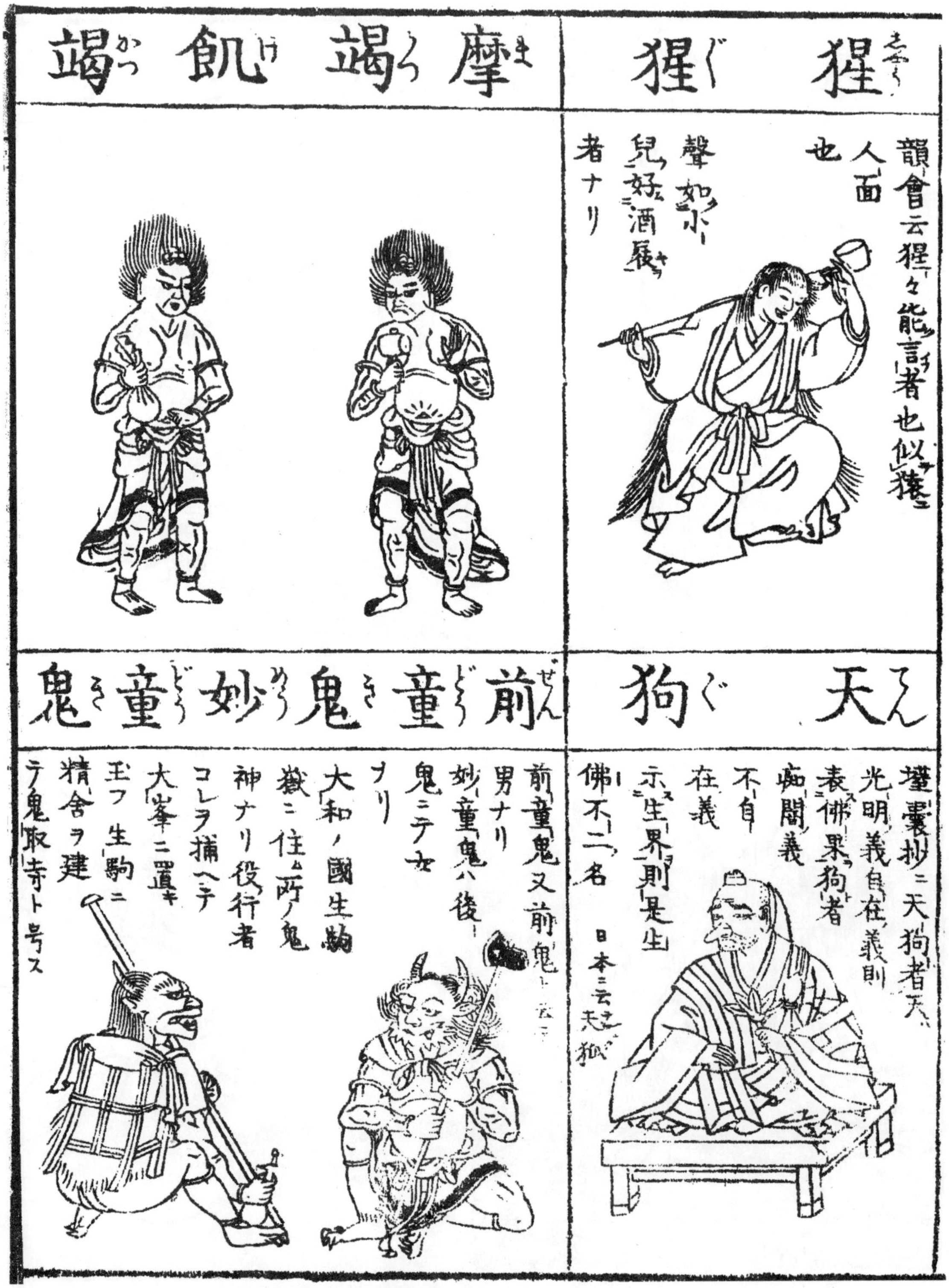

598. Zendōki, Myodōki
A pair of male & female goblins

596. Tengu
Long-nosed being

601. Okusen Sennin
Ascetic Okusen

599. Ten-nin
Celestial being

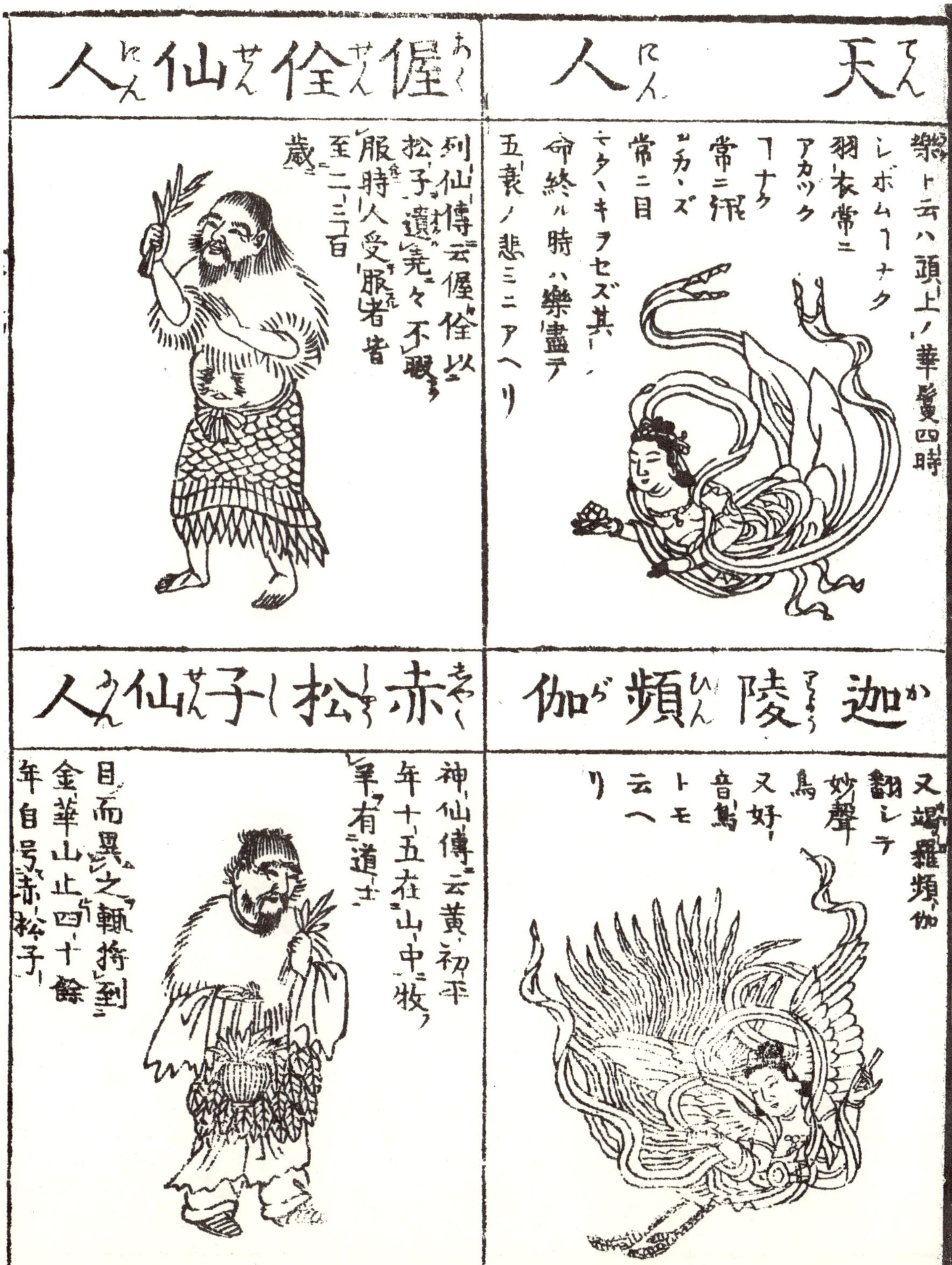

602. Shakushōshi Sennin
Ascetic Sekimatsu (Red -pine)

600. Karyūbinga
Kalaviṅka

605. Seiōbo
Queen Mother of the West

603. Fuchō sennin
Ascetic Fucho

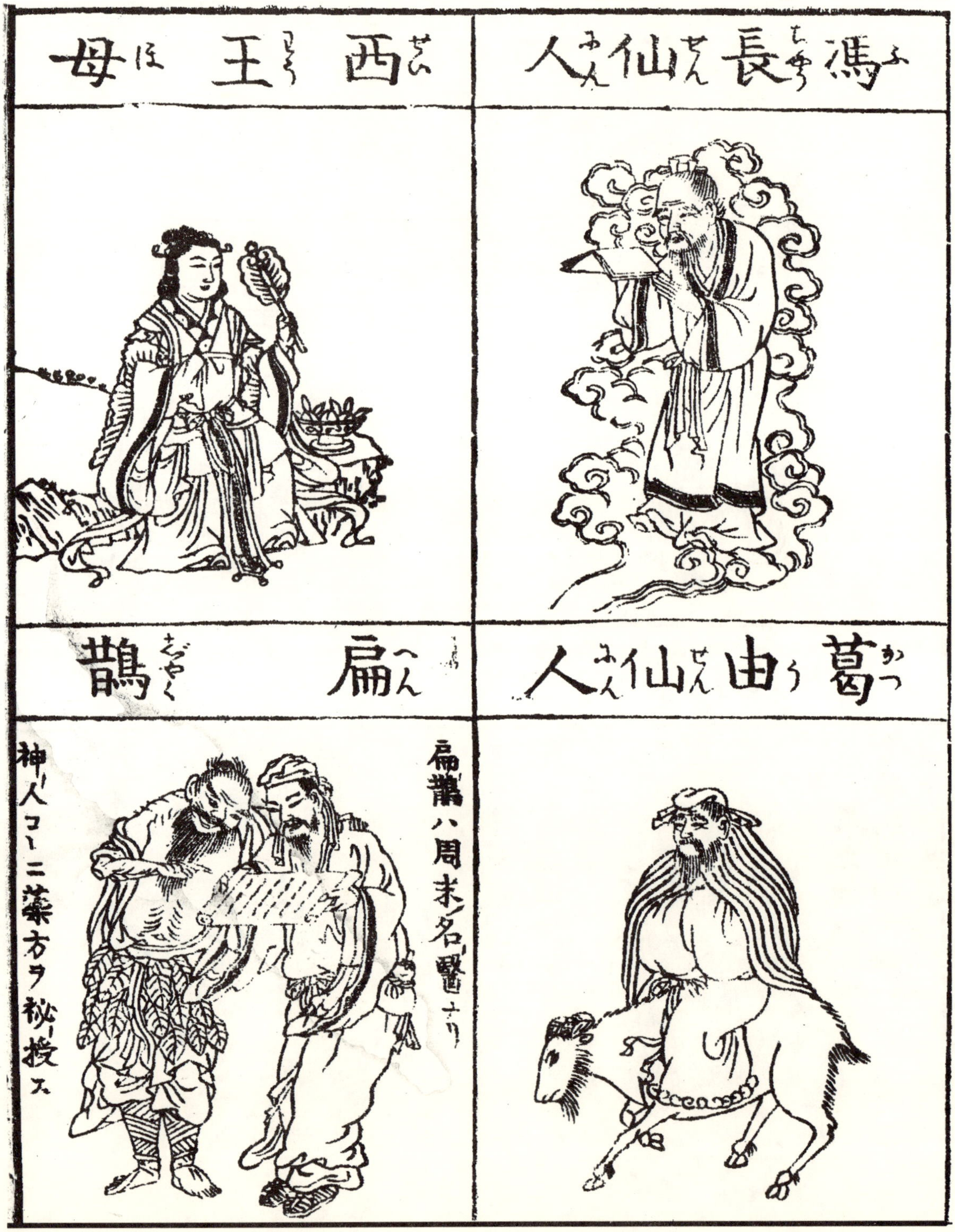

606. Henjaku
The Chinese Healer paired withJivaka

604. Katsuyu Sennin
Ascetic with Cap of Grass-cloth

§ 46. Jūroku Rakan
The Sixteen Arhats (607-622)

608. Kanakabassa Sonja, 2nd
Kanakavatsa

607. Batsurataja Sonja, 1st
Pindola Bharadrāja

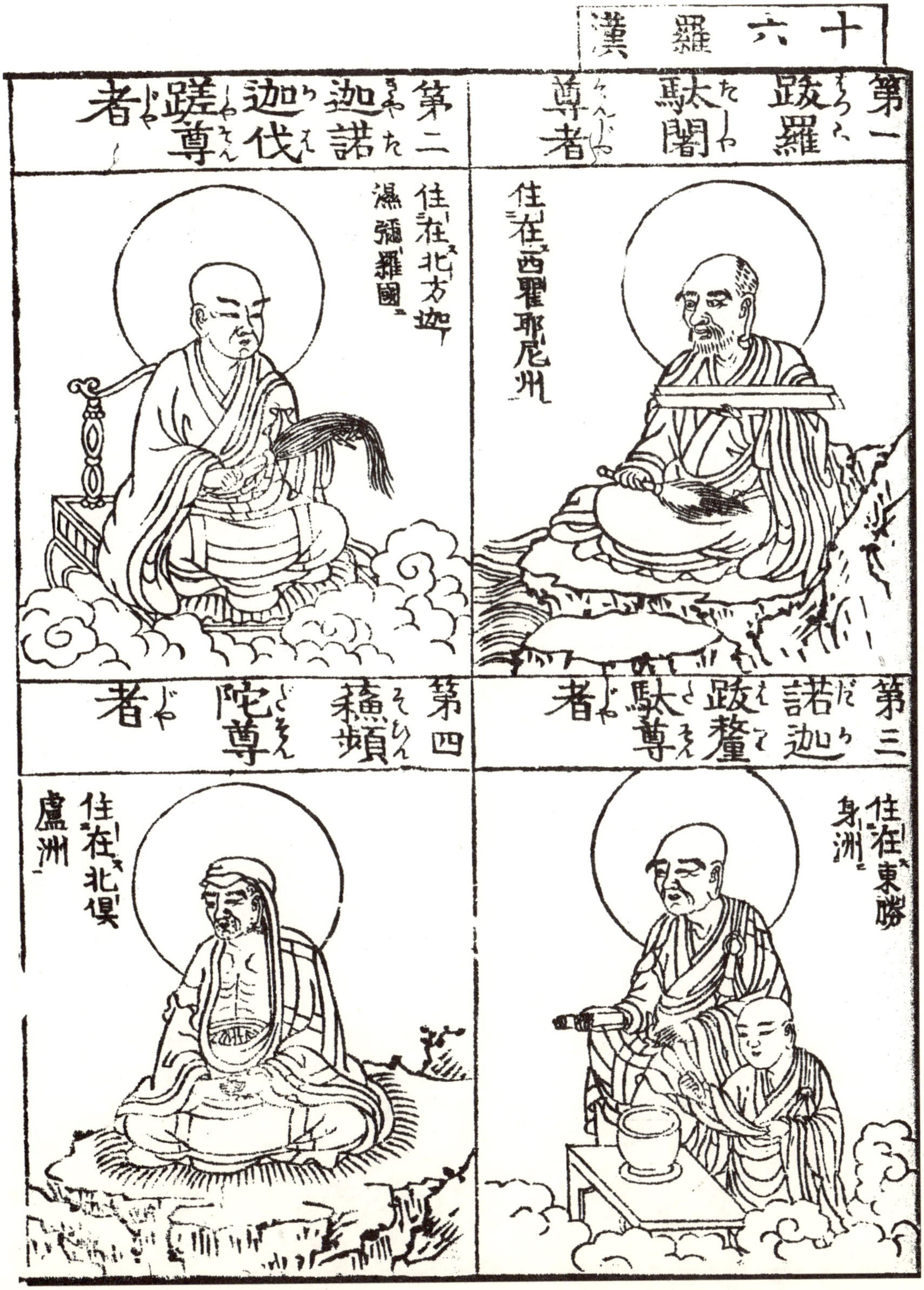

610. Sobinda Sonja, 4th
Subinda

609. Nakabarito Sonja, 3rd
Kanaka Bharadrāja

612. Badara Sonja, 6th
Bhadra

611. Nakora Sonja, 5th
Nakula

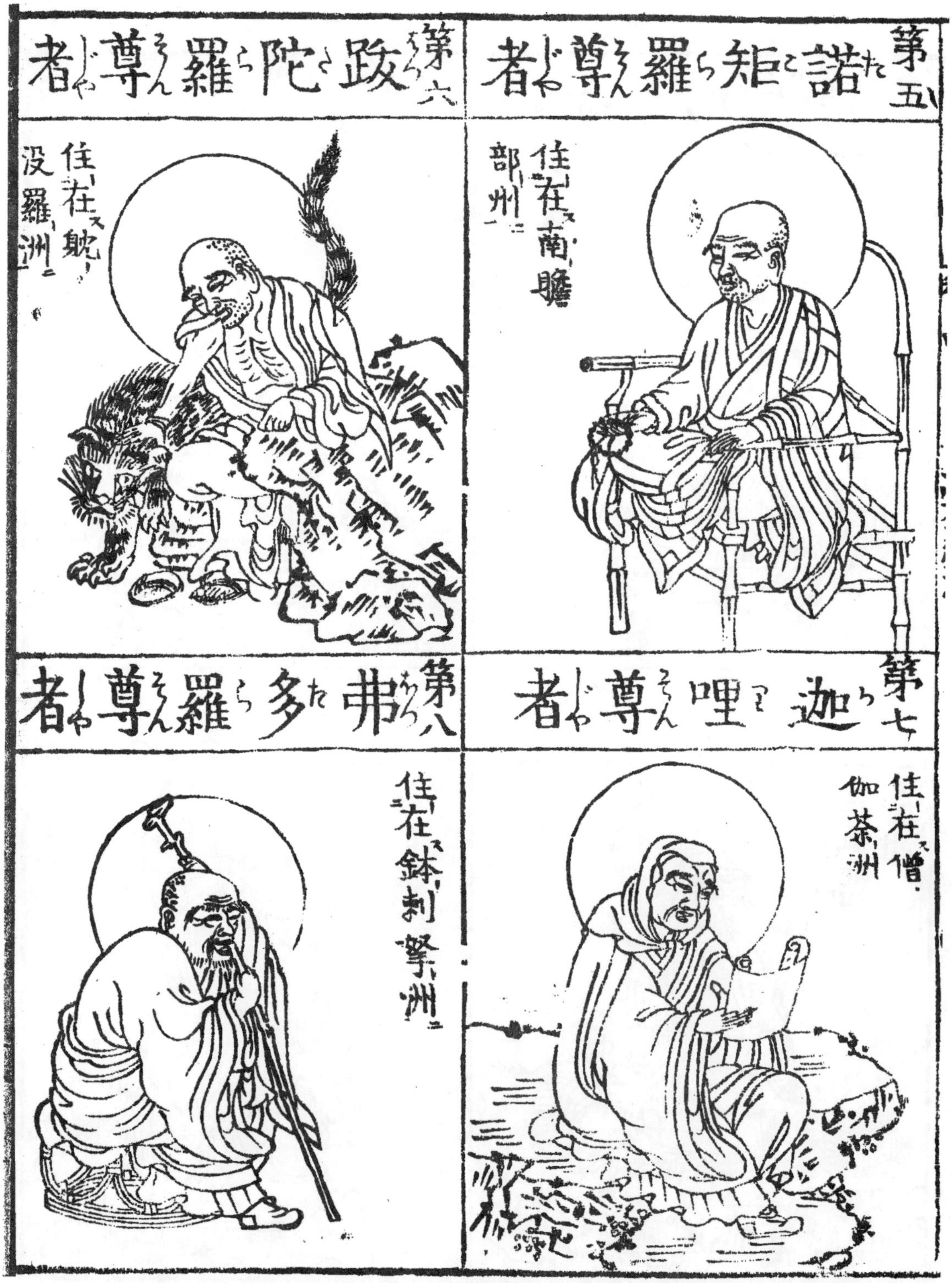

614. Butsutara Sonja, 8th
Putra

613. Kari Sonja, 7th
Kālikā

616. Handaka Sonja, 10th
Panthaka

615. Juhakuka Sonja, 9th
Jīvaka

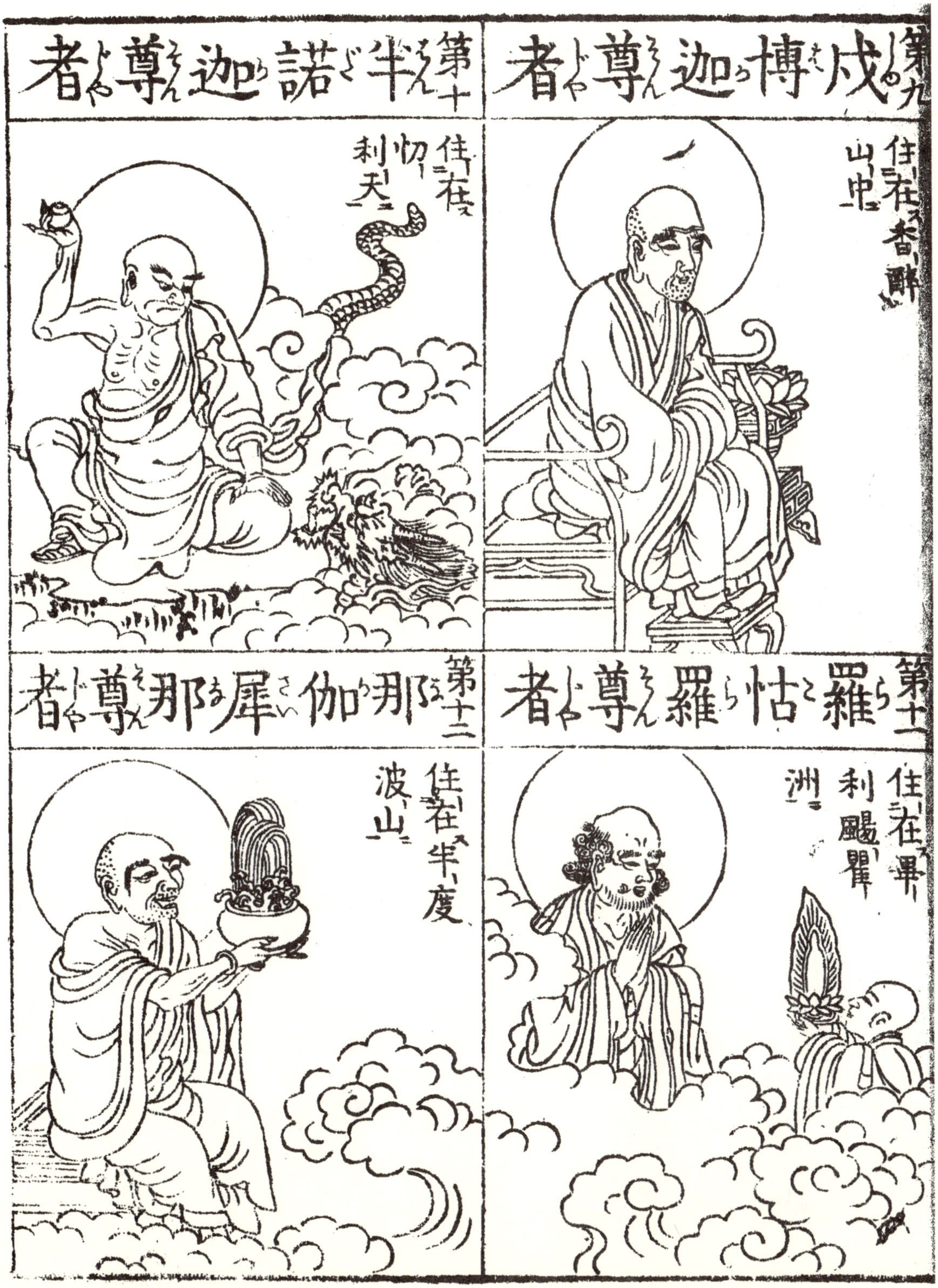

618. Nakasaina Sonja, 12th
Nāgasena

617. Ragora Sonja, 11th
Rāhula

620. Banabashi Sonja, 14th
Vanavāsin

619. Inkada Sonja, 13th
Iṅgada

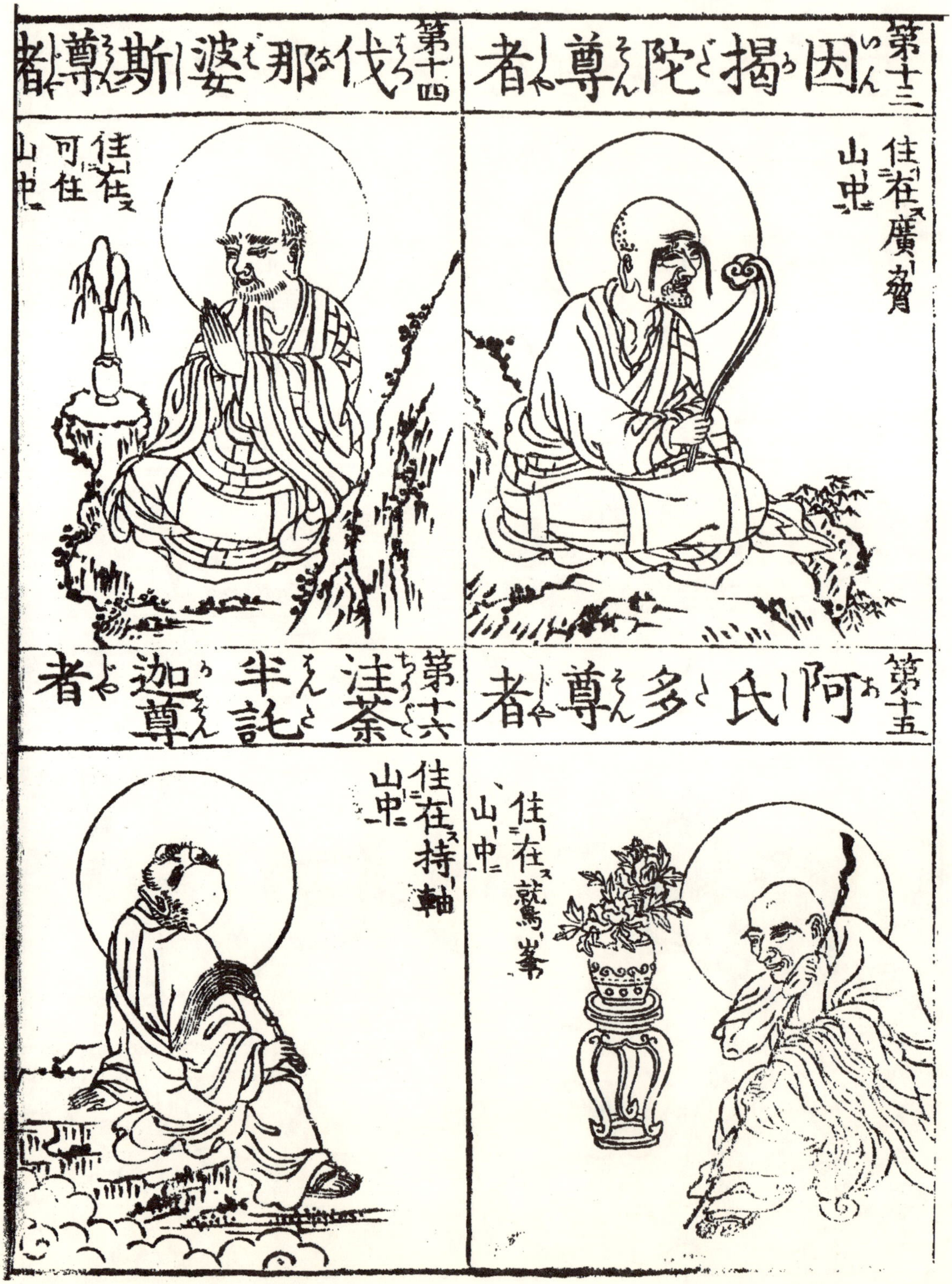

622. Chūda-hantoka Sonja, 16th
Cūḍapanthaka

621. Ashita Sonja, 15th
Ajita

§ 47. Jū Daideshi
The Ten Great Disciples (623-634)

625. Daikashō, 3rd
Mahākāśyapa

623. Sharihotsu, 1st
Śāriputra

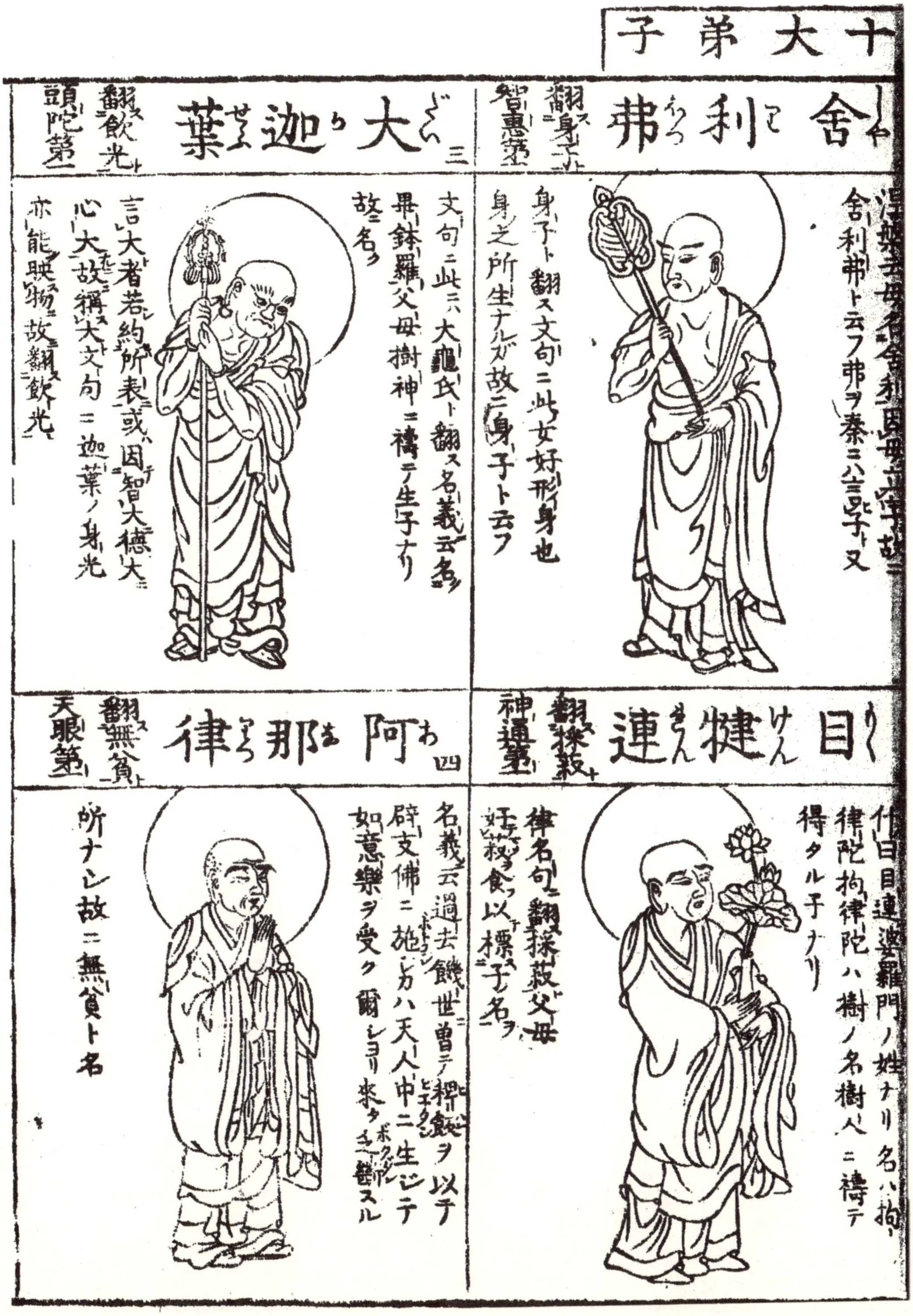

626. Anaritsu, 4th
Aniruddha

624. Mokkenren, 2nd
Maudgalyāyana

629. Kasenen, 7th
Kātyāyana

627. Shubodai, 5th
Subhūti

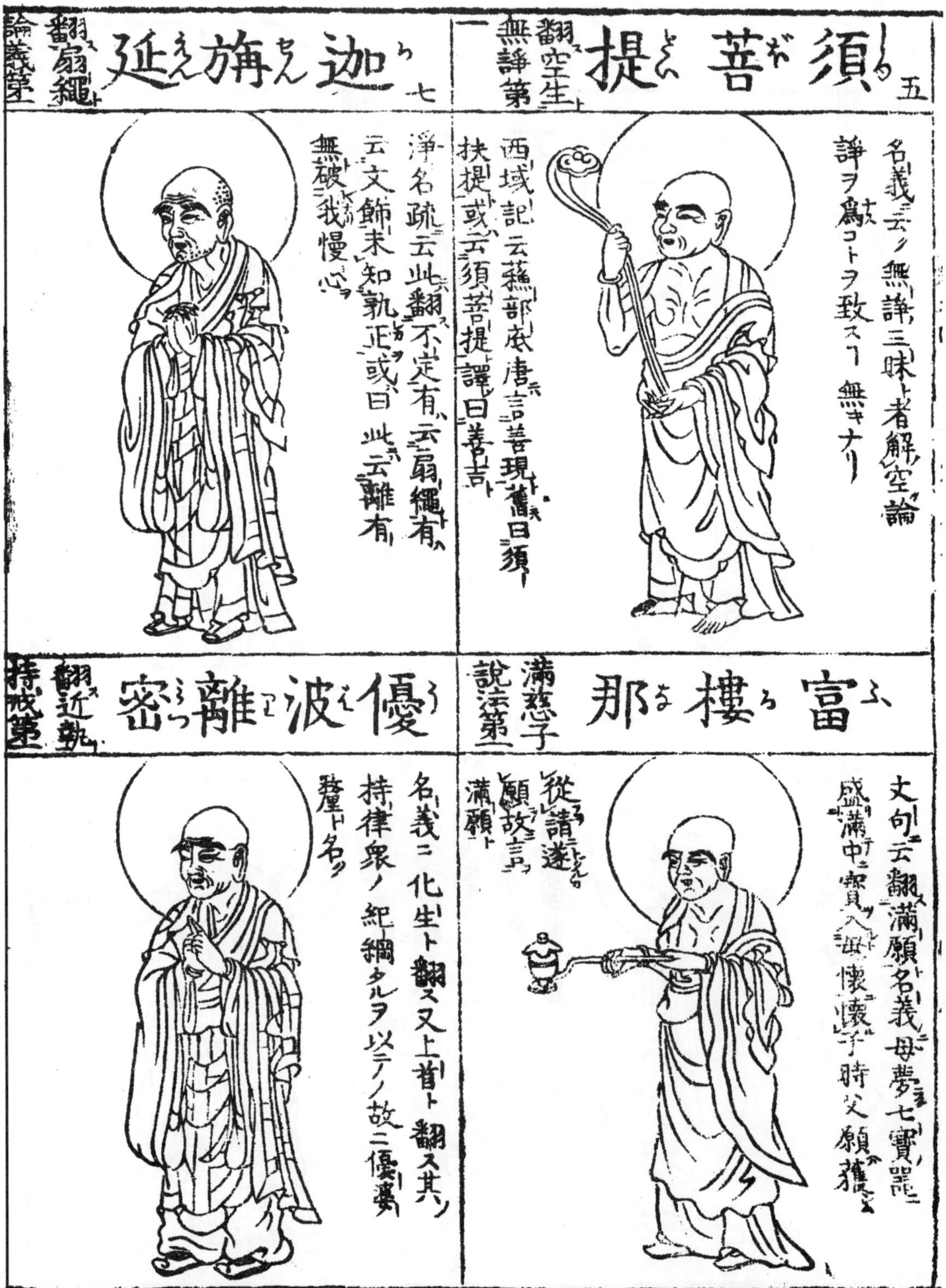

630. Upari, 8th
Upāli

628. Furuna, 6th
Pūrṇa

633. Yuima Doji
Vimalakīrti

631. Ragora, 9th
Rāhula

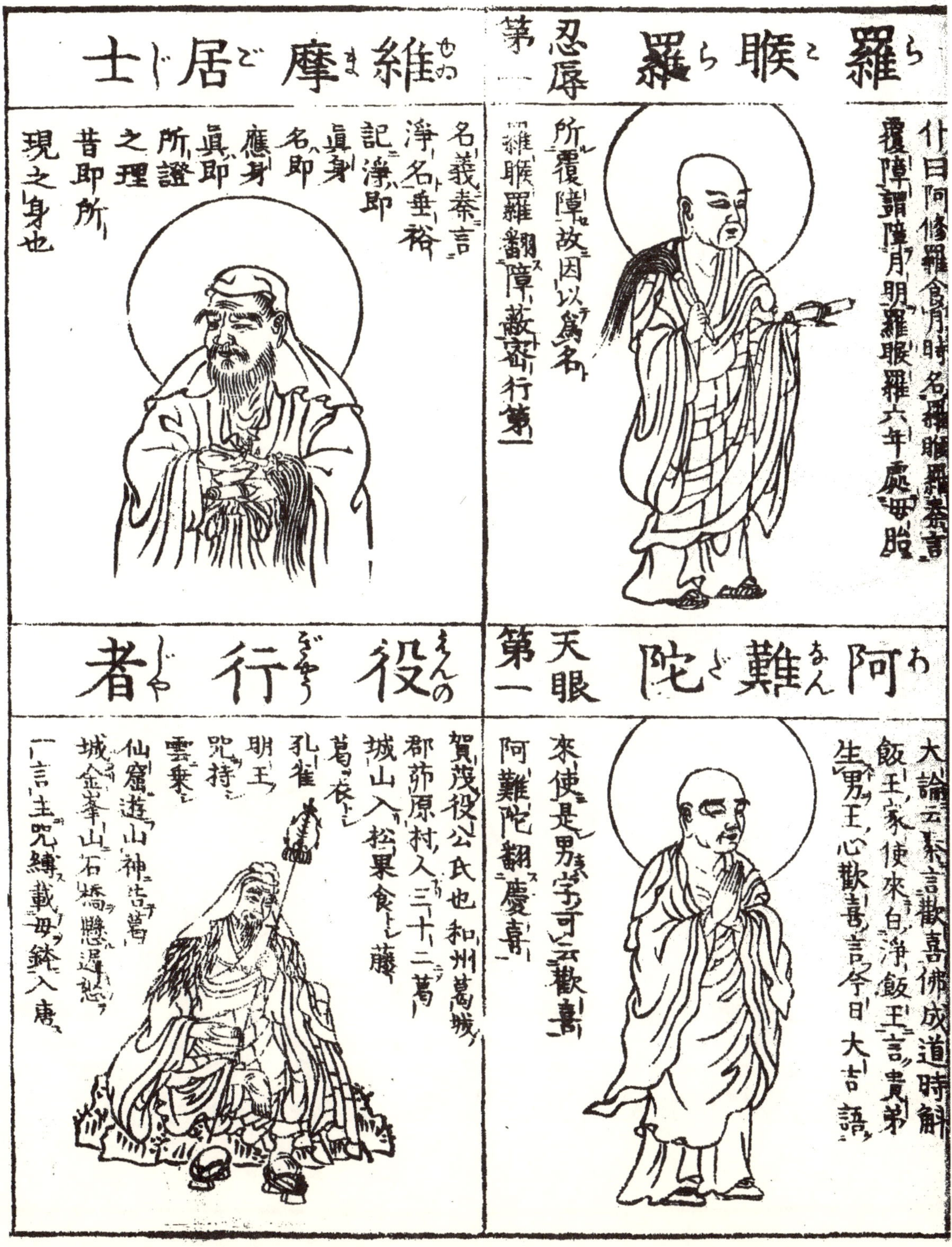

634. Enno Gyoja
Ācārya Enno Ozuno

632. Ananda, 10th
Ānanda

§ 48. Shotoku Taishi
Prince Shotoku

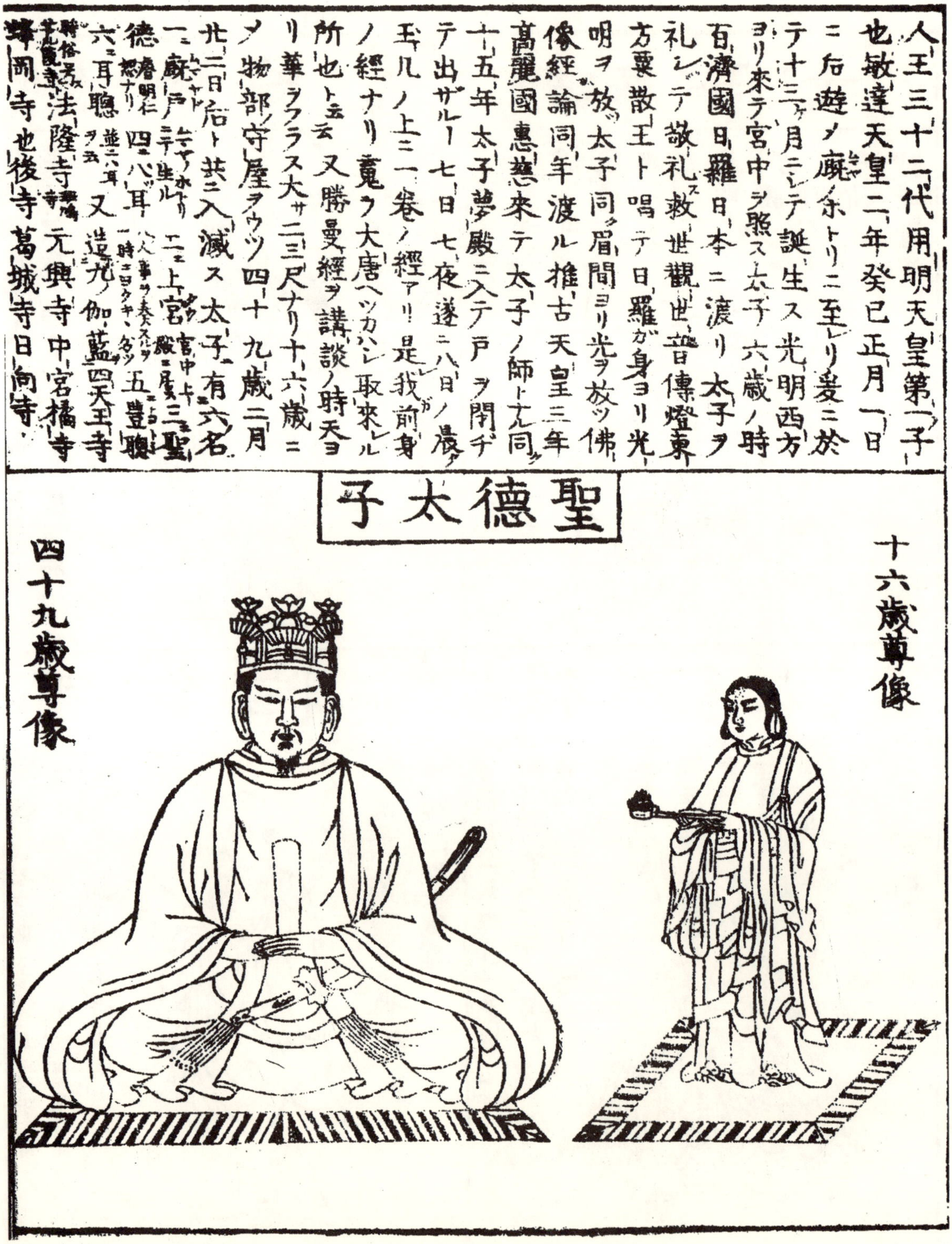

635. Jūroku Sonzō & Yonjūku Sonzō
Shotoku Taishi, at the age of six & 49 Years

增補諸宗

佛像圖彙

伍

5

Fascicle - V

The tittle of a book containing hymns in praise of Deities for young boys and girls, used during the Edō period.

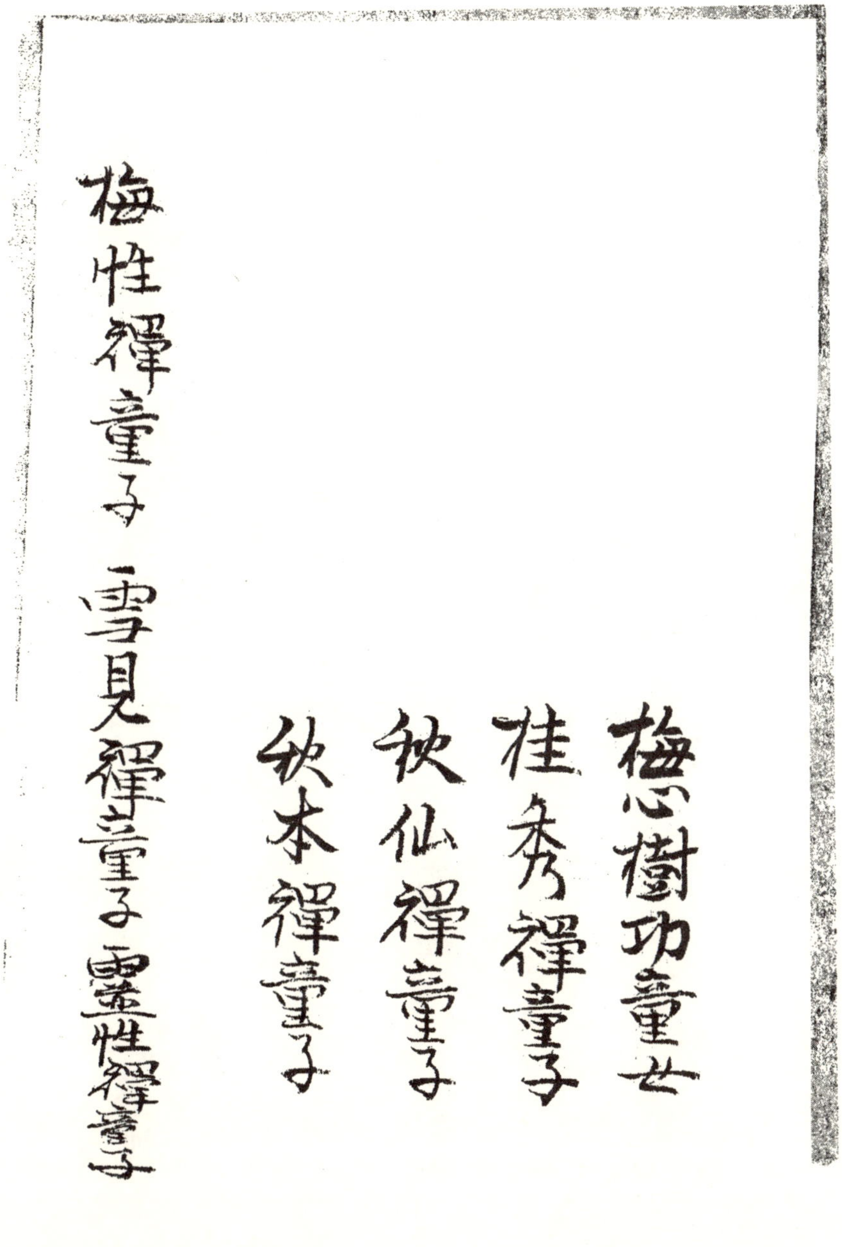
梅心樹功童女
桂秀禪童子
秋仙禪童子
秋本禪童子
梅性禪童子　雪見禪童子　靈性禪童子

§ 49. The Teachers of Various Sects (636-729)
Hosso shu
The Hosso Sect (636-639)

638. Shinrakoku Chihō Hōshi
Religious Teacher Chihō of Shiragi

636. Tenjikugohō Bosatsu
Dharmapāla Bodhisattva of India

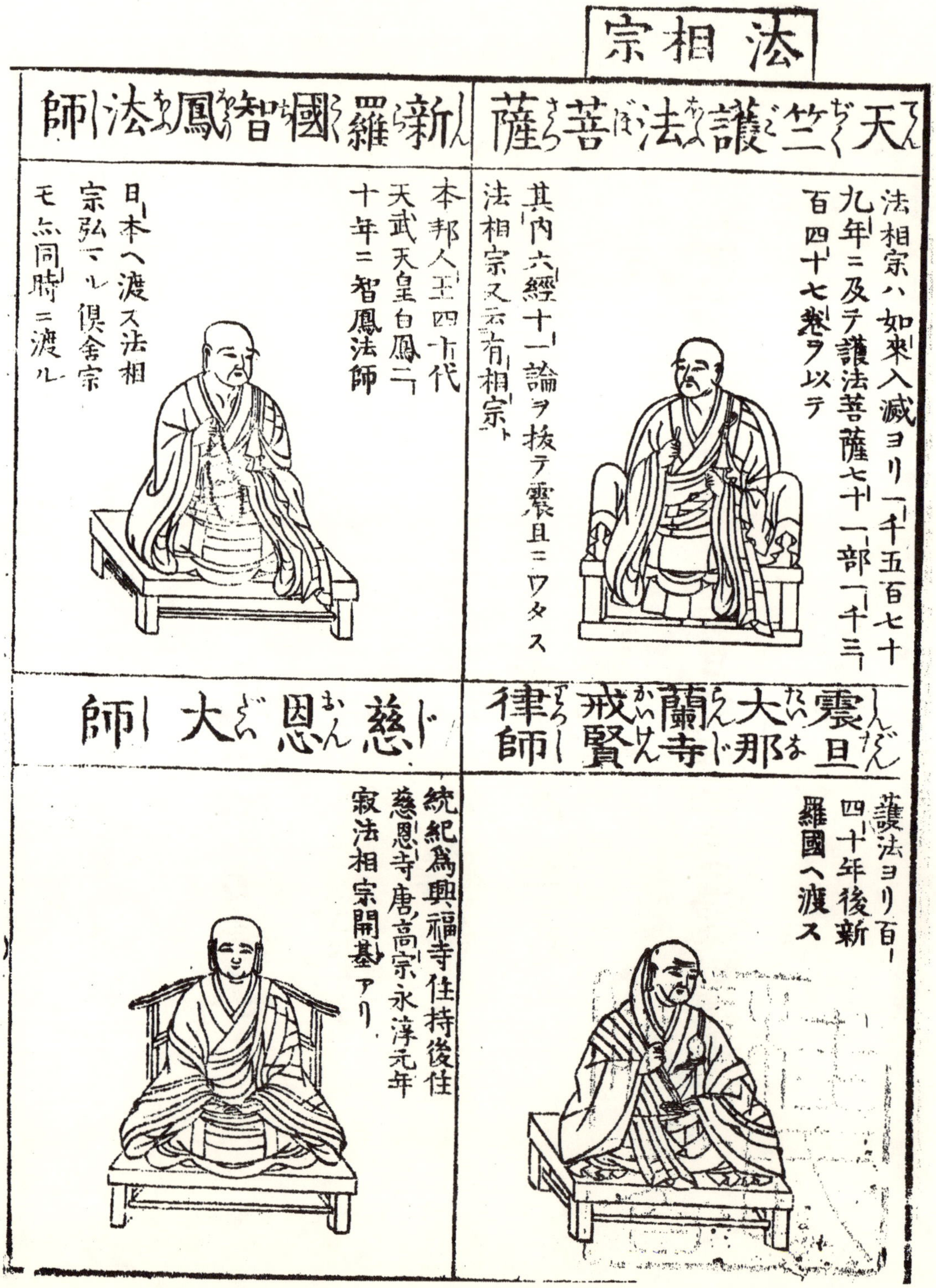

639. Jion Daishi
Grand Master Gi-en Kuei-chi Chinese

637. Shintan Dainaranji Kai kenritsushi
Chinese Karmakārka of Nālandā

Sanron shū
The Sanron Sect (640-643)

642. Shintan Kakuzōji Dōyū Oshō
Dōyū of Kakuzōji, Chinese High Priest

640. Tenjiku Seiben Bosatsu
Bhāvaviveka Bodhisattva of India

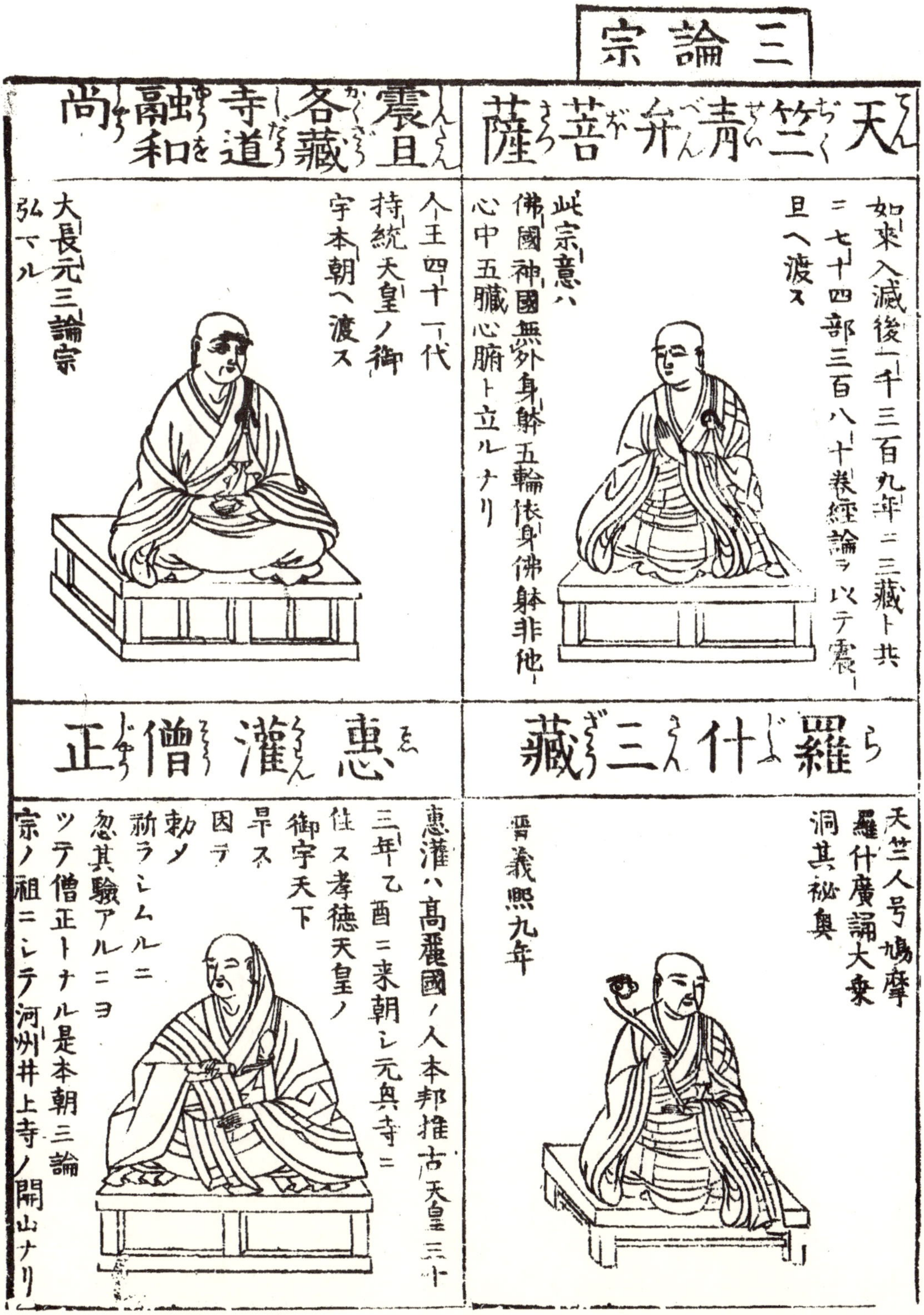

643. Ekan Sōjō
Korean Priest Ekan

641. Rajū Sanzō
Kumārajīva, the High Priest

Jojitsu shū
The Jojitsu Sect (646-647)

646. Tenjiku Batsuma Sanzō
Indian Bonze, Hariharman

Kusha shū
The Kuśa Sect (644-645)

644. Seshin Bosatsu
Vasubandhu Bodhisattva

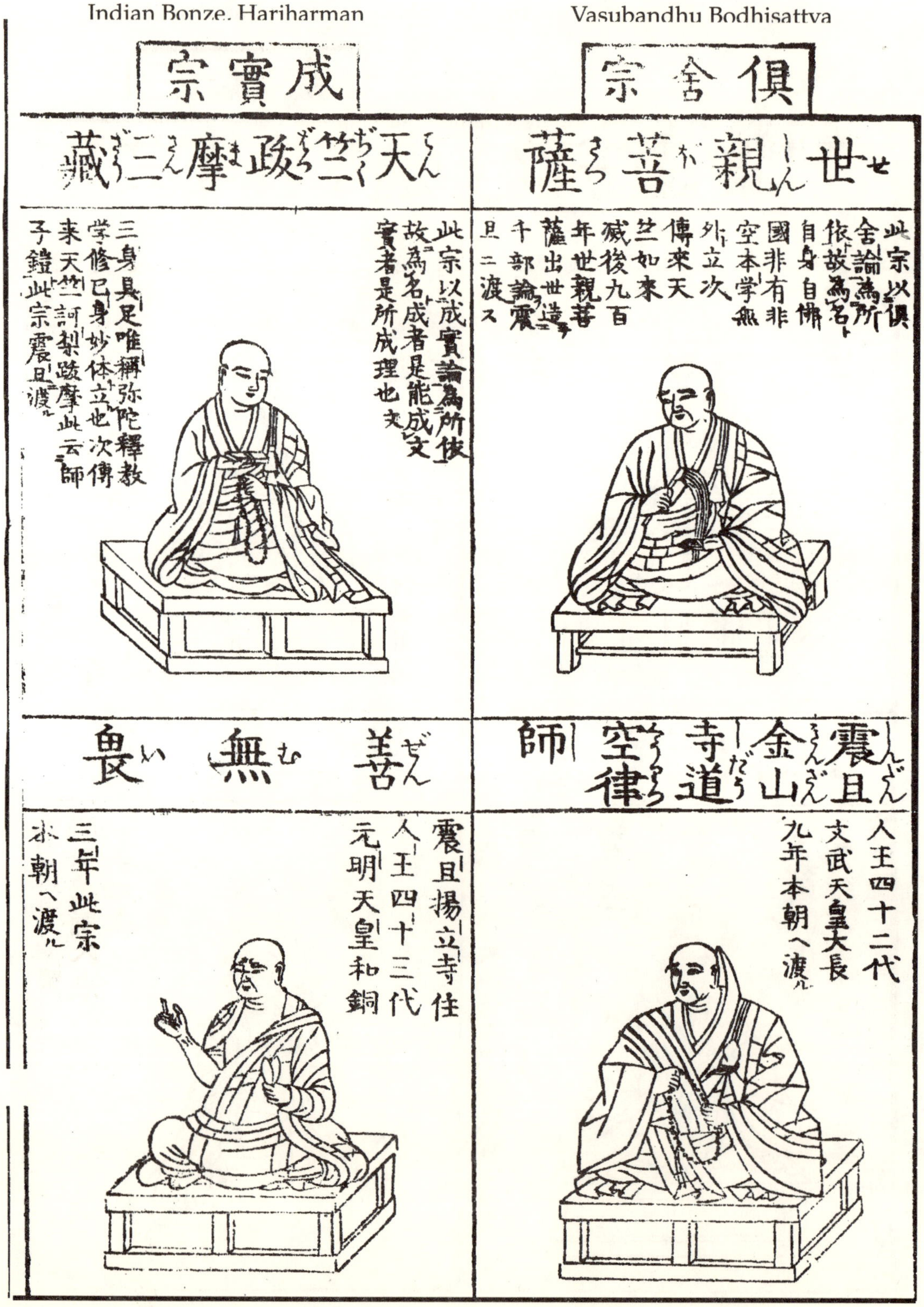

647. Zenmui
Śubhākarasiṁha

645. Shintan konzanji Dōkūritsūshi
The Chinese bonze of Konzanji temple

Ritsu shū
The Ritsu Sect (648-651)

650. Saidaiji Eizon
Priest Eizon of Saidaiji Temple

648. Tenjiku Kikuta Sanzō
Indian High Priest Dharmagupta

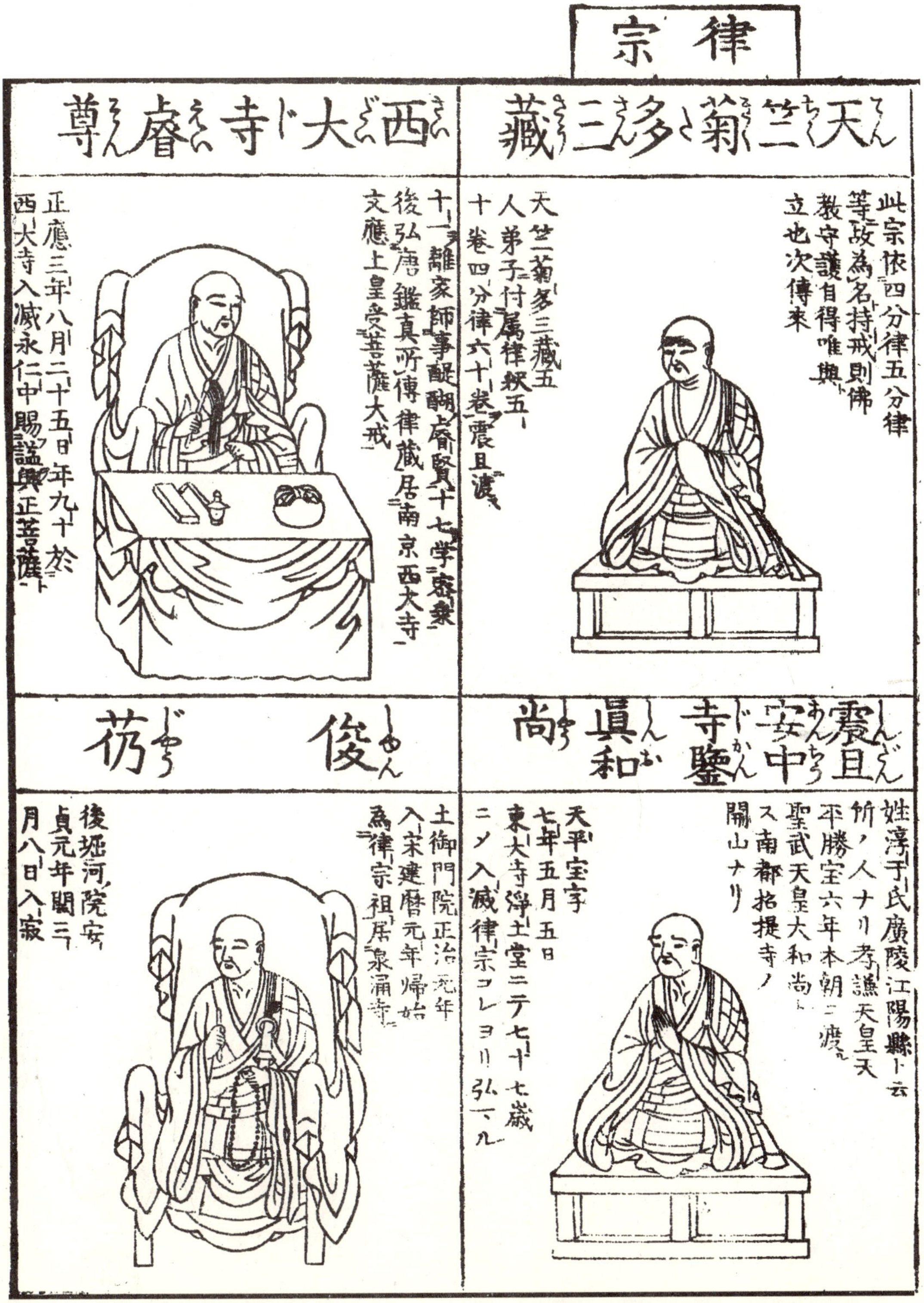

651. Shunjū
Bonze of Sennyūji temple

649. Shintan Anchūji Ganjin wāshō
Chinese bonze Ganjin of Anchūji temple

Tendai shū
The Tendai Sect (654-663)

654. Shintan Tendaisan Nangaku Daishi
Chinese Bonze Huisi of Nān-yuī

Kegon shū
The Avataṁsaka Sect (652-653)

652. Shintan Ryūkōji Kegon Oshō
Chinese priest of Ryū kōji

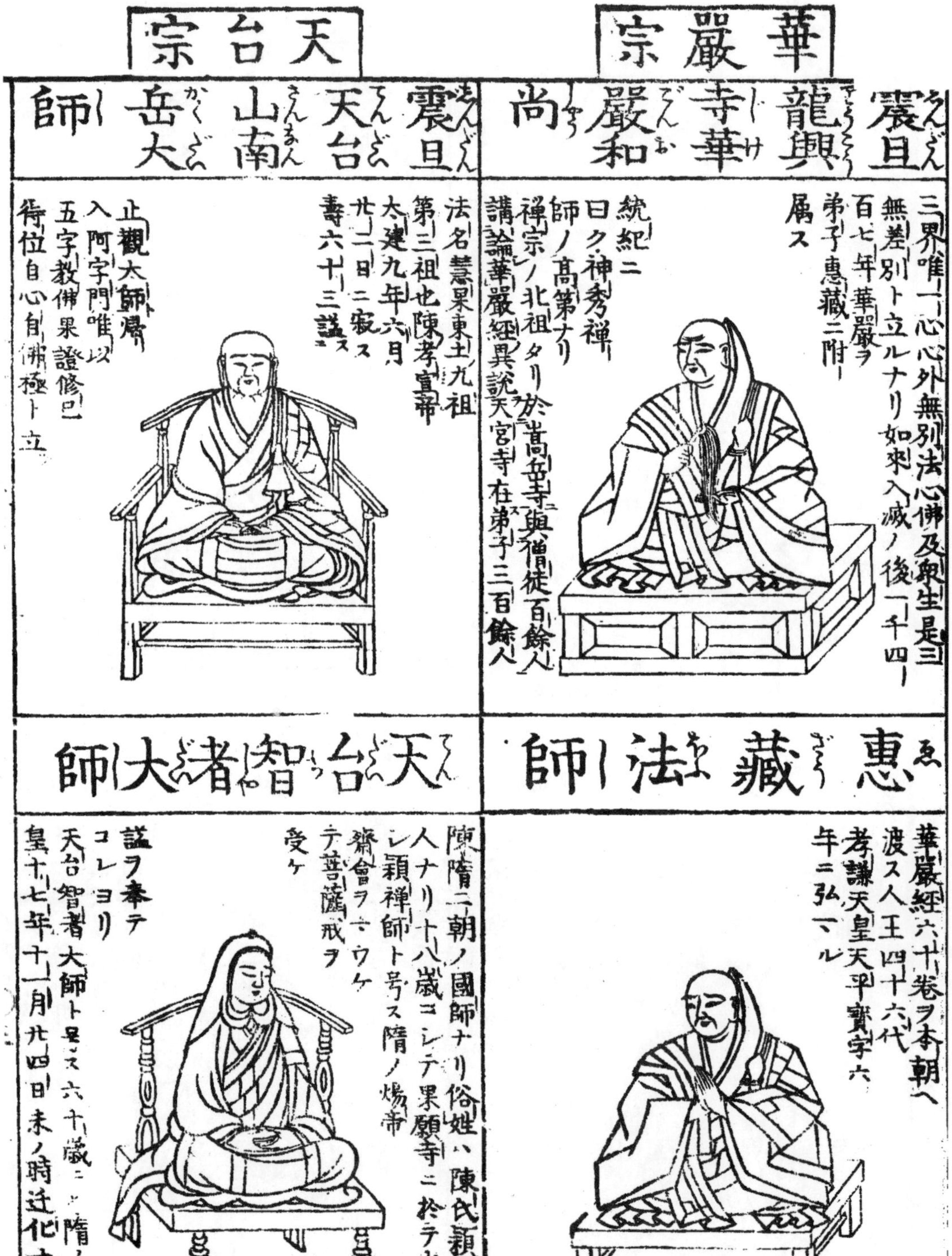

655. Tendai Chisha Daishi
Chihi chên of Tendai Sect

653. Ezō Hōshi
Bonze Dōsen of China

658. Dengyō Daishi
The Grand Master Saichō

656. Shōan Sonja
Honorable Monk Guān Ding

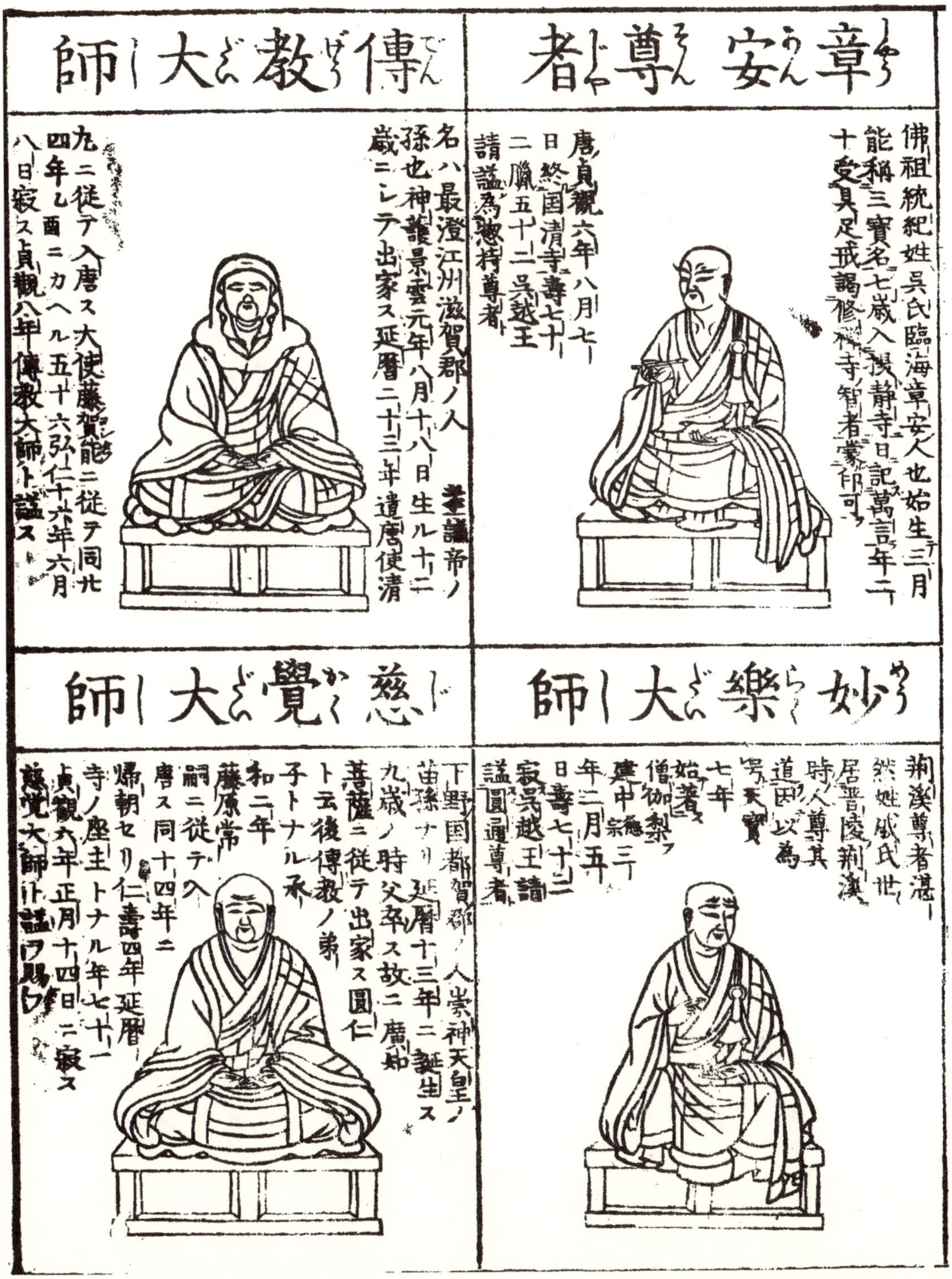

659. Jikaku Daishi
The Grand Master Ennin

657. Myoraku Daishi
The Grand Master Tannen (Zhanran)

662. Eshin Sozu
Assistant High priest Eshin

660. Ganzan Daishi
Penname of Monk Ryōgen

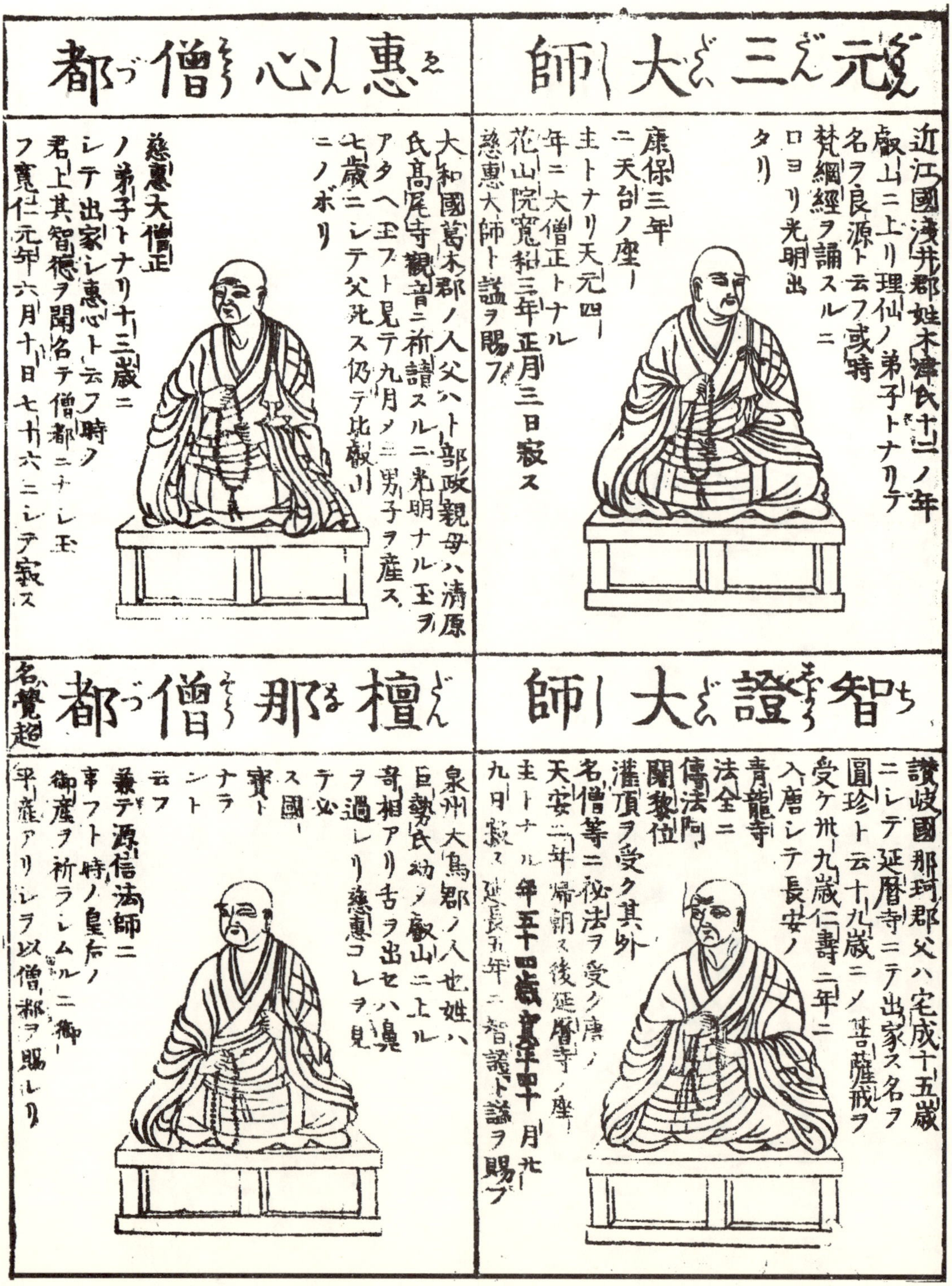

663. Danna Sozu
Monk Kakuun

661. Chishō Daishi
Posthumous name of priest Enchin

Shingon shū
The Shingon Sect (664-671)

666. Kongōchi Sanzō
Vajrabodhi, High Priest

664. Ryūmō Bosatsu
Nāgārjuna Bodhisattva

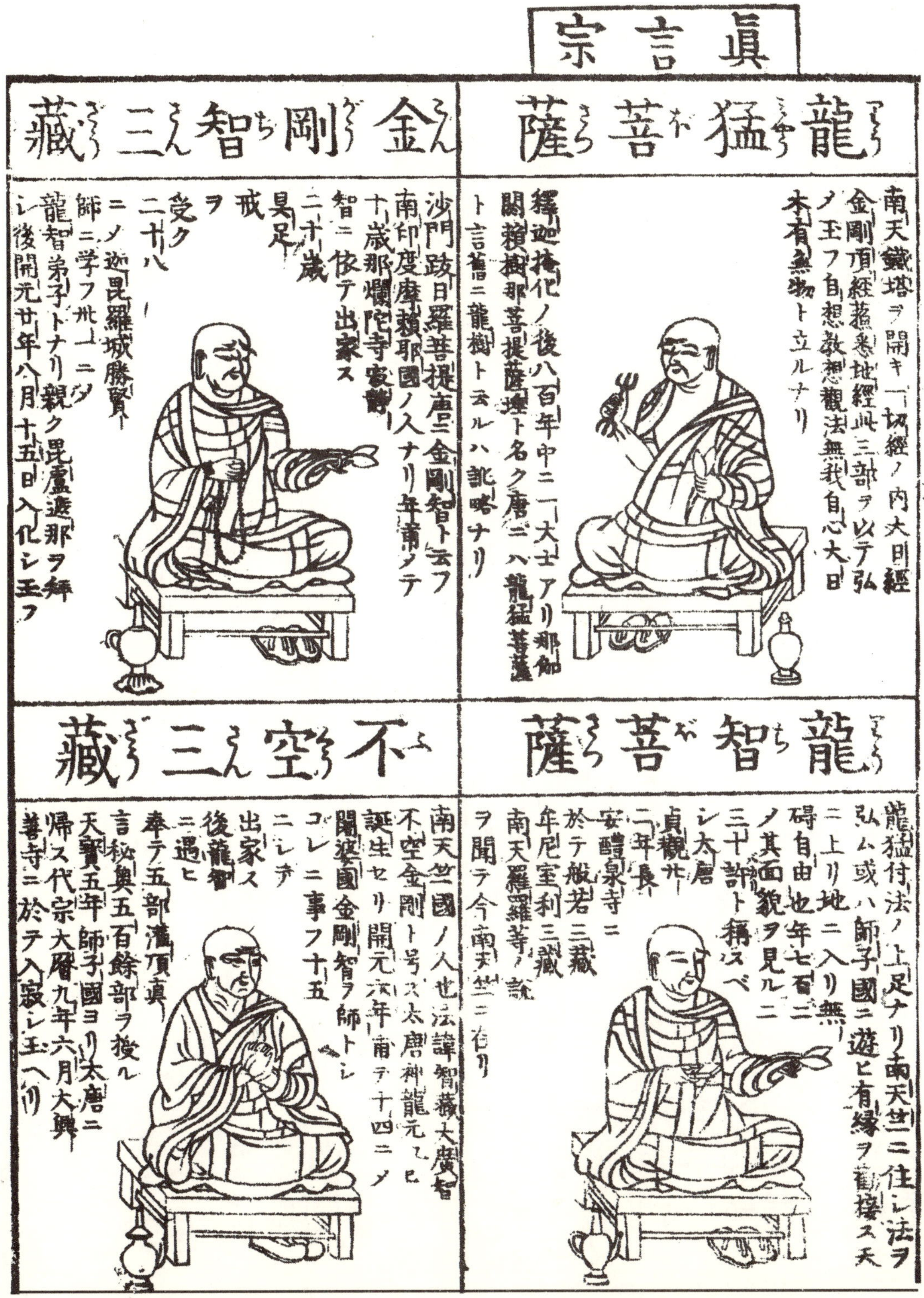

667. Fukū Sanzō
Amoghavajra, High Priest

665. Ryūchi Bosatsu
Nāgabodhi Bodhisattva

670. Keika Ajari
Hui-Guō Ācārya

668. Shazenmui Sanzō
Śubhākarasiṁha, High Priest

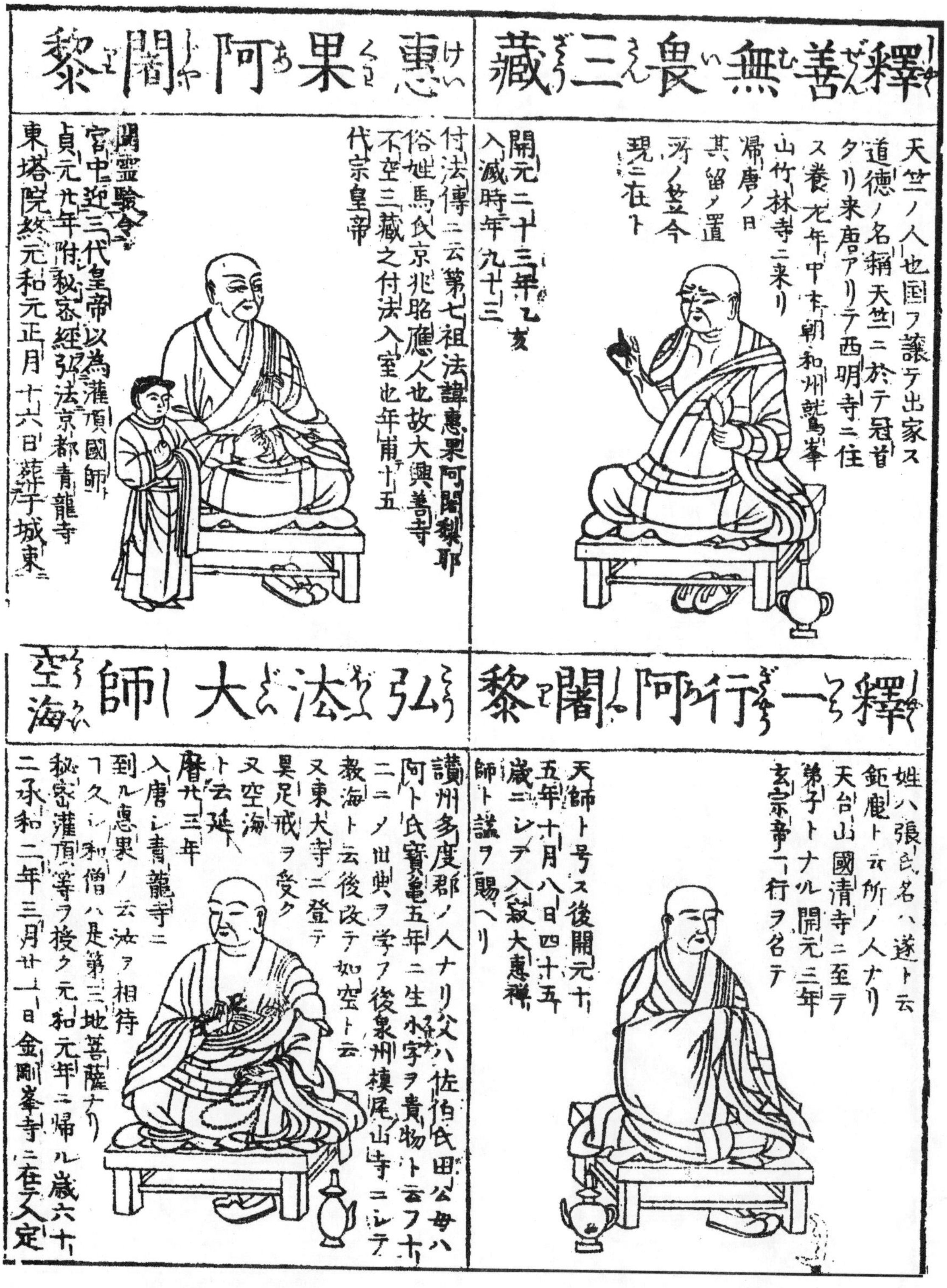

671. Kōbō Daishi
Grand Priest Kukai

669. Shaku Ichigyō Ajari
Yi-xing Ācārya

Zenshū Rokuso
The Six Patriarchs of Zen (672-677)

674. Sōsan Daishi Sonja
Grand Master Sosan

672. Tōdoshosō Bodaidaruma Sonja
Ayuṣmat Bodhidharma

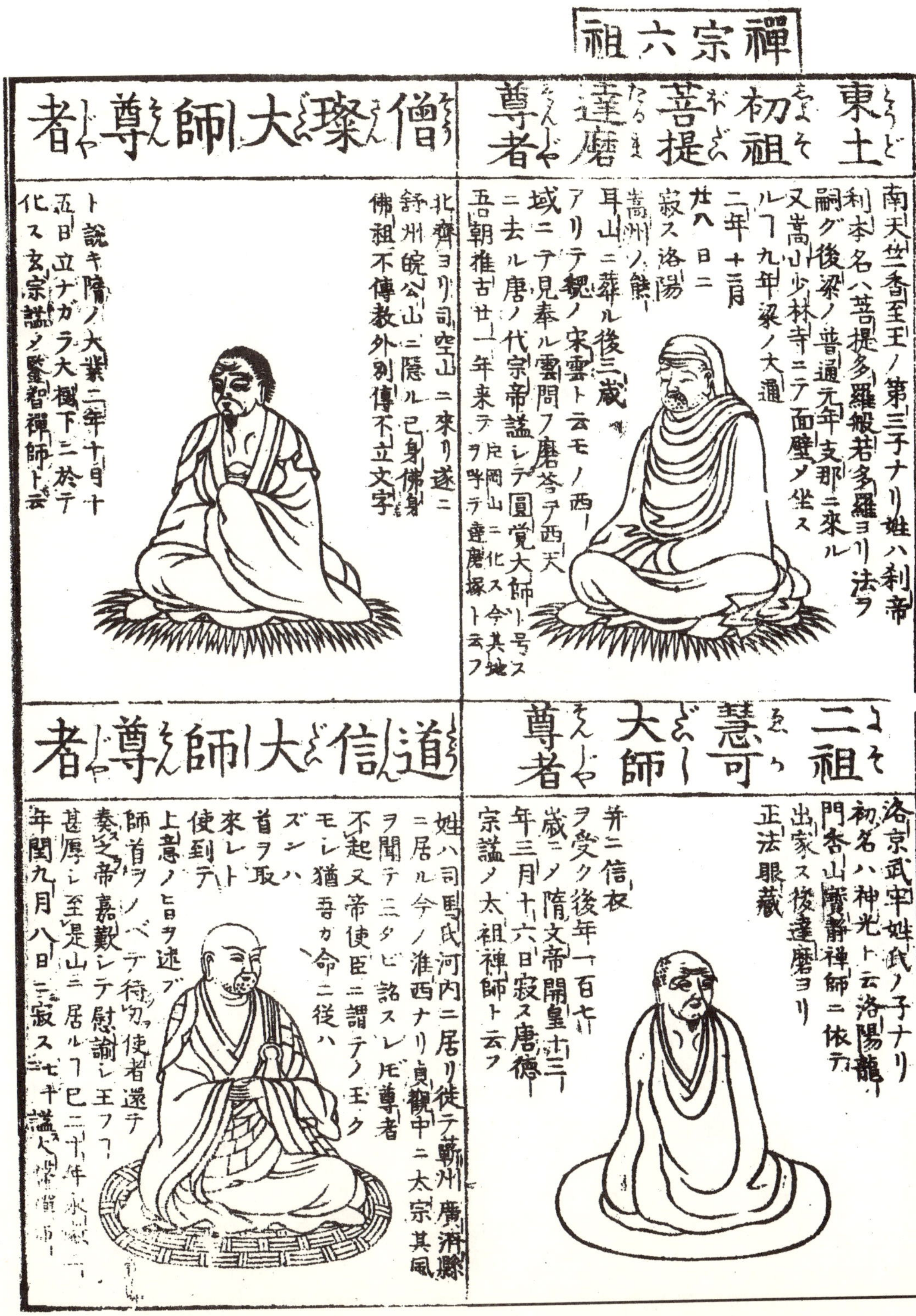

675. Dōjin Daishi Sonja
The Grand Master Dōjin

673. Niso Eka Daishi Sonja
Grand Master Hui-yuān

Jōdō shū Hasso
The Eight Pariarchs of Jōdō Sect (678-685) and Other Patriarchs (686-699)

678. Memyō Daishi

The Grand Master Aśvaghoṣa

676. Kōnin Daishi

The Grand Master Hung Jén

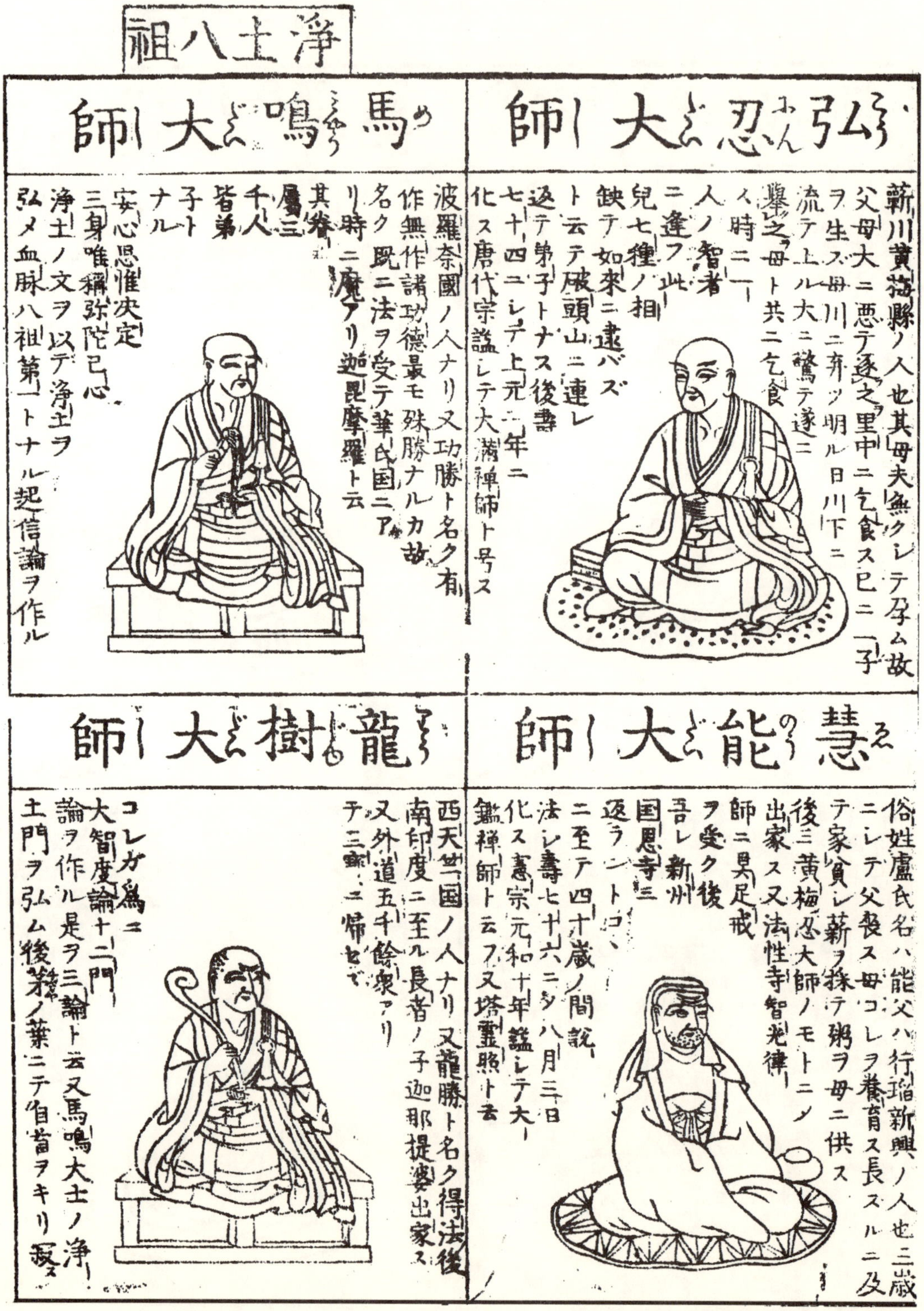

679. Ryūju Daishi

The Grand Master Nāgārjuna

677. Eno Daishi

The Grand Master Enō (China)

682. Donran Daishi
The Grand Master T'an-Luan

680. Tenjin Bosatsu
Vasubandhu Bodhisattva

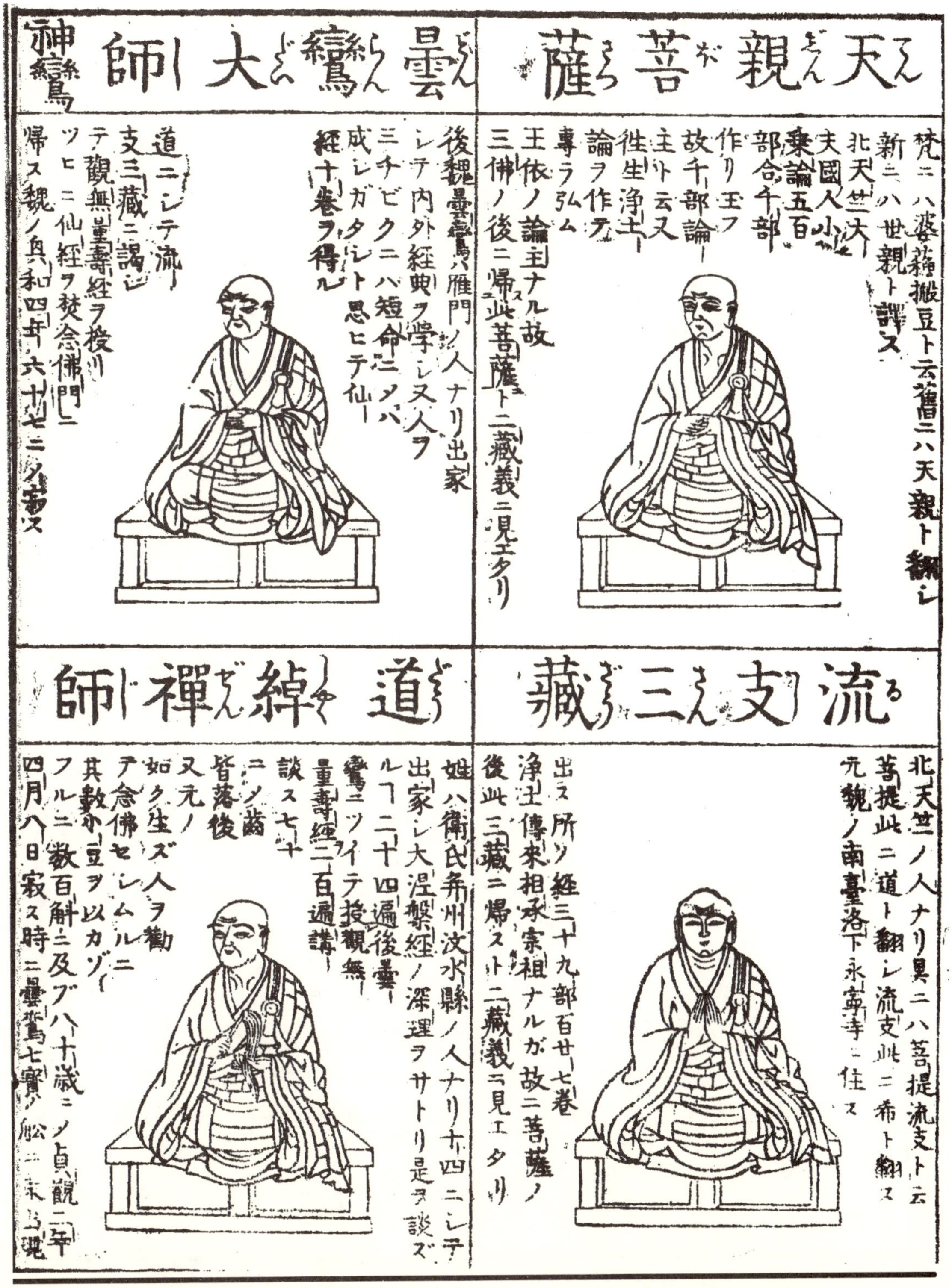

683. Dōshaku Zenshi
Tao-chō the Zen Master

681. Rushi Sanzō
Bodhiruci, High Priest

686. Shinran (Ikko shū)
Patriarch Shinran (Ikko sect)

684. Zendō Daishi
The Grand Master Shan-Tao

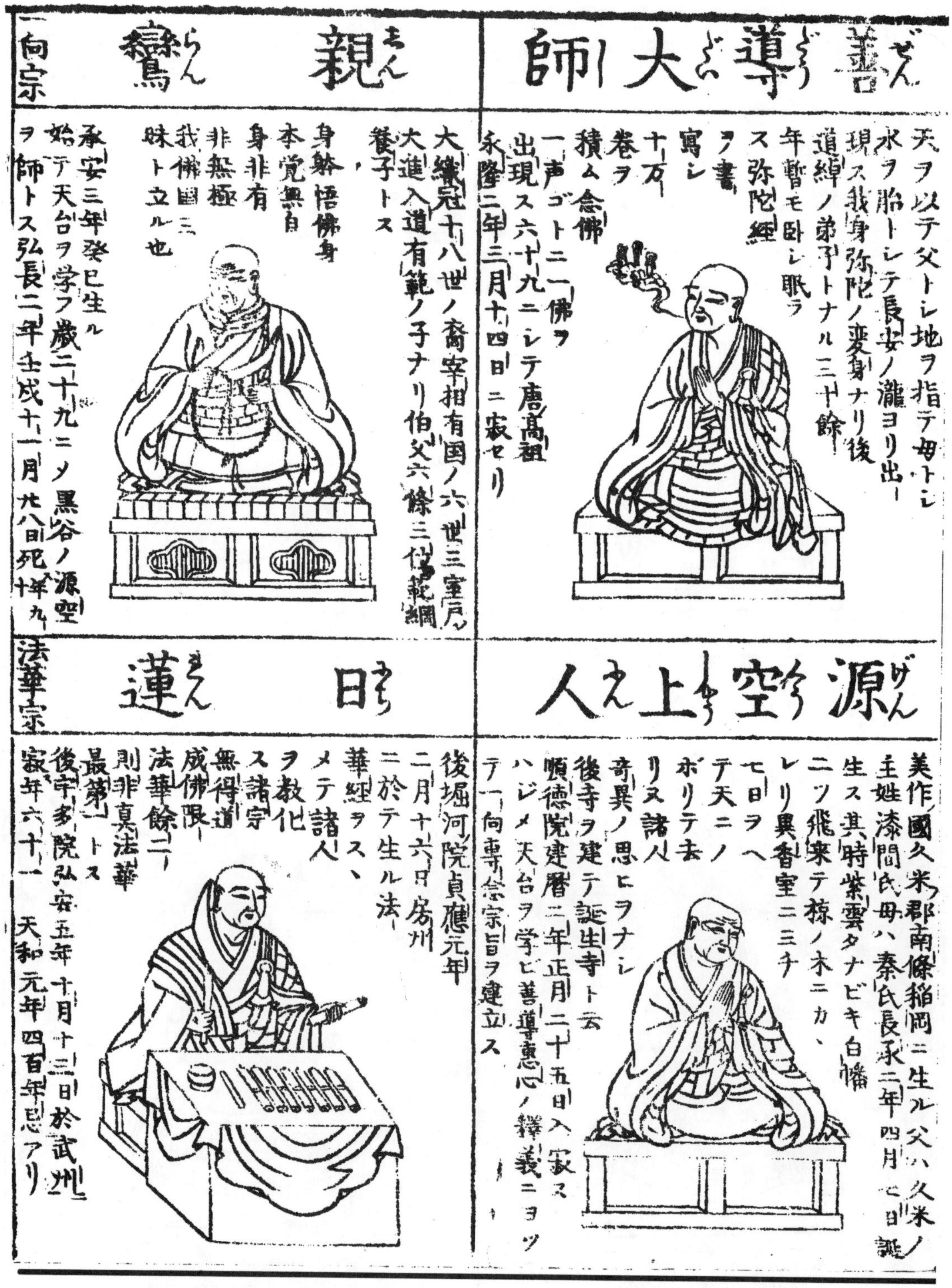

687. Nichiren (Hokke shū)
Patriarch Nichiren (Lotus sect)

685. Genkū Jōnin
The High Priest Genkū
(posthumous title of Hōnen)

692. Gyogi Daisōjō
Gyogi, the Great Priest

690. Baramon Sōjō
Great Brāhmaṇa Bodhisena

688. Kofukuji Gembō
Monk Gembo of Kofukuji temple

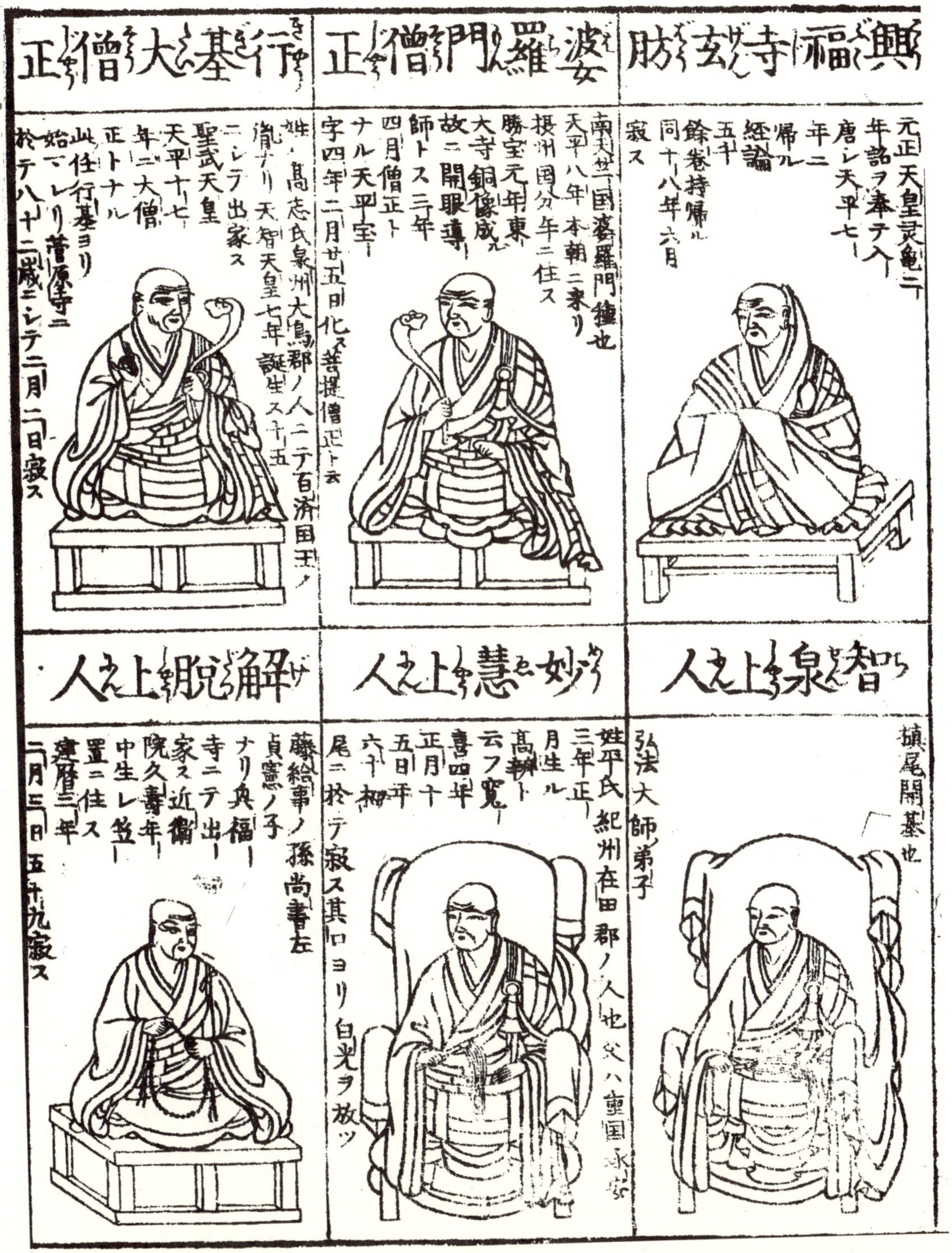

693. Gedatsu Jōnin
High priest Jōkei
(Hōsso sect)

691. Myō E Jōnin
High Priest Myōe
(Kegon sect)

689. Chisen Jōnin
High Priest Chisen
(disciple of Kobo Daishi)

698. Shōkū Jōnin
Priest Shōkū

696. Kōshō Bosatsu
Eizon Bodhisattva

694. Taichō
Priest Taicho

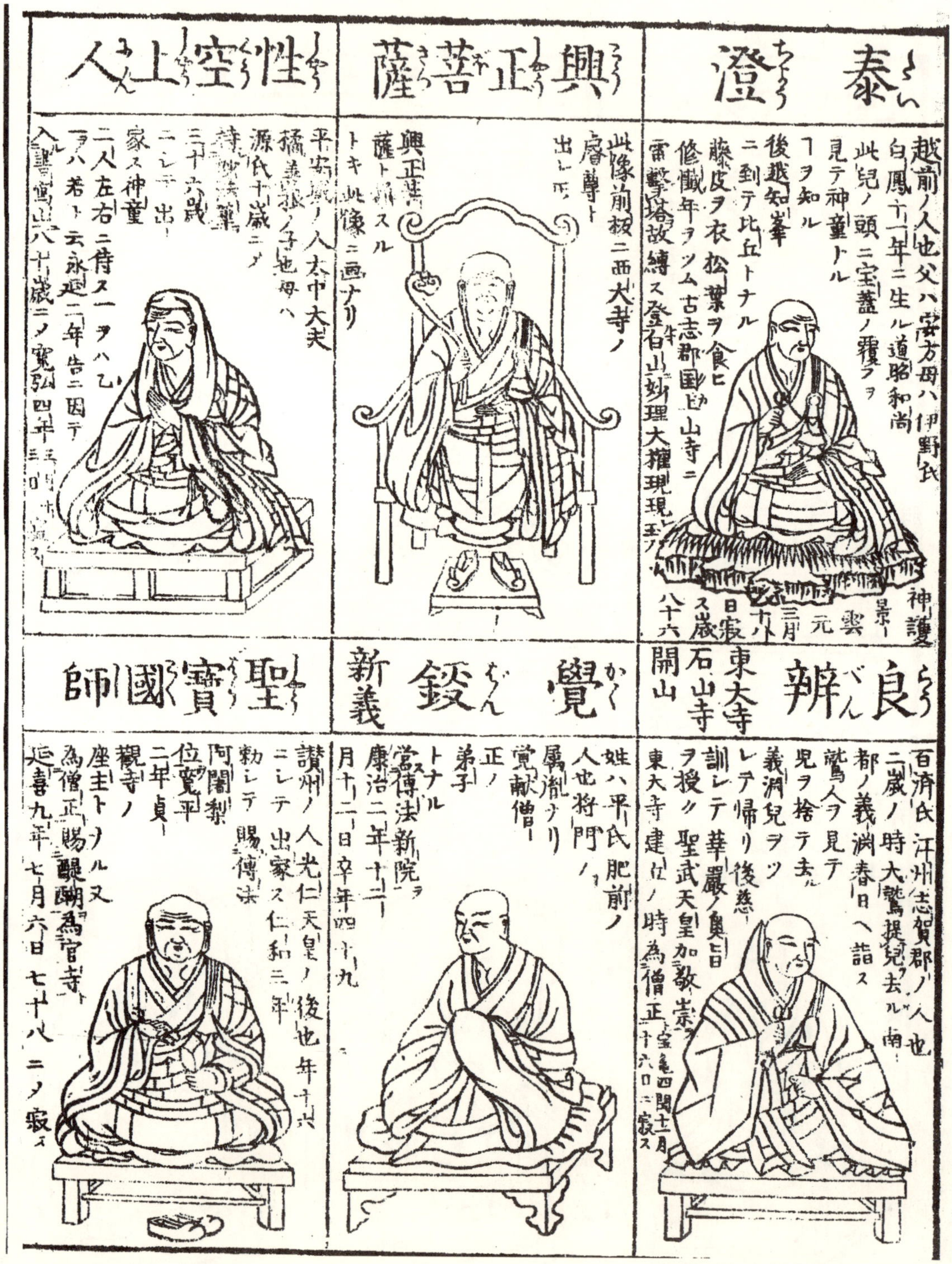

699. Shōbō Kokushi
Patriarch Shōhō

697. Kakuhan
Bonze Kakuhan of Shingi branch

695. Rōben (Todaiji Ishiyamaji Kaisan)
Priest Rōben, founder of Todaiji, Ishiyamadera

Go-zan
Patriarchs of Five Mountain Sect (700-729)

700. Rinzai Eshōzenshi
Zen Master Linji
of Rinzai

702. Dōgen Zenshi,
Sōtō Kaizan
Zen Master Dōgen,
Founder of Sotō

704. Reikisan
Tenryūji Musō
Priest Musō of Tenryūji,
Mt. Reikisan

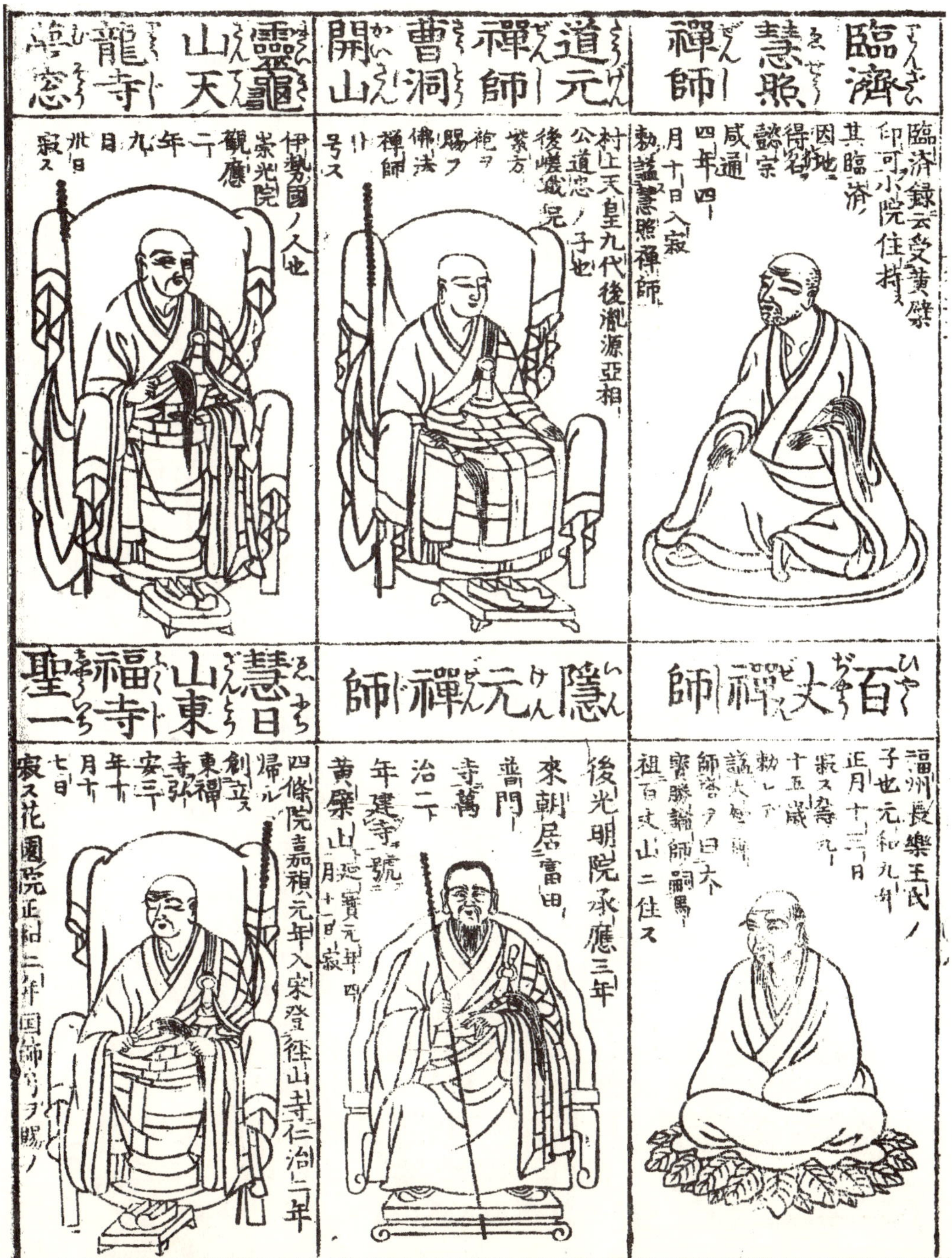

701. Hyakujō Zenshi
Zen Master Hyakujō Ekai
(of China)

703. Ingen Zenshi
Zen Master Ingen

705. Enichizan Tōfukuji shōichi
Monk Bennen of Tofukuji
temple, Mount Enichi

710. Daito Kokushi
Title of priest
Myō-Chō of Rinzai

708.Tōzan Kenninji Eisaiojō
Priest Eisai of Kenninji
Temple in Kyoto

706. Zuiryūzan Nanzen Fumon, Master Fumon (Sāmanta-Mukha) of Nanzenji Temple on Mt. Zuiryūzan

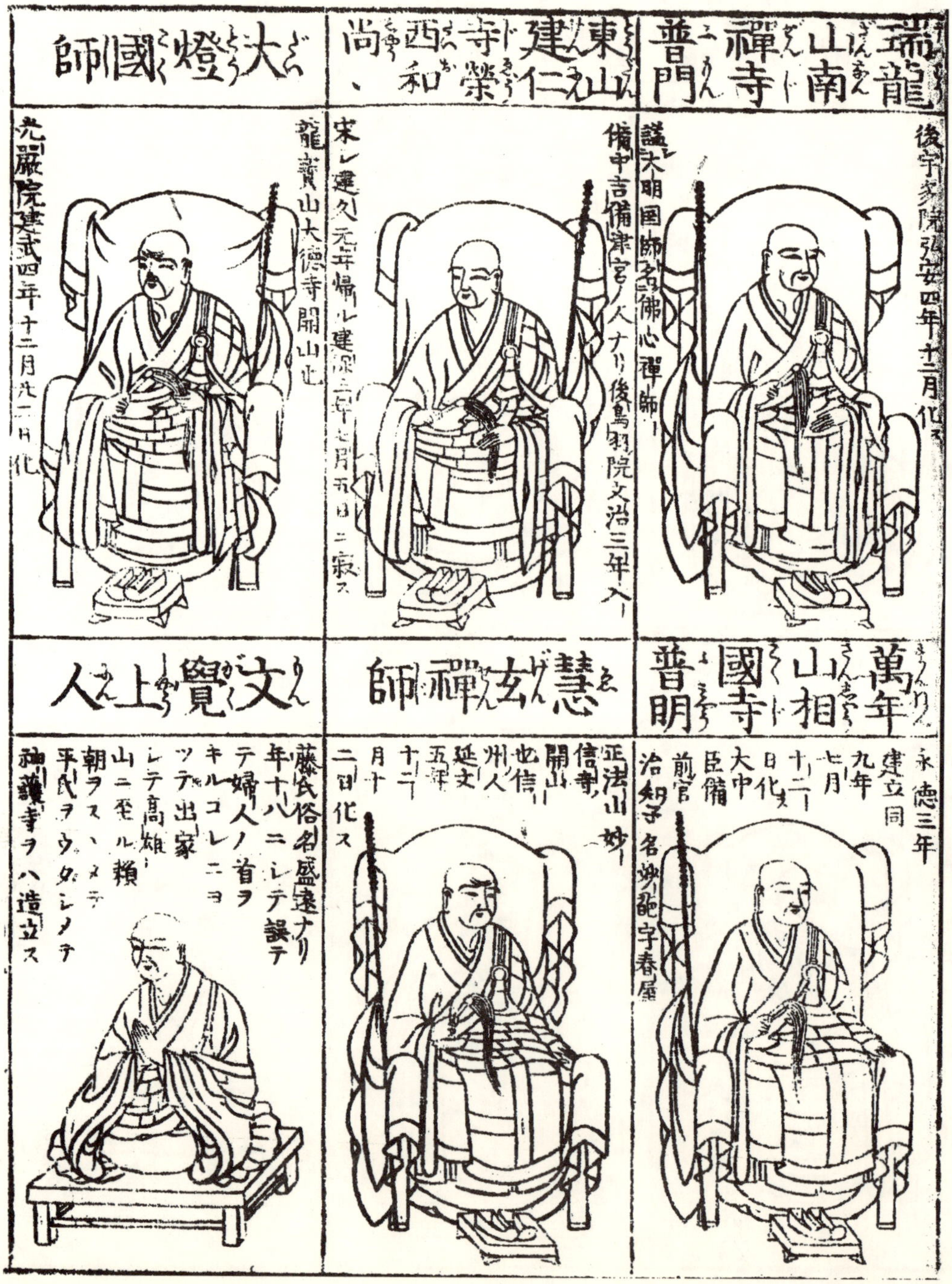

711. Mongaku Jōnin
Priest Mongaku

709. Egen Zenshi
Zen Master Egen

707. Mannensan Shōkokuji Fumyō
Monk Fumyō of Shōkokuji
Temple, mount Mannen

716. Ryōnin
Priest Ryōnin

714. Kūya Jonin
Priest Kūya (founder of Kūya school)

712. Chūjō Hōni
Nun Chūjō (Taimadera temple)

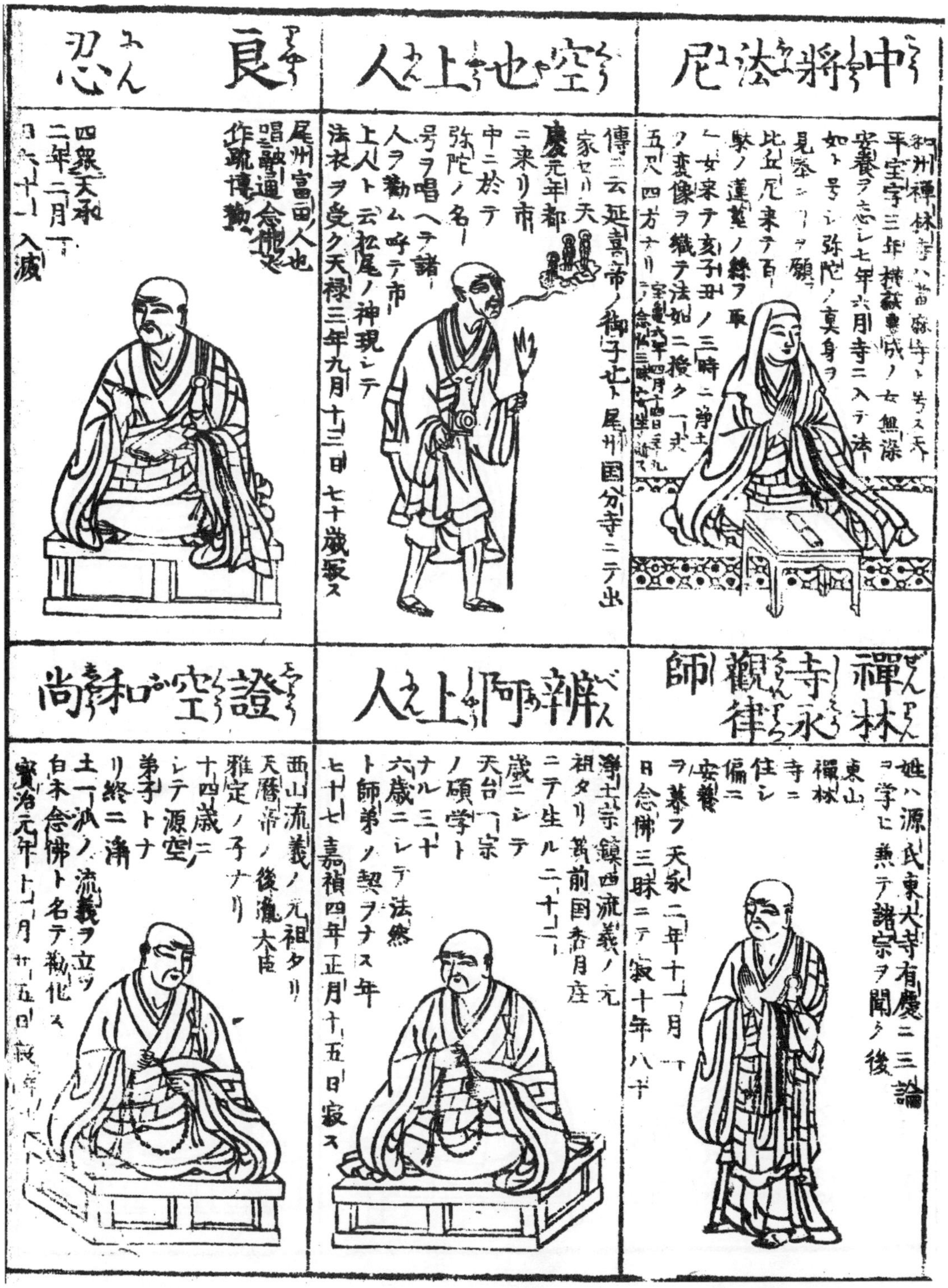

717. Shōkū Washō
Monk Shōkū (1177-1247)

715. Ben-A Jōnin
High Priest Benchō

713. Zenrinji Eikan Risshi
Monk Eikan of Zenrinji Temple

722. Ryōzen Kokua Jōnin
High Priest Kokua at Mt. Ryōzen

720. Ippen Jōnin
High Priest Ippen

718. Enchin Kiyomizudera Kaisan
Priest Enchin, the Founder of Kiyomizu Temple

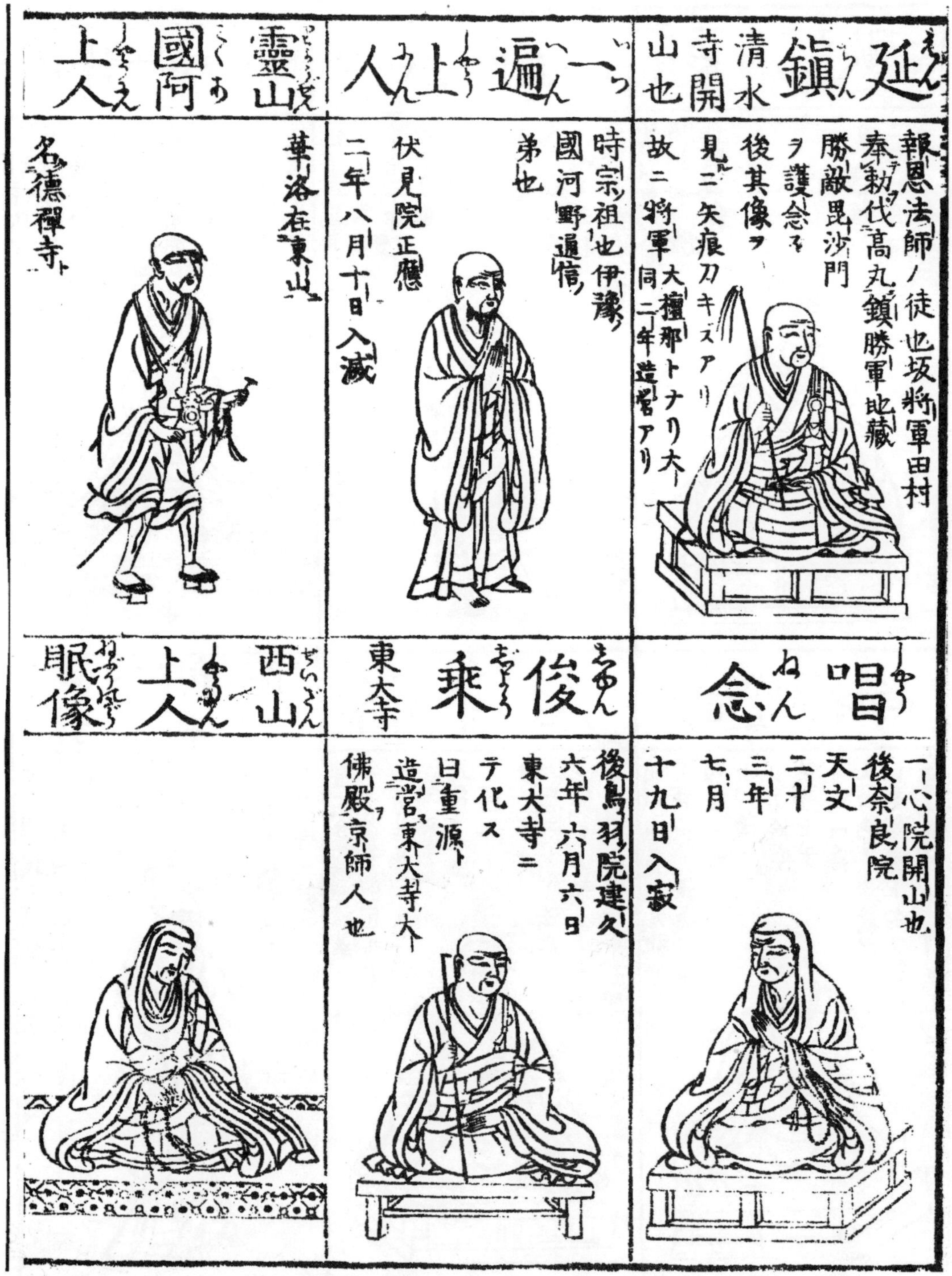

723. Zeizan Jōnin; Nemurizō
High Priest of Seizan

721. Shunjō Tōdaiji
Monk Chogen of Tōdaiji

719. Shōnen
Priest Nichiren

728. Shin Butsu, Bukkōji, Fukukōji Kaizan
Priest Shimbutsu, Founder of Temple Bukkōji and Fukukoji

726. Kakushin-Ni, Honganji, Ikko-shū
Nun Kakushini of Honganji temple, Ikkō sect

724. Nichizō, Myokenji Kaizan
Monk Nichizō, Founder of Myokenji temple

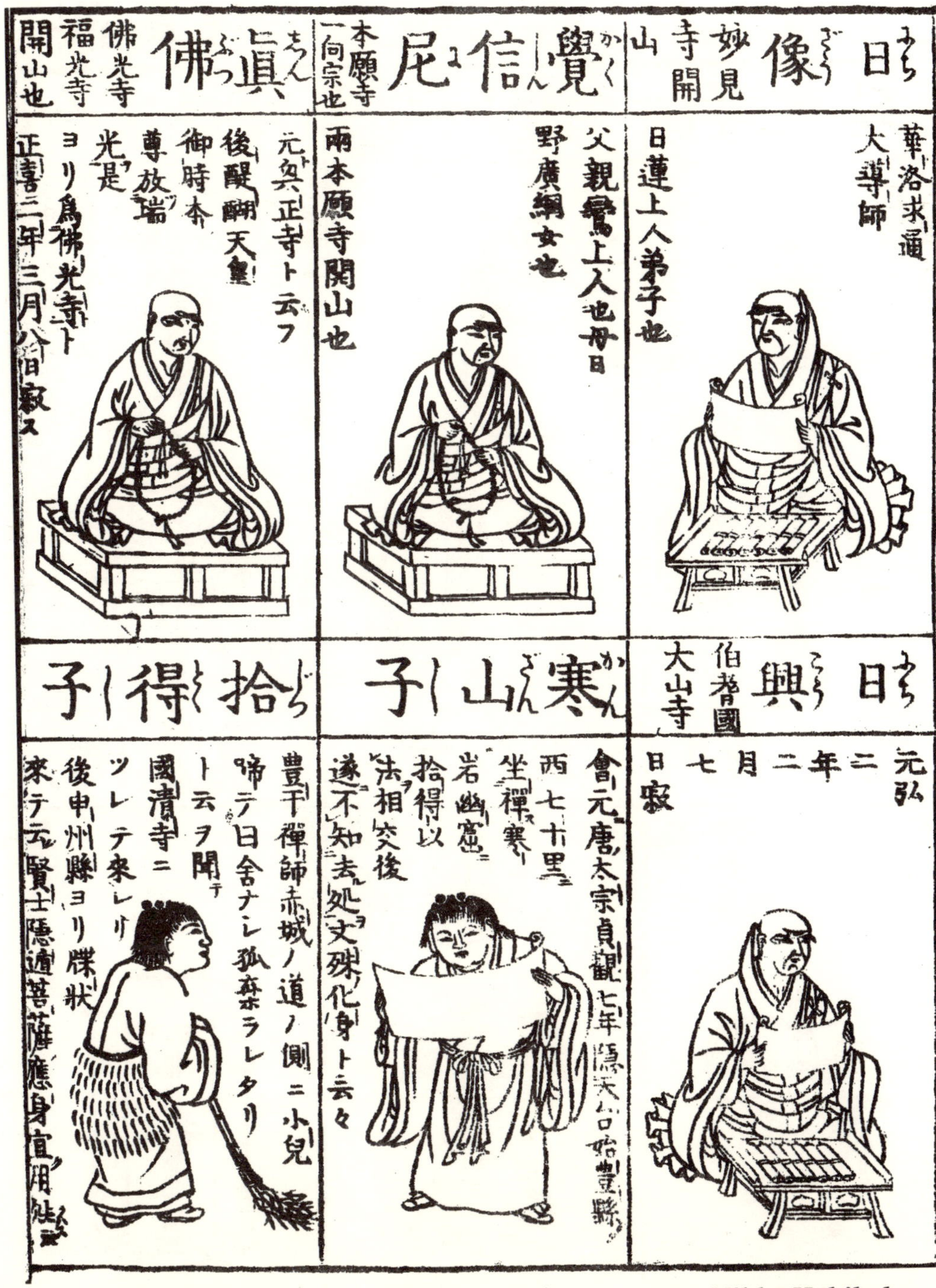

729. Jittoku Shi
Jittoku Kumāra

727. Kanzan shi
Kanzan Kumāra

725. Nikkō Hōkikoku Oyama Dera
Monk Nikkō of Oyama Temple in Hōki province

§ 50. Dōgu-bu
Implements and Accessories (730-825)

734. Yōraku
Decorative Accessories

732. Funa Gokō; Wagokō
Boat Shape Halo; round halo

730. Shari tō
Stūpa enshrining relics of Buddha

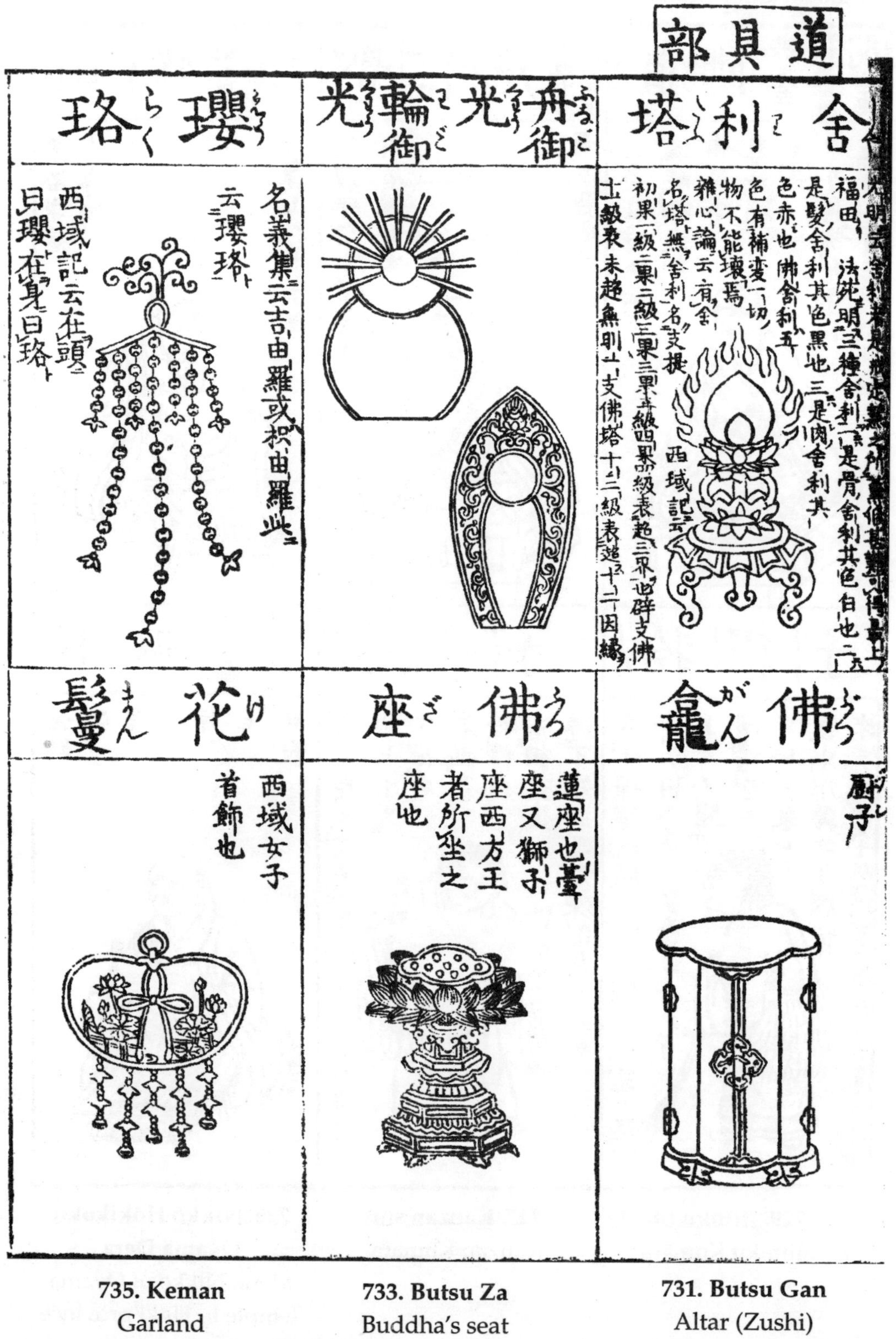

735. Keman
Garland

733. Butsu Za
Buddha's seat

731. Butsu Gan
Altar (Zushi)

740. Shō kane
Hanging Bell

738. Dōhan
Hanging banner

736. Tengai
Canopy

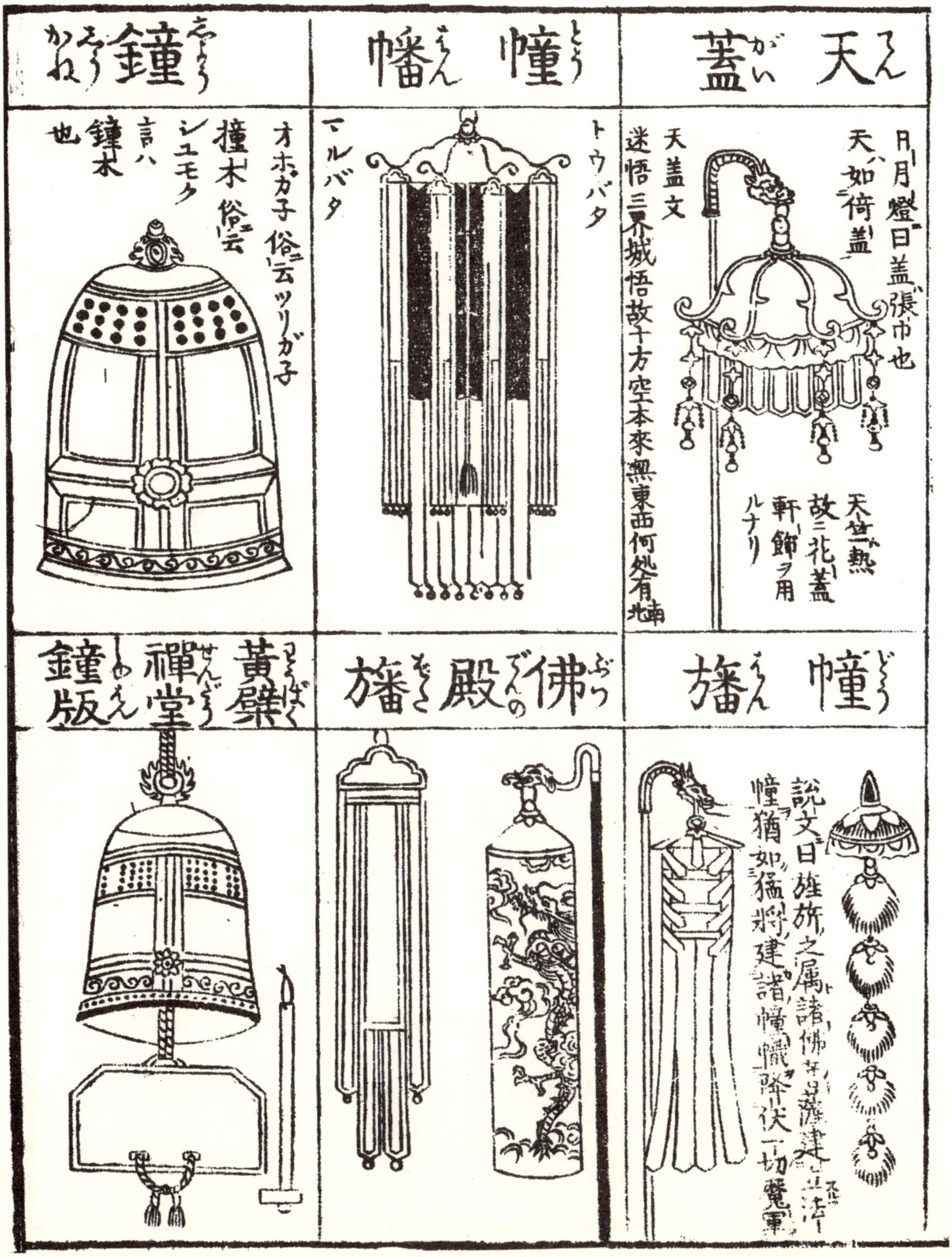

741. Ōbaku Zendō Shōhan
Golden bell of Zen hall

739. Butsuden Hata
Banner of the inner hall

737. Dōhan
Hanging banner

746. Kei
Chevron stone musical Instrument

744. Rei
Bell

742. Fūtaku
Wind chimes

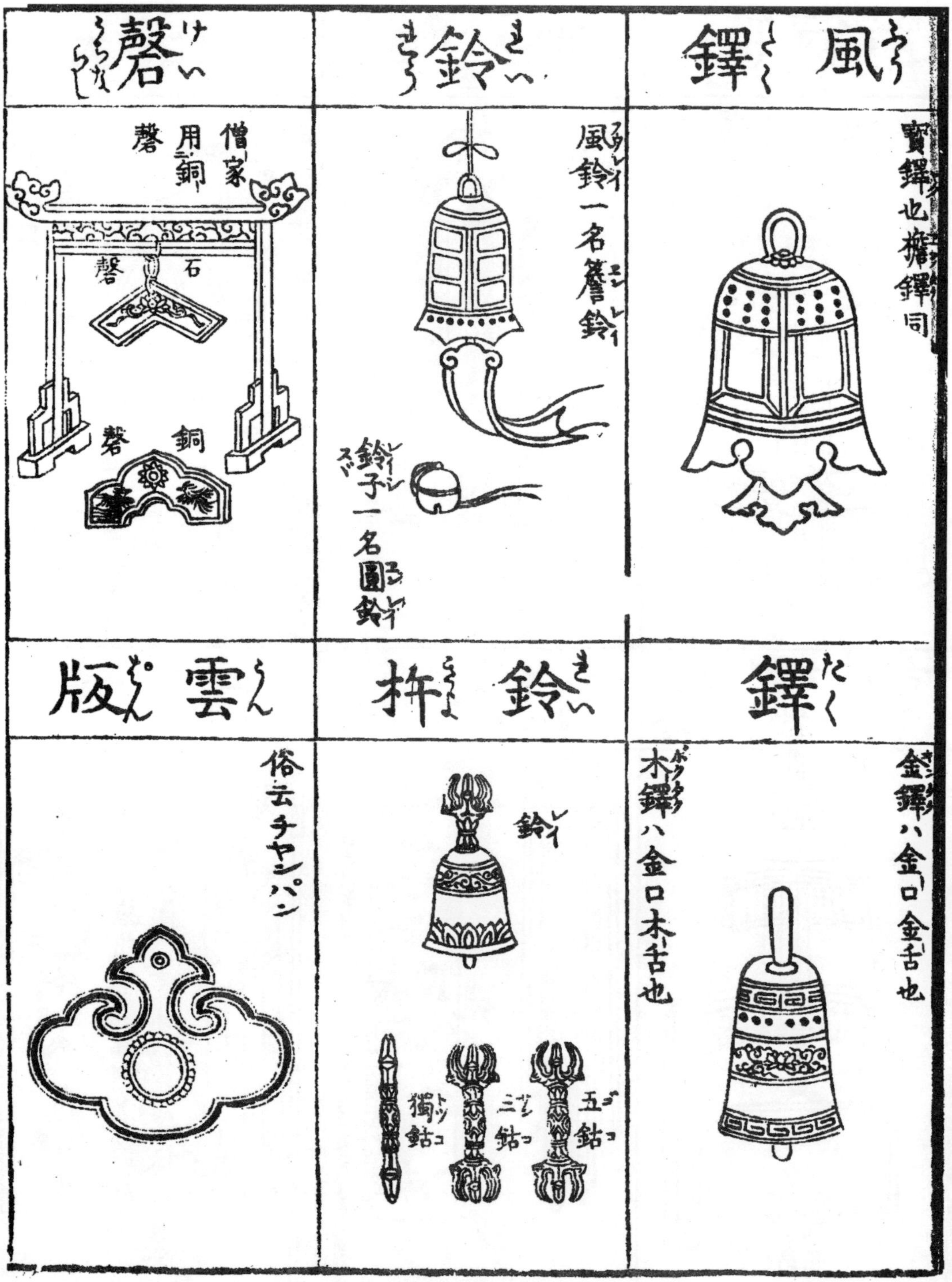

747. Unpan
Cloud-shaped bronze plate used as a gong in a monastery

745. Rei; shō
Bell and Vajra

743. Taku
Wooden and metallic chimes

752. Bustu zen Shoko
Drum and Bell in front of Buddha

750. Moku gyo
Fish-shaped wooden Drum

748. Dō bachi
Copper Bowl

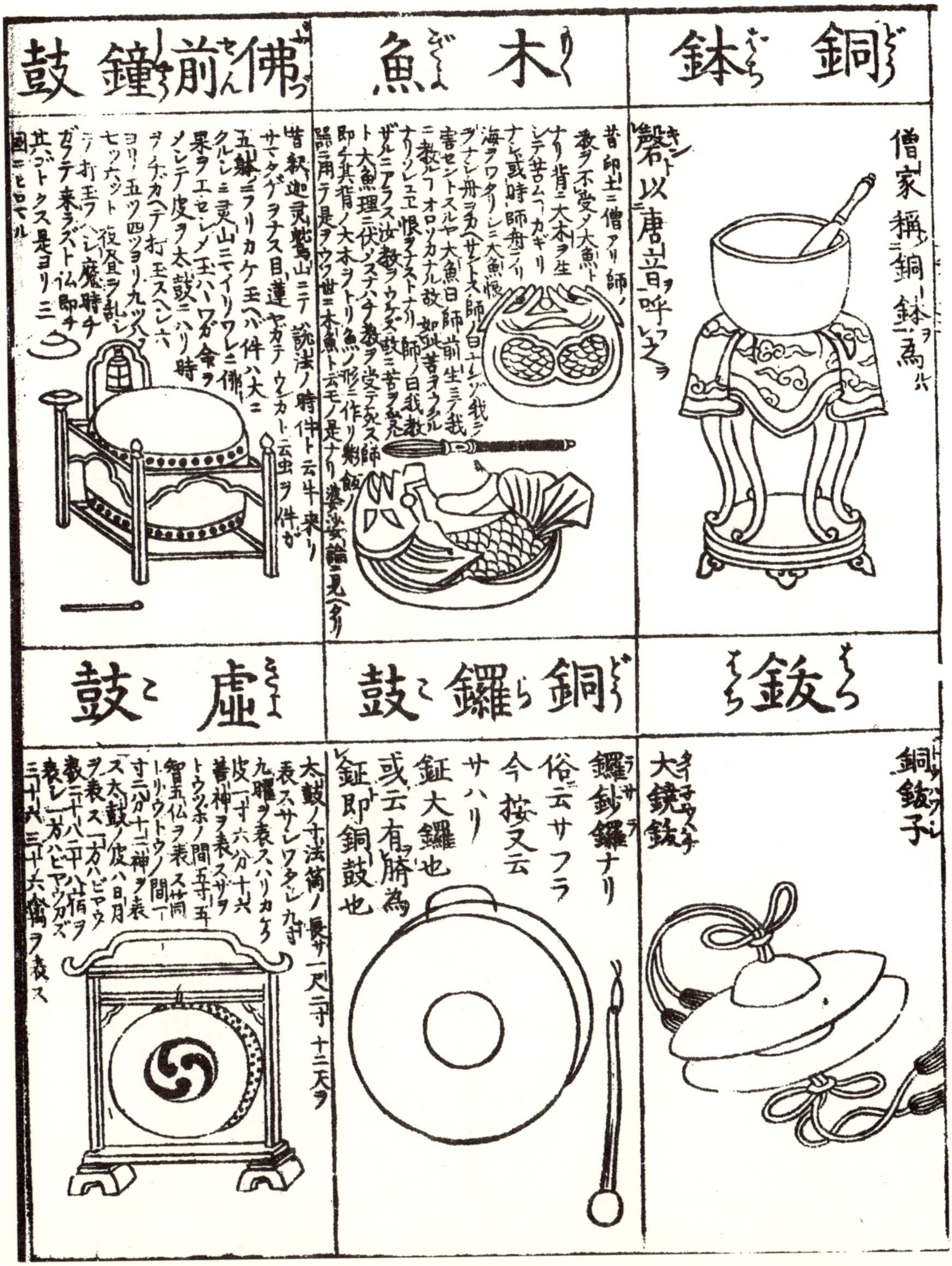

753. Kyoko
Drum

751. Dōrako
Gong

749. Hatsu
Cymbals

758. Hachi no ko-Sanban Ita
Wooden begging bowls for Monks

756. Saidō mae no hanteki
Bell of Dining Hall

754. Mei Tsui
Mallets

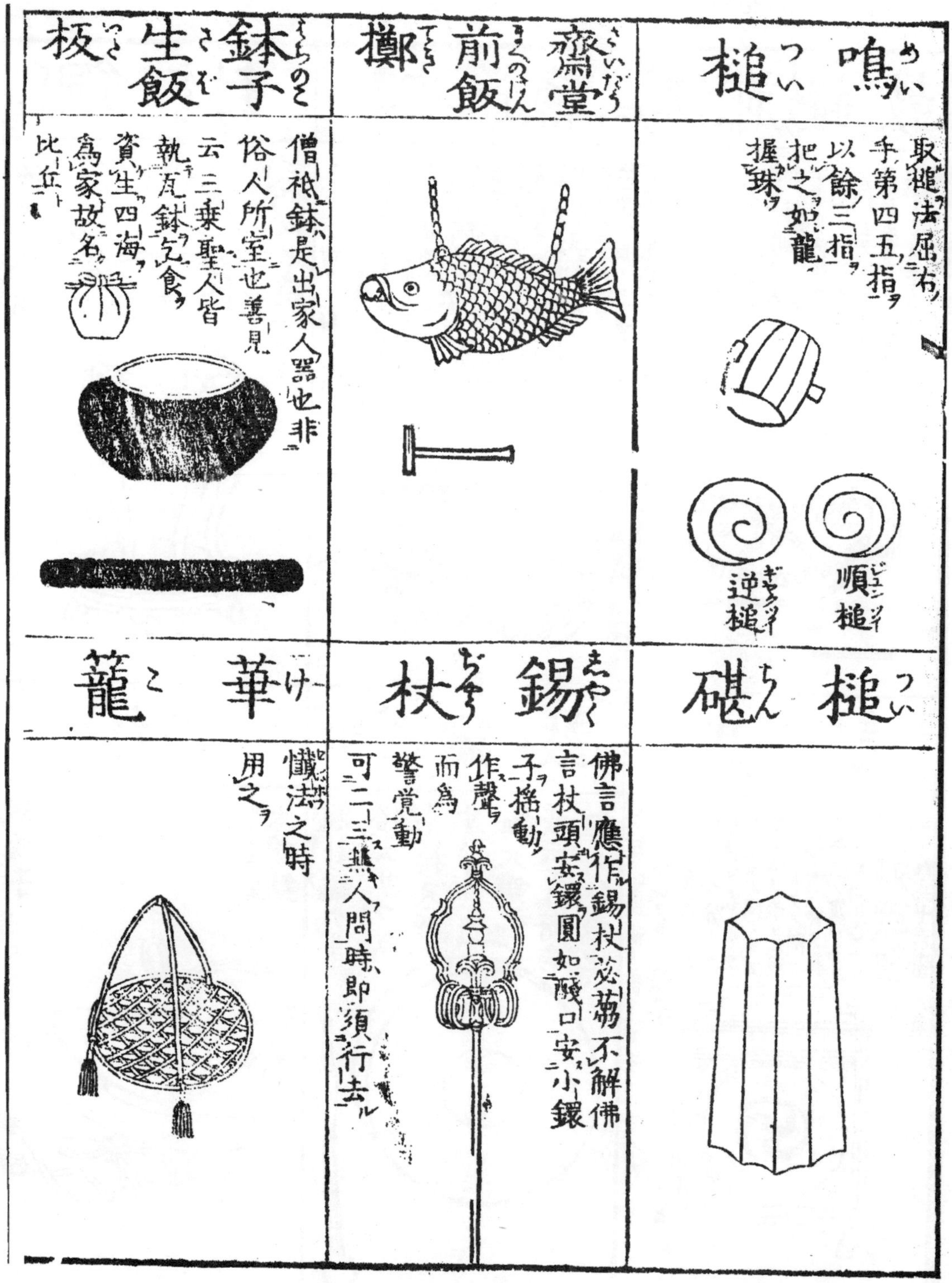

759. Keko
Flower Basket

757. Shakujyō
Staff of a Buddhist Monk

755. Tsuichin
Mallet and Wooden Block used in Zen Monastery

764. Kakushi
Trumpet

762. Gotō kaku
Wooden trumpet

760. Ko
Drum

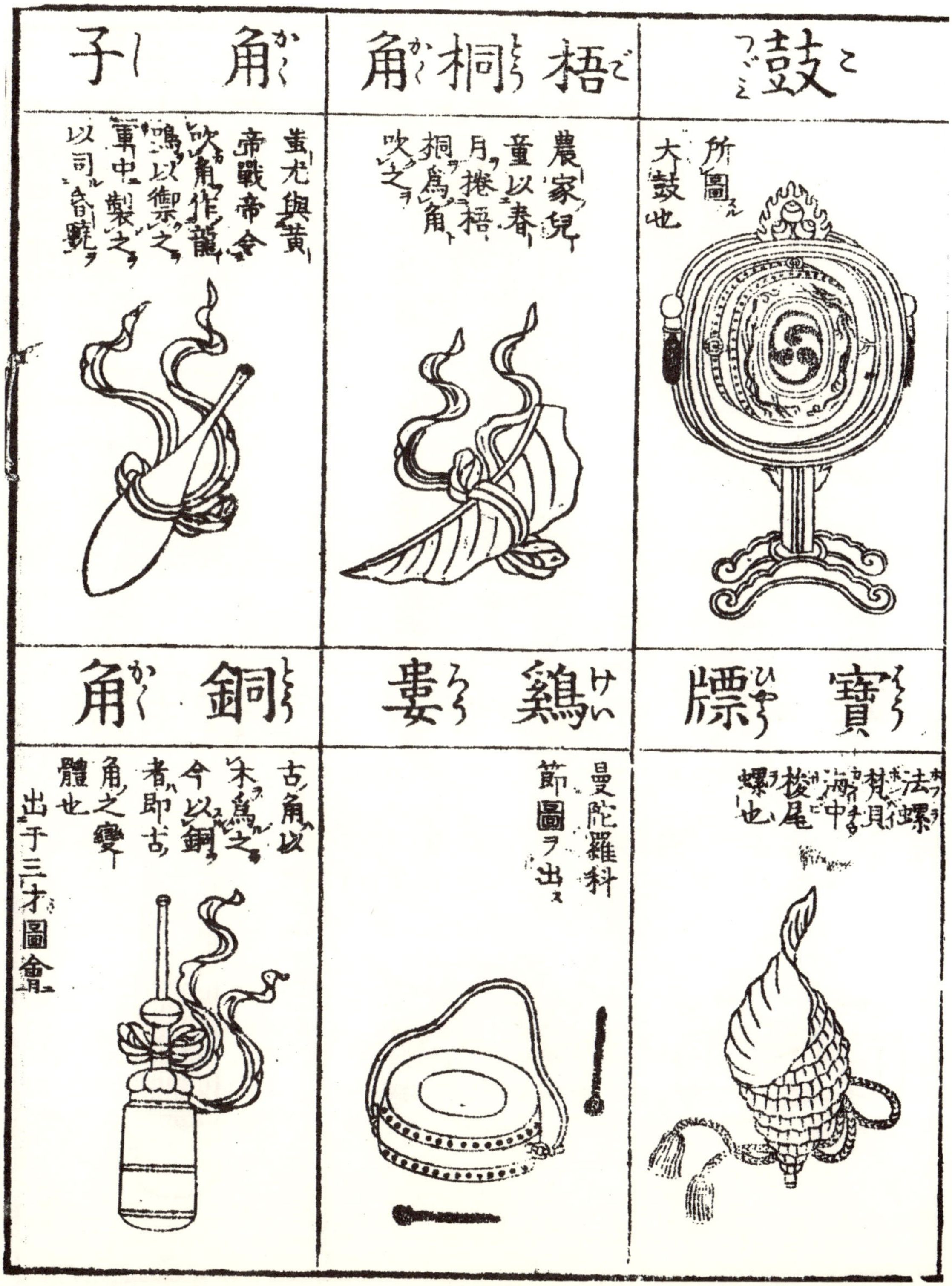

765. Dōkaku
Bronze trumpet

763. Keirō
Traditional Japanese Drum

761. Hōhyō
Conch

770. Kakko
Chinese shoulder Drum

768. Fue
Flutes

766. Ritsu
Pipe with twelve notes

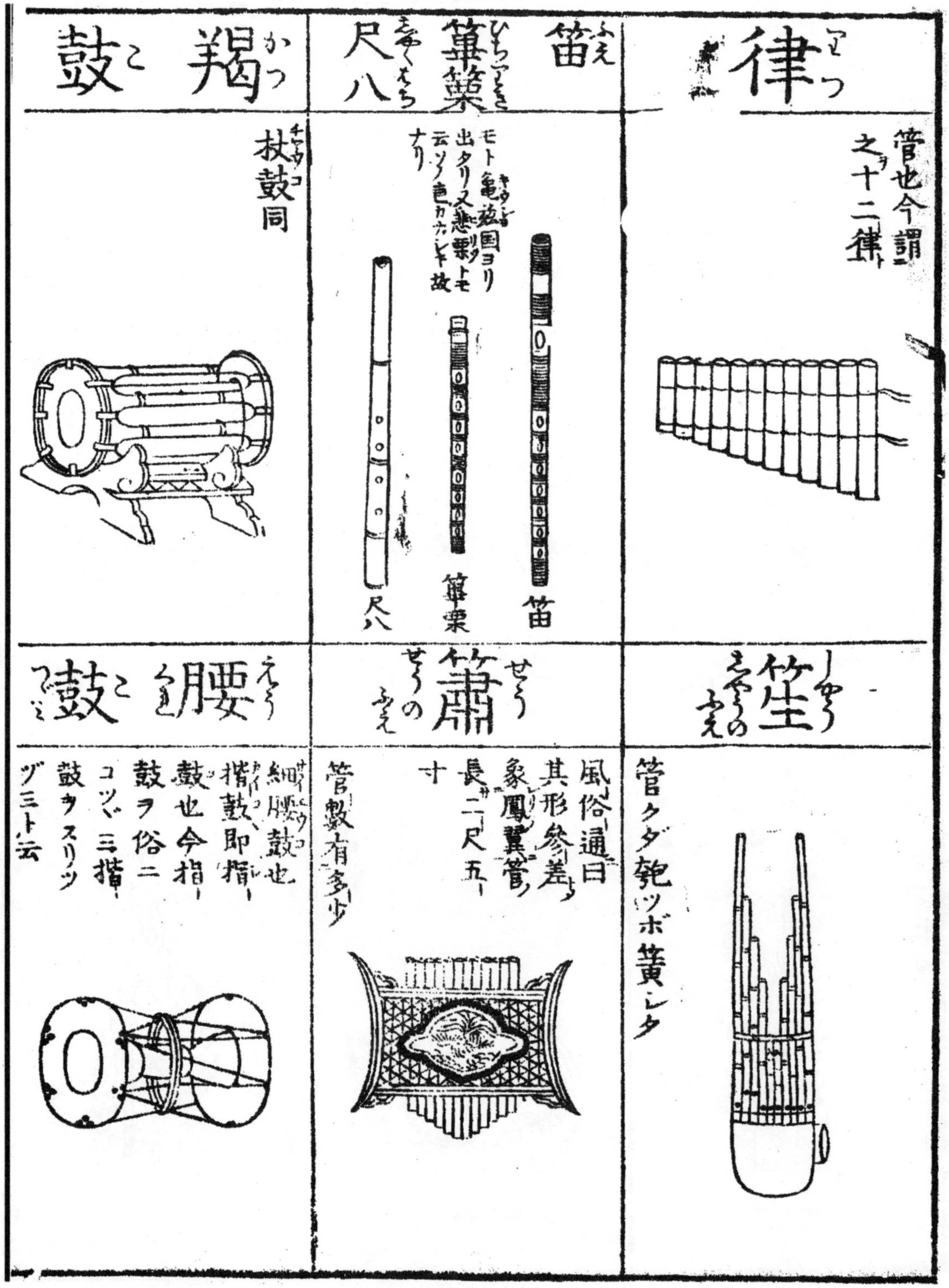

771. Yōko
Waist Drum

769. Shō no fue
Flute with several pipes

767. Shō
A reed flute

776. Gekkin
Round Moon-shaped Koto

774. Kūko
Japanese Harp

772. Kin/koto
A string musical instrument

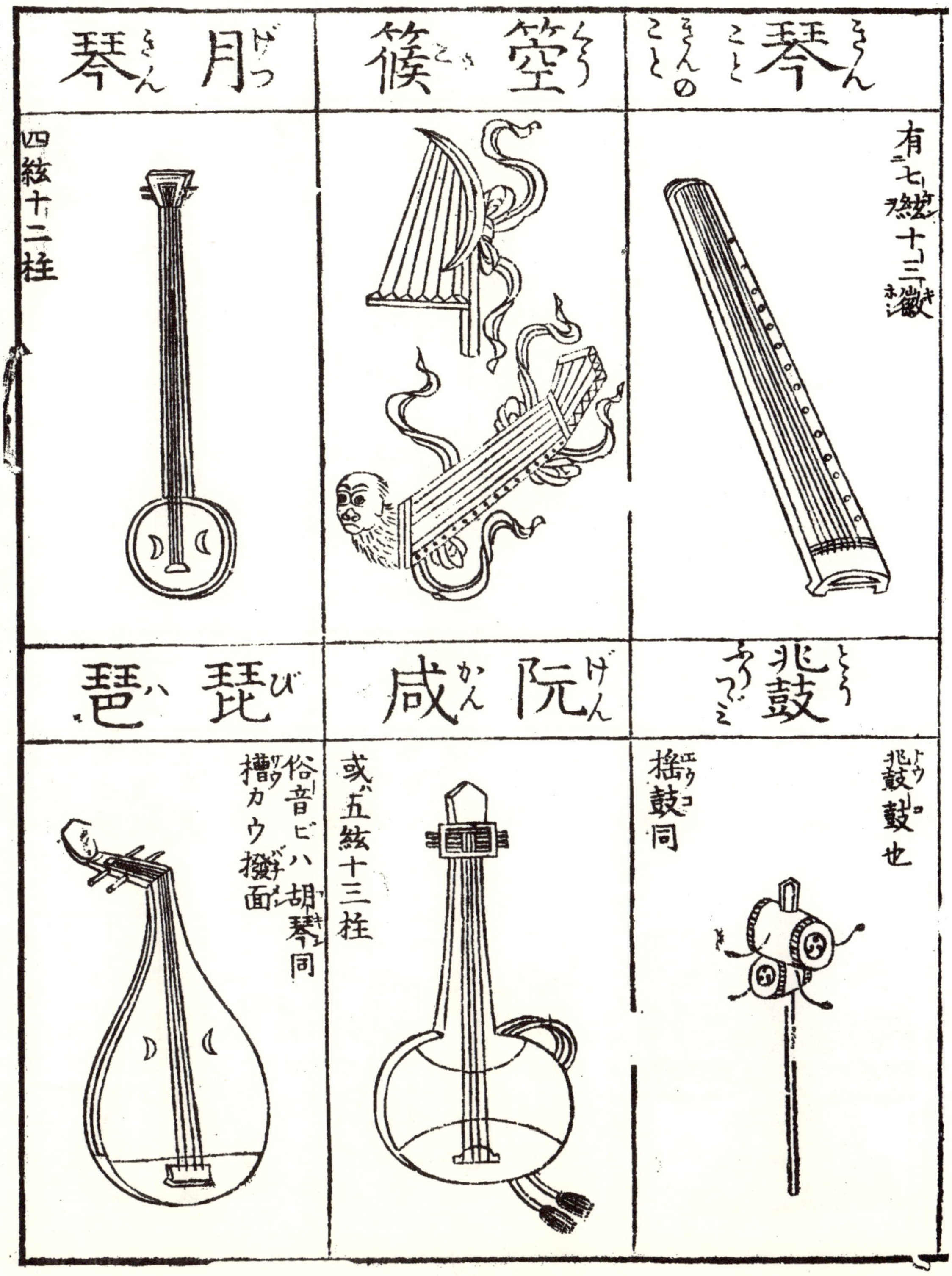

777. Biwa
Japanese lute

775. Genkan
Stringed instrument

773. Tōko
A Japanese drum

782. Dōe Soken
Coarse Silk Robe

780. Hō
Coat

778. Jikitotsu
Casual robe of Monk

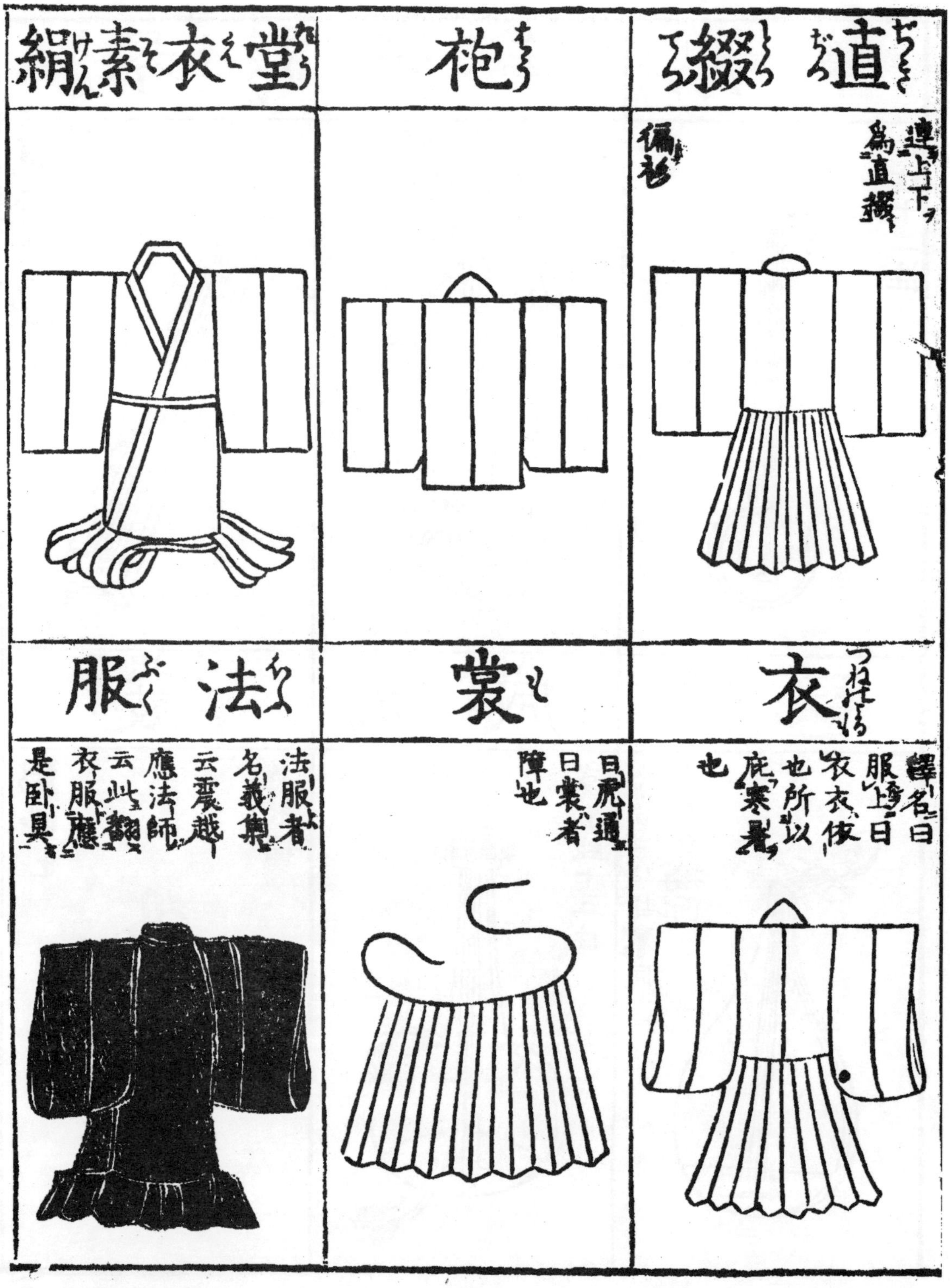

783. Hō Buku
Preacher's Robe

781. Mo
Skirt

779. Koromo
Robe

788. Rakushi
Shoulder-bag

786. Kesa (=kāṣāya)
Monk's Stole

784. Nijūgojō kesa
Monks stole with
twenty five pleats

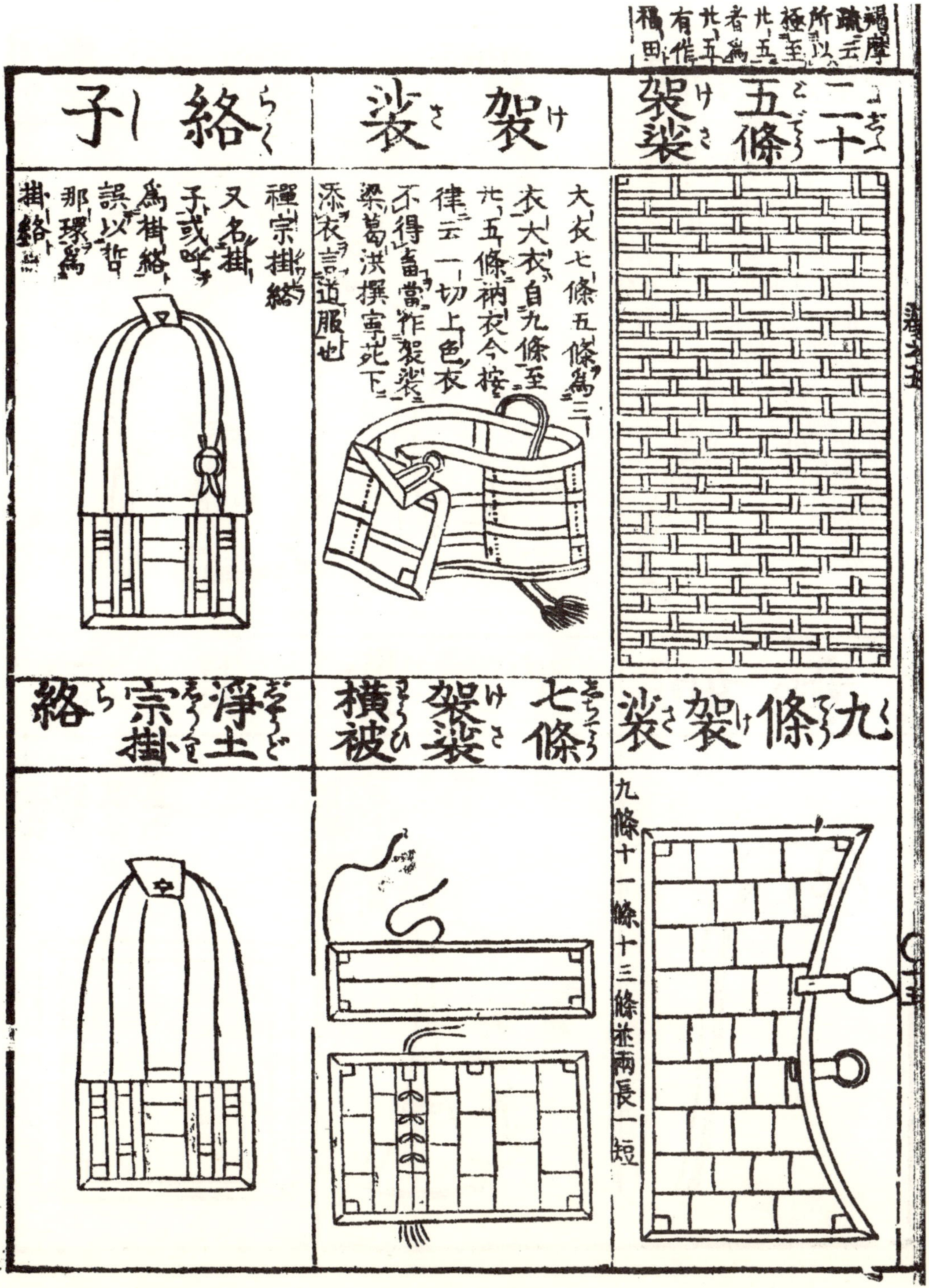

789. Jōdoshū Kakera
Shoulder bag of Jōdo sect

787. ShichiJō Kesa
Seven-pleated stole

785. Kujō Kesa
Nine-pleated Monk's stole

794. Bucchin
Clean speck

792. Bō
Cap

790. Kesa Suzuuke
Band for Bell on monk's Robe
1. Tendai 2. Shingon 3. Yamabushi at Honzan
4. Yamabushi at Tōzan

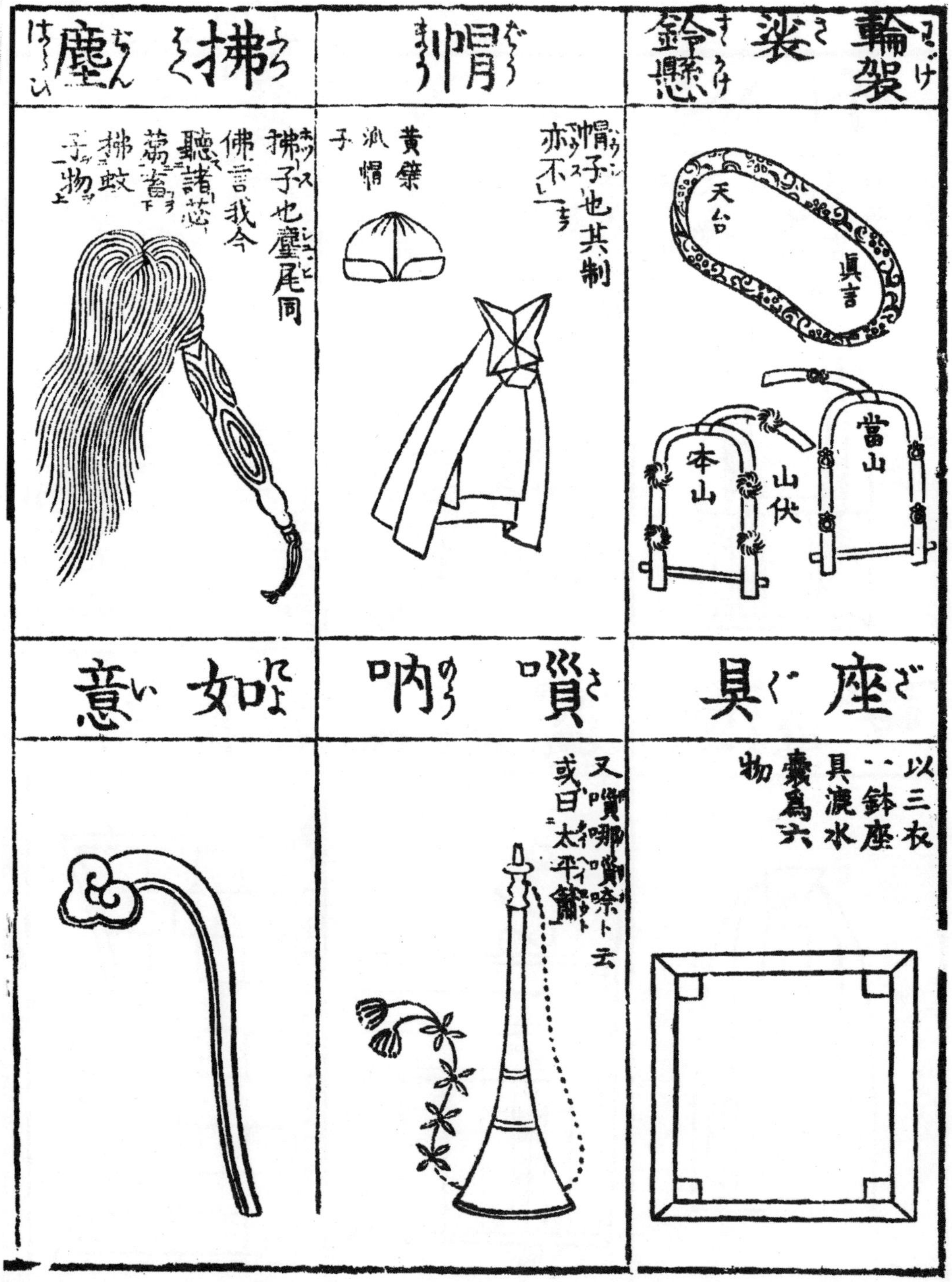

795. Nyoi
Anuruddha

793. Sanō
Pipe instrument

791. Za gu
Cushion

800. Sen
Japanese Fan

798. Zuzu
Rosary

796. Gomadan
Altar for Homa

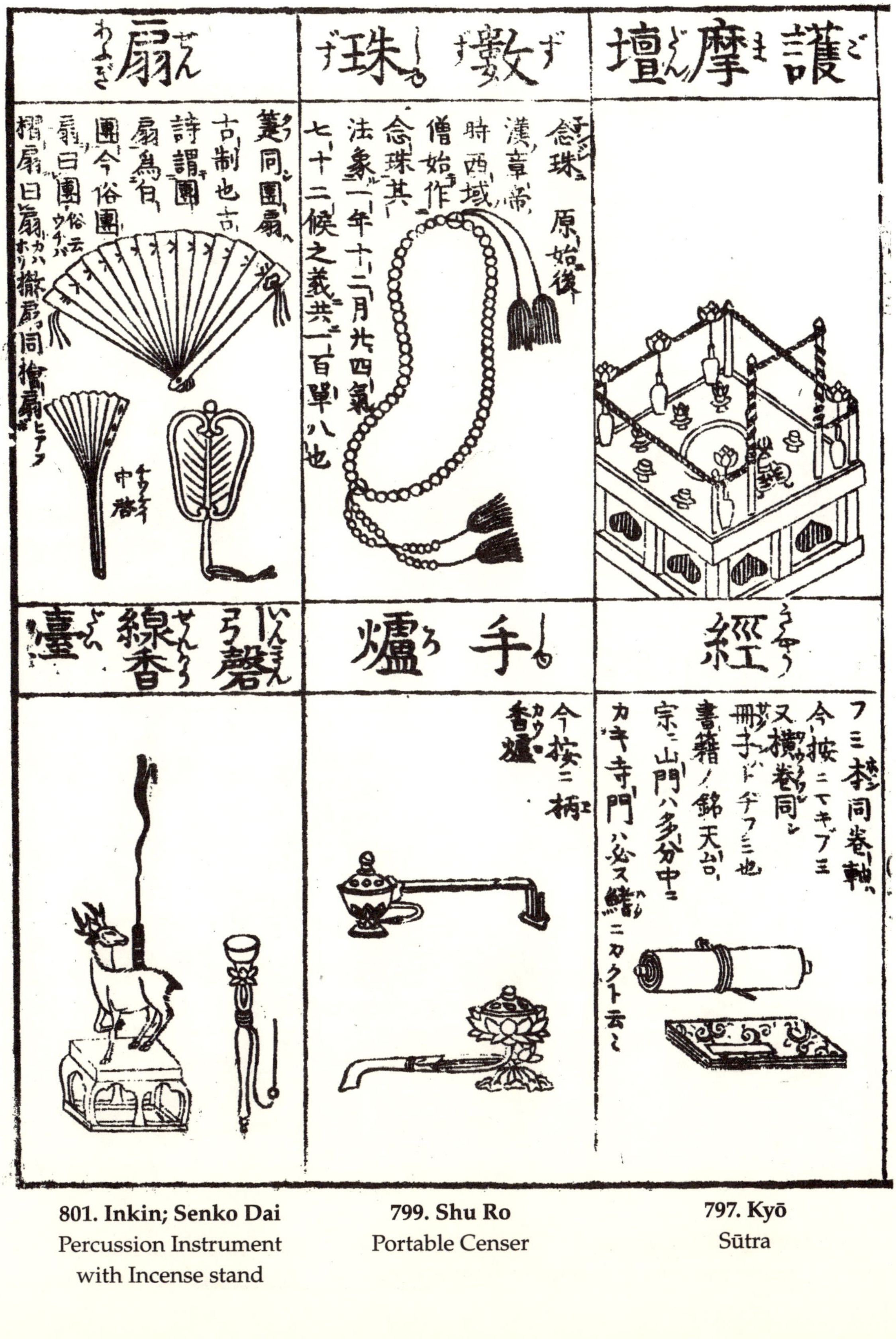

801. Inkin; Senko Dai
Percussion Instrument
with Incense stand

799. Shu Ro
Portable Censer

797. Kyō
Sūtra

806. Hanazara butsugu
Flower plates for a Buddhist Altar

804. Kabin
Flower vase

802. Tsuru Kame
Crane and Tortoise

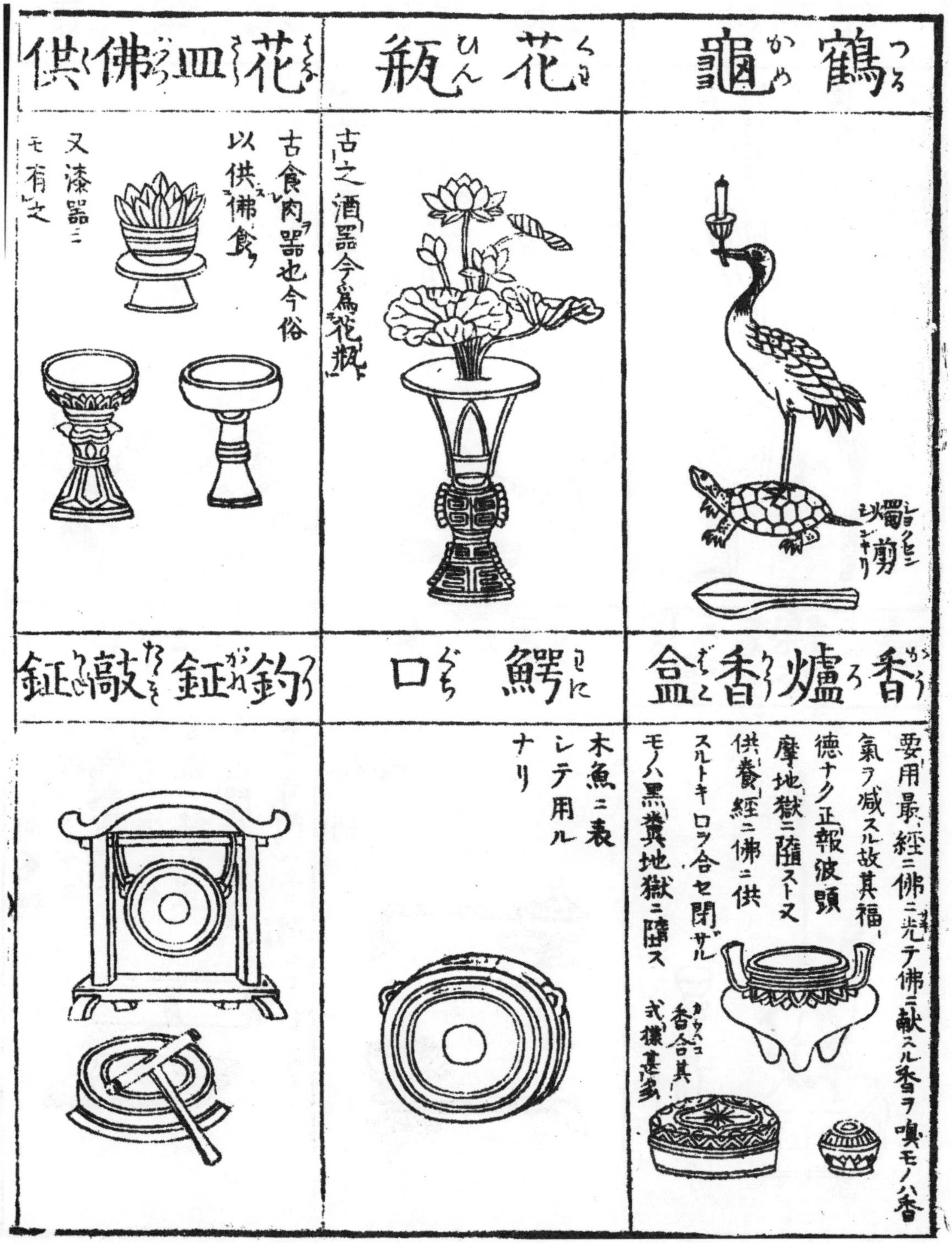

807. Tsuri gane; tataki gama
Hanging Ceremonial Gong in a temple

805. Wani-Guchi
Temple Gong

803. Kōro; Kobako
Censer and Incense-container

812. Kō za
Lecture Seat

810. Ihai; shusshō dai
Buddhist memorial Tablets;
A Stand to hold new boon

808. Tosoku
Candle Lighting

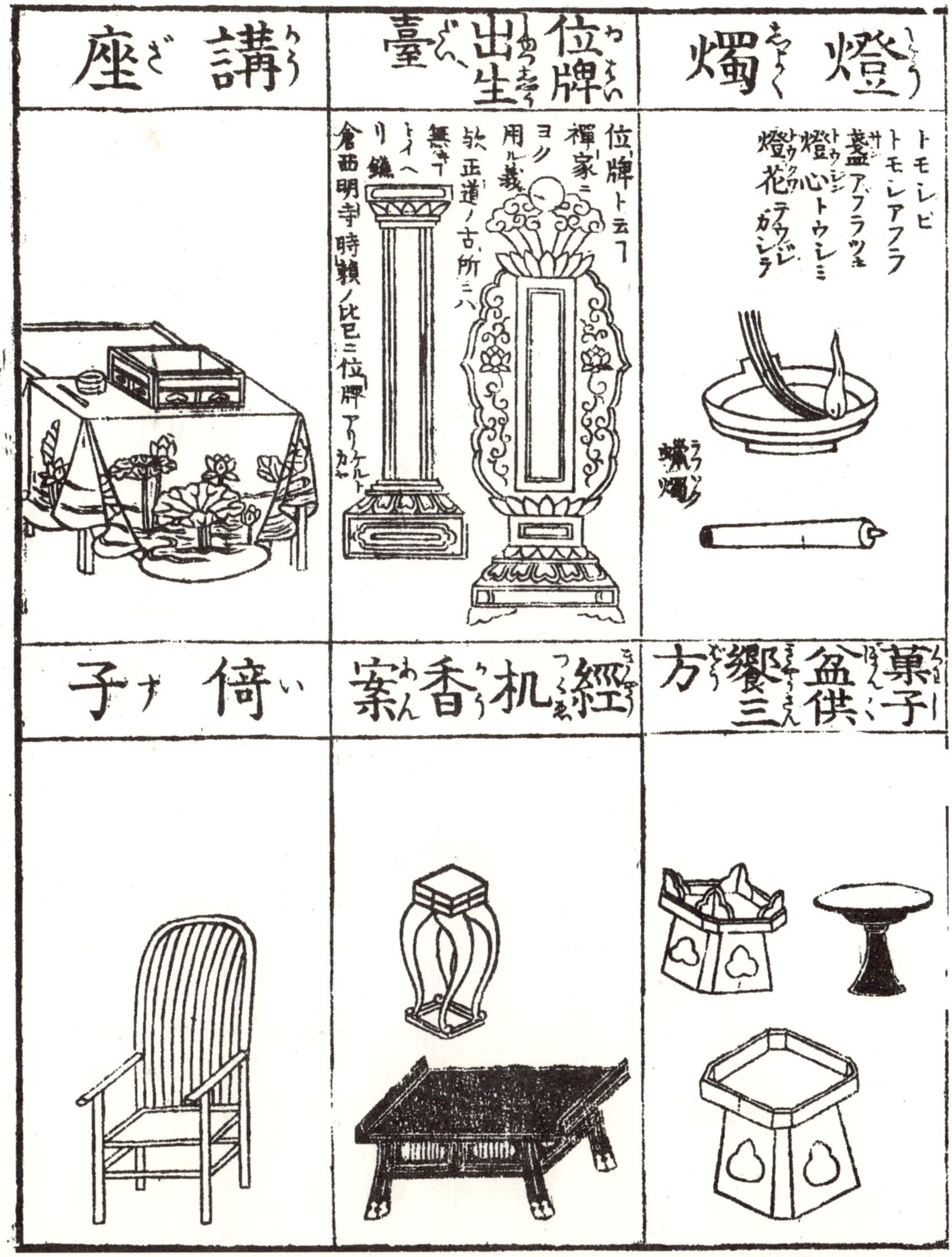

813. Isu
Chair

811. Kyō zukue
Table for Sūtras

809. Okashibon
Small wooden stands
for Dinner Service Cakes

818. Tōrō
Lantern

816. Ruri To
Vaiḍūrya Lamp

814. Mizukoshi Jōbin
Water strainer and pure water jar

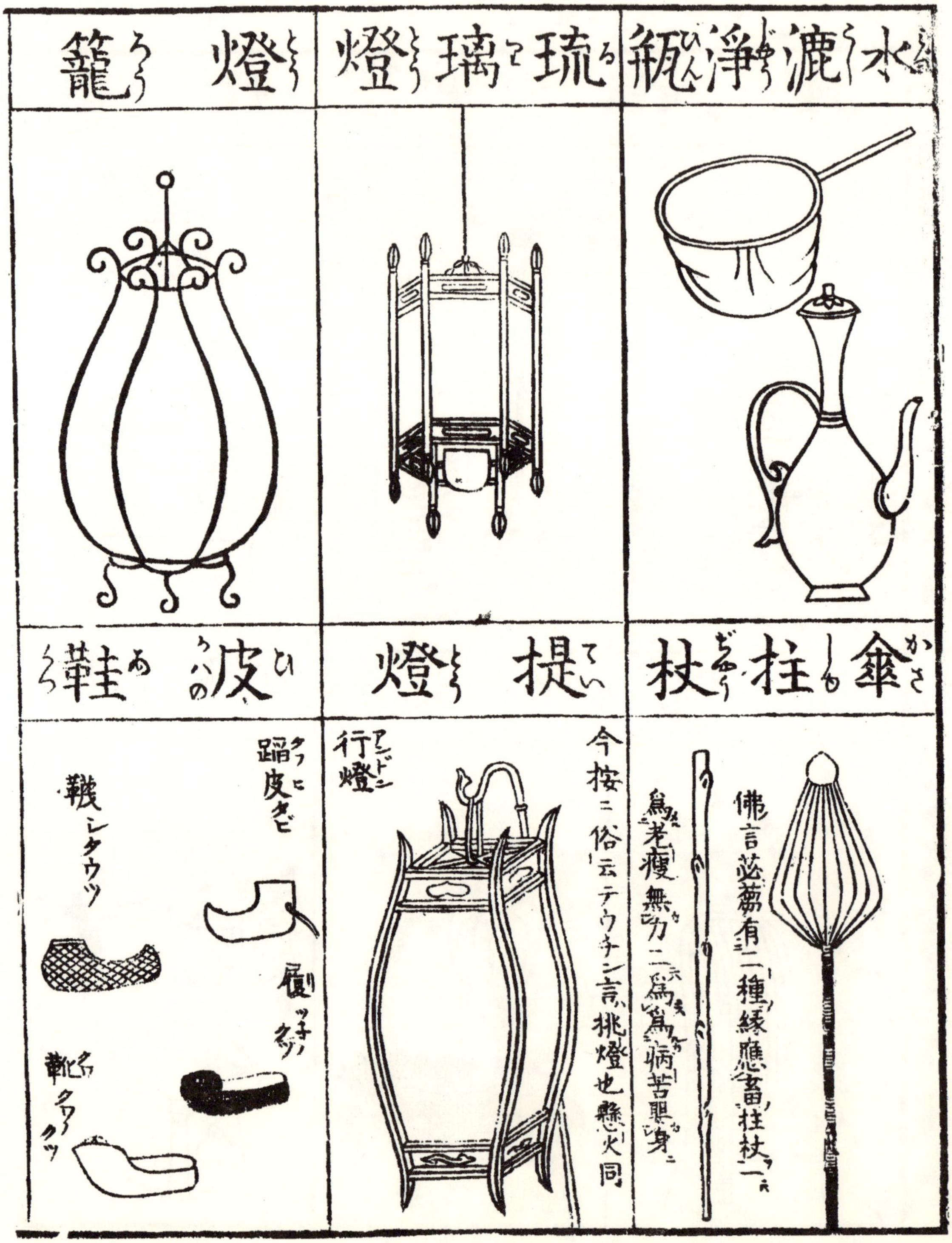

819. Hia
Foot wear

817. Teito
Hand Lamp

815. Kasa ; Shujō
Umbrella & Monk's wand

824. Gorin Sekitō
Five-stage stone, Dhātugarbha

822. Nagae no koshi
Palanquin

820. Sotoba
Stūpa

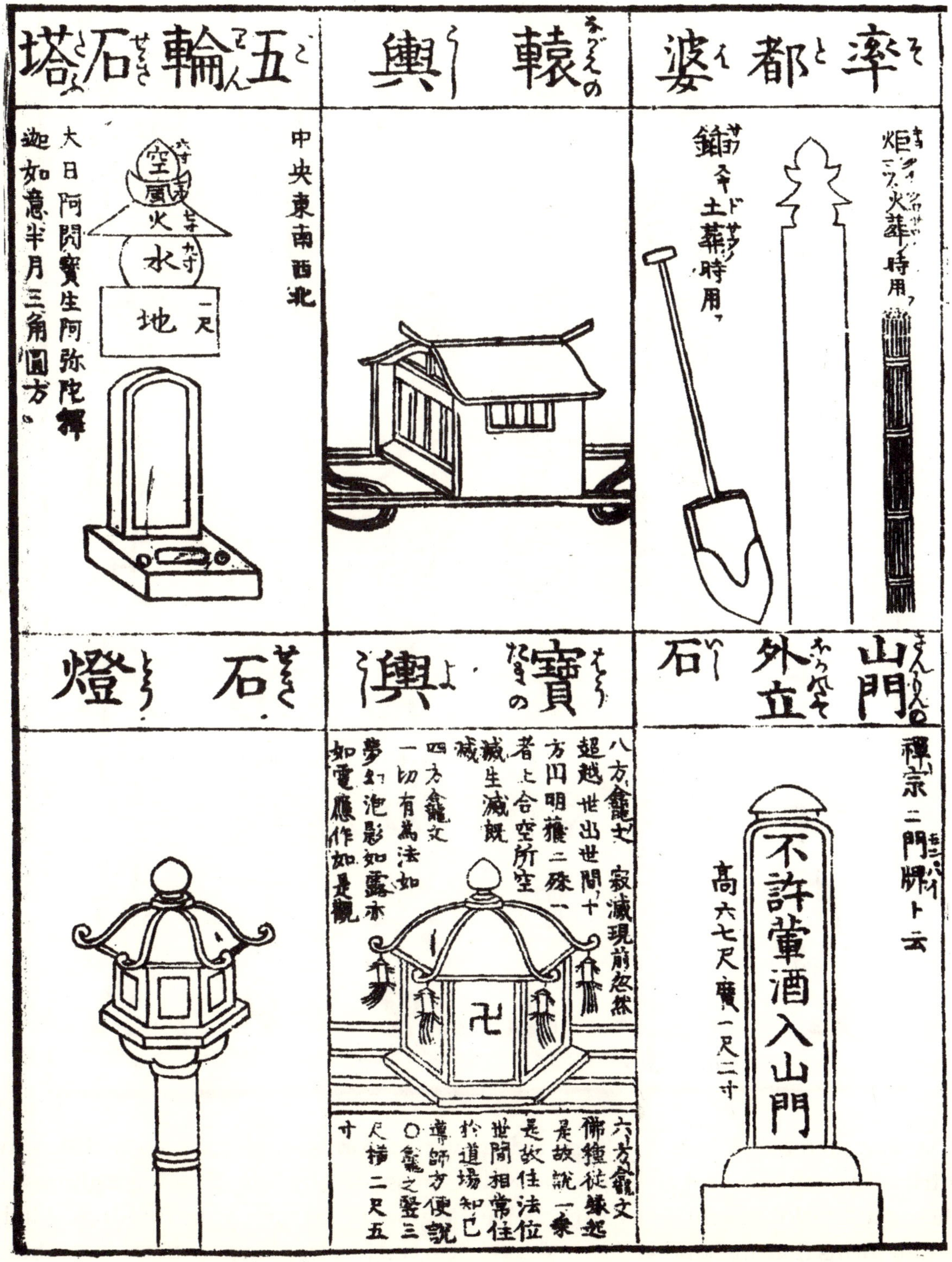

825. Sekitō
Stone Lantern

823. Hō yo
Jewelled palanquin

821. Sanmon no Tateishi
Milestone of a temple

Epilogue

夫諸尊名相其殊異最多
而所持器物亦品類不少
也以故釋氏猶未易詳況
庸流耶屬者圖畫諸尊妙
相要略因由於其傍刊刻
流布諸世矣嗟呼彌其名

The innumerable Arhats are depicted in varied forms, each one with distinctive attributes wich are symbolized by the objects possessed by him . Having a glimpse of these multifarious forms, one can conceive the grace of the numerous Buddhas. All the extant forms that are handed down to us are carved in accordance with their attributes on the wood blocks. Also, a concise commentary is added as per the omens of each one in order to spread the awareness among the common folk.

相明其因由淨信愈篤愈
增庶乎登菩提場之一助
云爾
元祿三龍集庚午仲秋
上澣寓指月軒義山跋

Thus this collection shall certainly present a vivid image of various Buddhas which in turn will help the readers to develop a deeper faith to attain the higher realm of Bodhi.

3rd year of Genroku (1690) Ryūshū, Kanoe, Uma, Full Moon of Autumn at my humble dwelling in Shigetsuk-Ken, Gizan.

I hereby pen the epilogue.

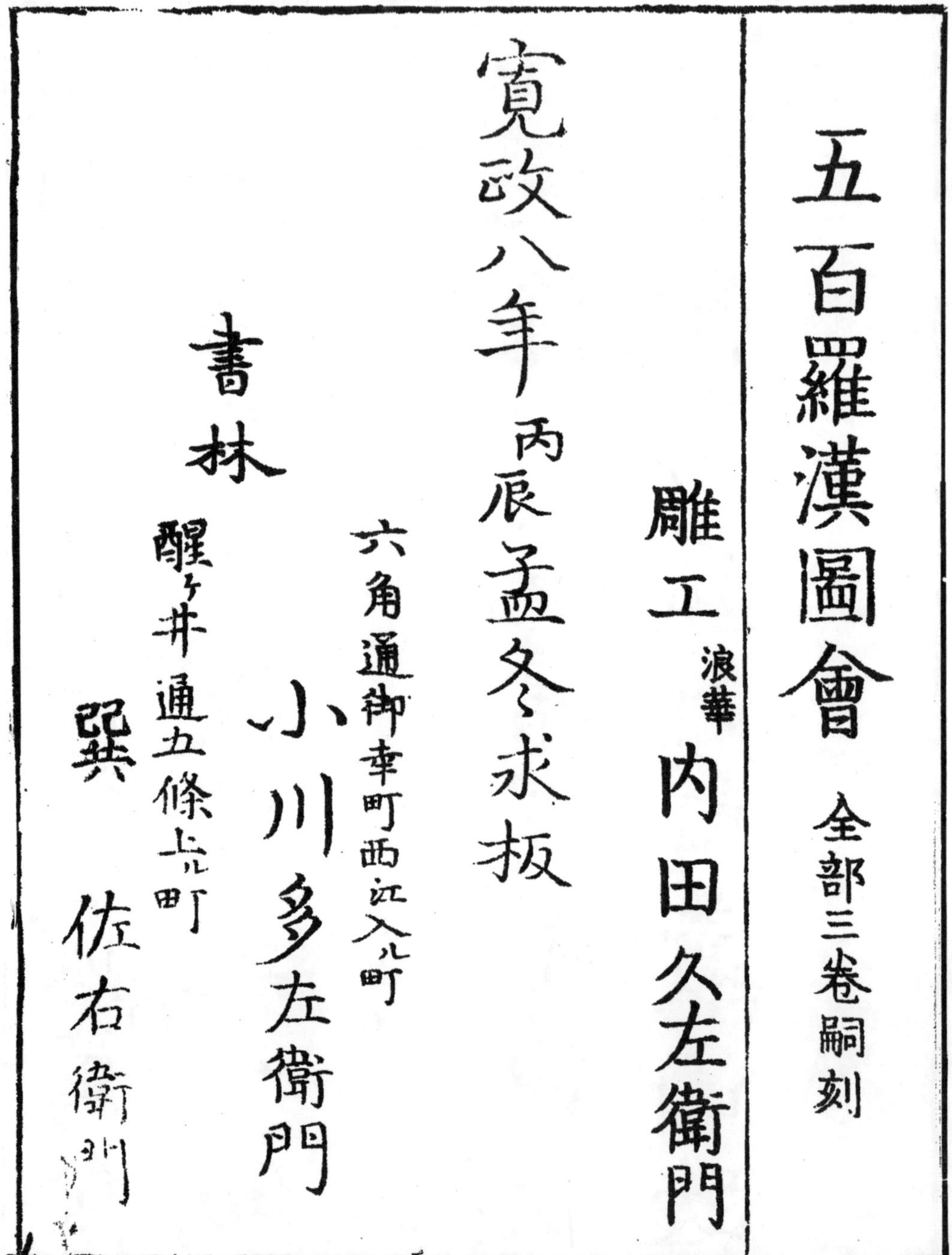

五百羅漢圖會　全部三巻嗣刻

雕工　浪華　内田久左衛門

寛政八年丙辰孟冬求板

六角通御幸町西江入ル町　小川多左衛門

書林　醒ヶ井通五條上ル町　巽佐右衛門

Gohyaku Rakan Zō: The Five Hundred Arhat Icons
Total Three fascicles in wood blocks; Artist: Uchida Kazaemon, Naniwa
The Order was made in 8th year of Kansei (1796), in the month of peak winter
By Ōgawa Tazaemon, Rokkaku Dōri, Gokōchō, Nishie Hairu machi
Publisher: Shorin, Samegai Dōri, Go jō, Agaru chō
Editor: Tatsumi Saemon

Alphabetical List of Japanese Terms

Alphabetical List of Sanskrit Terms